Gathering the Elements

GATHERING THE ELEMENTS

The Cult of the Wrathful Deity Vajrakīla according to the Texts of the Northern Treasures Tradition of Tibet

(Byang-gter phur-ba)

Vajrakīla Texts of the Northern Treasures Tradition
Volume One

by
Rig-'dzin rdo-rje
(Martin J. Boord)

WANDEL VERLAG berlin 2013

Khordong Commentary Series X

ISBN: 978-3-942380-10-2
A newly revised and expanded edition of the work formerly published as *The Cult of the Deity Vajrakīla*, Institute of Buddhist Studies, Tring 1993

Published by **WANDEL VERLAG** berlin, 2013

Second edition, 2016

Printed in Germany on FSC certified 100% acid-, wood- & chlorine-free long-lasting paper conforming to ANSI standard.

edition khordong is the publication series of the non-profit Khordong e.V. in Germany, published by **WANDEL VERLAG** berlin.
Please visit our websites:

Web:	www.khordong.net	www.wandel-verlag.de	www.tsagli.de
Contact:	edition@khordong.net	mail@wandel-verlag.de	

WANDEL VERLAG berlin 2013

CONTENTS

Incidental illustrations by Robert Beer are used with the artist's permission
Illustration of *sman rak gtor gsum* on p.320 © Jamyang
Other illustrations are from traditional sources or drawn by the author

ABBREVIATIONS

A,B,C,D,E	The five collections of Byang-gter Vajrakīla mss upon which the present study is based. See Appendix I
BRT	*The Black Razor Tantra*
CIHTS	Central Institute of Higher Tibetan Studies, Sarnath
BEFEO	*Bulletin de l'École Française d'Extrême Orient*
BHS	Buddhist Hybrid Sanskrit
GOS	Gaekwad's Oriental Series, Baroda
GST	*Guhyasamāja-tantra.* Ed., F. Fremantle, 1971
HT	*Hevajra-tantra.* Ed., D.L. Snellgrove, 1959
IASWR	The Institute for Advanced Studies of World Religions, Carmel, New York
IIBS	The International Institute for Buddhist Studies, Tokyo
JA	*Journal Asiatique,* Paris
JASB	*Journal of Proceedings of the Asiatic Society of Bengal*
JIABS	*Journal of the International Association of Buddhist Studies,* Madison
JRAS	*Journal of the Royal Asiatic Society,* London
LTWA	The Library of Tibetan Works & Archives, Dharamsala
MLB	Motilal Banarsidass, New Delhi
MMK	*Mañjuśrīmūlakalpa.* Ed., G. Sastri, 1925
NGB	*rNying ma'i rgyud 'bum.* Reproduced from a manuscript preserved at gTing-skyes dgon-pa-byang monastery, Thimbu Published in 36 vols., 1973-1975 Catalogue by E. Kaneko, Tokyo, 1982
NGMPP	Nepal-German Manuscript Preservation Project Staatsbibliothek Preussischer Kulturbesitz, Berlin
NSTB	*The Nyingma School of Tibetan Buddhism; its Fundamentals and History by 'Jigs-bral ye-shes rdo-rje.* Translation and annotation by G. Dorje and M. Kapstein (2 vols.), 1991
OUP	Oxford University Press
P	Peking *bKa'-'gyur* and *bsTan-'gyur* Catalogue and Index of the Tibetan *Tripiṭaka* kept in the library of Otani University, Kyoto Ed., D.T. Suzuki. Suzuki Research Foundation, Tokyo,1962
PTS	Pali Text Society, London
RAS	Royal Asiatic Society, London

RKP	Routledge & Kegan Paul, London
SBB	Sacred Books of the Buddhists, PTS, London
SBE	Sacred Books of the East. Gen. ed., Max Müller, Oxford
SDPT	*Sarvadurgatipariśodhanatantra.* Ed., T. Skorupski, 1983
SOAS	School of Oriental & African Studies, University of London
STTS	*Sarvatathāgatatattvasaṁgraha.* Ed., L. Chandra, 1987
SUNY	The State University of New York
T	Taisho edition of the Chinese *Tripiṭaka,* Taisho Issaikyo Ed., Takakusu Junjoro & Watanabe Kaigyoku Tokyo, 1924-1929
TPS	*Tibetan Painted Scrolls.* G. Tucci, 1949
VKMK	*Vajrakīlamūlatantrakhaṇḍa* (P.78)
WZKSA	*Wiener Zeitschrift fur die Kunde Südasiens,* Wien
ZDMG	*Zeitschrift der Deutschen Morgenländischen Gesellschaft,* Wiesbaden

INTRODUCTION

The present work surveys the cult of the wrathful deity Vajrakīla as represented by the literature and living tradition of the Northern Treasures (Byang-gter) school of Tibetan Buddhism. Divided into three parts, it focuses its attention, in turn, upon the Byang-gter (Part One), the *kīla* (Part Two) and the Byang-gter Kīla cult (Part Three).

Part One: the Northern Treasures

The first part seeks to trace the origin and development of the Northern Treasures Tradition and to indicate its vitality and relevance as a school of spiritual development within the modern world. Much of the information for this section is derived from Tibetan hagiographies dealing with the lineage of masters through whom the tradition has been transmitted, as well as from various notes and references to be found in the works of Western scholars. The latter works are mainly short papers on diverse topics, for this tradition until now has not been the subject of any major research.

In the eighth century CE, Tibet was the greatest military power in Central Asia and its control extended from what is now China and Iran to the Ganges River in India. Buddhist teachers had been visiting the country for some time but their influence had been fairly marginal. According to tradition, the learned scholar Śāntarakṣita had been invited to teach in the central provinces of Tibet but, being unable to establish the religion on any firm footing, he advised the king to invite Padmasambhava, a charismatic adept in the branch of Buddhism known as Guhyamantrayāna, the mystical path of secret utterances. Together, Padmasambhava, Śāntarakṣita and the king Khri Srong-lde'u-btsan (742-796) managed to integrate Buddhism into the Tibetan way of life and thus set the stage for more than twelve hundred years of Tibetan cultural development.

Before departing from Tibet, Padmasambhava was requested by his Nepalese consort Śākyadevī to leave further instructions for future generations. In response, Padmasambhava and the noble lady Ye-shes mtsho-rgyal together concealed religious teachings and material objects in secret locations all over the country. Empowering his close disciples to become the future masters of these hidden treasures (*gter*) when the time was right, Padmasambhava protected the treasures from the gaze of the unworthy by entrusting their safe preservation to the ancient spirits of the land. Often written on scrolls of yellow parchment in a symbolic script, only to be comprehended by the one intended to receive it, these religious instructions have subsequently inspired future generations by providing them with novel methods of meditation practice, as well as sacred objects of support, including ritual implements and prescribed substances of occult power, statues and paintings.[1]

The Byang-gter is concerned exclusively with the esoteric tenets of *guhyamantra* and thus its documentary records consist of largely psychological narrative replete with religious symbolism, a stream of apparently miraculous events brought about by wonder-working sages (*siddha*). It claims a place within the more general fabric of Buddhism by recognising each of its principal protagonists as the reincarnation of an earlier historical personality of acknowledged religious significance, the purpose of each rebirth being to carry on the work begun in a former life (sometimes several centuries earlier) on a deeper, more esoteric, level. These reincarnations, moreover, are said to have been prophesied by the earlier Buddhist masters and thus the importance of their roles in the grand design of Buddhist history is placed beyond dispute among the faithful. Among the many great disciples of Padmasambhava who later appeared in the Northern Treasures lineage are sNa-nam rdo-rje bdud-'joms, Nam-mkha'i snying-po, gNyags Jñānakumāra, rGyal-ba mchog-dbyangs, and Princess Pema-gsal. As for the 'treasures' of this school, they are found to consist of an admixture of extraordinarily profound and subtle methods of *śamatha* and *vipaśyanā* (yogic preoccupations of the earliest Buddhists, brought here to their apogee in the teachings of *atiyoga*[2]), together with magical rites of every weird and wonderful sort, so beloved of the medieval Indian *siddha* tradition. In particular, the Northern Treasures contain many prophecies which emphasise their importance for future descendants of king Khri Srong-lde'u-btsan and the preservation of Tibet as a homeland of Buddhism and haven of religious practice in the coming degenerate age.

According to the Byang-gter chronicles, cultic texts and practices concerning the wrathful deity Vajrakīla were among the many teachings transmitted to Tibetan devotees in the eighth century by the visiting

---

1 For a study of the rNying-ma *gter ma* tradition see Tulku Thondup, *Hidden Teachings of Tibet*. Wisdom Publications, London 1986

2 See Samten Karmay, *The Great Perfection (passim)*

Indian *siddha* Padmasambhava.[3] A number of these esoteric teachings, said to consist of sacred texts from India and oral instructions concerning them, were specifically entrusted to the *yogin* sNa-nam rdo-rje bdud-'joms before being sealed up in a casket, together with a vast quantity of other material, and hidden away for several hundred years in a cave in La-stod-byang to the north of the Brahmaputra river. When they were eventually rediscovered and revealed to the world in 1366, this particular collection of teachings became famous as 'The Northern Treasures' and the doctrines of Vajrakīla found among them were widely acclaimed as being of paramount importance.

As knowledge of the Byang-gter spread throughout Tibet, it gradually became established as a major religious system with over fifty monasteries propagating its teachings, chief among which was the mother monastery of rDo-rje-brag. Monks of this seminary, properly trained in its rituals, have always been highly prized for their religious expertise. One such monk, for example, was invariably required in the *sKu lnga* shrine in the Jo-khang in Lhasa, another at the *lHa mo khang* and eight in the *mGon khang* at the base of the Potala palace engaged in the worship of Mahākāla. Four monks from rDo-rje-brag annually performed the *'Gong po ar gtad* ritual for the suppression of demons at the Lhasa *Rigs gsum* shrine and the oracle of dGa'-gdong was regularly consulted to divine the whereabouts of deceased lamas.

Having surveyed the general history of the Northern Treasures school in Tibet, the chapter goes on to look at the particular lineage of Yol-mo sprul-sku in Nepal and concludes with a brief note on the Byang-gter monks and monasteries now established among the Tibetan refugee population of Northern India.

Part Two: the history and form of the vajra spike

The second part of this study consists of three chapters. In the first of these (Chapter Two) I have attempted to clarify the cultural milieu out of which the Kīla deity arose. To this end I have looked at the social context as well as the religious and have drawn upon both historical and mythological sources.

---

3 In the view of the Byang-gter tradition, the three principal recipients of these Kīla *upadeśa* were the king Khri Srong-lde'u-btsan, the noble lady Ye-shes mtsho-rgyal and the *yogin* sNa-nam rdo-rje bdud-'joms.

With regard to the name 'Vajrakīla': *vajra* as a prefix is almost ubiquitous within the Buddhist system of *guhyamantra*. Originally meaning 'the hard or mighty one' and referring in particular to the thunderbolt as a weapon of Indra, it subsequently became so intimately associated with the development of tantric ideas in Buddhism that the entire system of practice came to be known as the Vajrayāna or *Vajra* Vehicle. Indeed, as a symbol within the Buddhist *tantra* it is as pregnant with meaning as the very texts themselves. Characterised as *abhedya* 'unbreakable' and *acchedya* 'indivisible', the term may be said to represent nothing less than the full enlightenment of the *samyaksaṁbuddha* who himself came to be referred to as Vajradhara, "He who holds the *vajra*". The Sanskrit word *kīla* means 'nail', 'peg' or 'spike' and thus Vajrakīla may be taken to mean "the unassailable spike" or, on a higher level, "(He who is) the nail of supreme enlightenment".

The roots of *kīla* mythology, however, may lie buried deep within the pre-Buddhist religion of ancient India where, in the *Ṛgveda*, the story is told of the god Indra who slew the demon Vṛtra.[4] It is said that, at that time, Indra stabilised the earth and propped up the heavens and thus, at the outset, we have clearly discernible indications of a path along which a humble wooden stake might travel so as eventually to become deified as a terrifying god of awesome power, one by whom all demons are vanquished.

The idea of stabilising the earth by pinning it down with a *kīla* was taken up by architects and priests who projected a magical function onto the wooden pegs employed by them in the process of marking out a plot of ground chosen as the site for a temple or other building. Since Buddhists also used wooden pegs and lengths of string to mark out the ground plan of a *stūpa* or *vihāra*, they naturally enough also adopted the concept of those pegs as magically potent items. In particular, the pegs struck into the four corners of the site or around its periphery were regarded as estab-

---

4 The name Vṛtra derives from the root *vṛ* with the sense of "to surround, enclose, obstruct". Hence the noun *vṛtra* means restrainer, enemy or hostile host. It also stands as "the name of the Vedic personification of an imaginary malignant influence or demon of darkness and drought supposed to take possession of the clouds, causing them to obstruct the clearness of the sky and keep back the waters". M. Monier-Williams, *Sanskrit-English Dictionary*. We shall meet with the *kīla* as an implement employed in the magical control of weather below, Chapter Two.

lishing a protective boundary (*rakṣācakra)* capable of repelling all harm.[5] As it says in the *Āryamañjuśrīmūlakalpa* [p.693]:

> खदिरकीलकमष्टशतजप्तां कृत्वा चतुर्षु दिशासु निखनेत् । सीमाबन्धः कृतो भवति ॥
>
> Having prepared *kīla* of acacia wood, empowered by 108 recitations of *mantra*, they should be embedded in the four directions. That is the way in which the boundaries are sealed.

This idea may have been established in Buddhist practice at a remarkably early period because literary evidence for the use of the *kīla* as a magical implement is to be found in the *dhāraṇī*, some of which conceivably date right back to the third or fourth centuries BCE.

The earliest extant pegs of this type, in which the form of the *kīla* unambiguously reflects its identification with a wrathful divinity, are believed to have been carved in the first century BCE. They were discovered by the archeologist and explorer Sir Marc Aurel Stein among the debris associated with the ancient watchtowers situated at the south-west extremity of the frontier defence system to the north of Dūnhuáng. In the detailed reports of his expeditions, Stein describes a watchtower (which he identifies as T.VI.b) and the artefacts discovered there, among which are a number of *kīla* to which were originally attached loops of string. He describes these items as resembling tent pegs and exhibiting evident signs of having been pegged into the ground and yet "certainly not strong enough to have served as real tent pegs". Similar finds were made at the watchtowers T.VI.c and T.VIII. Some of these pegs bore Chinese inscriptions that could only make sense if read as personal names but no indication is given as to whether they might be the personal names of men

---

5 All that has a terrible aspect (*ghora*) is traditionally regarded in India as *vighna;* an impediment, obstacle, interruption, hurdle, difficulty or trouble. Indeed, the vast size of the problem of *vighna* led to its being associated with the boundary or circumference which, it is said, the Vedic Prajāpati finally overcame by taking control of the centre (an inconceivable subtlety totally devoid of extension) so that "the very root of (demonic) arrogance and conceit, viz. the vast size, ceased to have any meaning". V.S.Agrawala, "The Meaning of Gaṇapati". *Journal of the Oriental Institute,* Baroda, vol.XIII.1 (1963) 1-4. So, too, we will observe throughout this study that the *kīla* that protects the circumference is also the instrument through which the centre is conquered.

or gods. The evidence put forward by Stein for dating these finds to the first century BCE seems overwhelming.[6]

The theme of the apotropaic spike, having come to the surface in the early *dhāraṇī*, was subsequently developed extensively within the *kriyā-* and *yogatantra* of the later periods. Throughout this time spikes came to be employed increasingly in rituals of mundane sorcery which seem to have posed no moral dilemma for their perpetrators, even within a Buddhist context.

Although the *mantra* of Vajrakīla is to be found in the fundamental *yogatantra* STTS and, as pointed out by authorities on tantric practice, "the *mantra* is the god", the absolute deification of the sacred spike and its transformation into an awesome god of terrible wrath seems not to have been finally completed until the period of the *yoganiruttaratantra*. By this time the spike that brought death and destruction to its opponents came also to be regarded as the harbinger of liberation, a bestower of *nirvāṇa*. As a symbol of absolute stability, the paradoxical nature of the magic spike is expressed in the religious myth and ritual of the deity which everywhere depicts chaos as the natural condition of *saṁsāra*. The *maṇḍala* of the deified spike is a bloody charnel ground, in the centre of which dwells the god in a palace of skulls, astride a throne of demonic corpses. His sanguinary sport (*līlā*) is the archetype of violent behaviour, leading to a distinct antinomian trend in the religious ideals of his worshippers.

Within the sacred texts of both this deity and others like him, it is said that the function of 'wrathful compassion' is to kill sentient beings and thus apparently to violate one of the primary ethical precepts of Buddhism. The question naturally arises – Is this vile injunction to be taken literally, or is it symbolic? In fact, it is to be taken both ways. The major commentary on the *Kālacakra-tantra* says that provisionally (*neyārtha*) "a Buddha may kill those who are really committing the five immediacies, who break their vows, and who damage the teaching. But a *mantrin* who has not attained the five special knowledges (*abhijñā*) should not perform such fearful actions." On the definitive level (*nītārtha*), however, killing

---

6 M.A. Stein, *Serindia* (5 vols.), Oxford, 1921. Stein's description of the watchtower and his finds is to be found in vol.III 644-651 and the *kīla* themselves are depicted in plate LII (vol.IV)

More recent photographs of two of those *kīla,* currently housed in the British Museum, are to be seen in R. Whitfield & A. Farrer, *Caves of the Thousand Buddhas; Chinese Art from the Silk Route* 174

refers to the yogic practice of holding the semen at the top of the head.[7] Klong-chen-pa in his commentary on the *Guhyagarbha-tantra* says that the skilful *yogin* should kill wrongdoers and release them into an exalted realm, thus saving them from the certainty of rebirth in limitless evil existences. The rite itself has two main parts: (1) destruction of the evil body, speech and mind and (2) guiding the consciousness of the deceased to a 'Pure Realm' (*buddhakṣetra*). There is no hatred in the rite, only an altruistic mind of awareness and compassion.[8] As it says in the *Saṁvarodaya-tantra*, "Ah! Marvellous is the rite of killing. It kills the transmigration which is only imagination. It does not kill the mind recognising suchness (*tathatā*, the real state of things)."[9]

Finally, Śubhakarasiṁha says that 'killing' expresses the basic concept of the vow to cut away the life of all beings, where 'life' means 'beginningless ignorance and passion' (*kleśa*).[10]

The various biographies of those whose practised this magical art of slaying, however, provide us with evidence of occasional, all too human, lapses from such noble altruism. Mortal nature is such that there have inevitably arisen in the past certain self-centred, power-hungry *yogins* who have been tempted to turn this philanthropic 'white magic' into 'black' for their own nefarious purposes. In the chronicles of the Byang-gter, for example, is recounted the story of combative sorcery between Lang-lab and the translator of Rva, which is told below in Chapter Four.

Following the introduction of these ideas to Tibet, the *kīla* as a weapon of ritual magic became immensely popular among both Buddhist and Bon-po – both within the Kīla cult in which the deity Vajrakīla is worshipped, and independent of that cult.

To date there have been several western studies published concerned with the ritual *kīla* and the Kīla cult, although none of them could be called in any way major. The first book to be published was by John Huntingdon (*The Phur-pa; Tibetan Ritual Daggers*. Ascona, 1975) in which a number of ritual *kīla* are described in terms of length, weight, material of manufacture, etc. It contains almost nothing that has any bearing on the

---

7 M. Broido, "Killing, Lying, Stealing and Adultery; a Problem of Interpretation in the Tantras" 73

8 G. Dorje, *The Guhyagarbha-tantra* 918

9 S. Tsuda, *The Saṁvarodaya-tantra* 279

10 A. Snodgrass, *The Matrix and Diamond World Maṇḍalas in Shingon Buddhism* 481

present research. The second book is by Thomas Marcotty (*Dagger Blessing. The Tibetan Phurba Cult: Reflections and Materials*. Delhi, 1987) in which more is said concerning the rituals in which *kīla* are symbolically employed. This book also presents translated excerpts from four Tibetan texts, including the canonical *Vajramantrabhīrusandhi-mūlatantra* (P.467) but is, unfortunately, highly subjective in nature and riddled with unwarranted and spurious assertions. Its many shortcomings have been adequately brought to light by Cathy Cantwell in her review for the *Tibet Journal* XIV,2 (1989) 61-64.

Many other books have carried passing references to either the deity Vajrakīla or to symbolic *kīla* as encountered in iconography or ritual, foremost among which is the classic *Oracles and Demons of Tibet* by René de Nebesky-Wojkowitz. The large number of instances cited in this text clearly demonstrates the ubiquity of the ritual *kīla* as a magic weapon throughout the entire realm of Tibetan tantrism, especially following the importation from India of the cult of Vajrakīla. The several studies and text translations that have been published in more recent years, concerning the ritual techniques of the deity and the theoretical basis underpinning these techniques, serve to highlight the continuing relevance of the cult of Vajrakīla in the modern age.

Several papers have also been published in academic journals and the like which have a bearing on our topic. One of the most interesting of these is the study by Bischoff and Hartman[11] on the manuscript from Dūunhuáng listed as 'Pelliot tibétain 44'. This is said to be "possibly the oldest document in existence referring to Padmasambhava" and is considered by Prof. Tucci as a major proof of the *siddha*'s historicity. Its theme is the summoning of the Kīla *Vidyottama-tantra* from Nālandā University to the Asura cave in Nepal. In their introduction to the text, the translators deal with the problem of the widespread assertion in Tibetan literature that the Sanskrit term for *phur ba* is *kīlaya* (with or without a long *i*) when all dictionaries and Sanskrit works agree the word to be *kīla* (or *kīlaka*). I am convinced that this is due to an indiscriminate use by Tibetans of the dative singular *kīlāya*. This form would have been familiar to them in the simple salutation *namo vajrakīlāya* (homage to Vajrakīla) from which it could easily be assumed by those unfamiliar with the technicali-

---

11 F.A. Bischoff & Charles Hartman, "Padmasambhava's Invention of the Phur-bu." *Études tibétaines dediées à la memoire de Marcelle Lalou* 11-28 Paris 1971

ties of Sanskrit that the name of the deity is Vajrakīlāya instead of Vajrakīla. It should also be noted that the term *(vajra)kīlaya* is frequently found in Sanskrit texts (as well as in virtually every *kīlanamantra*) legitimately used as the denominative verb 'to spike', 'transfix', 'nail down', etc.

John Huntingdon made the assumption that the precursor of Vajrakīla was Mahākāla.[12] Such an identification appears quite plausible for Mahākāla is, indeed, one of the earliest wrathful deities to become clearly defined in the Vajrayāna pantheon and among his many epithets and guises he is widely renowned as the destroyer of obstructors and misleaders,[13] a role subsequently taken up by Vajrakīla. Mahākāla is, of course, a deity known to both the Buddhists and Hindus and in the opening chapter of the Hindu *Uḍḍīśa-tantra* there is given a rite for the destruction of an enemy which involves burying "a terrible pin made of copper" in the chest of his effigy. Sitting on a seat of tiger skin, the *yogin* should mutter the *mantra* "OṀ Honour to the Lord Mahākāla whose lustre is equal to the fire of destruction; Liquidate liquidate, destroy destroy this enemy of mine called So-and-so; HŪṀ PHAṬ SVĀHĀ".[14] Such a procedure differs in no way from its Buddhist counterparts. There is, furthermore, an attested Buddhist form of Mahākāla with *kīla* legs which was worshipped in Khotan,[15] a place known to have accepted early on the notion of the *kīla* as a god[16] and culturally connected via the 'silk route' with those Central Asian finds of Sir Aurel Stein. There is also the widespread opinion that ritual *kīla* evolved to a certain extent from tent pegs[17] and it is certainly true to say that tent pegs are viewed by *yogins* as *kīla*.[18] In rites of meditation, *kīla* are employed to effect a protective tent (*pañjara*) around an area that is to be kept ritually pure[19] and the special form of Mahākāla with the *kīla* feet is known as 'the Lord of the Tent' (Pañjaranātha). That god also has *garuḍa* wings and other details of iconography that match exactly those of the later Vajrakīla. On the face of it, therefore, one might sup-

---

12 John C.Huntingdon, *The Phur-pa* 32

13 More than one dozen rites of Mahākāla are to be found in the *Sādhanamālā.*

14 T. Goudriaan & S. Gupta, *Hindu Tantric and Śākta Literature* 120

15 René de Nebesky-Wojkowitz, *Oracles and Demons of Tibet* 51

16 R.E. Emmerick, *Tibetan Texts Concerning Khotan* 46-47

17 P. Pal, *Art of Tibet* 244 and *passim*

18 W.Y. Evans-Wentz, *Tibetan Yoga and Secret Doctrines* 324

19 J. Hopkins, *The Yoga of Tibet* 98-100

pose Huntingdon's theory of the identity of Mahākāla and Vajrakīla to be correct. In Chapter Two of the present work, however, I have drawn together several strands of literary evidence that clearly reveal not Mahākāla but Amṛtakuṇḍalin (a god also associated with the protection of boundaries) to be the precursor of Vajrakīla.

This identification of Amṛtakuṇḍalin with Vajrakīla remains valid even in the Byang-gter literature of a much later period. The short Byang-gter text *Phur pa'i dam can gnad rem*, for example, gives proper names to the Kīlas of the three families: Buddhakīla is called Yamāntaka, Padmakīla is Hayagrīva and Vajrakīla is Amṛtakuṇḍalin.[20] This grouping of three families (*kula*) belongs to the system of *kriyātantra*[21] and therefore indicates an early provenance for this material said to have been unearthed in 1366. Such primitive features are widespread in the Byang-gter literature and I see no reason to doubt that much of it could indeed have been brought to Tibet from India in the eighth century CE.

The Byang-gter text *sGrub thabs rgyun khyer* exemplifies the manner in which the *yogin* mystically identifies himself with the deity Vajrakīla as he takes the ritual nail into his hands. Thinking of himself as the single-faced, two-armed god with the lower half of his body in the form of a triple-edged spike blazing in a mass of fire, the *yogin* blesses the ritual *kīla* by contemplating that his right hand is the *maṇḍala* of the sun from which arise the *bīja* of the *pañcatathāgata* and his left hand is the *maṇḍala* of the moon emanating the *bīja* of their five consorts. Then, as his hands are brought together with *mantra,* the male and female buddhas unite and the *bodhicitta* of their union flows into the *kīla*. Rolling it between his palms, the *yogin* exhorts the *kīla* to fulfil the four magical acts. He places the deity Hūṁkāra on the top of the spike and Mahābala at its lower tip. Upon the upper 'vast knot' he places the *krodha* kings of the four cardinal quarters, and the kings of the intermediate directions are installed within its lower knot. Then, as the *yogin* rolls the empowered spike between the palms of his hands, he recites the *mantra* and simultaneously blesses the entire *traidhātuka* with 'liberation'.[22]

---

20 C8 99

21 Lessing & Wayman, *Introduction to the Buddhist Tantric Systems* 103

22 A29 199-200

Chapter Three of the present work discusses the iconographic details of the principal *kīla* deities in the retinue of the supremely wrathful Vajrakīla.

The 'history' of the *Vajrakīla-tantra* as described in cultic documents is outlined in Chapter Four. Although the several short Tibetan texts[23] (*lo rgyus,* 'chronicles') dealing with this subject may not be regarded as historical works according to our own definition of the term (they tell us, for example, that the doctrines of Vajrakīla were once taught in a cremation ground by a gigantic iron scorpion with nine heads), they nevertheless throw considerable light upon the subject. According to these traditional accounts, the canon of Vajrakīla arose in a previous aeon at a time when the buddhas felt impelled to subdue the arch-demon Rudra. The myth of the subjugation of Rudra in fact constitutes the central theme of the entire genre of wrathful *tantra* of *mahāyoga.* In the light of comparative literature and iconography, this myth may be regarded as indicative of the final formulation of *mahāyoga* tenets (including the cycle of teachings of Vajrakīla) as a conscious development designed to present a direct challenge to the perceived evils of the growing cult of Śaiva (Rudra) tantrism. The Buddhist view, however, is that the appearance of Rudra in the world is a skilful expedient (*upāya*) for the sake of those to be converted.[24]

Having been taught among the gods and *nāga,* the doctrines of Vajrakīla were transmitted to the human realm where they were spread in India by Indrabhūti, Dhanasaṁskṛta, Śrīsiṁha, Prabhahasti and an unnamed *kāpālika* brahmin. In Nepal they were taught by Śīlamañju and Śākyadevī. Śīlamañju is said to have taught a prostitute by the name of Śānti who, in her turn, transmitted the doctrines to Guṇapatala (a prince of Nepal) so that they then became widely known in that country[25] and Śākyadevī is said to have taught them to Dharmakośa by whom they were

---

23 As far as possible for this section I have drawn upon texts of the Northern Treasures tradition but, in fact, the 'history' of the deity as outlined here is broadly accepted (discounting endless variations of detail) by followers of all Vajrakīla lineages in Tibet.

24 Explained in detail by Klong-chen-pa in his commentary to Ch.XV of the *Guhyagarbha-tantra.*

25 gTsang mkhan-chen, *rDo rje phur pai' chos 'byung* 171. Nepalese *kīla* rituals and the spread in that country of the Kīla cult have, as yet, been inadequately studied. This lamentable situation will surely change as further Nepalese manuscripts are brought to light.

subsequently propagated throughout Oḍḍiyāna.[26] The doctrines are also said to have been taught in Khotan by Vairocana[27] and in Tibet by Padmasambhava, Vairocana and Vimalamitra. Since one of the stated aims of the Kīla doctrines is to provide a method "for the subjugation of all enemies and obstructors", the cult was readily able to assimilate troublesome local gods and demons wherever it spread. In particular, Padmasambhava is said to have employed the occult power of Vajrakīla to tame the spirits of the Himalayan regions on his journey to Tibet and convert them all to defenders of the Buddhist faith.

Part Two concludes with the observation that Indian traditions of Vajrakīla must have reached their peak in the early eighth century CE, just when the cult was transmitted to Tibet. In Tibet, subsequently, a large number of Vajrakīla lineages became firmly established, while in India worship of the deity seems to have been abandoned.

Part Three: the Byang-gter Kīla

The primary sources for this entire study are various collections of Byang-gter Kīla texts rescued from Tibet since 1959 and subsequently made available to a wider readership under the American Library of Congress PL 480 acquisition scheme.

(A) The first of these collections, the *Phur pa dril sgrub*, was published in Leh in 1973 as volume 75 of the *Smanrtsis Shesrig Spendzod* series and consists of manuscripts from the libraries of Padma Chos-ldan and sTag-lung-rtse-sprul rinpoche. From its short preface we learn that the Byang-gter tradition contains three cycles of teachings related to Vajrakīla. The largest (*rgyas pa*) is the Che-mchog (Mahottara) cycle in fifteen sections,[28] the medium (*'bring po*) is the sPu-gri (*Kṣura) cycle and the shortest (*bsdus pa*) is the Drag-sngags (Mantrabhīru).[29] The *Dril sgrub* is a com-

---

26 gTsang mkhan-chen, *rDo rje phur pai' chos 'byung* 170

27 Vairocana is held to have learned the doctrines of Vajrakīla in India from Śrīsiṁha. S. Karmay, *The Great Perfection* 25

28 In fact, however, only 13 of these 15 sections are to be found in the currently available Byang-gter literature as demonstrated, below, in this Introduction.

29 Of these three divisions, it would appear that the *mahottara* cycle is unique to the Byang-gter school, the black *kṣura* and *mantrabhīru* cycles being the common property of all Kīla lineages (each of which, however, has its own textual tradition).

bination of these three cycles with the proper name *Byang gter phur pa lugs gsum gcig tu dril ba'i chos skor*, "the religious cycle of the three traditions of Northern Treasures Kīla rolled into one". This name acts as a pun in Tibetan because Kīla meditation is accompanied by the ritual act of rolling (*'dril ba*) a symbolic nail between the palms of the hands. The collection itself comprises 364 folios (727 pages).

(B) The second collection, in two volumes, was published in Dalhousie in 1977 under the name *Phur-pa Texts of the Byang-gter Tradition*. The title page says that it is a reproduction of a rare collection of manuscripts held in the LTWA, Dharamsala. Its contents also encompass the three cycles listed above but, in 614 folios, it is the largest single collection of such literature that has so far come to light.

(C) The third collection was published in Darjeeling in 1984 with the title *Byang gter phur pa'i skor*. The reproduction of a manuscript on 288 folios belonging to Yol-mo bla-ma rdo-rje, it is similar in scope to both A & B.

(D) *Byang gter phur pa lha nag gi chos tshan* (*sNga 'gyur byang gter phur pa lha nag thun min yol mo lugs su grags pa*) contains a collection of 33 supplementary texts, chiefly dealing with the protectors of the cult, most of which are unique to this collection. Covering 225 folios, these texts were written and compiled in the early 17th century by bsTan-'dzin nor-bu, the third Yol-mo sprul-sku.[30] This neatly written manuscript in *dbu can* script was published by Tingkey Gonjang Rinpoche, Gangtok, 1994.

(E) Eventually, in 2002, after many years of research and collection, the Bod-kyi shes-rig zhib-'jub-khang in Chengdu was able to publish a set of 45 volumes entitled *dPal chen rdo rje gzhon nu'i chos skor phyogs bsgrigs* (*Phur pa phyogs bsgrigs*), within which are contained Tibetan Vajrakīla texts and teachings assembled from all lineages. Texts from the Northern Treasures cycle of Vajrakīla are mainly gathered together in volumes 12, 13 & 14 of this large compilation, and it is vol. 12 of this series that constitutes our Collection E. Except for a few minor changes

---

30 The importance of the Yol-mo lineage of the Northern Treasures is highlighted at the end of Chapter 1, below.

(noted in Appendix I, below), vols. 13 & 14 of this series are photographic reproductions of collections B & A, above.[31]

The title of every text contained in these five collections is listed together with its page number in Appendix I of the present work, thus facilitating reference to these original sources. The texts themselves are referred to throughout the present book by their sequence numbers: A1, A2, etc. All five collections include original material said to have come from the treasure trove of Zang-zang lha-brag, unearthed by the revealer Rig-'dzin rgod-ldem in the 14th century, as well as commentarial material, liturgical arrangements and the independent compositions of various historical holders of the lineage. The texts vary in length from those that merely cover a single side of a single folio to those that extend to over one hundred sides (50 folios). It is invariably the original *gter ma* material that is brief, the later compilations and commentaries tending to be more expansive. The *gter ma* material consists of a few texts of supposedly Indic origin not found elsewhere, as well as a large number of esoteric teachings on the Vajrakīla system said to have been taught by Padmasambhava to a select few among his close disciples. From the colophons of these texts, it would appear that Padmasambhava gave many of the teachings in Bhutan and that transcripts were also hidden there.

There are only two root *tantra*[32] at the heart of all this material, neither one of which is accompanied by any commentary. This would seem to reflect their transmission through a lineage more concerned with meditative experience and mystic praxis than philosophical theory.[33] The

---

31 In recent years, several of these Kīla texts have been republished in general anthologies of Byang-gter literature, newly edited by masters of the lineage in India and Nepal. For details of these modern collections, please refer to the bibliography.

32 These are the BRT on seven folios listed as A2, B31, C19 & E21, and the *Vajrakīlacittaguhyakāya-tantra* on ten folios found at A3, B10 & C1.
A31, C13, D16 & E15 are said to be the 21st chapter of a lost *tantra* called *Phur pa me lce'i 'phreng ba.*

33 Tāranātha claims that tantric adepts, in general, had no interest in philosophical speculation and the only religious works they composed were "great and small *sādhana* and empowerments as well as major and minor texts concerning *saṁpannakrama*. The *siddhas* themselves did not speak at all about commentaries and explanatory works ..."
David Templeman, *Tāranātha's Life of Kṛṣnācārya* 45

overwhelming mass of material in the collections is devoted to *sādhana* and ritual and there are also several chronicles that place these rituals within a more or less mythological context. These consist of both original *gter ma* texts and later elaborations.

Authors of the later texts range from the famous to the obscure. The most illustrious name, perhaps, is that of the Great Fifth Dalai Lama. A staunch supporter of the Byang-gter school, the Fifth Dalai Lama's recently published *Secret Visions* (Samten Karmay, London, 1988) show him to be a firm believer in the power of the ritual *kīla*. Better represented, however, is his disciple Padma 'phrin-las (1641-1718), traditionally regarded as the fourth incarnation of the Byang-gter's founder and widely acknowledged as the greatest scholar in the history of this school.

All the texts, other than those of collection D, are written in headless (*dbu med*) script with only a couple of exceptions, both of which are found in collection A. A45 is a short xylographed *sādhana* on six folios and A48 is a hand written ritual for turning away evil, calligraphed in *dbu can* on 24 folios. All the other texts abound with shorthand abbreviations as well as orthographic and grammatical irregularities so that deciphering and editing them has been a major task. The handwriting of collections A and B is quite similar (although not uniform throughout) and seems to conform to a type categorised by John Stevens as "originated by Vairocana the translator".[34] Collection C is not very different but I found it the most difficult to read. My chief native informant (prof. C.R. Lama of Viśvabharati University, West Bengal) describes the handwriting of A & B as "East Tibetan style" and I suppose C to have been written in Nepal (Yol-mo), where the Byang-gter tradition has long been established.[35] Collection E, of unknown provenance, is written in a more fluid hand. A particular

34 J. Stevens, *Sacred Calligraphy of the East* 75

35 Yol-mo in northeast Nepal (marked on maps as Helambu) is one of the seven "hidden lands" (*sbas yul*) deemed preeminently suitable as sites for meditational retreat, a "place where the Dharma will flourish after its disappearance in Tibet". Graham Clarke, "A Helambu History", *Journal of the Nepal Research Centre* IV (1980) 7. See also; *'Gu ru'i ga'u bdun ma; A collection of prophecies of Guru Padmasambhava on the location of the various treasure caches concealed for future revelations and the concealed lands destined for future gter-ston to reveal. From the Byang-gter discoveries of Rig-'dzin rgod kyi ldem-'phru-can and his tradition.* Reproduced from a rare manuscript from the library of Khanchung Rinpoche and published by Dorjee Tsering, Delhi, 1983. For a modern ethnographic account of life in that region see Graham Clarke, "Lama and Tamang in Yolmo".

problem, of course, is presented by the many *mantra* with which this kind of tantric literature is inevitably saturated. After so many centuries in isolation from their Indian matrix, these *mantra* which may originally have been encoded in formal Sanskrit interspersed with various vernacular phrases and nomenclature as well as the usual non-semantic *bīja* and expletives, are found within the manuscripts rendered more or less unintelligible in Tibetanized forms. Despite (or, in some cases, because of) the repetition of the most salient *mantra* in several texts so that we are thereby presented with an enormous number of variants from which to chose, a 'correct' reading could only be hoped for in a minority of the more obvious cases.

rNying-ma-pa literature

Only one of our source materials attempts to place the Northern Treasures Kīla doctrines within the context of rNying-ma sacred literature as a whole, and that is B4, the *Nor bu'i do shal* ('Necklace of Gems'), in 17 folios by 'Phrin-las bdud-'joms (1725-1789). This text was composed as an introduction to the doctrines of Vajrakīla for a group of his disciples about to become initiated into the cult. The author states at the outset his belief that a single Vajrayāna empowerment encompasses within itself every aspect of the path and goal. "For those who cannot grasp this immensity within a single *maṇḍala*", however, he says that the Buddha taught the two vehicles known as 'the causal vehicle of dialectics' (*mtshan nyid rgyu yi theg pa*) and 'the resultant *vajra* vehicle' (*'bras bu rdo rje'i theg pa*). The teachings of the former being contained within the *sūtra* and those of the latter within the *tantra.*[36]

The various *sūtra* and *tantra* followed by the rNying-ma-pa were translated into Tibetan from the languages of India, China and Central Asia, from the reign of Srong-btsan sgam-po (629-710 CE) up until the last of

---

36 B4 176

the early translators, Smṛtijñāna, in the tenth century.[37] Later, however, when the *bKa' 'gyur* and *bsTan 'gyur* were compiled as canons of sacred literature for the followers of the gSar-ma traditions, many of the early *tantra* were excluded on the premise that no Sanskrit original could be found as verification of authenticity. As a consequence, many followers of the New Translation schools (*gsar lugs*) tended to reject the rNying-ma texts as unrepresentative of the true teachings of the Buddha. Followers of the Old Translation schools, however, embrace all the texts of the *bKa' 'gyur* and *bsTan 'gyur* and study them in the monasteries, although the philosophical viewpoints of the old and new traditions often diverge from one another quite radically.

'Phrin-las bdud-'joms continues his explanation by saying that the two *yāna* known as 'the vehicle of cause' and 'the vehicle of result' may, alternatively, be considered under three rubrics as 'the vehicle which controls the source of suffering' (*kun 'byung 'dran pa'i theg pa*), 'the vehicle of the outer *tantra* of austere awareness' (*phyi dka' thub rig pa'i rgyud kyi theg pa*) and 'the vehicle of overpowering means' (*dbang bsgyur thabs kyi theg pa*).[38] Each of these three *yāna* has three divisions and thus there are the nine vehicles of the 1) *Śrāvaka*, 2) *Pratyekabuddha*, and 3) *Bodhisattva* (followers of the Hīnayāna and Mahāyāna *sūtras* that control the source of suffering through renunciation, wisdom and compassion), 4) *Kriyātantra*, 5) *Ubhayatantra*, and 6) *Yogatantra* (which, by means of austere awareness, gradually transform the universe and its inhabitants into a sacred *maṇḍala* populated with deities), 7) *Mahāyogatantra*, 8) *Anuyogatantra*, and 9) *Atiyogatantra* (which, respectively, emphasise the skilful means of the *utpattikrama*, the discriminative awareness of the *saṁpannakrama* and

---

37 It is said that during the time of persecution of Buddhism in Tibet in the early ninth century by king gLang dar-ma, lay tantric *yogins* were spared the excesses of ill treatment suffered by their monastic brethren because the king had been frightened by demonstrations of occult power displayed to him by the *kīla-siddha* Sangs-rgyas ye-shes.
T. Thondup, *The Tantric Tradition of the Nyingmapa* 153
gZhon-nu-dpal comments that those tantric adepts hid away the *śāstra*s and *sūtra*s that had been translated before the time of Ral-pa-can and it is thanks to them that the early doctrines survived the ensuing years of chaos between 901 and 973 CE. George Roerich, *The Blue Annals* 60-61

38 These three divisions are said to have been outlined in the *anuyoga* text *sPyi mdo dgongs pa'i 'dus pa* and elaborated by teachers in the sMin-grol-gling tradition. G. Dorje, *The Guhyagarbha-tantra* 18

the pristine cognition free of duality that is the great perfection of the final result).

'Phrin-las bdud-'joms then informs us that, within this ninefold scheme, the canon of Vajrakīla embodies the skilful means (*upāya*) of the *yoganiruttaratantra*, a general term for the teachings of the seventh, eighth and ninth *yāna.*[39] Generally in rNying-ma literature these three are known as 'the inner *tantra*', within which category the doctrines of Vajrakīla mostly pertain to *mahāyoga.*[40] They are classified as '*tantra* of skilful means' because of their strong bias towards enlightened activity (*'phrin las*) but this is not to say that they lack the view of transcendental wisdom (*prajñā*). As well as the *anuyoga* techniques discussed below in Chapter Eight, Kīla literature is thoroughly pervaded by the viewpoint and terminology of *atiyoga* (the system of rDzogs-chen)[41] and the Byang-gter cycle even contains two *sādhana* (A32 & A35) that purport to have been taught by Śrīsiṁha, one of the greatest luminaries of the *atiyoga* tradition.[42] It should be noted, however, that in at least one early *atiyoga* document, the word *kīla* is used disparagingly as an indicator of only the relative aspects of Buddhist religious practice: the accumulation of merit, contemplation and the purification of *saṁsāric* traces.[43]

"Furthermore", continues 'Phrin-las bdud-'joms, "in this country of Tibet having both early and later transmissions of the doctrine, especially with regard to the transmissions of *guhyamantra*, it is the early transmission of the Vajrayāna that has the two great systems of *bka' ma* and *gter ma*. Now within this system, the tantric doctrines of Vajrakīla under consideration here are classified as *gter ma* because they were taken out of hiding during a later period."[44]

---

39 B4 176-177

40 They are found under that heading, for example, in the NGB.

41 A fact already noted by Eva Dargyay, *The Rise of Esoteric Buddhism in Tibet* 35. In Chapter Three of the present work, in which the nature of the *kīla* as well as its form and function is explored, we note the *kīla* in both material (relative) and philosophic (absolute) guises: "Annihilating enemies and obstructors by means of symbolic *kīla,* grasping thoughts of ignorance are cut off by the actual *kīla.*" A47 471

42 The emphasis in both these *sādhana,* found in all three collections and dealt with below in Chapter Seven, is on the absolute, non-dual nature of the *kīla*.

43 S. Karmay, *The Great Perfection* 72

44 B4 177

Thus, with regard to the transmission of the doctrines, the received texts (*bka' ma*) of the rNying-ma school are divided into three categories: *rGyal ba'i dgongs brgyud* ('intentional lineage of the *jina*'), *Rig 'dzin brda' brgyud* ('symbolic lineage of the *vidyādhara*') and *Gang zag snyan brgyud* ('aural lineage of mundane individuals'). The discovered texts (*gter ma*) moreover, have three additional lineages called *bKa' babs lung bstan brgyud* ('lineage of prophetically declared spiritual succession'), *Las 'phro gter gyi brgyud* ('lineage of treasures of karmic maturation') and *Tsig brgyud shog ser gyi brgyud* ('lineage of transmitted words on yellow scrolls'). The Byang-gter doctrines of Vajrakīla are said to have been transmitted along all six of those lines.[45]

The Byang-gter Kīla texts

The received Byang-gter Kīla literature consists of a chaotic confusion of texts dealing in large part with ritual formulae and their magical correlates, the open-ended nature of which appears to imply no theoretical limit to their exegesis. Many of the texts may, at first, seem verbose and repetitive in their opening and closing, largely panegyrical, vignettes whilst remaining cryptic in the extreme with regard to central content. I have tried to reflect a little of the original literary flavour of the source materials in my study but have, of necessity, to a certain extent abbreviated the flowery rhetoric and opened up the more obscure passages in order to shed a modicum of light into the cryptic gloom. In order to facilitate cross-referencing this material with the data of other Buddhist schools, I have included a number of Sanskrit key terms in parentheses throughout the study, generally employing Tibetan terminology only when the Sanskrit appeared doubtful.[46] The Tibetan-Sanskrit equivalents of most of these words are to be found in the index.

Even though the texts overlap with much repetition of data, it is noted that a fresh element or novel twist is introduced with each retelling so that the material seems to grow in organic fashion quite unlike the lineally structured logical progression of modern western writing. The discrete

---

45 B4 178

46 Although based entirely upon Tibetan sources I am in no doubt that the material presented here has an Indic origin, as argued below in Chapter Two. It is understood, however, that the implications of these key terms gradually shift with time so that modern Tibetan usage may not coincide exactly with that of ancient India.

title applied to the individual sections of the literature and their idiosyncratic assemblage within the various collections here studied indicates a random structure to the whole within which any given text may or may not be included with impunity. The texts put forward an interconnected, self-sustaining dogma of symbols and ritual technique designed to serve as a means through which the initiate may both express this symbolic world and interact with it. Growing ever more skilful in this interaction, the *yogin* supposedly develops ritual power, the magical ability to control events in the world at large. Despite a preponderance of technical vocabulary and cosmological/religious dogma, the texts are clearly intended to convey not physical but rather psychological truths. Their purpose is conveyed to the emotion rather than the intellect so that the *yogin* realises their validity within his heart not his head. Indeed, it is axiomatic that mystical insight into the 'truth' of the *maṇḍala* is experienced by the *yogin* as a knowledge utterly free of propositional content. Such a result is a phenomenologically potent spiritual ecstasy equated with the higher *siddhi*. The meditator is imbued with a profound sense of well-being that is understood in the Kīla tradition to be the result of having banished the evil hordes of Māra beyond the confines of the *maṇḍala*, the *yogin*'s symbolic world. Within that context, the lower *siddhi* are indicated by omens encountered either in dreams, visions or the ordinary waking state. Thus, through his practice, the *yogin* learns to sustain the condition within which the world is experienced in the image of the sacred *maṇḍala* of Vajrakīla.

Although among Tibetans there exist several important lineages of Vajrakīla teachings, at no time during the writing of this book did I feel impelled to refer to parallel texts from traditions other than the Byang-gter, either to clarify my doubts or verify my conclusions. As I worked I found that each document studied, although presenting enigmatic riddles to ponder, shed fresh light on the significance of others in the cycle so that the entire tradition seemed to fit together like a jigsaw puzzle, each small text being meaningful only within the context of the whole.

The currently available collections of Northern Treasures Vajrakīla texts at the heart of the present study together comprise a total of over 250 separate titles, all of which are listed in Appendix I in the form in which they appear at the head of the texts themselves. When these texts are checked for duplications, however, their number is reduced by more than 50%. The collections also contain a few random texts that are not relevant to our purposes. B8, for example, is neither a Northern Treasures text nor does it relate to the Vajrakīla cycle. C37 is a Northern Treasures text but unrelated to the Kīla cycle. And so on. This leaves us with a core collection of little more than one hundred separate texts, the overwhelming majority of which claim to have been among the original treasures revealed by the *gter ston* Rig-'dzin rgod-ldem in 1366. To this essential core, carefully considered commentarial notes and supplementary prayers have been added in later years by named authors, so that the original gems of the tradition have been repeatedly polished and allowed to shine under different lights. Each of the individual collections contains texts that are not found elsewhere, as well as texts that it holds in common with one or more of the other collections. The full details of these correspondences are also listed in the Appendix.

The systematic ordering of the eight chapters of Part Three is based upon an arrangement set out in the very first of numerous minor commentaries to be found within this Northern Treasures Kīla literature, the *Phur pa che mchog gi them byang rin chen gter mdzod,* in which we are presented with a list of the essential elements of the Vajrakīla cycle.[47] Scarcely more than a single folio in length, this valuable text arranges the Byang-gter Kīla literature into five groups, each of which consists of three elements:

1) The fundamental elements that underpin the sacred tradition are the three called *rgyud* (*tantra*)*, dbang chog* (rites of initiation and empowerment, *adhiṣṭhānavidhi*) and *'phrin las* (ritual activities, equivalent here to *sādhana*).

2) The methods which are taught so that *yogins* may appropriate the *siddhi* of the deity are the three called *dKar po lam gyi sgron ma* (Lamp of the White Path), *bKa' nyan lcags kyi ber ka* (Iron Cloak of Attendants) and *Nag po dug gi 'khor lo* (Wheel of Black Poison).

3) The heart of the fierce activities is said to be the three called *zor* (a magic weapon to be hurled against the enemy), *sbyin sreg* (ritual burning, *homa*) and *mnan gtad* (forcing down, subduing).

4) For the benefit of *yogins* are taught the three called *tshe sgrub* (for the attainment of long life, *āyurvidhi*), *nor sgrub* (for the attainment of wealth) and *bza' tshogs* (the presentation of offerings for a sacramental feast).

---

47 Found independently as A1, also included within C15. Although the title of the text indicates a specific relationship to the *mahottarakīla* cycle, its analysis of the doctrines appears equally valid for the *kṣura* and *mantrabhīru* cycles.

5) As supplements to make up for any deficiencies are taught the method of making *sāccha* (*tsha tsha,* miniature reliquaries, the preparation of which fulfils broken vows), *rgyud rims* (*sic.*) and the *zur 'debs* (appendix).[48]

Only one of the texts at our disposal (E49, a short ritual composed by Padma 'Phrin-las) teaches an independent procedure for the attainment of wealth (*nor sgrub*), considered by the *them byang* to be an essential part of the Vajrakīla cycle and taught for the benefit of *yogins* under section 4. Collection A apparently once contained a wealth rite that focussed upon the deity Jambhala,[49] for the publishers of that collection have listed such a text between our A27 and A28. No such text is to be found there now, however, so that we are unable to ascertain whether that text was an original treasure text or not. E49 also focusses upon Jambhala but makes no reference to a 'root text.' It is quite possible that Padma 'Phrin-las composed his text solely in order to fill this gap. There remains also a question mark over the term *rgyud rims* in section 5. *Rims* means 'infectious disease' so the word is surely a misspelling (despite its recurrence at C15) of *rim* for *rim pa;* 'order, series, succession'. *rGyud rim* could then mean either the successive stages of tantric practice – the *bskyed rim* (*utpattikrama*) and *rdzogs rim* (*saṁpannakrama*) – or 'the succession of *tantra*' more commonly referred to as *brgyud rim,* the succession of masters through whom the tantric tradition was transmitted (*paramparā*). Among the texts in the various collections are found several *brgyud 'debs* (prayers to the lineage masters) and these could perhaps be thought of as "supplements to make up for deficiencies in the *yogin*'s practice". Our text C15 contains the words *rgyud rims* in its title and the text itself deals, among other things, with the transmission of the Vajrakīla doctrines from the primordial Buddha Samantabhadra to Vajrasattva, Vajrapāṇi, Karmendrāṇī,[50] Padmasambhava and finally to sNa-nam rdo-rje bdud-'joms who was the last to receive them before they were hidden away as treasures to be rediscovered by sNa-nam rdo-rje bdud-'joms' own later incarnation as a *gter ston.* This, however, is unsatisfactory and thus we are left with no original *gter ma* texts at all in

48 A1 2-3

49 Jambhala is a god of wealth popularly worshipped by Mahāyāna Buddhists in general, having no particular connection with the cycle of Vajrakīla.

50 E2 puts Vajravārāhī in place of Karmendrāṇī.

any of the collections that pertain unmistakably to either the category *nor sgrub*, the meaning of which is clear, or *rgyud rims,* the meaning of which is problematic. The remaining 13 sections of this 15-fold system of categorising the Northern Treasures Vajrakīla literature, on the other hand, are all well represented by precisely those texts which are generally to be found in common within collections A, B, C & E.

1) The first group of (a) *tantra,* (b) *adhiṣṭhānavidhi* and (c) *sādhana* are represented by:

(a) The two root *tantra* called *Śrīvajrakīlapotrihala-tantra* (*sic.*) (BRT, A2, B31, C19, E21) and the *Vajrakīlacittaguhyakāya-tantra* (A3, B10, C1, E3). These two *tantra,* which form the subject matter of our Chapter Five, present the fundamental mythology of the Vajrakīla cycle as accepted both within and without the Byang-gter school. The *tantra* from the black iron cache in the north is observed to correspond remarkably closely to the fragment included in the *bKa' 'gyur*, translated by the Sa-skya paṇḍita from a Sanskrit original thought to have been brought to Tibet by guru Padma himself.[51] The Mahottarakīla text from the golden southern cache puts forward the origin myth of the demon Rudra and the deity Vajrakīla as well as a paradigm for the fierce rites of the Vajrakīla cult utilising the device of questions and answers between Vajrapāṇi and the lord of the *maṇḍala*, a traditional format of Buddhist texts.

(b) The *Phur pa che mchog gi dbang chu* (A8, B12, C5, E8) and the *sPu gri nag po'i dbang chog* (A14, B63, C20, E30) are analysed in Chapter Six. These are the rites of empowerment enacted in terms of a symbolic palingenesis through which the *yogin* who aspires to membership of the Kīla cult may be introduced to its doctrines and authorised to participate in its sacred mysteries. Within this chapter the *yogin*'s 'price of admission' to the cult is considered[52] as well as those benefits he may seek to gain by his entry.

(c) The *Phur pa'i thugs kyi 'phrin las* (A45, B42, C35) and the *Dril sgrub kyi 'phrin las* (A36, &c.) are the fundamental rites through which

---

51 For these two texts, see my *A Bolt of Lightning from the Blue*, pp.79-90

52 By "price of admission" is meant not only the fee paid to the teacher at the time of empowerment but also the vows (*saṁvara*) and commitments (*samaya*) to which the neophyte is subsequently bound for the rest of his life. According to Śrīsiṁha, the essential *samaya* to be observed by initiates into the cult of Vajrakīla is that they should carry with them at all times a symbolic *kīla* made of iron. A32 227

the *yogin* expresses his commitment to the cult and through which he seeks to draw upon its power. Essentially these rites may be viewed as a reenactment of his own first ceremony of initiation (or 'empowerment') which, in turn, sought to recreate the primordial state of purity described in the deity's *tantra*. It is by means of these rites that the *yogin* seeks to transform his view of the world until he is able to maintain it in his mind as being nothing less than the deity's sacred *maṇḍala*.[53] His image of himself, meanwhile, has simultaneously to be transformed into that of the deity. This process of *sādhana*, known as *utpattikrama*, through which both the deity and his *maṇḍala* are generated, is examined in Chapter Seven.

In accordance with the tripartite schema ubiquitous in Buddhist tantric praxis, the *sādhaka* effects the total identification of himself with the deity by absorbing his mind in the *samādhi* of the deity, causing his speech "to resound with the unceasing recitation of *mantra*" and 'sealing' his body by *mudrā*.[54] The significance of this last term is by no means restricted to a simple 'gesture of the hands' but may include the physical placement of the practitioner in the deity's favoured abode (a fearful charnel ground where wild animals roam) where he dwells within a hut made of skulls, besmearing himself with ashes and drops of blood and grease, consuming the foodstuffs of the god (especially meat and alcohol) and wearing the deity's apparel of animal skins with ornamentation of bone.[55] Through this process of *utpattikrama* the *yogin* aims to gain direct and intuitive insight (the antidote to ignorance) and thus, as part of his *sādhana*, he is

---

53 In fact the distinction between 'the mind' and 'the world' is not much maintained in these texts. Although the theatre of *sādhana* praxis is generally the imagination of the practitioner himself (with body, speech and mind all having their role to play), in the black deity cycle the ritual is thematically projected upon the outer world whereas the *mahottarakīla* cycle deems it to occur almost entirely within the *yogin*'s own body. The anthropocosmos, however, is ritually homologised with the containing macrocosmos, especially with its underlying process of endless becoming based on ignorance and its resultant suffering, defined as birth in any realm under the sway of Māra.

54 Such a simplistic outline, however, is belied by the texts themselves within which the boundaries of 'self' and 'other', 'inner' and 'outer', remain remarkably fluid.

55 Vajrakīla meditation is concerned with the nature of *saṁsāra* and not *nirvāṇa*. HT I.X.34,36 describes the calmness of the innate (*sahaja*) specifically as being *nistaraṅga* "without waves" whereas the violently agitated nature of the Vajrakīla *maṇḍala* is repeatedly stressed. Indeed, the *maṇḍala* itself is stated in the *sādhana* to rest upon "a churning ocean of blood" indicative of the waves of *saṁsāra*.

instructed to "gulp down *saṁsāra*" and experience the one taste (*ekarasa*) of all phenomena and phenomenal processes. With the whole world in his belly he is no less than the god himself.[56] He has 'liberated' and 'blessed' all beings by killing them and, having gained control over worldly 'demonic' forces (the hosts of Māra), he has become master of his own destiny. Thus the *yogin* obtains the 'dual benefit' of the Mahāyāna: freedom from *saṁsāra* for others as much as for himself.[57]

2) The second group consists of three named texts. The *dKar po lam gyi sgron ma* (A9, B15, C6, E9) examined in Chapter Eight describes the climax of the *utpattikrama* process. Building on his success in appropriating for himself the outward appearance of the deity, the *yogin* now purifies his internal nature until it, too, becomes 'divine' in the process known as *saṁpannakrama* brought about by close meditation upon light.

The *bKa' nyan lcags kyi ber ka* is found as A10 & E10 and the *Nag po dug gi 'khor lo* as A11 & E11. In collections B and C, however, the two texts are found together under a single title as B19 & C7. These documents are studied in Chapter Nine together with related texts of the black deity cycle which detail the manner in which the *yogin,* having achieved total self-identification with the deity and being thus empowered to "roll the ritual nail between the palms of his hands", may strive to bring all 'lesser' spiritual beings[58] under his majesty. Once adept at controlling those powers, the *yogin* is able to dispatch them against his enemy in a display of violent sorcery. This chapter, then, is permeated with the darkest images of witchcraft and yet the texts themselves claim to rank among the most profound of spiritual practices. Much of their content is almost indistinguishable in kind from that encountered in the grimoires of late medieval Europe where procedures of black magic are taught for gaining

---

56 This expansion of the *yogin*'s perception from that of a merely theoretical knowledge of the dynamic principles of existence (such as the 12 *nidāna* and so on) to a first-hand (if interiorised, mystical) experience of the totality of created being is enhanced by his psychic 'growth' to a gigantic form of many colours with nine heads and 18 arms in which he holds all manner of symbolic attributes, etc.

57 The sequential stages of *utpattikrama* meditation are analysed in full detail in volume two of this series: *A Roll of Thunder from the Void.*

58 These "lesser spirits" are included within the mythology of the Vajrakīla cult as local deities who, having submitted to the authority and power of Vajrakīla (in the guise of Padmasambhava or other adept) were subsequently given seats around the periphery of the Vajrakīla *maṇḍala.*

the upper hand in a struggle for power over the forces of nature, personified in the guise of 'elementals' or mischievous sprites. Publicly disavowed by Buddhist hierarchs throughout the course of religious history, these texts nevertheless claim huge rewards for those sorcerer *yogins* who master their apparently appalling methodology.

3) All of the collections link *zor, sbyin sreg* and *mnan gtad* together within the single text called *mNan sreg 'phang gsum* found at A13, B20, C11 & E12. Under these three rubrics, dealt with in Chapter Ten, the hitherto highly introspective yogic procedures for the destruction of foes are simplified and recast in the form of rituals that readily lend themselves to the involvement of the *saṅgha* as a whole. In particular, this group involvement may be coordinated in the monastic masked dances (*gar 'cham, nartana*), during which participants don the divine accessories specifically "designed to set the individual free from any naturalistic expression, so that all the codified elements (gestures, postures, utterances) may fall into place with the structural rigor of a veritable body writing".[59] Thus the mythology of the Kīla cult is transmitted in the form of sacred drama to the wider audience of lay faithful, whose pious offerings support and maintain the monastic establishments enacting these colourful rites.

4) The *rDo rje phur pa'i tshe sgrub* is found at A18, B22, C12 & E13 while the *bZa' tshogs* is found at A23, B24, C14 & E17. There are no root *nor sgrub* texts to be found in any of the collections. Chapter Eleven therefore investigates the two remaining techniques said to be of direct benefit to the *yogin* in his personal life: the means to prolong his youth and vitality, and the contemplations through which he may bless all that he eats and drinks.

---

59 M. Thevoz, *The Painted Body* 90. The impersonal nature of the rites in the case of the Vajrakīla cult is further reinforced by their scatological nature. The painted faces of the Kīla sorcerers make play with "the very things (modern man) is so intent on averting; the dissociation of the body, the break-up of the physiognomy, the release of wild impulses, the disintegration of the Ego" (*ibidem* 25). In this remarkable book, Thevoz points out that the function of makeup has always been essentially magical and that ritual body decorations "are all polarized by the supernatural world, by the magical powers that govern and order reality, by their reference to the elemental forces and primordial causes which are external to and dissimilar to the society of man." (p.33)

5) *Sāccha* are taught at A24, B24, C14 & E19 and additional notes (*zur 'debs*) at A28, B25, C16 & E20. The final chapter of the book is dedicated to an investigation of these procedures through which the *yogin* is instructed to make up for any deficiencies in his practice and pays particular attention to the symbolic value of the various sacraments utilised within the Kīla cult for the celebration of community feasts (*gaṇacakra*). Spontaneously generating the Vajrakīla *maṇḍala* within his body, speech and mind, each *yogin* presents his own defilements (*kleśa*) as offerings to the deities. He thus seeks to eradicate from himself all traces of imperfection, "the obscurations to enlightenment", and achieve the divine purity of his goal. His oath of *bodhicitta* is fulfilled by contemplatively offering a boundless quantity of blood (= *prajñā*) and nectar (= *upāya*).

Throughout this study it is observed that the religious system of the wrathful deity Vajrakīla requires its followers entirely to abandon all preconceived views of the mundane world and immerse themselves instead in a world of symbols, a fantastical model that adheres solely to its own internal system of logic based upon earlier Buddhist concepts of cosmology and psychology. That model, it is claimed, will liberate the *yogin* who is successful in its realisation so that he may dwell in a state of permanent bliss. More than that, however, it will also bestow upon him a number of occult powers which may be used at his discretion for the benefit and ultimate liberation of all his fellow creatures. The work concludes with the observation that it is this 'intention of great compassion' that is offered as the legitimising factor for the inclusion of the cult within the general framework of Mahāyāna Buddhism[60] and points to a profound psychology underlying its somewhat bizarre approach to the age-old problem of man's quest for enlightenment and spiritual fulfilment.

60 The Mahāyāna ('Great Vehicle') is so called by its adherents precisely because of the emphasis it places on great compassion (*mahākaruṇā*). Within the way of *guhyamantra*, this great compassion takes the form of such magical activities as the slaying of demons – acts considered to be great expedients (*mahopāya*) for the ultimate benefit of all living beings.

Part One

THE NORTHERN TREASURES

CHAPTER ONE
The Byang-gter Tradition

Although a significant force within the rNying-ma group of religious traditions in old Tibet, very little as yet has been published in the west concerning the Byang-gter and its revealer dNgos-grub rgyal-mtshan. Brief references to the Byang-gter tradition, the fortunes of which have suffered a severe decline in the modern age since the invasion of Tibet by the communist Chinese, are to be found in a number of textbooks on the history of Buddhism in that country, especially those written from the rNying-ma-pa point of view, but no western scholar to date has attempted an exhaustive study of the subject.

A condensed history of the tradition is to be found in the form of an anonymous English language foreword to the *dGongs pa zang thal,* Leh 1975, and the biography of its *gter ston* as compiled by dDud-'joms rinpoche in his rNying-ma-pa history has been translated by Gyurme Dorje and Matthew Kapstein, NSTB I 780-783. Eva Dargyay in her earlier publication, *The Rise of Esoteric Buddhism in Tibet* 129-132, also utilised bDud-'joms' biography, comparing it with the version of sKong-sprul padma-gar-dbang from the *Rin chen gter mdzod.* Further information is to be found in a pamphlet entitled *A Brief History of Dorje Tag Monastery in Tibet and its Lineage holders*, written by sTag-lung-tse-sprul rinpoche and published in Leh, 1985, as well as among the notes to the many translations of Byang-gter ritual texts produced by prof. C.R. Lama of Viśva-bharati University, West Bengal, in collaboration with James Low. More recently, a paper by Jeremy Russell and Tsepak Rigzin entitled "Taglung Tsetrul Rinpoche, Dorje Drak and the Northern Treasure Tradition" was published in the *Chos Yang* journal from Dharamsala in order to commemorate the reestablishment in India of rDo-rje-brag Monastery, the chief monastery of the Byang-gter tradition.

The present account is based primarily upon three Tibetan texts: (1) The biography of our *gter ston* as told in the *sPrul sku rig 'dzin rgod kyi ldem 'phru can kyi rnam thar gsal byed nyi ma'i 'od zer*, written by Nyi-ma bzang-po. One redaction of this text is to be found in the *Byang gter lugs kyi rnam thar dang ma 'ongs lung bstan*, published by Sherab Gyal-tsen & Lama Dawa, Gangtok, 1983, and a second redaction, reproduced from a manuscript in the possession of Dilgo Khyentse Rinpoche, was published in Paro, Bhutan, in 1985. (2) The *Rig 'dzin ngag gi dbang po'i rnam thar,* written by Dalai Lama V and published in vol. 37 of the *Smanrtsis Shesrig Spendzod Series,* Leh 1972, and (3) the autobiography of bsKal-bzang padma dbang-phyug, entitled *lHa rigs kyi btsun pa bskal bzang padma'i ming can rang nyid kyi rtogs par brjod pa 'jam gnyen utpal gzhad pa'i dga' tshal gzhon nu byung ba'i yid 'phrog*, published as vol. 43 of the same series in 1973. Also of interest is our text B4, the *Byang gter phur pa'i dbang gi lo rgyus* by 'Phrin-las bdud-'joms of Yol-mo.

Derived as it is from these Tibetan hagiographies rather than contemporary historical documents, this short chapter cannot pretend to the status of 'proper historical research' and the picture presented herein may seem to some to have about it an air of fanciful romance. Its Tibetan sources take for granted a view of life that is the norm within their own culture – an 'otherworldly' view quite removed from the prevailing 'rational materialist' outlook of the modern west. As pointed out recently by Michael Aris, "Indeed one does not need to look very far into Tibetan literature of any period to see that every traditional account rests on a fundamental basis of magic".[61] In my opinion, however, the Tibetan concern is less with magic than with psychology, for the devout hagiographer sees it as his primary function to record the all-important 'inner' or subjectively experienced aspect of the situation he chronicles.

The various sources offer conflicting dates for the episodes with which they are concerned and I have chosen to deal with them by the simple expedient of deciding the most probable in the light of all the 'evidence' before me. Disparate views are to be found in the footnotes. The outline as I have given it, however, is important in that it collates for the first time all that has so far been published on the Byang-gter tradition in European languages and it is my hope that perhaps the present survey will inspire future scholars to delve more deeply into its fascinating history. It is offered here in brief simply in order to provide a context for the materials that constitute the focal point of my research: the cult of Vajrakīla as it is found within this Northern Treasures tradition.

Concealment of the treasures

In the various biographies of the treasure revealer dNgos-grub rgyal-mtshan (1337-1408) it is said that his *dharmakāya* form is Samantabhadra and his *sambhogakāya* form is Vajrasattva. His *nirmāṇakāya* career com-

---

61 M. Aris, *Hidden Treasures and Secret Lives* 1

menced in India, where he manifested in more than two dozen incarnations[62] before he was born in Tibet as rDo-rje bdud-'joms of the sNa-nam clan in gTsang-rong.

Also known as sBa khri-zher, while still a young man rDo-rje bdud-'joms became the minister for religion in the court of the eighth-century ruler of Tibet and great Buddhist patron, king Khri srong-lde'u-btsan. When this king was advised to request the assistance of Padmasambhava in the founding of bSam-yas monastery, he entrusted sNa-nam rDo-rje bdud-'joms, together with Chims Śākyaprabhā and Shud-pu dPal gyi seng-ge, to be his messengers and deliver the invitation to India. Having gained permission in India from King Sūrya of Magadha, the three companions set off with Padmasambhava on their homeward journey to Tibet, but they travelled together only as far as Nepal. Announcing his intention to subdue the gods and demons of the Himalayan passes, the precious guru sent the three messengers back to Tibet, while he remained behind in Nepal. After Padmasambhava tarried yet again in Mang-yul, on the Nepalese border, Khri srong-lde'u-btsan impatiently dispatched rDo-rje bdud-'joms and further envoys back to the border, where they offered the guru gold dust as an incentive to return with them quickly to central Tibet. "Is this a gift from the King of the City of Ghosts (Pretapurī)?" he asked and, to their dismay, Padmasambhava threw the dust into the wind. Then, giving each of the envoys a measure of rocks and soil, the guru transformed these things into gold and jewels so that they were overwhelmed with faith.

Following his arrival in Tibet, Padmasambhava gave a large number of esoteric instructions to sNa-nam rdo-rje bdud-'joms who remained one of

---

62 Dalai Lama V lists the prior incarnations of the Byang-gter *gter ston* in India and Nepal as: (1) Samantabhadra, the *dharmakāya,* (2) Vajrasattva, the *sambhogakāya,* (3) Vajragarbha, the *nirmāṇakāya* who gathered together all the doctrines of esoteric Buddhism, (4) Khye'u-chung she-la rog-po, (5) rGyal-sras deva bzang-skyong, (6) Byang-sems ye-shes snying-po, (7) bKa'i-sdud-po Nam-mkha'i mdog-can (alias Vajragarbha II), (8) sKye-rgu'i bdag-mo, (9) mKha-'gro bde-ldan-ma, (10) mKha-'gro rig-byed bde-ma, (11) Yid-byin (sbyin) dpal, (12) the Dharma minister Blo-gros-mchog, (13) Byang-sems nam-mkha'i snying-po, (14) Sems-dpa' chen-po nor-bu 'dzin-pa, (15) bDe-ba'i rdo-rje, (16) Drag-po gtum-po, (17) Śākyamitra, (18) the *bhikṣu* Zhi-ba'i snying-po, (19) lha-lcam Mandāravā (Yid-'dzin lha-mo), (20) the beer-seller Vinasā, (21) the Dharma minister Ye-shes-gsal, (22) bTsun-mo 'od-'chang-ma, (23) bDe-ba'i 'byung-gnas, (24) the *ḍākinī* Gar-gyi dbang-phyug (Narteśvarī), (25) the *ḍākinī* Suṣatī (bDe-'byung II), (26) Ded-dpon ka-kha-'dzin, and (27) the Nepalese Jinamitra.

his five innermost disciples[63] throughout the period of his most intense teaching activity. When the guru bestowed upon him the empowerment of the Eight Great Herukas, rDo-rje bdud-'joms' flower fell onto 'Jig-rten mchod-stod. While meditating in a dark cave, he had a vision that the construction of the temple at bSam-yas was nearly completed, so he emerged through a small chink in the rock, leaving behind a large passageway. While practising the Vajrakīla *sādhana* in the Has-po-ri retreat centre, he cut off thought at its root and demonstrated his attainment by embedding his *kīla* into solid rock. He is renowned as having travelled in the sky as fast as the wind and passing unhindered through a mountain. Under the name Khri-zher of sBa, rDo-rje bdud-'joms was also one of the early translators who made the dangerous journey to India to bring back scriptures and, together with Ye-shes dbang-po and other skilled *lo-tsā-wa*, he translated numerous texts of the *vinaya*.

The particular magico-religious instructions entrusted by guru Padma to sNa-nam rdo-rje bdud-'joms were calculated to be of vital importance for the protection of the future descendants of king Khri Srong-lde'u-btsan. Thus it was that they were all carefully concealed in chosen locations as a treasure to be revealed in the future for the benefit of Tibet in general and for the welfare of the royal line in particular.

According to the *gSal byed nyi ma'i 'od zer*, an extensive biography of the *gter ston* written by his direct disciple Sūryabhadra,[64] among the many Dharma treasures that Padmasambhava concealed for the benefit of future generations is a special set of three that are intended for the benefit of the king of Gung-thang and his teacher (priest and patron, *yon mchod*), as well as for the benefit of all future sentient beings. A prophetic scroll which was extracted from one of the keys (*lde mig*) speaks of an occasion when prince Mu-khri btsan-po, in the company of sNa-nam rdo-rje bdud-'joms and Ye-shes mtsho-rgyal, turned to the guru Padmasambhava and asked, "Khye ma ho, Precious Guru! In the final period of time, the lineage of my sons will be reduced to the level of common folk in Mang-yul gung-thang. At that time, when the end of the dynasty is close at hand, where will this store of treasures which protects through the compassion of the master himself be hidden? Who will be appointed as the guardian of

---

63 *Las can dag pa'i 'khor lnga,* 'the fortunate circle of five', consisted of sNa-nam rdo-rje bdud-'joms, king Khri Srong-lde'u-btsan and his son prince Mu-khri btsan-po, Nam-mkha'i snying-po and the lady Ye-shes mtsho-rgyal.

64 Nyi-ma bzang-po (Sūryabhadra), belonged to the lineage of the Se clan, who had their seat at dPal-ldan brgya-mkhar gsang-sngags-gling.

those treasures? When will be a good time for the concealment of the treasures? And, for the one destined to reveal them in the future, what will be the key for their extraction?" To which Padmasambhava replied, "Listen well, royal majesty. All those who are possessed of faith and devotion will always be protected by my compassion. In particular, with regard to the three noble treasures that are set aside for the king and the inhabitants of Tibet, to the north of this place there is a mountain endowed with auspicious virtues. In accordance with the prophesy, we must go there. Oh, you three disciples possessed of good fortune, cast aside your doubts and assiduously pay attention to me now with faithful concentration." So saying, the guru uttered a forceful HŪṀ from his mouth and three visions arose in his companions. One of them saw the guru himself with one face and two hands, dancing with his legs spread wide in the depths of a blazing mass of blue black fire, his body as splendid as Mount Meru. Another saw the guru mounted upon a white lioness disappearing into the sky, while the third saw three faithful people arise, riding upon rainbows of five-coloured light. Then, in an instant, with a snap of the fingers, the master and his three faithful followers arrived on the peak of Mount bKra-bzang. Then the *ācārya* Padmasambhava moved his hands in the gesture of summoning (*ākarṣaṇamudrā*) and turned his face to look southwest. There, amidst gathering clouds of rainbows, a white *ḍākinī* dressed in a cloak of silk appeared in the sky. In her hands she carried a jewelled container, from which she took out three hard white stones (*'dzeng rdo*), a handspan in length, and presented them to the hands of the *ācārya*. With a smiling face, the guru spoke to his three faithful followers, "Listen to me, you faithful people of Tibet! For the protection of all those who live in Tibet, there are three especially important treasure stores concealed in three different locations. Inside a mountain resembling a heap of poisonous snakes, four treasures for the protection of the king are concealed within the stomach of a black poisonous snake. These have been entrusted to four very powerful treasure lords. In the area of Mang-yul, sun and moon are destined to arise together." Thus he spoke.

Within a maroon wooden box, one span in height and four spans in width, fashioned by three foreign lords from China, Nepal and mKhar-brag (?), is concealed a treasure called 'four teachings necessary for the king' (*rje la dgos pa'i chos bzhi*). These include one hundred instructions (*upadeśa*), as beneficial as the stalks of medicinal plants, which promote the happiness of Tibet by prolonging the lifespan of the king and extending his dominion; one hundred instructions of evil *mantra*, as pernicious as stalks of poisonous plants, which can be used in order to turn aside the enemies of the king and slay them; one hundred instructions on the cycle of practices of the four limbs of approach and accomplishment (*sevā-sādhana*), as well as skilful methods for the king to compose Dharma laws which will ensure the welfare of beings in this life and in the future; and one hundred instructions on Samantabhadra, as profound as the sky, so that the king, having provided great and powerful advantages for beings in this life, will attain enlightenment in his next. These four treasuries of one hundred instructions, together with the *kīla* called Srid-gsum bdud-'dul (Controller of demons in the three worlds), which was used in ritual by Padmasambhava when he attained *siddhi* in Yang-le-shod, Nepal, hammered from seven sorts of iron by dPal-rtsegs, a blacksmith from Mon; and also the *kīla* called Sras-tshogs nyi-ma (Sunshine of a host of sons), which was used to subdue enemies and obstructors at sTag-tshang seng-ge bsam-'grub in Bhutan, hammered from five sorts of iron by a blacksmith from India; and the *kīla* called 'Bar-ba-mchog (Supreme radiance), carved from the wood of a 'Dza-la nag-po tree from Ha-shang-ya in China, which was held by Padmasambhava when he beheld the face of Vajrakīla at dPal chu-bo-ri; and the *kīla* of ritual service (*sevā*), carved from the wood of an acacia tree (*khadira*), which was used by the lady Ye-she-mtsho-rgyal to slay seven demons of the extremities when they appeared in the guise of ravens at the cave of dPal chu-bo-ri; and the *kīla* of ritual service belonging to sNa-nams rdo-rje bdud-'joms, carved from the hard wood of a thorny tree from the land of Ge-sar-khrom, which he used to extinguish a blazing fire at Has-po-ri; and also the wish-fulfilling jewel called Nyi-ma lnga-shar (Fivefold Sunrise), which had been offered as a reciprocal gift to king Khri Srong-lde'u-btsan by the Indian emperor Dharmapāla (reigned over northern & eastern India *circa* 770-810), together with six small tufts of hair from the heads of Padmasambhava, Ye-shes mtsho-rgyal, king Khri Srong-lde'u-btsan, prince Mu-khri btsan-po, sNa-nam rdo-rje bdud-'joms and Nam-mkha'i snying-po, so that each scroll of instructions was accompanied by consecrated articles – every aspect of the teachings that a person could require: instructions for Tibet in general together with small scrolls of prophesies necessary for particular individuals and so on – a treasury of Dharma topics beyond imagination were sealed with a black poisonous snake forged from molten copper, and all were concealed on the southeast slope of Zang-zang lha-brag.

Furthermore, within a maroon coloured wooden box were placed an activity *kīla* (*karmakīla*), 18 inches in length, which had been used in ritual by guru Padma; a turquoise called Nyi-ma 'od-'phro (Emanating sunlight) which had been worn on the throat of the lady Ye-shes mtsho-rgyal; 51 paper scrolls predominantly containing instructions for clearing away mental defilements (*kleśa*); and seven scrolls concerning the razor-like malign *mantra*, enclosed within a reliquary amulet (*ga'u*) made of leather. This box was sealed with a mongoose and a victory banner, and concealed in a jewel-like rocky mountain in Mang-yul.

A paper scroll extracted from one of the keys says:

> On a rocky mountain resembling a heap of jewels,
> A treasure like the wish-fulfilling gem
> Is concealed with the seal of Vaiśravaṇa
> And entrusted to the treasure lord who bears a red spear.
> Hidden at the appropriate hour,
> It will ripen and liberate those who have good karma.

And it is also written: Hidden within a wooden box there is a statue of Padmasambhava, self-arisen from stone, which bestows great bliss on anyone who sees, hears about, touches or thinks of it; together with a five-pronged *vajra* which had been offered by king Indrabodhi; a skull cup filled with nectar that had been offered by Vajravārāhī; and 21 scrolls. This box has been sealed with a *kīla* and hidden in the cave of Yang-le-shod in Nepal.

And, in a second scroll, it is written:

> Within a rocky cave, endowed with auspicious blessings,
> At a time of advancement along the path of awakening,
> Hidden in the hollow of the vast knot of a *kīla*,
> [A treasure was] entrusted to three obedient protectors
> And hurriedly concealed in the hours of daylight.

The keys to those treasures are three standing stones (*rdo ring*). Sealed in the hollow of stone containers and within amulets of copper and bronze, having been inscribed in ink of charcoal, they stand as the right eye, mouth and heart of mount bKra-bzang.

And it is also written in the scroll cited above:

On the eastern slopes of mount bKra-bzang,
An emanation of sNa-nam rdo-rje bdud-'joms,
Endowed with the feathers of a vulture,
Will appear in a secret manner, possessed of great compassion.
Extracting three deposits of treasure,
he will bring great benefit to beings.
Endowed with good karma by maintaining his *samaya* vows,
That one is the son of myself, Padmasambhava.

As for those three standing stones of white *'dzeng brag*,
They are the keys to three treasure deposits
That will be hidden on this mountain:
One will be concealed as the eye –
It is the mirror of luminous clarity for the phenomenal world.
One will be concealed as the tongue –
It is the symbolic key of secret *mantra*.
One will be concealed as the heart –
It is the key of the resultant meaning.

As the guardian of those treasures, the watchful sentry
Bu-le nor-bu bzang-po protects them.

Thus it was prophesied.

In 1173 sNa-nam rdo-rje bdud-'joms was born again in Tibet, this time as Byams-pa-dpal (dPal-bo Āḥ Hūṁ), the translator of Khro-phu. Living as a tantric householder, he travelled to sPa-gro in Bhutan, where he revealed a number of Dharma treasures which have since become lost.

Rediscovery of the hidden treasures

In 1337, on the tenth day of the first month of the fire ox year, he was reborn in the area known as gNyan-yul (the place of snake demons) or Tho-yor nag-po (the country of the black stone cairn), to the east of mount bKra-bzang in La-stod-byang. In this incarnation he was given the name dNgos-grub rgyal-mtshan. Upon his body were seen many auspicious marks including sacred seed-syllables (*bīja*) on his heart, the sign of a conch shell on his throat, and black and white moles (*sme ba, tilaka*) upon his head.

dNgos-grub rgyal-mtshan's mother, Jo-lcam bsod-nams khye-'dren, was a lady of noble descent and his father sLob-dpon bdud-'dul (Sri-'dul-dpal) belonged to the family of sNa-mo-lung living on the estate (*gzhi kha*) of sNa-mo whose ancestry was said to trace back to the Mongolian king Gur-ser.

sLob-dpon bdud-'dul was a tantric *yogin* with expertise in the practice of the *Phur bu ze'u smug gu*, an early cycle of the deity Vajrakīla, and the young dNgos-grub rgyal-mtshan studied these doctrines together with those of the Māyājāla and Mātaraḥ and so on under his tutelage. He demonstrated remarkable skill in both understanding and practice from a very early age, perfecting the *samādhi* of Vajrakīla by the time he was eight years old. Following the death of his father he continued to be educated by his mother.

When he was just 11 years old, three feathery growths appeared on the top of his head and when he was 23 there were five. Because these growths looked like the feathers of a vulture, he became famous as rGod kyi ldem-'phru-can ('the one with vulture's feathers'). These extraordinary signs had been foretold in the prophecies and were regarded with awe as the marks of a truly special being. He also became known as *Rig 'dzin chen po* (*mahāvidyādhara*) and this is the title which has been held ever since by each of his successive incarnations.

In 1364 a lama by the name of Mang-lam bzang-po grags-pa[65] unearthed a number of treasure texts at Gyang Yon-po-lung. Among these texts were eight related to the concealed treasures of Zang-zang lha-brag and prophesies concerning Rig-'dzin rgod-ldem, who was born nearby, as the one destined to reveal them. These texts included the essential inventory (*snying byang*) entitled *Man ngag gnas kyi don bdun ma*. In the new year (February/ March 1365) bZang-po grags-pa entrusted these texts to sTon-pa bsod-nams dbang-phyug[66] and two companions with instructions to pass them on to "a *yogin* carrying a statue or rosary in his hand" that supposedly they would encounter to the east of the Zang-zang mountain and who would begin to engage them in a conversation concerning the king of Gung-thang, legitimate heir of the ancestral rulers of Tibet.

---

65 Renowned as a hermit (*ri khrod pa*), bZang-po grags-pa was proclaimed to be an emanation of Prince Mu-khri btsan-po.

66 A *vinaya* master involved in the ordination of Rin-chen 'byung-gnas, the eighth holder of the throne of sTag-lung. G. Roerich, *The Blue Annals* 634

A week or so later, as the three travellers were eating their meal on the bank of a stream near Brag-lung monastery in northern gYas-ru, rGod-ldem-can arrived there from sNa-mo-lung carrying in his hands a brass image of Vajrakīla and a rosary. "Have you heard that lord bKra-shis-lde (the king of Gung-thang) died today?" he asked. "This is not good. Has the very essence of the earth gone bad?" As he spoke, the three travellers realised that all the requirements of the prophecy were fulfilled and so, recognising him as the one they sought, they handed over all the treasure scrolls and a sealed letter of good wishes.

Upon his return to sNa-mo-lung, Rig-'dzin rgod-ldem interpreted the rising of the planet Jupiter in the eighth lunar mansion[67] as a sign that the time had come to take out the key to the treasures. At the first crack of dawn on the eighth day of the snake month in the year of the fire horse (1366), there came from the east a beam of white light "like the trunk of the wish-fulfilling *kalpalatā*" that struck the summit of Mount bKra-bzang and a spot beneath that was indicated by a light fall of snow. Thus, from the vicinity of three standing stones (*rdo ring*) within a cavity of hard white rock (*'dzeng brag dkar po*) beneath the summit of Ri-bo bkra-bzang, rGod-ldem-can unearthed the next link in the chain of the Northern Treasures in the form of seven paper scrolls (*shog ril*). In order to compensate for the removal of these scrolls, Rig-'dzin rgod-ldem buried another treasure in their place and the resultant cavity known as rLung-gseng ('Windy Hollow') is reported to be still in existence today.[68] During the new year celebrations on the following year, as Rig-'dzin rgod-ldem reached the age of thirty, a tree spontaneously grew up there which is also thought to have remained until now.

Two months later, on the fourth day of the sheep month 1366, Rig-'dzin rgod-ldem was engaged in the rite of bestowing upon his disciples the *abhiṣeka* of Vajrakīla. During the preliminary section of the rite, just as he was establishing the *maṇḍala* of deities within the bodies of his disciples, the guru arose and led his followers up into the mountains that look like a heap of poisonous snakes (*dug sbrul spung 'dra*). The texts describe the air as sweetly scented and filled with rainbows as Rig-'dzin rgod-ldem guided his disciples to the southwest face of the mountain where the atmosphere glowed with ruby-red light in the splendour of the

---

67 This auspicious configuration marked the birth of the Buddha. *Buddhacarita* I.9, II.36

68 NSTB I.780

setting sun. They climbed up to a mountain cave and, leaving two disciples[69] stationed beneath the entrance, rGod-ldem-can went inside and began to pray. As the sky grew dark following the setting of the sun, the rock cave began to tremor and shake as a sign that the master of the treasures (*gter bdag*) had arrived. At midnight they lit a number of butter-lamps and by their light the group was able to discern upon the rock the clear image of a *viśvavajra*. When the guru pressed beneath that mark with his paper scroll (the symbolic key to the treasures) it seemed to open like a door onto a triangular chamber within which they found a pale blue snake with a yellow belly, as thick as a man's arm. It was lying in a coil with its face to the southeast upon a square blue stone, the top of which was marked in nine sections with silver coloured nails so that it resembled the back of a tortoise. The coils of the snake looked like an enormous eight-sided precious stone and upon its heart were three gem-like excrescences from which were extracted a roll of paper and a symbolic jewel (*rin po che'i rtags tsam cig*).

Resting upon the blue stone slab, concealed within the serpent's coils, lay a maroon leather casket, the fivefold repository of the Northern Treasures.

From the central compartment of deep red leather, Rig-'dzin rgod-ldem took out the *Kun bzang dgongs pa zang thal* cycle in four volumes, which subsequently became among the most famous and revered of all the expositions of *atiyoga* doctrines in Tibet. From within this section he also took out the teachings of *Bla ma rig 'dzin gdung sgrub* and other texts related to the *sādhana* of *guru, deva* and *ḍākinī,*[70] together with the *atiyoga* texts of Vajrakīla and three *kīla* wrapped in maroon silk, thirty paper scrolls wrapped in blue silk, together with hair from the heads of guru Padma and his disciples and other sacred articles (*byin rlabs kyi rdzas*).

The front (eastern) compartment of the box was fashioned of white conch shell and contained texts of the *rGyu 'bras la ldog pa* cycle (putting an end to cause and effect) as well as teachings on the similarity of the awakened mind to the sky (*dgongs pa nam mkha' dang mnyam pa'i chos*) and the root *tantra* texts of the *Ka dag rang byung rang shar* cycle concerning the natural presence and arising of primordial purity.

---

69 Named in the biography as bLa-ma Do-pa-ba Sangs-rgyas bstan-pa & Rig-'dzin mgon-po.

70 Known as 'the three roots' (*rtsa gsum*) of tantric practice.

The golden southern chamber of the chest contained teachings on the fourfold practice of approach and attainment of the deity (*snyen sgrub rnam pa bzhi'i chos*) and the texts of the *gSang sgrub guru drag po rtsal* and *bKa' brgyad drag po rang byung rang shar.* These important ritual cycles became famous "like the sun and the moon" due to the brightness and clarity that they induced within the minds of those who practised them. Also in this chamber were found texts relating to Vajrakīla in his form as Mahottarakīla with nine faces and 18 hands.

From the western compartment of red copper, Rig-'dzin rgod-ldem took out the *rTen 'brel khyad par can* and the *Phyi sgrub 'gro ba kun grol*[71] which form part of the *rTen 'brel chos bdun* cycle. These teachings are said to be as pure and fragrant as the trunk of a sandalwood tree (*tsan dan gyi sdong bu lta bu'i chos*). He also took out a volume in which were found the *rTa mgrin dregs pa dbang sdud* (gaining control of inimical forces through the power of Hayagrīva), the *'Khor 'das dbang sdud* (overthrow of *saṁsāra* and *nirvāṇa*) and the *Lha chen* (Mahādeva) teachings, as well as a further volume containing the *Byang chub sems dpa'i spyod dbang* (authentic practices of a bodhisattva).

Within the black northern compartment of iron were found the most violent of all the wrathful ritual texts. Many Vajrakīla texts were taken from this chamber of the box, together with other teachings concerning "grinding the enemies and obstructors to dust" (*dgra bgegs thal bar rlog pa'i chos*), texts said to be as pernicious as the stem of a poisonous plant (*dug gi sdong po lta bu*). Eight treatises on the compounding of ritual medicine (*sman gyi tshad byas pa*) were also found there, as well as further commentaries (*upadeśa*) and instructions on 'thread cross rituals' (*mdos*)[72] but not all of these texts were transcribed and disseminated.

---

71 Several texts from this group have recently been published as *Illuminating Sunshine*, Wandel Verlag, Berlin 2012

72 Both Ramon Prats ("Some Preliminary Considerations Arising from a Biographical Study of the Early *gTer-ston*" 259) and Tulku Thondup (*Buddha Mind* 110) say that rGod-ldem-can is revered by the Bon-po as a *gter ston.* None of my sources, however, list any Bon-po doctrines among his discoveries, unless these are hinted at by the words "*mDos* ... and further *upadeśa*", and it seems to me that there may be some confusion here between Rig-'dzin rgod-ldem & the Bon-po *gter ston* Dpon-gsas khyung rgod-rtsal. Dpon-gsas khyung rgod-rtsal was born in the same area as Rig-'dzin rgod-ldem and revealed several similar texts, but was contemporary with his predecessor dPal-bo Āh Hūṁ.

Deposited in the four corners of the cave were found to be precious treasures dedicated as offerings to the guardian protectors, including the four soul turquoises of the king (*rgyal po'i bla gYu bzhi*) and other jewels. These precious offerings were left undisturbed.

Taking away the five treasuries of teachings (*mdzod lnga*), Rig-'dzin rgod-ldem organised each of the sections into one hundred and one parts and rearranged the folios of yellow paper (*shog ser po ti*) into pairs like mother and son, marked with the seed-syllables (*bīja*) of the four guardian goddesses of the gates. He then taught the doctrines contained therein to his chosen pupils.

These teachings became known as the Byang-gter or Northern Treasures in order to distinguish them from the Lho-gter (Southern Treasures) that had been revealed in previous centuries by Nyang-ral nyi-ma 'od-zer (1136-1204) and Guru chos-dbang (1212-1270). Together, these three *gter ston* are widely renowned in Tibet as the Body, Speech and Mind emanations of the great teacher Padmasambhava himself, and thought to be the three greatest treasure revealers of all. Indeed, the *sGron ma rnam gsum* states that "Any person who has a connection with just the spittle or urine of Rig-'dzin rgod-ldem will generate faith and devotion and proceed towards liberation."

Rig-'dzin rgod-ldem unearthed the keys to numerous 'hidden lands' (*sbas yul*), in which people could live in happiness in the peaceful pursuit of Dharma, and he is personally credited with the discovery of seven of these sacred places.[73] Entering Sikkim ('Bras-mo gshong) through the southern passageway of mChod-rten nyi-ma[74] in the year of the female ox (1373), Rig-'dzin rgod-ldem is said to have worked miracles there and blessed the 'White Rock Cave' of bKra-shis-lding as a powerful place for meditation. The Chronicle of the rulers of Sikkim describes a local cult dedicated to the holiest mountain in that vicinity (Gangs-chen mdzod-lnga) as contained in the work of a later Byang-gter *gter ston*, Shes-rab me-'bar. Sacred dances in honour of the deities thought to reside on the five peaks of that mountain are annually performed by royal command on

---

73 Listed by Dalai Lama V as: 'Bras-mo-gshongs, bDe-ldan skyid-mo-lung, sBas-pa padma'i-tshal, Rol-pa mkha'-'gro-gling, rGyal-kyi mkhan-po-lung, Lha'i pho-brang-sdings and Gro-mo-khud.

See also my translation of Rig-'dzin rgod-ldem's *General Introduction to the Hidden Lands* at www.khordong.de

74 See my "Pilgrim's Guide to the Hidden Land of Sikkim" *Bulletin of Tibetology* 39(1) Gangtok 2003

the full moon day of the seventh Tibetan month and Rig-'dzin rgod-ldem himself recovered further *gter ma* from the central peak. This secondary revelation was in the form of images: one of Padmasambhava in wrathful guise and one of the goddess mThing-kha. Letters announcing these discoveries were dispatched to Tibet, suspended from the necks of vultures.

Apart from the *gter ma* which he himself revealed, Rig-'dzin rgod-ldem held the key to other lists of hiding places (*them byang, kha byang*) and was thus instrumental in the unearthing of many more texts and powerful cult objects.

In harmony with the prophecies that describe the treasures of Zang-zang lha-brag as being of particular importance to the dynastic descendants of Khri Srong-lde'u-btsan, in 1389 at the age of fifty-two, Rig-'dzin rgod-ldem was appointed the role of personal preceptor to the king of Gung-thang, Khri-rgyal mChog-grub-lde, who gave him possession of the region of Ri-bo dpal-'bar in Mang-yul. As an offering to the sovereign, the guru presented the *kīla* called Srid-gsum bdud-'dul, which had been used by Padmasambhava himself when he attained *siddhi* in Yang-le-shod, together with other precious treasures and innumerable teachings and empowerments.

Thinking to benefit future generations, Rig-'dzin rgod-ldem also concealed a certain portion of his personal *gter ma* on Ri-bo dpal-'bar.

Opening the door to the hidden land of sKyid-mo-lung, a 'place of great happiness' (*bde ldan*), rGod-ldem-can also concealed portions of his *gter ma* there. During his time in gTsang, Rig-'dzin rgod-ldem-can founded the monastery of Se-bkra-bzang that became the seat of his son and heir to his lineage, rNam-rgyal mgon-po. This monastery later became the seat of the Se-ston line of incarnations.

The special cult object that seems to be endowed with great power for all holders of the Byang-gter phur-pa lineage is named in our texts as 'the precious *Gong khug ma*.' It remains unclear as to whether this is a text or a ritual *kīla* that was always carried by the *siddha* Padmasambhava and inherited from him, together with appropriate oral instructions, by Ye-shes mtsho-rgyal.[75] In either case it is reckoned to represent the power of Vajrakīla and embody the essence of the Vajrakīla doctrines.

Rig-'dzin rgod-ldem passed away in Zil-gnon, Sikkim, at the age of seventy-one in 1408, the year of the male earth mouse. The large number of teachings and special tantric precepts that he handed down to posterity were transmitted through three lineages known as the Mother, Son and Disciple lines. The successive holders of these doctrines are renowned as having attained many higher and ordinary *siddhi*.

Maintaining the continuity of the tradition

Having thus established the school of the Northern Treasures in Tibet, Rig-'dzin rgod-ldem remains, to this day, committed by his vows as a *bodhisattva* to propagate these teachings so long as they continue to serve the needs of humanity. Thus, in accordance with his religious precepts, he is said to have been reborn in the year of the water monkey in mNga'-ris glo-bo as the *gter ston* Legs-ldan bdud-'joms rdo-rje (1512-1625?).[76] His father, the *tāntrika* 'Jam-dbyangs rin-chen rgyal-mtshan, was considered to be an emanation of Legs-ldan nag-po, the main protector of the ancient spoken teachings of the *mDo gongs pa 'dus pa* (*Gongs 'dus*), in the rituals of which he was a renowned scholar and adept. His mother was 'Gro-lcam khrom-pa-rgyan.

Legs-ldan bdud-'joms rdo-rje and his elder brother, the mNga'-ris paṇ-chen Padma dbang-rgyal (1487-1542),[77] together received the empowerment of the *dGongs 'dus* cycle from their father and the three of them, father and sons, took a great interest in the study and practice of these

---

75 *Gong khug* means either a small pouch worn around the neck or the breast pocket of a shirt, etc. In either case, the *Gong khug ma* is that which was always kept by Padmasambhava close to his heart. Some indication that the item referred to here is indeed a ritual *kīla* is found in the *gter ma* revelations of mChog-gyur gling-pa where guru Padma is described as having a *kīla* of bell metal in his right hand with which the *māra* and *rākṣasa* are subjugated, a *kīla* of teak wood (*khadira*? Tibetan not supplied) with which the devoted disciples are protected, and an iron *kīla* worn around his neck which is indivisible with the deity. Erik Schmidt, *The Great Gate* 124

C.R. Lama, on the other hand, insists that the *Gong khug ma* is a condensed ritual text.

76 Traditional sources push these dates back by one *rab byung* cycle, i.e. 1452-1565, but both sets of dates are problematic.

77 Cf. Eva Dargyay, *The Rise of Esoteric Buddhism* 156-160 and NSTB I 805-808, for a potted biography of this lama.

teachings. More than a century later, when Padma 'phrin-las (see below) came to compose his own ritual manual for the empowerment rites of this cycle, he incorporated much material from the notes that they had written.

The two brothers, Legs-ldan rdo-rje and Padma dbang-rgyal, became disciples of sNgags-'chang śākya bzang-po,[78] who instructed them in the teachings of the Northern Treasures, bestowing upon them the complete series of empowerments and commentaries. At their first meeting, Śākya bzang-po gave a treasure text to Legs-ldan rdo-rje concerning the great *stūpa* of Boudhanātha in Nepal. Visiting that holy place, some years later, Legs-ldan rdo-rje and his brother returned to Tibet via sKyid-grong in order to visit Śākya bzang-po in Ri-bo dpal-'bar. Legs-ldan rdo-rje then stayed in sKyid-grong, immersing himself in a lengthy retreat under Śākya bzang-po's guidance.

In 1527, Legs-ldan rdo-rje was staying with this teacher Śākya bzang-po in the monastery of bDe-grol in Byang ngam-ring, at which time he took a solemn oath to maintain the teachings of the Northern Treasures in all their purity. It was his intention thereafter to return with his master to Ri-bo dpal-'bar, there to seclude himself in solitary retreat for a period of ten years. The right circumstances for the fulfilment of this wish were not present at that time, however, and he returned instead to central Tibet with his brother Padma dbang-rgyal.

At the monastery of bSam-yas, the two brothers met up with the 'Bri-gung *gter-ston* Zhig-po gling-pa gar-gyi dbang-phyug-rtsal (1524-1583).[79] The three lamas together performed a series of joint consecration and empowerment rituals which brought about a period of happiness and prosperity for the people of Tibet, which lasted for 13 years.

Legs-ldan rdo-rje is famed as the revealer of three further volumes of teachings,[80] unearthed at lCags-zam chu-bo-ri and other places, supplementing the original Northern Treasure revelations of rGod-ldem-can. The extraordinary length of his lifespan is attributed to his accomplishment of the *Tshe sgrub bdud rtsi 'khyil pa* practice, still celebrated every

---

78 sNgags-'chang śākya bzang-po (dates uncertain) was the first in the line of Yol-mo-ba sprul-sku, about whom more will be said below, p.63*ff*

79 One of the *snang sog gong gsum*, the teachings of this lama did not find favour with Dalai Lama V. See below, p.60

80 *Thugs rje chen po 'khor ba dbyings grol* (1 vol.), *Tshe sgrub bdud rtsi 'khyil pa* (1 vol.), and *Drag po dbu dgu* (1 small vol. including teachings on *'Jam dpal, Zhi drag & Phyag rdor*, etc.)

year with a week long retreat in the fourth Tibetan month by the monks of rDo-rje-brag, the Mother Monastery of the Northern Treasures tradition. His ritual cycle of Avalokiteśvara, *'Khor ba dbyings grol*, is also practised on an annual basis for seven days in the seventh Tibetan month.

Among his disciples was Nam-mkha' brgya-byin, the reincarnation of his own precious teacher Śākya bzang-po.

In the later period of his life, Legs-ldan rdo-rje settled at gSang-sngags theg-mchog-gling in La-stod byang and, at the age of 113 years, amidst many wonderful signs, he dissolved into the clear light of emptiness and great bliss.

His elder brother, the mNga'-ris paṇ-chen Padma dbang-rgyal, a renowned scholar and adept in the Byang-gter lineage, established a temporary monastery around his mountainside retreat cave, to which he gave the name Evaṁ lcog-sgar.

Anticipating the future expansion of his encamped community of Evaṁ lcog-sgar monks, Padma dbang-rgyal composed a strict code of conduct[81] to be followed by all who dwelt there. In this way, the teachings of the *vidyādhara* householder rGod-ldem-can came to be the central field of study for a community of ordained *bhikṣu*. Encouraged by the *gter ston* Shes-rab 'od-zer, Padma dbang-rgyal continued to build up both the fabric and the reputation of this religious community and eventually established the monastery of Thub-bstan gser-mdog-can.

The teachings of the Northern Treasures, central to the curriculum of this community, were further supplemented by Padma dbang-rgyal's own *gter ma* discovery, the cycle of *Rig 'dzin yongs 'dus,*[82] within which it is written: "In the southeast direction of the world, nine sons will be born to the demoness rNo-myur nag-mo and they will overthrow the world. In particular, in Tibet, this land of snows, forty years from now there will arise nine evil ministers and nine emanations of Māra, nine outer noble ladies, nine inner noble ladies, nine servants, nine commoners, nine messengers, nine lords and nine military commanders – nine groups of nine making 81 in all – and they will drag living beings down to misery."[83]

---

81 *bsGrigs kyi bka' yig rdo rje 'bar ba gzi byin.* Padma dbang-rgyal also composed the renowned *sDom gsum rnam nges* in which he demonstrated the interrelationship of the *prātimokṣa, bodhisattva* and *mantra* vows.

82 *Bla ma bka' brgyad yongs 'dus chos skor*

83 As told by Dalai Lama V in his biography of mNga'-ris paṇ-chen 468-469

Padma dbang-rgyal, famed as an incarnation of the religious king Khri Srong-lde'u-btsan, died at the age of fifty-six in the village of 'On-sme-thang.

Six years later, in 1548, the Rin-spungs ruler of Central Tibet appointed Zhing-zhag tshe-brtan rdo-rje as governor of gTsang province. The new ruler chose to settle in the castle palace at bSam-'grub-rtse (Zhigatse). He soon broke from his Rin-spungs masters, however, and proclaimed himself to be the king of gTsang. Then, together with his nine sons, as prophesied in the *Rig 'dzin yongs 'dus,* Tshe-brtan rdo-rje gradually took over all of Central Tibet, dBus and gTsangs. The problems that this created for the followers of the Northern Treasures school, loyal to the ancient rule of Tibetan kings, were soon to become apparent.

Following the death of Padma dbang-rgyal, his reincarnation was recognised by his younger brother Legs-ldan-rje in the form of a prince, bKra-shis stobs-rgyal dbang-po'i-sde (1550-1607) from the aristocratic family of Byang-pa. bKra-shis stobs-rgyal's father was Nam-mkha' rin-chen, of the royal family of Mi-nyag rtsa-shing, and his mother was Chos-skyong 'dzom-chen, from the governing family of Lhasa. bKra-shis stobs-rgyal lived in peaceful luxury, as befits a *sprul sku* prince, receiving a thorough education in both religious and secular affairs. Among his teachers were Legs-ldan bdud-'joms rdo-rje and the *lo chen mchog gi sprul sku*, Ratnabhadra.[84]

When he was 29, however, the noble house of Byang became involved in a dispute with Zhing-zhag tshe-brtan rdo-rje, as a result of which, bKra-shis stobs-rgyal and his brother Nam-mkha' rgyal-mtshan were expelled by force from their home in Byang ngam-ring to the province of dBus. Laughing at his victims, Zhing-zhag tshe-brtan rdo-rje made mockery of bKra-shis stobs-rgyal by jeering at his name (*sTobs*, 'strength, power'), calling him a powerless country-boy, now banished to the realm of hungry ghosts. In return, bKra-shis stobs-rgyal replied, "You, whose name is *Zhing* ('field'), are a perfect example of 'the ten fields to be destroyed'[85] and I banish you to the mouth of Rāhu!" Cursing him thus, bKra-shis stobs-rgyal performed the wrathful rites of Rāhu and so on, including

---

84 Lo-chen Ratnabhadra, founder of Ri-bo gru-'dzin monastery in gZhad Valley, was a teacher of the Jo-nang school. We will meet him again, below, as father of Yol-mo-ba sprul-sku III.

85 *bsGral ba'i zhing bcu.* This marks him out as an enemy of Dharma, suitable for destruction by means of the wrathful rites. See, below, note 692 For more on this topic, see *A Bolt of Lightning from the Blue* 223

many recitations of Yamāntaka, with the result that Zhing-zhag tshe-brtan rdo-rje died a short while later.

Among the writings of this great master bKra-shis stobs-rgyal is to be found a prophesy concerning a future treasure-revealer whose destiny it would be to become king of all Tibet in his fifth incarnation:

> Twenty-five [treasures] and five special treasures of mind
> Will be revealed, through pure aspirations,
> By your fifth incarnation,
> Oh present king of the black-headed race.[86]

The significance of this prophesy was soon to become apparent.

During his exile in 'Phyong-rgyas (later to be the birthplace of the Great Fifth Dalai Lama), bKra-shis stobs-rgyal fathered a son to the 'Phyong-rgyas princess, Yid-bzhin dbang-mo. This son, Ngag-gi dbang-po (1580-1639), of whom more will be said below, was recognised as the third incarnation of Rig-'dzin rgod-ldem.

Meanwhile, however, with regard to the illegitimate government in gTsang: Although this regime was remarkable for its secularism, it maintained close ties with the Sa-skya, Jo-nang and Karma bka'-brgyud Buddhist schools. At the same time, the gTsang rulers' relations with the burgeoning dGe-lugs school were less friendly. This predicament worsened further when, in 1578, the dGe-lugs abbot of 'Bras-spungs Monastery, bSod-nam rgya-mtsho (1543-1588), converted the Mongol leader Altan Khan and all of his subjects to Buddhism. In honour of his guru, Altan Khan bestowed the hitherto unknown title of Dalai Lama upon Sod-nam rgya-mtsho, who became known as Dalai Lama III while his two previous incarnations were posthumously awarded the title so as to become Dalai Lama I and Dalai Lama II. This new allegiance marked the beginning of a long struggle for patronage and support between the dGe-lugs-pa and Karma-pa schools, continuing throughout the lifetime of Dalai Lama IV, Yon-tan rgya-mtsho, (1589-1616).

---

86 Dudjom Rinpoche, *The Nyingma School of Tibetan Buddhism* 822-823

Furthering the work of his predecessor, bKra-shis stobs-rgyal unearthed three important cycles of teachings[87] from within a cave in gTsang-rong and became famous for his religious activities in both Khams and China.

With the support of his religious patron Pho-bo bka'-gnam rgyal-po, bKra-shis stobs-rgyal continued to build up the mountainside retreat centre mNga'-ris paṇ-chen evaṁ lcog-sgar which he now renamed Guru padma'i evaṁ lcog-sgar.

Travelling through eastern Tibet, bKra-shis stobs-rgyal was warmly welcomed at the monastery of Kaḥ-tog, which, at that time, was the most important rNying-ma-pa monastery in Khams. When requested by the assembly of Kaḥ-tog to say the prayers for an offering of tea to the three roots, bKra-shis stobs-rgyal spontaneously composed a hymn in honour of his predecessor, Padma dbang-rgyal, exhorting the listeners to emulate his great qualities (*rig 'dzin mnga' ris paṇ chen po'i mtshan dpe la yod pa'i legs pa'i lam ston*). This prayer began to be recited on a regular basis at Kaḥ-tog, but then the words were changed so that it became a hymn in praise of the teacher of Kaḥ-tog, gTsang-pa padma rgyal-mtshan. Becoming angry at this insult, bKra-shis stobs-rgyal performed the wrathful rite of *Nyi zla nag po'i rlung khor* so that the hapless teacher from gTsang was ousted by his patrons, became a homeless wanderer and eventually died of a 'virulent contagion of demons' (*rims gdon drag po*). Despite this rather violent altercation, however, history records the journey as one in which "the welfare of all beings was extensively promoted by means of the holy Dharma" (*dam pa'i chos kyis 'gro don rgya cher spel*).[88] It was probably during this trip to Khams that bKra-shis stobs-rgyal went to Dar-rtse-mdo and founded the small temple there that would eventually become the easternmost branch of rDo-rje-brag Monastery.

As for his son, the third incarnation of the *mahāvidyādhara* rGod kyi ldem-'phru-can: With the death of Zhing-zhag tshe-brtan rdo-rje, it was time for bKra-shis stobs-rgyal to return to his home in Byang ngam-ring with his princess Yid-bzhin dbang-mo, where she gave birth to Ngag-gi dbang-po chos-rgyal rdo-rje in the year of the iron dragon (1580).

---

87 These are the *Tshe sgrub sku gsum rig 'dus*, the *Karma guru'i chos skor* and the *Ma rgyud khrag rlung ma* (*Ma rgyud snying po don gsum*)

88 Biography of mNga'-ris paṇ-chen 497 (See above, note 83)

In the early part of his life, Ngag-gi dbang-po performed so many beneficial deeds for the people of Bhutan (Mon), Kong-po, Khams and China that the emperor of China respectfully bestowed upon him the rank of *Ho thog thu*, the highest imperial honour for an incarnate lama.

At the age of nineteen, Ngag-gi dbang-po moved the residence of Evaṁ lcog-sgar to the central province of dBus where, in the year of the earth pig (1599), he founded the monastery Guru padma'i evaṁ lcog-sgar thub-bstan rdo-rje-brag. Since then, that monastery has been the main seat of learning for the lineage of the Northern Treasures and the see for all successive incarnations of its *gter ston*.

The name rDo-rje-brag derives from the natural image of a *viśvavajra,* which was clearly discernible in the surrounding hills.[89] This auspicious location, abundant with wonderful signs and marks, was formerly visited by guru Padma himself, as well as by Nga'-ris paṇ-chen padma dbang-rgyal, and the area is considered to be especially beneficial for tantric practice. A handprint and footprint of Padmasambhava, both deeply imprinted in solid rock on the face of the mountain at the back of the monastery, are worshipped by pilgrims to the site as sources of blessing and inspiration and, when Padma dbang-rgyal spent the night there, he felt that his lifespan had been increased by a dozen years.

During the lifetime of its founder it perhaps housed more than two thousand monks[90] and, growing even larger in later years, it became one of the principal rNying-ma-pa monasteries in Tibet. Even so, Rig-'dzin Ngag-gi dbang-po was not satisfied with what he had been able to achieve by the end of his lifetime and he entrusted further plans for its development to his 'heart son' (leading disciple) bsTan-'dzin nor-bu of Yol-mo.

In 1617, Ngag-gi dbang-po bestowed an empowerment of long life upon a new-born child who was destined to attain immortal renown as the Great Fifth Dalai Lama (1617-1682).

---

89 According to the *Vaiḍūrya phreng ba*: Behind the monastery stands a dark red *vajra* mountain which rises up to touch the sky. The triangular shape of the mountain is an auspicious sign that all tantric activities performed in that place, especially the wrathful rites, will be accomplished without hindrance and, on its peak, the clear outline of a turquoise *viśvavajra*, from which the monastery derives its name, remained visible until it was reduced to rubble by the invading Dzungar Mongols in 1718.

90 This figure is given by Rigzin & Russell. Tarthang Tulku (*Crystal Mirror* V) gives the figure as 200, whilst Wylie (*The Geography of Tibet*) and Ferrari & Petech (*mKhyen-brtse's Guide*) give 400. Tarthang Tulku also mentions that, at this time, the monastery had three incarnate lamas.

Foretold in numerous Dharma treasures as the actual embodiment of the compassion of Avalokiteśvara and the enlightened activity of king Khri Srong-lde'u-btsan,[91] the fifth Dalai Lama was born in the year of the fire snake as a son of the rNying-ma-pa family of the dukes of 'Phyong-rgyas stag-rtse, home of the ancient Tibetan monarchy. His father was Mi-dbang bdud-'dul rab-brtan, a descendent of the royal line of Za-hor, and his mother Kun-dga' lha-mdzes was a daughter of the *khri dpon* of Yar-'brog. Born amidst many auspicious signs and omens, his life was filled with auspiciousness and joy from the outset.

When Yon-tan rgya-mtsho, Dalai Lama IV, died at a suspiciously young age, the search for his reincarnation was prohibited by the administration in gTsang. Despite this prohibition, however, Dalai Lama V was secretly recognised when he was just one year old. Shortly after this, his father was imprisoned at bSam-'grub-rtse by the king of gTsang, accused of complicity in a plot against the government, and the young *sprul sku* was taken by his mother to her family castle in Yar-'brog. The young Dalai Lama never saw his father again and, as time went by, it became necessary to establish a small army of Mongol soldiers around him as bodyguards.

Having been recognised as the incarnation of the fourth Dalai Lama by Paṇ-chen bla-ma bLo-bzang chos-kyi rgyal-mtshan, the boy was brought to the monastery of 'Bras-spungs at the age of four in 1622 where he took his first set of vows (*upāsaka*) and was installed upon the lion throne with the name bLo-bzang rgya-mtsho. At the age of eight he was ordained as a novice monk, and he became a fully ordained *bhikṣu* in 1628, aged eleven.

As he grew up he came to receive the full series of tantric authorisations of the Northern Treasures tradition (some of which were said to have been received directly from the deceased master bKra-shis stobs-rgyal in mystic visions[92]), as well as the unbiased teachings of his own (dGe-lugs-pa) and other schools.

With dKon-mchog chos-'phel (1573-1644) of gLing-smad, foretold by guru Padma as the incarnation of rNgog lo-tsā-ba, the young Dalai Lama studied the great texts of Buddhist philosophy, mastering all of them with ease. Subsequently, under the greatest teachers of his time, he studied the

---

91 The three great Dharma rulers of Tibet, according to popular tradition, were: Avalokiteśvara (manifest as Srong-btsan sgam-po), Mañjuśrī (Khri Srong-lde'u-btsan), and Vajrapāṇi (Khri Ral-pa-can).

92 See Samten Karmay, *Secret Visions* 66, 74, etc., also 34 where it is said that guru Padma himself gave Dalai Lama V instructions in the Byang-gter.

various arts and sciences, such as grammar, poetic composition, astrology and divination, so that he became renowned as a *mahāpaṇḍita*. Receiving empowerments and instructions in all the major tantric cycles of the old schools and the new, he became a fully awakened Dharma master and a true manifestation of buddhahood in this degenerate world. He upheld the purity of his vows of *prātimokṣa, bodhisattva* and *guhyamantra* without the smallest blemish and the catalogue of his studies (*gsan yig*) fills four volumes.

Referred to clearly in the prophetic verse of bKra-shis stobs-rgyal, cited above, during his lifetime the fifth Dalai Lama revealed a total of 25 treasures which pertain, for the most part, to the corpus of the Byang-gter – the sacred system to which he had been introduced at birth and within which he was encouraged to further his spiritual development by repeated visitations of lineage holders, including the deceased bKra-shis stobs-rgyal himself.

The epoch into which he was born was a troubled one in Tibetan history, during which the country was torn apart by religious and political rivalries. Certainly, at this time, the prophesied rebirth of the ancient line of kings would be a great blessing for the people.

In the language of the Dalai Lama's biography, "the lords of Chog-tu, Be-ri and gTsang became confused by demons who established wrong views in their minds and thus they became enemies of Dharma, suitable to be overthrown by the wrathful rites.[93] It then happened that, in accordance with the prophesies and as a result of his past actions, the *cakravartin* king bsTan-'dzin chos-kyi rgyal-po (the Mongolian warlord Gushri Khan, leader of the Qoshot Mongols), came to the province of dBus in central Tibet where he developed profound faith in the Lord Lama as soon as he set eyes upon him, so that the hair of his body quivered and he took the feet of the Dalai Lama upon the crown of his head. He then gathered together his army and dispatched those enemies of Dharma to the realm of Samantabhadra."[94]

---

93 Regarding the ten categories of those suitable to be destroyed by the wrathful rites (*bsgral ba'i zhing bcu*), see below, note 692

As for the mighty warlord Gushri Khan, "the very essence of bravery and courage," he is believed to have been the reincarnation of Phyag-rgya zil-gnon, a rNying-ma-pa specialist in the wrathful rites of Yamāntaka.

94 Sangs-rgyas rgya-mtsho, *Life of the Fifth Dalai Lama* 260-261

In 1641,[95] when the Dalai Lama was just 24 years old, Gushri Khan, having overthrown those three rebellious provinces, offered all that he had conquered, both secular and religious, to the dominion of the Dalai Lama. Later, in 1652, the Dalai Lama travelled to Peking at the invitation of Shun-chih, the Manchu emperor of China, who proclaimed him Lord of the Doctrine and installed him as the imperial preceptor. Thus the vow-holding monk became the *de facto* king of all Tibet, its foretold ruler, and he united the country under one banner for the first time since the collapse of the royal dynasty, eight hundred years previously. Restoring peace and prosperity to his people, he showed himself to be the least sectarian of religious leaders. Receiving the Karma-pa Chos-dbyings rdo-rje at the Potala Palace, a welcome reconciliation was effected so that all factional fighting was brought to an end[96] – and his successive incarnations have upheld the happiness and welfare of a greater Tibet down to the present time.

As recounted in his *Secret Biography*, the Dalai Lama experienced throughout his life a series of mystic visions (*gzigs snang*), in the course of which were revealed to him a number of Dharma treasures which became known as the 'Twenty-five Teachings Sealed for Secrecy' (*gsang ba rgya can du gsol ba'i chos sde nyi shu rtsa lnga*). Many of these visions were connected with doctrines of the Northern Treasures tradition and involved masters of the lineage (both living and deceased), and two of the 'seals which keep them secret' relate directly to the deity Vajrakīla, a deity that also looms large within the visions themselves. During one such ecstatic experience, the Dalai Lama was granted the empowerment of Vajrakīla by the *mahāsiddha* Prabhahasti, by whom Padmasambhava himself had been empowered in India almost nine centuries earlier. On that occasion, Prabhahasti displayed the *maṇḍala* of deities within his heart and no sooner had the ritual *kīla* been placed into his hands than the Dalai Lama began to dispatch messengers, with instructions to drag forth the *dam sri* demons so that they may be destroyed. So important was the deity Vajrakīla to the Dalai Lama that, much to the disapproval of his personal attendants, following a visionary empowerment bestowed upon him

---

95 Iron serpent year (1641) according to the Dalai Lama's biography, although other sources give the year of the water horse (1642) for this event.

96 For political reasons, however, Dalai Lama V took control of several Bon monasteries in central Tibet and banished the Jo-nang order to A-mdo. He later reinstated the Bon, giving it public recognition so as to restore it to it's place in the religious and political affairs of the country.

in 1642 by bKra-shis stobs-rgyal dbang-po'i-sde, he adopted the habit of wearing a ritual *kīla* stuck into the belt of his monastic robes. Later, when he decided to move the seat of his new government from 'Bras-spungs to Lhasa, the Dalai Lama instructed the monks of rNam-rgyal monastery to enact sacred dances outlining the black deity *maṇḍala* of Vajrakumāra upon the site, and thus the ritual 'taming of the earth' was performed for his new Potala palace and all the local gods and demons were brought under control by the circle of 51 blood-drinkers of the Vajrakīla *maṇḍala*. This took place in 1645, when the Dalai Lama was just 28 years old.

In his youth, the Dalai Lama had been introduced to the rDzogs-chen view, meditation and practice by dKon-mchog lhun-grub. As his root teacher, he accepted Chos-dbyings rang-grol of the great family of Zur (1604-1669), who had been nurtured as a *sprul sku* by Rig-'dzin ngag-gi dbang-po since the age of nine years and was a renowned master of the Northern Treasures tradition of Rig-'dzin rgod-ldem. Throughout the whole of his life, this was the tradition in which the Dalai Lama always had the greatest faith.

In fact, the Dalai Lama's personal support of the rNying-ma schools in general is quite evident in many of the changes which he made to the structure of religious and political authority during the course of his lifetime. Several of the important ceremonies of state, newly instituted during his reign and subsequently performed annually in Lhasa for centuries, clearly reveal their Old School antecedents and he also sponsored the carving of a large number of xylographic blocks for the preservation and dissemination of texts of the early translations. His own writings, also, (amounting to 235 titles in 24 volumes) include many prayers and meditations designed to be incorporated into the rituals of the Northern Treasures and other early cycles. In the reports of his visions recorded in his *Secret Biography* (which, uniquely among his works, was never carved onto wooden blocks and printed), the Dalai Lama states that Legs-ldan rdo-rje appeared to him several times and gave him specific instructions to propagate the teachings of the Northern Treasures. After that, he received visionary empowerments and guidance in the Byang-gter tradition from both the recently deceased Ngag-gi dbang-po and his long dead father bKra-shis stobs-rgyal, and it is clear that he regularly performed the ritual practices of the Northern Treasures throughout his lifetime.[97]

In his *Secret Biography* it is recorded that, at the age of 35 years, on the 23rd day of the 11th month in the year of the iron rabbit (1651), a group of five dancing *ḍākinī* with *ḍamaru* drums and hand bells appeared in the sky before him leading a long white cloud, at the end of which was the master Padmasambhava. In order to instruct the Dalai Lama in the doctrines of the Northern Treasures, Padmasambhava presented him with his heart practice (*thugs sgrub*) by appearing in the form of Guru drag-po-rtsal (one of the most important teachings of the Byang-gter). Upon the crown of his head stood an especially wrathful form with nine faces and eighteen arms, and he was surrounded by a retinue of deities and an outer circle of Dharma protectors. Furthermore, within an unprecedented divine palace situated inside the 'vast knot' of his large ritual *kīla*, the Dalai Lama could clearly see all the deities in the *maṇḍala* of Vajrakīla. Entering into that palace, he found a gathered assembly of tantric heroes and heroines, all dancing, and so he joined in the dance. Within the recesses of a chapel in that place, a throne had been set up, upon which was seated a maroon coloured *rākṣasa* demon holding aloft a mirror in his hand. "Look into this mirror!" he commanded and, having done so, the Dalai Lama saw all the countries such as India, China, Nepal, Oḍḍiyāna, Śambhala, and so on, most clearly and distinctly. He then understood with certainty that his vision had taken him to the pure land of the Copper Coloured Mountain (Zangs-mdog dpal-ri).[98] There, on top of a mountain shaped 'like the handle of a *kīla* of control' (i.e. like a tall, upturned bowl), stood a three-storeyed palace. The lower storey was occupied by the precious teacher of Oḍḍiyāna in his activity manifestation as the Karma guru, teaching the profound means of averting the hosts of Māra. In the middle and upper storeys of the palace, he appeared in various guises to be worshipped by sentient beings.

---

97 Two sections of the secret teachings: Eight ('sealed by the kiss of sun & moon', containing prophesies) and Nine ('sealed by the Kīla', containing rituals), were taught to the Dalai Lama by bKra-shis stobs-rgyal during a Byang-gter retreat focussing on the teachings of Legs-ldan rdo-rje.

98 The Copper Coloured Mountain is situated on the island of Cāmaradvīpa, to the southwest of our world. It is inhabited by *rākṣasa* demons, kept under control by Padmasambhava himself who is believed to reside there currently as their king in the form of the dark maroon demon on the throne.

Then the Dalai Lama was taken behind a bright veil of white light, like a curtain, where he encountered Ye-shes mtsho-rgyal, white in colour and adorned with ornaments of bone, who acted as his support (consort) for the empowerment of wisdom-knowledge (*prajñā-jñānābhiṣeka*). This empowerment brought his psychic channels (*nāḍi*) and subtle drops (*bindu*) to the state of ultimate perfection, so that a very special experience of bliss and emptiness was generated within his mindstream. After that, he went immediately to a castle where he encountered a maroon coloured woman, blazing brightly and looking a little fierce. She took him into her mouth and swallowed him, and he was transformed into rDo-rje gro-lod in her womb. Emerging from her birth canal, the Dalai Lama maintained the divine pride of himself as the deity rDo-rje gro-lod and understood that, even though he himself rested in the state of clear light within which all illusory appearances had come to an end, the entire triple world of phenomenal appearances existed within his belly. This vision lasted for as long as it takes to drink a cup of tea.

When it was all over, a disembodied voice gave ominous warning of trouble arising after three lifetimes,[99] so the Dalai Lama then prepared a ritual thread cross (*mdos*) for the restoration of broken vows, dedicated to the protectress Rematī (dPal-ldan lha-mo).[100]

When the goddess arrived, galloping across the sky, the whole Earth shook and trembled violently. Then five *ḍākinī* appeared in the sky before him, their bodies shining like crystals – white, yellow, red, green and blue. Their leader, white in colour, gave some teachings on the different classes of *māra* and the means of averting difficult circumstances, at the end of which she carried the Dalai Lama in her womb until they reached a cave in a *vajra*-shaped rocky mountain that seemed to rise precipitously up into the sky. Within that cave they entered a palace of the gods where they found an ordinary-looking *yogin* that the Dalai Lama knew must really be

---

99 It should also be noted that, throughout his visions, the Dalai Lama received many prophetic warnings concerning future interferences to be caused to his work by troublesome *dam sri* demons. In particular, the wild spirit called Shugs-ldan arose at this time, following the murder of Grags-pa rgyal-mtshan, and remains a cause of trouble to the present day.

100 The Dalai Lama received visionary teachings on dPal-ldan lha-mo from the Byang-gter master bKra-shis stobs-rgyal. Subsequently, this goddess became not only the chief personal protectress of the Dalai Lama himself but, in accordance with the prophesies concerning the importance of the Byang-gter tradition for the welfare of Tibet, has remained to this day the main protector of his dGa'-ldan pho-brang theocratic government.

Padmasambhava himself. That *yogin* placed several volumes of books upon the Dalai Lama's head, granting him mystic empowerments and blessings and, when this was over, that *yogin* dissolved into light and became absorbed into the Dalai Lama's heart.[101]

A religious commentary on the significance of this single day's visions could fill a book, and it is recorded that all of his visions and their meanings were transmitted by the Dalai Lama to his favourite disciple, Rig-'dzin padma 'phrin-las.

Throughout the course of his life, the Dalai Lama built a vast number of shrines and temples, fully endowing each one with all the paraphernalia of worship in accordance with his visions. Following the Byang-gter predictions concerning the restoration of the ancient lineage of kings, he also sponsored Bon priests to perform regular rituals for the good of the land and his people, for the Bon continued to honour the old gods of the soil so that the countryside remained fertile and productive, just as it had been in the days of the kings. And he rebuilt the decayed temples of the early dynastic period, renewing them with fresh consecrations, and endowed them with monastic communities. He put a golden roof on the temple of Mount Chu-bo, and another on the Yum-bu bla-sgang, as well as a crown on the statue of Mahākāruṇika in the Jo-khang, and so on. Among the countless gifts of statues and other works of art offered as part of this restoration process, it is recorded that he bequeathed pennants of pearls and precious stone as well as an iron lattice fence to an ancient *maṇḍala* of Vajrakīla.

Meanwhile, in 1639, at a time when the Dalai Lama was still only 22 years old, the *mahāvidyādhara* of rDo-rje-brag Monastery, Ngag-gi dbang-po, died.

Two years later, in the year of the iron snake at Mon-mkhar rnam-sras-gling, the birth of bLo-bzang padma 'phrin-las theg-mchog dbang-gi rgyal-po (1641-1718) was marked by an unusually high number of auspicious portents and he was recognised as the fourth in the line of *mahā-*

---

101 *rGya can gyi 'khrul snang rnams gsal bar bkod pa mthong ba don ldan* (Visions and their Significance, being the elucidation of the visions recorded in the Sealed Volume)
Text I in *Secret Visions of the Fifth Dalai Lama* 182-183

vidyādhara. After the ceremony of his re-enthronement by his former disciple bsTan-'dzin nor-bu of Yol-mo, Padma 'phrin-las became a disciple of the Great Fifth Dalai Lama, from whom he received both *śrāmaṇera* and *bhikṣu* vows.

Universally acknowledged as the greatest scholar in the lineage of the Northern Treasures, bLo-bzang padma 'phrin-las studied intensively under some of the greatest teachers of his day,[102] receiving the empowerments and commentaries of a large number of tantric doctrines from both the old schools and the new. Revising and greatly extending the teachings of his own incarnation line, the Northern Treasure school of rDo-rje-brag, he gathered together all of the teachings that had been handed down in the three streams of transmission from the original *gter ston* (the Mother, Son and Disciple lineages), uniting them into a single line. He composed a number of new treatises and worked extensively to arrange the ritual texts of the Byang-gter in proper liturgical order, supplementing the original texts with extra parts wherever necessary. Correcting such errors as had arisen in the transmission, he reinstated earlier traditions of ritual activity that had become lost or confused, such as the proper systems of chanting, laying out the *maṇḍala*, preparing the sacrificial *bali* cakes and so on, filling 13 volumes with his work.

In his autobiography, Dalai Lama V repeatedly refers to Padma 'phrin-las as "the best of reincarnate ones" and "spiritual son of supreme virtue," and it is evident that Padma 'phrin-las was his favourite disciple. The Dharma treasures of the Dalai Lama, the 'Twenty-five Teachings Sealed for Secrecy' spoken of above, were all transmitted to Padma 'phrin-las who incorporated much of their highly esoteric ritual lore into his own Northern Treasures school of rDo-rje-brag.

It could also be said that Rig-'dzin padma 'phrin-las himself was instrumental in bringing about some of these visions. Thus, for example, on the 20th day of the fourth month in the year of the water hare (1663), as a long-life ritual was being performed by Padma 'phrin-las on behalf of his master, a vision of Amitāyus and his consort arose which subsequently blessed the Dalai Lama by becoming absorbed into his body.

---

102 Among whom were Zur-chen chos-dbyings rang-grol, bKa'-gyur-ba bsod-nams mchog-ldan, Khra-tshang-ba blo-mchog rdo-rje, gTer-chen 'gyur-med rdo-rje, lHa-btsun nam-mkha' 'jigs-med and Se-ston thugs-mchog 'od-'bar.

Throughout this period, with the patronage and support of the Dalai Lama, huge new rNying-ma monasteries were founded throughout central and eastern Tibet, the two monasteries of rDo-rje-brag and sMin-grol-gling in central Tibet being of particular significance, so that the years of the Dalai Lama's reign saw an increase in the general fortunes of the rNying-ma-pa with a clearly marked tendency towards such larger monastic institutions.

During this period, also, for primarily political reasons, Padma 'phrin-las produced extensive writings on the *anuyoga* system of 'Sūtra Empowerment' (*mdo dbang*), based on the *anuyogatantra* entitled *dGongs pa 'dus pa'i mdo* (*Sūtra of the Gathering of all Buddha's Intentions*). Historically, the *dGongs 'dus* provided much of the mythological and doctrinal structure for the orally transmitted teachings (*bka' ma*) of the rNying-ma-pa and, as a result, by the 17th century the *dGongs 'dus* empowerment had become a grand ceremony that was thought to embody the very heart of the *bka' ma* transmission. One hundred years previously, in his former life as Legs-ldan rdo-rje, Padma 'phrin-las had received this important cycle of teachings at a young age as one of the special transmissions of his father 'Jam-dbyangs rin-chen rgyal-mtshan and, having incorporated it into the curriculum of study for the Byang-gter community of E-vaṁ lcog-sgar, had become one of its chief proponents. The lineage of *bka' ma* teachings, however, became severely disrupted in the century that followed, as the E-vaṁ lcog-sgar community was persecuted by the lords of gTsang. In this life, now that the community had become settled in the monastery of rDo-rje-brag, it was time to reestablish these important ritual practices, integrating them once more into the Byang-gter curriculum of study. Accordingly, in 1664, Padma 'phrin-las received the full empowerment of this cycle from Nyang-ston khra-tshang-pa,[103] including the esoteric instructions, practical techniques and authoritative seal of entrustment. "The master arrived at rDo-rje-brag in the early morning," writes Padma 'phrin-las, and, "inaugurating procedures with the Vajrapāṇi empowerment, he went through the rituals in due sequence until he came to the rite for seizing the ground (*bhūparigraha*) for the *maṇḍala* of the Gathered

103 Also known as sMan-lung-pa bLo-mchog rdo-rje (1595-1671). This same teacher had previously granted the empowerment to the Great Fifth Dalai Lama, from whom he received the honorary title *ti shih*. It was at the Dalai Lama's special request that the empowerment was being bestowed upon Padma 'phrin-las at this time in such a manner as to make him a major lineage-holder at the age of 23.

Great Assembly. At this point, the great lama put on his costume of secret gown and wide-brimmed *thang zhu* hat and so forth, and took up his *vajra* and bell, some white mustard seed and the far-reaching lasso to banish all obstructions. Then, when he assumed the role of the Lord of Vajra Wrath, the sign of a blazing *viśvavajra* shone forth from each of the soles of his two feet. Shouting HŪṀ HŪṀ with his speech and adopting a threatening posture and formidable gaze, such was the power of his incredible splendour that there was one amongst us who, unable to endure it, was caused to faint. Realising that holy lama to be the genuine *vajra* anger of the Blessed Buddha, faith and devotion arose within me and, when he unfolded his roaring wings, I saw him clearly as the actual deity."[104]

Having thus received the empowerment so that the teachings of his former incarnation and his family could once again become an important part of the Evaṁ lcog-sgar curriculum of study, Padma 'phrin-las was urged by his teachers to spread its message widely. The Dalai Lama, especially, requested that he compose a new ritual for the performance of the Gathered Great Assembly ceremonies. This endeavour took more than a dozen years to complete and eventually (in 1679) resulted in a massive manual in three volumes entitled *Embarking on the Ocean of Maṇḍala: Empowerment Ceremonies of the Sūtra which Gathers all Intentions* (*'Dus pa mdo'i dbang chog dkyil 'khor rgya mtsho'i 'jug ngogs*). He also compiled a new collection of the biographies of the masters of the *dGongs 'dus* empowerment lineage. By these means, it was hoped that control of this key ritual system would be taken away from the Dalai Lama's enemies and tilt the balance of political authority in his favour. This project also represented a power shift within the rNying-ma school that paralleled the wider change to the new Dalai Lama government. Previously, under the rule of the gTsang kings, the main central Tibetan rNying-ma lineage enjoying royal patronage was that stemming from the *gter ston* Zhig-po gling-pa, passing through Sog-bzlog-pa and Gong-ra lochen amongst others. After Dalai Lama V's takeover, this group fell out of favour while the new monasteries of rDo-rje-brag and sMin-grol-gling

---

104 Rig-'dzin padma 'phrin-las, *'Dus pa mdo dbang gi bla ma brgyud pa'i rnam thar ngo mtshar dad pa'i phreng ba* 413

were established. Padma 'phrin-las' new ritual manual reflected this change in royal patronage.[105]

On the fourth day of the first month of the water dog year (1682), Padma 'phrin-las sent a message to the Regent Sangs-rgyas rgya-mtsho at the Potala, informing him of bad omens concerning his teacher, the Great Fifth Dalai Lama. He insisted that certain rites should be performed for the benefit of his health and recommended a retreat which the Dalai Lama followed eleven days later. During this retreat, the Dalai Lama died at the age of 65 on the 25th day of the third month 1682. The fact of the retreat, however, facilitated keeping the news of the Dalai Lama's death from all his rivals for a further fifteen years, and his fragile new government of the dGa'-ldan pho-brang continued to function unimpeded so that it was in a position of strength by the time that his successor, the sixth Dalai Lama, was announced and enthroned at the age of fourteen.

Rig-'dzin padma 'phrin-las himself was killed in 1718 when the invading Dzungar Mongols razed his monastic seat of Thub-bstan rdo-rje-brag to the ground.[106]

The fifth incarnation of Rig-'dzin rgod-ldem was bsKal-bzang padma dbang-phyug (1720-1770), born at Nyag-rong lcags-mdud in the district of sPo-'bor-sgang in southeastern Tibet to a family claiming descent from the ancient lHa dynasty of Tibetan monarchs. Following his installation at

---

105 The *dGongs 'dus* empowerment writings of gTer-bdag gling-pa, produced at sMin-grol-gling just a few decades later, approach the subject in an entirely different style – greatly simplifying the elaborate ceremony in an attempt to make it more suitable for the general public and render it more easily manageable for a festival format. With the most secret tantric elements removed, the unwieldy manual was divided into smaller parts that could be distributed among separate groups of ritual specialists within the monastery. In this way, both the preparations and the actual performance became streamlined so that the entire ceremony could be completed in just three days. This new system, backed by a rigorous historical study that provided unprecedented detail on the ritual tradition, culminated in 1691 when hundreds of leading rNying-ma masters throughout Tibet were invited to a grand unveiling at sMin-grol-gling. The project was highly successful, and today sMin-grol-gling's ritual manuals are standard at all rNying-ma monasteries other than those affiliated with rDo-rje-brag. (Jacob Dalton, *The Uses of the dGongs pa 'dus pa'i mdo in the Development of the rNying ma School of Tibetan Buddhism*, University of Michigan, 2002)

106 See L. Petech, *China and Tibet in the Early Eighteenth Century;* and Snellgrove & Richardson, *A Cultural History of Tibet,* for details of this troubled historical period.

rDo-rje-brag, he thoroughly repaired all damage to his monastery and further increased its size by erecting new buildings and installing sacred images. His own visionary teachings (*dag snang*) include the *bKa' 'dus chos kyi rgya mtsho* and the *Padma drag po* meditations upon the guru in ferocious aspect.

After him came Khams-gsum zil-gnon (Kun-bzang 'gyur-med lhun-grub rdo-rje, the sixth incarnation),[107] born at gSer-tog in the region of Dar-rtse-mdo where stands the easternmost branch monastery of the Byang-gter tradition; and Ngag-dbang 'jam-dpal mi-'gyur lhun-grub rdo-rje (the seventh) who came from rNam-sras-gling in Mon-mkhar. Although Khams-gsum zil-gnon received teachings on a secret longevity practice in pure visions, both of these lamas died while still quite young.

The eighth *mahāvidyādhara* of rDo-rje-brag was bsKal-bzang bdud-'dul rdo-rje, born in upper La-yag in lHo-brag. Famous for his skill in fierce tantric rites, he is said to have repulsed the invading Gorkha army by means of his occult power, for which service to his country he was rewarded by the government with the title *Hu thug thu*.

Thub-bstan chos-dbang mnyam-nyid rdo-rje, the ninth successor to the throne, was born near Lhasa in the fifth month of the wood monkey year (1884). He passed away in the year of the water monkey, 1932.

The present incumbent is Thub-bstan 'jig-med rnam-grol rgya-mtsho, who was born in Lhasa in 1936. Recognised as the tenth incarnation of the *gter ston*, he was ordained as a monk by Ra-sgreng rinpoche, the regent after Dalai Lama XIII. As well as studying the Byang-gter tradition with 'Go-tsha mkhan-chen Theg-mchog bstan-'dzin, a disciple of his predecessor, he has been taught by mKhan rinpoche of sMin-grol-gling and bDud-'joms rinpoche.

Despite the overthrow of Tibet by the communist Chinese, rNam-grol rgya-mtsho has remained in Tibet where he has lately been active in the rebuilding of his monastery which was almost completely devastated during the 'cultural revolution'.

---

107 Biographical outlines for the remaining incarnations are taken from sTag-lung-tse-sprul rinpoche, *A Brief History of Dorje Tag Monastery* 12-13

Five incarnations who upheld the Northern Treasures in the hidden land of Yol-mo, the Grove of Lotuses Ringed by a Wall of Snow, Nepal

As an appendix to our history of the Byang-gter tradition in Tibet, here, now, is the curious tale of the upkeep of the great *stūpa* Bya-rung kha-shor (Boudhanātha) in the Kathmandu Valley. The original construction of this great *stūpa* was undertaken in a bygone age by an old woman, a retired keeper of geese and poultry, together with her four sons, their servant, an elephant and a donkey. When the *stūpa* was complete, the servant made a vow to be born in Tibet as a minister of religion and so it happened that, as a result of the merit of that great act of construction, he was reborn in the eighth century as Padma gung-btsan of 'Gos, Dharma minister to Khri Srong-lde'u-btsan. In that lifetime, upon being informed of the wonderful qualities and deep significance of that great *stūpa* in a land beyond the ring of snow mountains, he made a further vow to maintain that *stūpa* in good repair. All of this can be read elsewhere.[108] Of particular interest to us here, is the fact that the series of Yol-mo-ba sprul-sku, whose stories are told below, continue the servant-minister reincarnation line through to the end of the 18th century. With regard to the recognition of the subsequent incarnations in this line, it is a tradition that each child must exhibit at birth, some visible signs of one who, in a former life, carried heavy burdens on his back.

Yol-mo-ba sprul-sku I
sNgags-'chang Śākya bzang-po
(15th century)

An incarnation of 'Gos Padma gung-btsan, the great Minister for Religious Affairs at the court of king Khri Srong-lde'u-btsan, Śākya bzang-po was born in southern La-stod at Gram-pa-ljongs (Gram-so-rdzong) into a family of tantric lineage holders. Studying with many of the great Dharma masters of his day, such as Nam-mkha' dpal-ldan of Kong-po, Nam-mkha' rgyal-mtshan, Sangs-rgyas bstan-pa (uncle of the *gter ston* Rig-'dzin rgod-ldem), O-rgyan dpal-bzang from gTsang and Padma gling-

---

[108] See next note.

pa, he learned the doctrines of both the old and new schools. Receiving innumerable transmissions, he became knowledgeable in both *bka' ma* and *gter ma*. Meditating at the Byang-gter site of Ri-bo dpal-'bar, he achieved success in all his practices.

Whilst at bSam-yas monastery in the year of the water monkey (1452), Śākya bzang-po received predictions from the *ḍākinī*, as a result of which, from within the red *stūpa* in the southwestern corner of the great courtyard of bSam-yas, he took out *gter chos* including the *Zhig gsos lung bstan gyi shog ril*, and another concerning Bya-rung kha-shor *stūpa* at Boudhanātha in Nepal. This latter text, in its original form of mystic formulae, had been discovered centuries earlier by Lha-btsun sngon-mo, who had been directed in prophetic visions to rewrite the text in ancient script on yellow paper scroll and reconceal it within the lion throne of the red *stūpa*.[109]

With the blessings and support of Kun-dga' grags-pa of Kong-po, Padma gling-pa and Kun-dga' rin-chen, Śākya bzang-po then went on a pilgrimage to the sacred sites of the Kathmandu valley where he restored the Bya-rung kha-shor *stūpa* at Boudhanātha, building it up into the form which it bears to this day, thereby fulfilling a vow he had made in the presence of Padmasambhava during his earlier incarnation as 'Gos Padma gung-btsan. He also supervised a major restoration of the great *stūpa* at Svayambhūnāth, in which a *cakra* and spire were placed on top of the edifice by gTsang-smyon (the crazy *yogin* of gTsang) Sangs-rgyas rgyal-mtshan (1452-1507). The date of this repair, patronised by King Ratna Malla of Nepal and his minister 'Dza'-drag, is given as 1504, just three years before Sangs-rgyas rgyal-mtshan's death.[110]

In Nepal, Śākya bzang-po is said to have discovered sacred relics of the early Nepalese king 'Od-zer go-cha, and in Lha-sa he also discovered Dharma treasures which included some of the great works of Srong-btsan sgam-po.

Becoming famous as a revealer of treasures, Śākya bzang-po gathered disciples in gLo-bo (Mustang) and in Byang ngam-ring, the political centre of the province of La-stod byang. It was in Ngam-ring, while he was teaching at the monastery of bDe-grol, that Śākya bzang-po received

---

109 *mChod rten chen po bya rung kha shor gyi lo rgyus thos pas grol ba.* English Translation by Keith Dowman, *The Legend of the Great Stūpa*, Berkeley 1973

110 Concerning the *yogin* Sangs-rgyas rgyal-mtshan, see E. Gene Smith, "The Life of Gtsang smyon Heruka," *Among Tibetan Texts* 59-79

the teachings of the Northern Treasures from the Master of bDe-grol, Thugs-sras nam-mkha' rgyal-mtshan (1454-1541), himself a disciple of Sangs-rgyas dpal-bzang. Following the instructions revealed in the treasures of Rig-'dzin rgod-ldem, Śākya bzang-po pierced 'the wall of snow' (*gangs kyi ra ba*) to the south of Gung-thang and opened up the 'hidden land' (*sbas yul*) of Yol-mo, the Grove of Lotuses (*padma'i tshal*). Described in the revelations of Rig-'dzin rgod-ldem as a most auspicious location, abundant with medicinal herbs and pure glacial water, suitable as a dwelling place for those with good karma, the treasure texts go on to warn that the area has, as its natural inhabitants, countless *ḍākinī* and local sprits (*kṣetrapāla*) who would be greatly offended by any improper conduct that threatened to pollute their pure land.[111] There, in accordance with a prediction given to him by mChog-ldan mgon-po, Śākya bzang-po founded and supported Yol-mo's first monastery of Tsu-ṭi (Cūḍā, 'Head Crest'), and the final years of his life were spent in this hidden valley of Yol-mo gangs-ra. It is unfortunate that this first monastery of Yol-mo was burned to the ground during the 16th century and many of Rig-'dzin rgod-ldem's original treasure documents (*gter shog*) and precious substances (*gter rdzas*) were lost in the flames.

sNgags-'chang Śākya bzang-po bestowed the complete teachings of the Northern Treasures upon the brothers mNga'-ris paṇ-chen and Legs-ldan rdo-rje, both of whom were his disciples, and was thus a vital link in the Byang-gter transmission. All the people of mNga'-ris and Gung-thang benefitted greatly from his enlightened activities.

At the royal court of Mang-yul gung-thang,[112] Śākya bzang-po was appointed preceptor to the prince Kun-bzang nyi-zla grags-pa (1540-1560) and, before his death, Śākya bzang-po gave clear indications to his circle of disciples concerning his next life, instructing them to seek his rebirth "among the descendants of mNga'-bdag."

---

111 As described in the *Yol mo'i snying byang*

112 Mang-yul is the huge area which includes the kingdom of Gung-thang and stretches to the west as far as sPu-hrang (mNga'-ris-skor-gsum). Prior to the 18th century it was also known as lower mNga'-ris (mNga'-ris-smad). The monastic estate at Ri-bo dpal-'bar had been bequeathed to Rig-'dzin rgod-ldem by Khri-rgyal mChog-grub-lde (see above) in 1389.

Yol-mo-ba sprul-sku II
Nam-mkha' brgya-byin
(16th century)

Although the biography of Nam-mkha' brgya-byin is known to have been written by Yol-mo-ba sprul-sku III, it appears that no copy of this text has survived to the present time. The details of his life are, therefore, fairly sketchy.

Born in the southeastern province of Lho-brag, in the family known as dGa'-thang nub-ma, Nam-mkha' brgya-byin was the 14th descendant of mNga'-bdag nyang-ral nyi-ma 'od-zer. This name was given to him at the time of his first ceremony of refuge, when a lock of his hair was taken by Rin-chen phun-tshogs (Ratnalakṣmi) (1509-1557) of the 'Bri-gung bka'-brgyud school.

His main teacher was the *mahāvidyādhara* Legs-ldan bdud-'joms rdo-rje, under whose guidance he mastered the tradition of the Northern Treasures, and he also studied under the *gter ston* Zhig-po gling-pa (1524-1583).

Just as his predecessor had done, Nam-mkha' brgya-byin was involved with reconstruction work of the Bya-rung kha-shor *stūpa* in the Kathmandu valley in the fulfilment of his previous prayers of aspiration.

Appointed to the royal court of Mang-yul gung-thang, he became spiritual preceptor to the young king bSod-nams dbang-phyug-lde (1577-1627). His Dharma legacy was also bestowed upon his heart disciple, O-rgyan don-grub of Nyang.

At one time he managed to cure the *lo chen mchog gi sprul sku* (Rig-'dzin phrin-las dbang-phyug) of a life-threatening disease. Years later, towards the end of his life, Nam-mkha' brgya-byin composed his final testament (*zhal chems*) and also wrote to this lama, sending him a stainless mirror within which it was hoped that the Lo-chen sprul-sku would be able to see portents concerning his future incarnation. As it happened, following the death of Nam-mkha' brgya-byin, the Lo-chen sprul-sku himself became the father of his next incarnation.

Yol-mo-ba sprul-sku III
bsTan-'dzin nor-bu *alias* sTobs-ldan shugs-'chang-rtsal
(1589-1644)

bsTan-'dzin nor-bu, the third incarnation of sNgags-'chang Śākya bzang-po, was born in kLu-lnga rgyal-grong, situated near the ancient golden roofed temple of Bu-chu[113] in the eastern province of Kong-po. He was the son of Rig-'dzin phrin-las dbang-phyug and lady Kun-bzang dbang-mo. While very young he recalled his previous incarnations, exhibited remarkable abilities, and had inspired visions. He was recognised by his former disciple O-rgyan don-grub, who subsequently became his teacher.

Travelling to Myang in central Tibet, bsTan-'dzin nor-bu took the lay vows of an *upāsaka* with Zhwa-dmar Karmapa Chos-kyi dbang-phyug and received the name Karma thub-bstan snying-po rnam-par-rgyal-ba'i-sde. Later in life, he also took full ordination as a *bhikṣu* under this master. He relied on masters of the Karma-'brug-pa school and Lo-chen 'Gyur-med bde-chen (1540-1615), a descendant of Thang-stong rgyal-po.

Whilst still very young, bsTan-'dzin nor-bu was invited by the Malla king Śivasiṁha to come to the kingdom of Nepal. There, with the patronage of Śivasiṁha, he once again consecrated and restored the great *stūpa* of Bya-rung kha-shor, just as he had in his previous lives, and a shower of flowers fell down from the sky. Wishing to provide for the newly installed caretaker of the *stūpa*, bsTan-'dzin nor-bu touched the cleft of a rock with his forefinger and a spring of fresh water arose there.

Moving from Kathmandu to Yol-mo, and then across the mountains to Tibet, he was welcomed as an honoured guest at the court of king bSod-nams dbang-phyug-lde in Gung-thang, and in the bSam-grub-rtse palace of the *sde srid* ruler of gTsang, Karma phun-tshogs rnam-rgyal. His purpose in moving to central Tibet, however, was in pursuance of his studies and these he undertook seriously in Nyin-byed-gling and at the dGa'-ldan byams-pa'i-gling Monastery in Ngam-ring. It is reported that he was greatly revered by the prince of gTsang when he gave Dharma teachings at Ngam-ring.

bsTan-'dzin nor-bu's main residence was the monastery of gCung ri-bo-che in western gTsang, founded by Thang-stong rgyal-po, and it was there

113 Bu-chu gser-kyi lha-khang was built by Khri Srong-btsan sgam-po as one of four temples that restrain the outer limits (*mtha' 'dul*) by pressing down upon the right elbow of the chthonic ogress of Tibet.

that he studied the practices of the *Kālacakra-tantra* under the guidance of Lo-chen 'Gyur-med bde-chen. Since then, that monastery has continued to transmit the teaching lineage of his younger brother, Phyag-rdor nor-bu.

Returning from his studies in Nyin-byed-gling, in 1617 bsTan-'dzin nor-bu met Rig-'dzin ngag-gi dbang-po in sMan-thang, who empowered him as a holder of the Byang-gter tradition and cleared his mind of all mundane theorising. Hitherto, bsTan-'dzin nor-bu had developed great skill in logic and debate, which had caused his mind to become hardened and arrogant so that he had begun to have doubts concerning the wrathful rites of slaughter and the purity of the sacred *samaya* substances for the *gaṇacakra* rituals and so on. Cured of these scholarly misconceptions, he thereafter became the chief disciple ('heart son') of Ngag-gi dbang-po.

Proceeding to Mang-yul, bsTan-'dzin nor-bu established a retreat centre at Ri-bo dpal-'bar and was appointed royal preceptor to the king, bSod-nams dbang-phyug-lde. This king had but one daughter, Lha-gcig by name, who became the consort of bsTan-'dzin nor-bu. She bore him a daughter called Nor-'dzin dbang-mo, whose body bore the visible signs of a *ḍākinī* and she was acclaimed as the reincarnation of Ma-cig rva-ma. At the age of 24, with an abundance of marvellous omens, she ascended to the sky realm of Khecarī and with her death the royal line of the kings of Gung-thang came to an end.

Engaging himself in profound meditation, bsTan-'dzin nor-bu received pure visions and predictions, in which it was said that he should go to a power place of Padmasambhava and engage in meditation upon the great guru in peaceful aspect. It was foretold that, as a result of this, any marvellous attainment for which he might wish would be bestowed upon him in reality. Being handed a scroll of paper by a *ḍākinī*, who also gave him the secret name sTobs-ldan shugs-'chang-rtsal, bsTan-'dzin nor-bu proceeded to rGyang yon-po-lung,[114] the site from which the original key to the Byang-gter had been revealed, where he was able to take out further treasures of the wrathful guru rDo-rje gro-lod from their place of concealment. Settling into a 'great cave of attainment' (*sgrub phug chen po*) in order to perform a series of meditations on the guru (*Rig 'dzin gdung sgrub*), as he had been instructed, bsTan-'dzin nor-bu was visited by the

---

114 An area of meditation caves, of great importance to the Northern Treasures tradition, in the vicinity of the ancient temple of Grom-pa-rgyang, built by Khri Srong-btsan sgam-po as one of four temples that restrain the corners (*ru bzhi*) by pressing down upon the left hip of the chthonic ogress of Tibet.

goddess Rematī in the form of a *ma mo* queen and an image of the great guru arose by itself upon the rock wall of his cave, which remains there to this day. At one time, while he was propitiating the fearful guardian of the teachings, the great planet Rāhū, the Sharp and Swift Active Messenger (*rNo myur las kyi pho nya*),[115] all the people in the valley below saw a mass of fire blazing from his cave. Not understanding that this was, in reality, the presence of the circle of great planets who had come as guests to feast upon the offerings of flesh and blood, the head man and all the commoners came up the hill to see what was happening.

Upon his return to the central province, bsTan-'dzin nor-bu was entrusted by his master Ngag-gi dbang-po with the care of rDo-rje-brag monastery. Following the death of his master, he became responsible for identifying the reincarnation and ensuring the continuance of the Byang-gter tradition of rDo-rje-brag. All of this was successfully accomplished, just as required, and bsTan-'dzin nor-bu himself performed the enthronement ceremony of Rig-'dzin padma 'phrin-las (1641-1718) just a few years before the end of his life.

Among those who came to him as students, bsTan-'dzin nor-bu gave the name Rig-'dzin stobs-ldan dbang-po 'chi-med rgya-mtsho'i-sde to one that he recognised as a further incarnation of the bodhisattva Lha-lung dpal-gyi rdo-rje, the ninth abbot of bSam-yas, who assassinated king gLang-dar-ma in 842.[116] The one he called his "heart son" was Nam-mkha' kun-bzang, the eldest son of Tshe-dbang bsod-nams rgyal-po (see below). This disciple spent much of his life engaged in renovating the ancient temple of Mangs-yul byams-pa-sprin. bsTan-'dzin nor-bu also became the teacher of Zur-chen Chos-dbyings rang-grol (1604-1669), the great master who later transmitted the system of the Northern Treasures to both the fifth Dalai Lama and his illustrious disciple, Rig-'dzin padma 'phrin-las.

---

115 This practice is a Dharma treasure of Padma las-'brel-rtsal (alias *gter ston* Rin-chen tshul-rdor, born 1228).

116 This is also tied in to the story of the Bya-rung kha-shor *stūpa*, the framing narrative of the Yol-mo-ba sprul-sku series of rebirths. The elephant, having worked so hard during the construction of the *stūpa*, felt stupid and frustrated by his inability to formulate a worthy dedication prayer at the completion of his tasks. Instead of a prayer, therefore, he uttered a curse that he should be reborn as a destroyer of the Dharma. A nearby crow, understanding the awful karmic retribution that would be accrued by the elephant, compassionately prayed to be reborn as his assassin. In due course of time, the elephant and crow were reborn as king gLang-dar-ma and the bodhisattva Lha-lung dpal-gyi rdo-rje.

At a meeting with the young Dalai Lama, bsTan-'dzin nor-bu made a prophesy that he would journey eastwards, invited by someone with different customs, language and lifestyle. Six years later (four years after the death of bsTan-'dzin nor-bu), the Dalai Lama was invited to Beijing by the emperor of China.

In the Tārā cave at rTa-nag, Yol-mo-ba sprul-sku bsTan-'dzin nor-bu received *gter ma* teachings from the *ḍākinī* in pure visions, but he reached the end of his life without the conditions becoming suitable for bringing these forth as treasures.

His collected teachings (*gsung thor bu*) fill one volume.

Yol-mo-ba sprul-sku IV
Zil-gnon dbang-rgyal rdo-rje *alias* Zla-ba mgon-po
(1647-1716)

The father, Rig-'dzin stobs-ldan dbang-po, who had been a student of Yol-mo-ba sprul-sku III, was the chief lama in the monastery of rGya-gling in gTsang. Following the death of Ngag-gi dbang-po of rDo-rje-brag in 1639, however, he was appointed superintendent of all the monasteries in Rong-khag-dgu and sent to Nepal to live at the great *stūpa* Bya-rung kha-shor. Whilst resident there, he was instructed in a dream by rDo-rje-legs-pa and the raven-faced Karma-Mahākāla to find a wife "of captivating beauty with the name Bande." These and other clear indications led quickly to his finding a local woman with the name Bhi saṅgha dpal, whom he took as his consort. Thereafter, sTobs-ldan dbang-po maintained the regular worship of the *stūpa*, fulfilling all his duties in proper fashion. On one occasion, he had an evil premonition in his dreams in which he saw the spire of the *stūpa* collapsing towards the north. Shortly after this, he received a letter from Phyag-rdor nor-bu, the younger brother of his teacher, Yol-mo-ba sprul-sku III, with the sad news that his teacher had died.

Sometime later, following dreams and indications, sTobs-ldan dbang-po and his consort travelled to La-stod gram-pa-ljongs, the birthplace of the first Yol-mo-ba sprul-sku, Śākya bzang-po. From there they returned to the monastery of rGya-gling in gTsang and it was in that place that, on the full moon day of the first Tibetan month in the year of the fire pig, their son Zla-ba mgon-po was born amidst a host of wondrous signs as the fourth in the line of Yol-mo-ba sprul-sku. Returning to Gram-pa-ljongs, the magical power (*siddhi*) of the new incarnation was invoked when a nearby lake flooded and the stricken residents implored the young *sprul sku* to turn back the flow of its waters. "Our former teacher, the great *tāntrika* Śākya bzang-po, held sway over all the local spirits and demons," they cried, "and now you must command them to obey you!" Accordingly, the child incarnation circumambulated the lake by being carried on the back of his attendant and the waters of the lake receded.

For a while, the family stayed at sKyid-grong in Mang-yul but, at that time, possession of the valley territory was disputed between the ruler of Kathmandu, the Dalai Lama's government in Lhasa and the king of Gorkha. Due to this political unrest, in 1651, while the child was still only four years old, the family moved to 'Gyes-phug and settled down in the monastery of Sa-sprin. Being met by *sprul sku* Phyag-rdor nor-bu, the younger brother of Yol-mo-ba sprul-sku III, and others, further tests were subsequently carried out in order to confirm the veracity of his status as the genuine Yol-mo-ba rebirth. Having satisfied all the investigators, Zla-ba mgon-po was presented with the four treasure scrolls (*gter shog ril bzhi*) of rGyang yon-po-lung and enthroned at the age of five years as Yol-mo-ba sprul-sku IV.

Receiving, in due order, all the empowerments and oral instructions from his father, by the time he was nine years old Zla-ba mgon-po had been introduced to the nature of his own mind and was the holder of the complete series of empowerments and oral instructions of the *rdzogs chen* cycle of *dGongs pa zang thal*. It is said that, within a single year he had memorised such texts as the *Mañjuśrīnāmasaṅgīti* and the five teachings of Maitreya, and had mastered all the arts and crafts of painting, sculpture and calligraphy, as well as the traditional styles of liturgical chanting, ritual music, sacred dance and so on, necessary for the performance of the tantric rites.

At the age of twelve years, Zla-ba mgon-po offered the first lock of his hair (*gtsug phud phul*, ie. took *upāsaka* vows) to the fifth Dalai Lama, who gave him the name Zil-gnon dbang-rgyal rdo-rje and bestowed upon him all the empowerments and oral instructions of the outer, inner and secret practices of the Northern Treasures.

As a student, he also received teachings from the mNga'-ris gter-ston Zla-ba rgyal-mtshan,[117] otherwise known as Padma gar-dbang-rtsal or

---

117 See *Crystal Mirror* XI 265-266 for details of this teacher, many of whose treasure revelations had first been discovered by Rig-'dzin rgod-ldem, by whom they had been reconcealed for a later generation.

Gar-dbang rdo-rje (1640-1685), among whose many *gter ma* discoveries was the important Vajrakīla cycle known as the sPu-gri reg-gcod.

Taking Nor-'dzin dbang-mo, the daughter of *sde srid* Tshe-dbang rab-brtan, as his consort (*karmamudrā*) they lived together in the family home at Mang-yul sa-sprin. Much of his life, however, was spent travelling throughout central and southern Tibet, Yol-mo and Kathmandu, at the invitation and request of the various local rulers. With their patronage, he established many temples, monasteries and retreat houses in those places, which he endowed with works of art. Bestowing consecrations and empowerments in every place he visited, he brought the great blessings of maturation and liberation to the local population. It is recorded, for example, that, during the fire-dog and fire-pig years (1706-1707), Zil-gnon dbang-rgyal rdo-rje was resident at the great *stūpa*, where he engaged in his religious practice and replaced the damaged wooden structure of the *harmikā*. In the following year he established the monastery of bSam-gtan-gling at Rag-ma in the valley of Mang-yul skyid-grong and, in 1709, he renovated and reconsecrated the old temple of Ri-bo dpal-'bar. Whenever he would bestow a consecration, the outer and inner aspects would merge within the harmonious purity of his mind and the compassion of all the buddhas and bodhisattvas would flow from his body as visible rays of light, to melt into the objects of the consecration, like fine rain falling upon the ocean.

The chief of his disciples was *gter dbon* Nyi-ma seng-ge. On the occasion of his empowerment into the *maṇḍala* of Byang-gter rig-'dzin gdung-sgrub, a shower of flowers fell down from the sky and the *maṇḍala* of empowerment was enclosed within a tent of light.

Among other disciples who carried on the transmission of his lineage were Rig-'dzin tshe-bdag rdo-rje and the throne-holder (*zhabs drung*) of rDo-dmar, Mi-'gyur rdo-rje of gNya'-nang, who was born in 1675. A renowned master of the Northern Treasures, 63 of Mi-'gyur rdo-rje's texts survive, including his mystical songs of realisation and a guide to the hidden land of the Crescent Moon Celestial Gateway (gNam-sgo zla-gam).

Zil-gnon dbang-rgyal rdo-rje was the author of a number of minor works (*thor bu*) which were subsequently gathered together by his disciples and transmitted as a single-volume collection (*gsung thor bu*). A volume of his 'autobiographical reminiscences',[118] which includes five

118 *sPrul pa'i rig 'dzin chen po zil gnon dbang rgyal rdo rje'i phyi nang gsang gsum gyi rnam thar*

large texts in which he records his various visionary experiences and Dharma activities, was also kept in the library of the dGon-pa-byang sprul-sku.[119]

Yol-mo-ba sprul-sku V
'Phrin-las bdud-'joms *alias* Karma bdud-'joms
(1725-1789)

At the close of the 15th century, at the request of the king of Gung-thang, the *gter ston* Rig-'dzin bstan-gnyis gling-pa (1480-1535) revealed a Dharma treasure from its place of concealment in Ri-bo dpal-'bar. This was one of the 'further treasures' (*yang gter*) that had been unearthed from Ri-bo bkra-bzang by Rig-'dzin rgod-ldem and buried again in Ri-bo dpal-'bar for future discovery. bsTan-gnyis gling-pa received the teachings of the Northern Treasures from Śākya bzang-po, which he transmitted to his son Tshe-dbang bsod-nams rgyal-po. Tshe-dbang bsod-nams rgyal-po also studied the Northern Treasures under Yol-mo-ba sprul-sku II, and this interrelationship of the two lines continued from generation to generation.

The fifth generation descendant of bsTan-gnyis gling-pa was *sngags 'chang* Nyi-ma seng-ge (1687-1738), the 'heart son' of Yol-mo-ba sprul-sku IV. Born in the area of sKyid-grong in Tibet, Nyi-ma seng-ge lived the life of an ascetic yogin (*bya btang brtul zhugs*) during the years of persecution by the invading Dzungar Mongols. During a sojourn in the Kathmandu Valley, he averted the course of a deadly epidemic by applying the Northern Treasures teachings called *Nad bdag stobs 'joms kyi man ngag* and, in reward for this great feat, he was granted gifts of land in Yolmo by Jaya Jagajjaya Malla, the king of Kathmandu, the title deeds of which were inscribed on copper plate. In 1723, Nyi-ma seng-ge built a temple on the summit of Mount Yang-ri-ma and, in 1727, he founded the temple of Padma chos-gling at rTa-brgyad-gyang village, a relatively affluent settlement at an altitude of 9,300 feet on the slope of that same mountain. Ever since then, the family lineage (*gter dbon*) of bsTan-gnyis gling-pa has been the chief father to son line producing the lamas of that

---

119 dGon-pa byang, near the Sikkimese border, is the seat of a branch line of Yol-mo-ba sprul-sku that began in the wake of Zil-gnon dbang-rgyal's death.

temple. His son 'Phrin-las bdud-'joms accordingly became head lama of Padma chos-gling upon the death of Nyi-ma seng-ge in 1738.

Due to the excellent spiritual qualities exhibited by 'Phrin-las bdud-'joms in early childhood, he was soon recognised as Yol-mo-ba sprul-sku V, the reincarnation of Zil-gnon dbang-rgyal rdo-rje. This identification was later verified by auguries at the great *stūpa* Bya-rung kha-shor.

'Phrin-las bdud-'joms was first taught to read and write at the age of eight by his mother Chos-nyid rang-grol, daughter of rDo-dmar zhabs-drung mi-'gyur rdo-rje, from Brag-dkar rta-so in southern Tibet. He was then instructed in the system of the Northern Treasures by his father, *sngags 'chang* Nyi-ma seng-ge. This early home schooling took place in the cave of Ca-thang in gLang-'phrang, referred to in the treasures of his grandfather as the hidden land of the Crescent Moon Celestial Gateway (gNam-sgo zla-gam).

'Phrin-las bdud-'joms studied under several lamas of the rDo-dmar-ba spiritual lineage, referred to as 'spiritual brothers' (*sku mchad*), including his uncle Padma rdo-rje (the head lama of the lineage), Padma gsang-sngags bstan-'dzin, and 'Gyur-med o-rgyan gsang-sngags bstan-'dzin. Of these, the most important was rDo-dmar-ba rig-'dzin chen-po Padma rdo-rje. While still a child, 'Phrin-las bdud-'joms accepted the vows of a novitiate (*dge bsnyen*) from this lama at Byams-pa-sprin, northwest of sKyid-grong, and received the name Rig-'dzin 'Phrin-las bdud-'joms.

Like his father, and as with all his incarnation predecessors, 'Phrin-las bdud-'joms travelled extensively between Yol-mo, southern Tibet and the Kathmandu Valley. In 1748, while he was staying in Mang-yul byams-pa-sprin, he heard that the Kaḥ-thog rig-'dzin tshe-dbang nor-bu (1698-1755)[120] had arrived in Kathmandu. Hurrying there to meet that most important lama, 'Phrin-las bdud-'joms met with Tshe-dbang nor-bu at the Kiṁdol Vihāra, near Svayambhūnāth. Spending one month in Nepal renovating the Bya-rung kha-shor *stūpa*, it was there that 'Phrin-las bdud-'joms received many of his teachings from the Kaḥ-thog rig-'dzin, including a special transmission of Mahākāruṇika.

'Phrin-las bdud-'joms wrote several commentaries on the practices of the Byang-gter phur-pa,[121] and arranged the order of their rituals.

---

120 For the life of Kaḥ-thog rig-'dzin tshe-dbang nor-bu, see *Crystal Mirror* XI 304-305

121 His *Byang gter phur pa'i dbang gi lo rgyus legs par bshad pa nor bu'i do shal* (B4) is relied upon extensively in chapter IV of the present work.

He was married to the daughter of the head lama of Brag-dkar rta-so, from where his mother came, and later in his life also became the head lama of that monastery. Already the head lama of Padma chos-gling, 'Phrin-las bdud-'joms was also the head lama of two more monasteries in Yol-mo: gNas-shar-le'u-dgon in the east and rDzong-dkar at the northern end of the valley. He was actually in residence at this latter place when the Nepalese invaded the region in 1788. The monastery of Padma chos-gling in rTa-brgyad-gyang was quite clearly the poorest of the three establishments.

Among his students was Mi-pham chos-kyi dbang-phyug (born 1775), the *sprul sku* of Brag-dkar rta-so who composed a biography of Tshe-dbang nor-bu and wrote several texts associated with Northern Treasures practices, and also Tshe-dbang 'chi-med mgon-po (1755-1807), the scribe of 'Phrin-las bdud-'joms' (mainly auto-)biography. This biography was later augmented by one of his sons who took up residence in the monastery of Brag-dkar rta-so. Another of 'Phrin-las bdud-'joms' sons was regarded locally as the reincarnation of his teacher Tshe-dbang nor-bu, referred to above. On his deathbed he sent two of his sons back to the monastery of Brag-dkar rta-so, their mother's home, and it was there that one of them later finished writing the biography.

From this biography we learn that 'Phrin-las bdud-'joms put a lot of effort into caring for his family endowment, the Padma chos-gling monastery of rTa-brgyad-gyang. He restored the fabric of the building in 1770 and was obviously much concerned about the moral laxity of its inhabitants, commenting that it had become "the street for all beings" and referring to it as an "empty shell." He states that the religious obligations and code of the temple were not being carried out, and that the senior religious notables were taking wives and so on. He also regrets that he did not know how to set matters aright, because the lifestyle of those around him was neither that of laymen nor that of religious men. On his deathbed, however, even while instructing his sons not to let the seat of the bsTan-gnyis gling-pa lineage become a ruin, it is clear that he expected two of them to go to Brag-dkar rta-so and gNas-shar-le'u-dgon, in Tibet, rather than to stay on in Yol-mo.

Spiritual succession at the family temple in Yol-mo apparently continued through the son(s) of a second wife of 'Phrin-las bdud-'joms whom he had married at Byams-pa-sprin. This second wife was of the rDo-dmar-ba lineage.

'Phrin-las bdud-'joms regarded himself as Tibetan and refers to the Nepalese as *mon pa*. He was used to conducting relations with the Tibetan, the Newar and then the Gorkha kingdoms. His is the only biography so far recorded concerning a lama born in Yol-mo. The succession of Yol-mo-ba sprul-sku ended with 'Phrin-las bdud-'joms and there is no local written account of the continuation of the spiritual lineage after his son.

In 1792, three years after the death of 'Phrin-las bdud-'joms, the Chinese invaded Nepal from sKyid-grong and imposed the terms of a treaty. From then, up until the successful reinvasion of the sKyid-grong and gNya'-lam areas by Gorkhāli soldiers under the Rānas in 1855, all of those outlying districts within the area to the north of the Kathmandu Valley and south of the passes into Tibet, were regarded as, if not within an area of Tibetan influence, then outside the immediate control of the Nepalese.

Northern Treasures studies in Tibet

In general, the religious tradition of rDo-rje-brag and its affiliate monasteries includes daily recitations from the *Chos spyod rab gsal* collection of Byang-gter prayers, the entire volume of which is memorised by every monk.[122] More able students undertake arduous meditative retreats focussed upon the 'outer, inner and secret' *sādhana* of the Byang-gter[123] and then the study of the wrathful deities including Yamāntaka and Vajrakīla. All inmates are expected to train in the arts of ritual chanting, music and dance, drawing the *maṇḍala* in coloured powder, sculpting the intricate *bali* cakes and the weaving of *mdos.*[124] Regular examinations are held in the *sūtra* and *tantra* throughout the year, for the course of study includes all branches of Buddhist knowledge, not merely the special revelations of the Byang-gter.

On the day of the first half-moon of each year, at the end of the new-year celebrations, the *saṅgha* of rDo-rje-brag gather together in order to spend a week practising the Byang-gter *tshe sgrub* rituals for the health

---

122 Cf. C.R. Lama, "The Twelve Months in the Life of a Monastery", in which the annual cycle of practice at 'Khor-gdong-dgon is discussed.

123 *Phyi sgrub thugs rje chen po 'gro ba kun grol, Nang sgrub rig 'dzin gdung sgrub & gSang sgrub drag po rtsal*

124 The expertise of the Brag-thog monks in this art is mentioned in Snellgrove & Skorupski, *The Cultural Heritage of Ladakh,* Vol.1 102

and longevity of the world. This is accompanied by meditation upon Sukhāvatī, the Western paradise of Amitābha, whose empowerment is bestowed upon the entire assembly on the day of the first full moon.[125]

On the new moon day of the second month, the *bhūmividhi* is performed in preparation for the elaborate construction of the Avalokiteśvara *maṇḍala*. The deity is then worshipped for seven days, at the end of which he is presented with the concluding *homa* offerings and his empowerment is bestowed upon the assembly.

During the third month, five days are devoted after the first half-moon to the *Zhi khro* cycle of Karma gling-pa and at the end of the month the *maṇḍala* of Vajrasattva is constructed in accordance with the *Thugs kyi me long*, a revealed treasure text of Gar-dbang rdo-rje.

The fourth month begins with a week-long practice of Legs-ldan-rje's *Tshe sgrub bdud rtsi 'khyil ba* cycle and the worship of *sKu gsum rigs sdus*. A token of the 'longevity nectar' produced during these rites is always presented to the Dalai Lama. From the 10th to the 14th, the peaceful and wrathful deities of the *dGongs pa zang thal* are worshipped and one thousand butter-lamps are offered on the day of the full moon in honour of the Buddha's birth, enlightenment and entry into *parinirvāṇa*. The month ends with a three day *gtor zlog* ritual.

Throughout the early part of the fifth month, rehearsals of the musicians and dancers are held in preparation for the elaborate worship of *Bla ma gsang 'dus*[126] which is performed on the tenth day. The rites of *Srog gi spu gri* are performed on the eighth and a *gaṇacakra* offered on the ninth in accordance with the texts of *Rig 'dzin gdung sgrub*. This is followed in the evening by the dances of the *daśakrodha* kings. Crowds of pilgrims gather to witness the spectacular masked dances of the *Guru mtshan brgyad* on the tenth day and to receive an empowerment of long life. The worship of *Bla ma gsang 'dus* continues in the temple through the 11th and 12th days and this is followed by the rites of *Drag po rtsal* on the 13th and those of *Guru yon tan gter mdzod* on the 14th.

The fourth day of the sixth month is set aside for the offering of one thousand butter-lamps and the *poṣadha* ceremony for the restoration of damaged vows is performed on the full moon day of the 15th. The summer retreat for all the monks begins on the 16th, during which time all the

---

125 For the Northern Treasures Sukhāvatī text, *sMon lam zhing gi yon tan ma*, see Martin Boord, *Illuminating Sunshine* 259*ff*

126 Revealed by the early *gter ston* Guru chos-dbang.

known 'Words of the Buddha' (*bKa' 'gyur*) are recited. From the 21st to the 27th, the elaborate rite of *'Khor ba dbyings grol* is performed using a *maṇḍala* constructed of coloured powders. This culminates in a peaceful *homa* and the bestowal of empowerment.

The seventh and eighth days of the seventh month are spent preparing the intricate offerings required for the five day cycle of rituals to be performed from the ninth. This begins with the worship of *Rig 'dzin gdung sgrub* on the ninth day and continues with an empowerment of *Bla ma gsang 'dus* on the tenth, the Nyang system of *Guru drag po* on the 11th, the Byang-gter *Guru drag po* on the 12th and a final *gaṇacakra* ceremony of *Guru yon tan gter mdzod* on the 13th. During the morning of the 20th, the *bhūmividhi* is performed so that the *maṇḍala* of Vajrakīla may be constructed throughout the evening. The remainder of the month is then devoted to the worship of this deity,[127] concluding with the casting of the *bali* on the 29th day and the performance of four types of *homa* rite on the 30th. Following the rite of accepting the *siddhi*, the accumulated annual donations to the monastery are distributed among the monks.

The eighth and ninth months are generally taken as a holiday but during this period a delegation consisting of the abbot and ten monks have traditionally gone to Lhasa in order to spend four weeks blessing (*gYang 'gug*) the government with the rites of *Nor bu mchog rgyal* and *Dur bdag*.

From the 17th to the 30th of the ninth month, 22 monks from rDo-rje-brag would reside in the southern gate shrine of bSam-yas monastery, as guests of the *rDzong dpon*, where they would perform the Yamāntaka rites called *'Char kha nag po*.

On the 19th day of the 11th month, those monks whose duty it is to attend upon the *mahāvidyādhara (gzim chung pa)* perform the *bhūmividhi* as a prelude to laying out the coloured powder *maṇḍala* of either the Byang-gter *bKa' brgyad khro rol* or the Zhang-khrom *Tshe bdag* cycle, alternating the one with the other on successive years. The main ritual practice then continues from the 22nd to the 28th and the rite of hurling the *zor* takes place on the 29th. On the final day of the month, *bali* offerings are made and they perform the rite of accepting the *siddhi*.

---

127 Apart from this annual ten-day festival in his honour, Vajrakīla is worshipped daily in his own chapel called Srid-gsum rnam-rgyal on the premises of rDo-rje-brag.

The latter half of the 12th month is especially devoted to rituals concerned with casting out the demons of the old year (*dgu gtor*). The most elaborate preparations of the site, the *maṇḍala* and the ritual offerings are made in accordance with either the *bKa' brgyad khro rol* or the *Tshe bdag* texts, these being alternated annually as before. The main *gtor zlog* rites begin on the 22nd day and continue until the end of the month, accompanied by dances on each of the four final days.[128] To mark the end of the Tibetan year, the rites conclude with particularly auspicious prayers of benediction and the practice that "Averts the Lord of Death", as taught by Padma 'phrin-las.

rDo-rje-'brag monastery maintains very strict discipline. Alcohol and meat are forbidden. If meat is to be used in a ritual offering, it must be from an animal that has died a natural death, rather than from one that has been slaughtered.

Beginning with the *gter ston* himself, who travelled extensively throughout Tibet during his lifetime, the teachings of the Byang-gter have spread to all parts of the Tibetan Buddhist world. Its doctrines have formed a part of the study curriculum in a large number of unrelated monasteries and its own establishments have numbered over 50, both large and small, from Brag-thog-dgon in Ladakh to Yol-mo-gangs and Shar-pa in Nepal,[129] bKra-shis-lding and others in Sikkim, and rDor-brag-dgon in Dar-rtse-mdo.

As the power and importance of rDo-rje-brag monastery grew in Tibet so the number of incarnation lineages within its hierarchy increased.[130] Second in command to the Rig-'dzin chen-po are the rGyal-sras sprul-sku

---

128 The main *sgrol 'cham* and *zor 'cham* being elaborately performed on the 29th day.

129 Byang-gter rituals are widely known and practised throughout Nepal, especially by the Tamang among whom the tradition was propagated by bsTan-'dzin nor-bu, the third Rig-'dzin yol-mo-ba sprul-sku, in the 17th century. Yol-mo and its temples are described in C. Jest, *Monuments of Northern Nepal* (UNESCO, 1981) 80-90. A brief description of Brag-thog-dgon is to be found in Snellgrove & Skorupski, *Cultural Heritage of Ladakh* Vol.1 132. In recent years, a new branch monastery of rDo-rje-brag has been established near Leh, the capital of Ladakh.

130 See the introduction to the *dGongs pa zang thal* (Leh 1973) for a list of these incarnation lineages and also for a comprehensive list of Byang-gter monasteries throughout Tibet.

and the Chu-bzang sprul-sku, who serve as the Regent holders of the throne during the minority of the Rig-'dzin chen-po or between his incarnations.

It will be remembered that the Great Fifth Dalai Lama took particular interest in the Northern Treasures tradition of rDo-rje-brag, partly because the holders of its lineage were blood descendants of the ancient Dharma kings. Guru Padmasambhava made it clear that if this lineage were not supported and upheld, it would be detrimental for the country of Tibet, and thus the rNam-rgyal Monastery of the Dalai Lama and the gNas-chung and dGa'-gdong grva-tshang of the state oracles of Tibet follow the Northern Treasures tradition of rDo-rje-brag.

Second state oracle

Among these monasteries, of particular interest is the small establishment of dGa'-gdong-dgon, the seat of the second most important (after gNas-chung) oracle in Tibet. It is the function of the resident medium of that monastery to act as a mouthpiece for the protective deity Shing-bya-can.[131] This *yakṣa* 'With a Wooden Bird' is a member of the sKu-lnga group[132] and the particular guardian of the people of Mi-nyag, the ancestral home of the Sikkim royal family and thus closely associated with the Byang-gter tradition. In a prophesy concerning the invasion of Tibet by the Mongols, the *Padma bka'i thang* recommends that this deity be invoked as a powerful protector.[133]

Shing-bya-can is described as dwelling in a palace of gold to the south under the appellation 'King of Good Qualities' (*yon tan gyi rgyal po*). Black in colour with one face and two hands, he wields a battle axe and a snare and rides a black horse with white heels. He wears a cloak of snake and tiger skins and a cane hat covered with *garuḍa* skin. His queen is the black gSer gyi spu-gri-ma who has a single face and four hands in which she holds a sword, red banner, lance and trident. She wears a garment of rough yellow silk with a belt of snakes and a black silken headdress. She roams around at night on a donkey with a red spot on its forehead.

Accompanying the royal pair are an 'emanation' of light blue colour, their 'minister' Bya-rgod thang-nag, who has the appearance of a young

---

131 René de Nebesky-Wojkowitz, *Oracles and Demons of Tibet* 5, 109-115, etc.

132 Consisting of Pe-har, the oracular deity of gNas-chung-dgon, and his four companions.

133 Douglas & Bays, *The Life and Liberation of Padmasambhava* Vol.2 392

upāsaka carrying a *vajra* and hammer, and their train of messengers consisting of long-tailed monkeys, grey-haired apes and rats.

Noted for his particular power in controlling the weather, the human medium of this deity (the dGa'-gdong chos-rje) has traditionally been employed by the government of Tibet in this capacity. Of greater import, however, is his supposed ability to trace the movements of deceased religious dignitaries and thereby render great assistance to the various monastic officials (*bla brang*) in search of their high priest's reincarnation. During their initial meeting with the medium, the petitioners would generally not disclose the actual details of their quest, these being put directly to the deity himself only after the medium had entered his oracular trance. Part of the reason for keeping their mission secret is that not all parents were found to be happy at the prospect of losing their child simply because he had been 'recognised' as the rightful occupant of the lama's throne in some far away monastery.[134]

dGa'-gdong-dgon in Tibet was home to approximately 175 monks. The oracle, a married man whose family domicile lay only a few hundred yards from the monastery, was apparently expected to enter a state of trance in order to fulfil his role as Shing-bya-can's mouthpiece as often as twice a week. All the preparatory work for the ritual trance being the responsibility of the monks, the medium would go to the monastery only after everything had been made ready. Donning the elaborate costume of the deity, he would then be questioned by the interested parties and expected to deliver his prediction(s). The spectacle of the trance would be witnessed by any number of persons but the information divulged by the deity would be kept secret – even from the medium himself who would have no recollection of events after the trance had ended. Indeed, the medium would generally fall into a faint following his ordeal and, even after regaining consciousness, would continue to experience nausea and severe abdominal pains for some time.

The role of the medium being an inherited one, the present dGa'-gdong chos-rje, bsTan-'dzin dbang-grags, was selected for the title from among the six eligible sons of the late oracle because he was sickly and slightly insane, such attributes being favourably regarded as indicative of a good candidate for the gruelling task of offering his body on a regular basis as host to a powerful foreign spirit. Afraid of causing offence to the deity, bsTan-'dzin dbang-grags accepted the role for which he had been chosen

---

134 Daniel Barlocher, *Testimonies of Tibetan Tulkus* Vol.1 310-324

and began a period of ritual purification[135] under the guidance of the senior dGa'-gdong monks. He is now settled with his wife in Dharamsala, actively involved there in building up the new dGa'-gdong monastery.

The Byang-gter Tradition in the modern world

When the communist Chinese began to invade Tibet from the east in 1949, the Khor-gdong gter-chen sprul-sku, bla-ma 'Chi-med rig-'dzin (1922-2002), was one of a number of rNying-ma-pa scholars that heeded the prophetic warnings of Padmasambhava and chose to move for safety to India – ten years before the influx of Tibetan refugees that followed the flight of the 14th Dalai Lama in 1959. In Kalimpong he served as a consultant to René de Nebesky-Wojkowitz during the writing of *Oracles & Demons of Tibet* and then, in 1954, Lama 'Chi-med rig-'dzin was appointed head of the Department of Indo-Tibetan studies at Viśvabharati University in Śāntiniketan, West Bengal. He remained in this post from 1954 until his retirement in 1987, during which time he was invited by Giuseppe Tucci to act as a visiting professor in Rome, and then by Helmut Hoffmann to teach in Munich.

Attracting the interest of a few European students and disciples through the 1970s, C.R. Lama (as he came to be called) embarked upon an ambitious programme of translation and teaching the sacred texts of the Northern Treasures tradition from his home in Bengal. In 1978, Lama 'Chi-med rig-'dzin travelled to the UK in order to give religious instruction in the Byang-gter system of Vajrakīla and the first tantric empowerments of that system ever to have been bestowed in the Western world. From that time until his death in 2002, Lama 'Chi-med rig-'dzin propagated the Byang-gter and the lesser-known treasures of Khor-gdong throughout Europe and the wider world. Near Darnkow in Poland, C.R. Lama founded a large *dgon pa* and retreat centre called 'Gro-phan-gling, which has since been the site of the complete transmission of the Northern Treasures by sTag-lung-tse-sprul rinpoche. He also founded the Khor-gdong Monastery in Siliguri, India, inaugurated in 2002.

---

135 During the interviews recorded with Daniel Barlocher (*supra*) he stated that he could easily avoid ever becoming the deity's medium (a role which he had not at that time actually begun to perform) by the simple expedient of adopting a dissolute lifestyle so that the deity would naturally refuse to enter his morally contaminated form.

Of particular importance to the Byang-gter tradition in modern India is the incarnation lineage of sTag-lung-tse. The fourth incarnation in this line is the present sTag-lung-tse-sprul rinpoche, bShad-grub nyin-byed 'phrin-las bzang-po, born in 1927. The foremost authority of the Byang-gter in India today, 'Phrin-las bzang-po was educated as a *sprul sku* in his early childhood at rDo-rje-brag monastery in Tibet, under the tutelage of rDo-brag rig-'dzin mNyam-nyid rdo-rje and Chu-bzang bstan-pa'i nyi-ma. At the age of 23 he became its elected abbot, a post which he held for six years.

Leaving Tibet in 1959 among the thousands of refugees fleeing from Chinese aggression, 'Phrin-las bzang-po was invited to act as the abbot of the only Byang-gter monastery in India at that time, Brag-thog-dgon in Ladakh. After that he moved to Śimla in Himachal Pradesh, where he successfully reestablished Evaṁ lcog-sgar rdo-rje-brag Monastery in exile in India. He also established a small *dgon pa* in the mountains to the north of Śimla, as well as a new Byang-gter monastery in Ladakh, called Thubs-bstan mdo-sngags chos-'khor-gling, in Chog-lam-sar, near to the capitol city of Leh.

In 2012, sTag-lung-tse-sprul rinpoche was invited to act as the supreme head of the rNying-ma-pa schools in India, so that the Northern Treasures tradition is currently being widely promoted among the Tibetan community in exile. In a bid to make these teachings better known to the outside world at large, on 8th November 2012 the exile Tibetan community of rDo-rje-brag monastery launched the internet social media website https://www.facebook.com/HisHolinessTaklungTsetrulRinpoche. It is to be hoped that this fresh exposure to the modern world will boost the fortunes of the Northern Treasures and result in the increased availability of the texts of this tradition, edited and published in India and Nepal.

Among the 25 close disciples of Guru Rinpoche, Nam-mkha'i snying-po gained complete realisation through the practice of Yang-dag heruka, following which he exhibited many miracles, such as riding on the rays of the sun. A *yogin* who was living at Lho-brag mkhar-chu in southern Tibet in the 17th century was recognised by Dalai Lama V as the incarnation of Nam-mkha'i snying-po and this name was subsequently applied to all of his incarnations. The present Nam-mkha'i snying-po rinpoche VII established a monastery in Bumthang, in central Bhutan, known as mKhar-chu dgon-pa, where he now resides. As the heart son of *skyabs rje* sTag-lung-tse-sprul rinpoche, from whom he received the entire transmission of the *Rin chen gter mdzod*, Nam-mkha'i snying-po and his monastery uphold the tradition of the Northern Treasures. The monastery houses about 200 monks and includes a philosophical school (*bshad grwa*), a retreat centre and a monastery for yogins, where about 25 inmates remain in retreat and practice. There are also plans to start a nunnery.

Since the 15th century, the incarnation line of Byang-gling sprul-sku have also practised and maintained the Northern Treasures lineage of Buddhist teachings. Before rDo-brag rig-'dzin chen-po Padma 'phrin-las united the three main practice traditions that were taught by Rig-'dzin rgod-ldem, the Byang-gling sprul-sku was the head of the branch which originated from the *gter ston*'s wife (the so-called Mother lineage).

The XIth & XIIth Byang-gling sprul-sku engaged extensively in the practices of the Byang-gter and established the Northern Treasures tradition in Byang-gling monastery.

Under the leadership of Byang-gling rinpoche, the lineage carried on today at Shes-chen byang-chub-gling on Vancouver Island in British Columbia is the tradition of the Northern Treasures and Byang-gling rinpoche himself has initiated a worldwide search for missing and hitherto unknown texts of the Northern Treasures tradition – the Northern Treasures Text Archival Project.

VĀSTUVIDYĀ

the arrangement of 32 deities

preparation of the ground for the construction of a Buddhist monastery according to the *Kriyāsaṁgrahapañjikā* by Kuladatta:

WEST

SOUTH

NORTH

नीलदण्ड	दुर्जय	वज्रस्फोट	भीम	प्रचण्ड	महाबल
रत्नशिखर	महोदर	त्रैलोक्य-प्रसाधक	पद्मान्तक	जय	पदनिक्षेप
पलाल	प्रज्ञान्तक	the *vajrācārya* stands in the centre		वीरविक्रम	वज्रावेश
वज्रपाश	कनिख्रोध			अमृत-कुण्डलिन्	वज्राट्टहास
अन्तचर	मेघनाद	यमान्तक	महाविजय	विजय	वज्रविदारण
टक्किराज	दुर्निरीक्ष	वज्राशनि	वज्राङ्कुश	विद्रापक	अचल

EAST

Part Two

THE KĪLA

CHAPTER TWO

The ritual kīla as a magic weapon and its apotheosis as Vajrakīla, a wrathful deity of the Vajrayāna pantheon. The assimilation of a Vedic myth and its subsequent development within the context of tantric Buddhism.

Vedic antecedents

According to the first book of the *Ṛgveda*, the demiurge Indra employed a *kīla*-like weapon before the world came into being in order to slay the primordial cosmic serpent Vṛtra, within whose coils were trapped 'the waters of life'.[136] As the primeval ocean was released life began, thus revealing the *kīla* as an instrument of paradox: a weapon having the power of both life and death. As a religious emblem it appears to kill and yet it creates life.

It is also said that during his act of creating the world, Indra pinned down the earth and propped up the heavens. Prior to that, earth and heaven were not separated. Thus the spike can be seen to possess a cosmic dimension as a weapon that spans both earth and heaven. The special function of its lower part is to stabilise the earth, while its upper part leads to the realm of the gods.[137]

These early themes remain discernible to the present day within the complex mythology of the Buddhist *kīla*. The idea of a spike that kills and liberates, a spike that strikes into the earth and reaches up to heaven, seems quite quickly to have become absorbed into Buddhism and eventually arose as the focal point of a tantric cult dedicated to the worship of the esoteric deity Vajrakīla who bears as his special symbol the ancient pointed spike adopted as a powerful instrument of ritual and magic.

A preliminary step towards the Buddhist assimilation of the *kīla* was probably the annual circumscription of an area within which the *saṅgha*

---

136 See; F.B.J. Kuiper, "Cosmogony and Conception: a Query" in *History of Religions* X (1970) 91-138. Cf. S. Kramrisch, *The Presence of Śiva* 29*ff*

137 A function often ascribed to mountains, popularly regarded in Indo-Tibetan culture as natural manifestations of the *indrakīla*.

An apotropaic aspect of the spike is also to be noted in the *Atharvaveda* ritual of hammering acacia pegs into the ground in order to drive out demons of illness. G.U. Thite, *Medicine; Its Magico-religious Aspects According to the Vedic and Later Literature* 148, Poona 1982

would have been expected to remain for the duration of the summer season rains retreat. As the monks were engaged in pegging out the boundaries of their sacred domicile with wooden stakes and lengths of cord, they would undoubtedly have wished those boundaries to remain secure against the onslaughts of Māra, who could be relied upon to try and disturb their meditations. Thus, as the stakes were hammered into the ground, the myth of Indra *versus* Vṛtra may have come to mind and been recast in Buddhist form.

Any demarcation of a circumference automatically creates a centre and, for all practical purposes, a wooden stake is again the natural implement with which to mark out the central spot.

Architecture

Indian treatises on temple architecture describe a number of operations for which the use of wooden pegs is required. For the most part these pegs are nailed into the earth in order to establish the outline of the building to be constructed. The texts simply describe the distances that are required to lie between these wooden pegs and the manner in which the whole area is to be divided up by further stakes and lengths of string so as to facilitate the delineation of the full temple plan upon the ground. Of course there is nothing extraordinary in any of this. We may suppose that similar instructions would have been included in a text devoted to the planning of a medieval kitchen garden, had any such tract been written. A temple, however, is consciously dedicated to the divine and so we may reasonably expect any mythological aspect adhering to the form or function of a wooden spike to be more expressly stated in a treatise on architecture than in a gardening manual.

The initial prescription in such treatises is to locate, by astrological methods, the earth-dwelling *nāga* within whose domain the architects wish to construct their edifice. It is then possible to stabilise the building site by fixing that *nāga* with a *kīla* judiciously driven into the earth.[138]

---

138 R. Mayer, "Observations on the Tibetan Phur-ba and the Indian Kīla" 167. This practice of *vāstuvidyā* is condemned as a vile art in the *Dīgha Nikāya* I.9 & II.87 etc. According to Trevor Ling, its purpose was to ascertain before building a house whether or not the site is haunted by spirits.
T. Ling, *Buddhism and the Mythology of Evil* 19

Stella Kramrisch,[139] likening the temple to an image of a god, says that the *āmalaka* (high dome) of the building is regarded as the head and that the *brahmarandhra* (foramen in the skull) is pierced by the *kīla* which fixes the *stūpikā* (finial). This corresponds closely to the Vaiṣṇavite tantric meditation in which the *vajrakīla* is contemplated within a thousand-petalled lotus in the crown of the *yogin*'s head. There it pierces the centre of the six-pointed *mahāyantra,* an emblematic figure resembling the six-pointed *dharmodaya* pierced by the tip of the Buddhist 'cosmic *kīla*' (*bhavakīla*).[140] The central axis of the Buddhist *stūpa*, also, is known as *indrakīla*[141] and this has the function of stabilising both the earth and the edifice itself.

So far, then, we have seen the *kīla* or wooden stake as both boundary marker and holder of the centre, where 'centre' refers not to a single point but to a vertical axis indicated by wooden stakes both above and below. We have also noted that Indra used a *kīla* to bring about liberation from a hostile force and that the ground where a *kīla* is implanted is considered to be firmly fixed and held in a stable condition with the upright line of the peg itself acting as a conduit to the realm of the gods.

In the lexicons we observe the word *indrakīla*[142] to include 'door bolt' among its several meanings and in later Buddhist writings this word came also to mean the threshold of any door or gate, be it the entrance to house, palace or city.[143] Robert Mayer mentions certain pillar-like *indrakīla* which function as boundary markers indicating the rule of law within and separating the enclosed area from the lawless wilderness of no-man's land without. In the case of the royal palace he shows them as markers of special reserved areas for which royal authority is required before admission can be gained.[144] The prevailing form of these pillars is octagonal in cross

---

139 S. Kramrisch, *The Hindu Temple* 359

140 *Brahmasamhitā* V.2. A. Avalon (ed.), *Tantrik Texts* XV

141 John Irwin, "The Axial Symbolism of the Early Stūpas" 21 In A.L. Dallapiccola (ed.), *The Stūpa* 12-38

142 Sir M. Monier-Williams, *A Sanskrit-English Dictionary* 166

143 F. Edgerton, *BHS Dictionary* 114. See also the *Pāli-English Dictionary* of the PTS where identical meanings are ascribed to *indakhīla*.

144 R. Mayer, (*op.cit.*) cites the work of Lily de Silva, Jan Gonda and Charles Malamoud (among others) in order to show the pillar *indrakīla* to be a conflation of the door peg (*indrakīla*) with the sacrificial post (*yūpa*).

section, the very shape described in Vajrayāna commentarial texts as the one required for the columns supporting the *toraṇa* at the entrance to a tantric *maṇḍala.* Lily de Silva links the placement of the *indrakīla* with the establishment of the *bodhimaṇḍa,* about which she says (quoting from the *Pūjāvaliya*): "(it) is a great fortress protected by the majestic wall of the ten *pāramitā,* extending up to the cupola of the Brahmā world. Even Māra with his vast array of forces could not get past this formidable barrier."[145] When we come to deal with the tantric rites of the *kīla* we shall observe how ten *kīla* form just such a formidable barrier against Māra and his hordes, surrounding and enclosing the sacred palace (or fortress) of the *bodhimaṇḍala.* In the rite of initiation through which this protective power is transmitted, these ten *kīla* are explicitly associated with the ten *pāramitā.*[146] Thus the *kīla* which marks the boundary is now seen to be associated with the protection of the enclosure against intrusion.

A 'border' or 'threshold', of course, need not necessarily be visibly located in space. The threshold of a house, palace or city is perhaps more tangible than the threshold of life and death but the latter, too, provides us with themes that have since become incorporated into the general mythology of the *kīla* as an instrument of magic. One such theme is derived from popular folklore at a great remove from the lofty Vedic tradition of Indra *versus* the chthonic Vṛtra. This is the idea of the *vetāla,* a picturesque topic which bears all the hallmarks of a Haitian voodoo cult nurtured in the fertile ground of village superstition.[147]

Vetāla: ghouls at the limit of life and death

The term *vetāla* ('zombie', corpse animated by rites of black magic) was perhaps coined by the Buddhists, because these creatures made their first appearance in Indian literature within the *Daśabhūmika-sūtra,*[148] the *Suvarṇaprabhāsottama-sūtra*[149] and the ten-sectioned *vinaya* of the

---

145 Lily de Silva, "The Symbolism of the Indrakīla in the Paritta Maṇḍapa" 248

146 See below, Chapter Seven

147 The voodoo-like technique of bringing harm to an enemy by piercing his effigy with spikes is a significant feature of the later *kīla* rituals dealt with in detail in Part Three of the present work.

148 Ed. Rahder, Paris and Louvain (1926) 45

149 Ed. J. Nobel, Leipzig (1937) 104 & 107

Sarvāstivādins.[150] Later references are to be found in the Buddhist *dhāraṇī,* such as the *Mahāmāyūrī* and the *Pañcabuddhoṣṇīṣa-dhāraṇī,* and *vetāla* are placed in the entourage of Śiva by the Śaivites of Kashmir.[151] In the first chapter of the *Vimalaprabhā* they are described as naked and emaciated, holding curved knives (*kartṛkā*) and skull cups in their hands and uttering fearful howls of *phaṭ!* Fire issues from their mouths and they are said to be cruel-minded eaters of human flesh.[152]

In a number of Buddhist tantric treatises, the *krodharāja* Yamāntaka is said to have as his queen the mistress of these un-dead monsters called (appropriately enough) Vetālī. In the earlier texts, however, she is known as Śmāśānikā ('Frequenter of the Charnel Ground', another fitting name for a ghoul) and such is her name in the Byang-gter Vajrakīla cycle. Vetālī is said to have appeared in person to Kantali, a stitcher of rags, after he pierced his finger with a spike, and she become his guru. Kantali's success in following her instructions quickly elevated him to the rank of *mahāsiddha.*[153] Vetālī also occurs in the circle of eight *ḍākinī* (Gaurī and the rest) found in the *maṇḍala*s of Hevajra, Jñānaḍākinī, Heruka, Yogāmbara, Vajraḍāka and others. Her seat in the circle is in the western direction of all these *maṇḍala* and her colour is given as red/black.[154]

In Chapter XXVI of the *Mañjuśrīmūlakalpa* (MMK) (widely acknowledged as probably the earliest of all Buddhist *tantra*), two rites are given through which one may seek to animate a corpse and attain the *vetālasiddhi.*[155] According to the *yogin* Kāṇha, who was himself apparently adept at this art, this is one of the *siddhi* to be counted among 'the eight

---

150 T.1435, first translated into Chinese in 404 AD by Kumārajīva

151 K. Dowman, *Masters of Mahāmudrā* 326, says that Vetālī, the mistress of these ghouls, was worshipped by the Kāpālikas in Orissa at the popular Kāpālinī Temple of Bhubaneswar.

It is also said that Vetāla and Bhairava were twin sons born to Tārāvatī after she had been raped by Śiva.

W.D. O'Flaherty, *Asceticism and Eroticism in the Mythology of Śiva* 69

152 J. Upadhyaya, *Vimalaprabhā* Vol.1, p.9. On p.8 of that text they are listed among the two groups (or the extended group?) of the eight great fears (*aṣṭaghora*) and are identified with *piśāca*. Such an identity, however, is not attested elsewhere.

153 K. Dowman, *op.cit.* 325-328

154 As described in the *Niṣpannayogāvalī*

155 MMK 292

great accomplishments' (*aṣṭamahāsiddhi*).[156] Narrative accounts of the *modus operandi* are to be found in the *Kathāsaritsāgara*[157] and other sources,[158] all of which portray the rite very much in accordance with the details given below. This would seem to indicate that the practice of this peculiar occult art eventually became widespread, partly due perhaps to the fascination that it held for the more macabre elements in the public imagination. Having successfully animated the corpse, the *sādhaka* was free to employ it as his servant. In the Blue Annals[159] we read that the scholar Vāgīśvarakīrti gained the *siddhi* of great memory from a *vetāla*.

In both of the descriptions given in the MMK, it is said that the *yogin* should perform this rite on a corpse in sound condition (*akṣatāṅga,* 'with unbroken limbs'). Such a corpse (according to the first rite) should be

---

156 This unusual occult accomplishment is not included among the *aṣṭamahā-siddhi* either in the *Sādhanamālā* or any other source consulted by me, unless it be equated with the *siddhi* of the sword (see below, note 164). It is listed as a minor *siddhi* in the *Vajrabhairava-tantra* (B. Siklós, 95). For the biography of Kāṇha see David Templeman (1989), within which Kāṇha's list of eight *siddhi* is to be found on p.14.

157 Somadeva, *Kathāsaritsāgara* Book XII Chapter LXXIII. English translation by C.H. Tawney *Ocean of the Streams of Story,* Delhi (reprint, Munshiram Manoharlal) 1968

The popular "Twenty-five tales of the *vetāla*" (*Vetālapañcaviṁśati*) contained within this work are thought by A.W. Macdonald to be of Buddhist origin (*Matériaux pour l'étude de la littérature populaire tibétaine: Éditions et traduction de deux manuscrits tibétains des "Histoires du cadavre"* Presses Universitaires de France, Paris 1967 pp.16-17). Several Sanskrit versions of these tales are known, the earliest still extant having been composed by Kṣemendra *circa* 1037 and included in his *Bṛhatkathāmañjarī.* Other versions were composed by Śivadāsa, Jambhaladatta and Vallabhadāsa, and translations exist in many Indian vernaculars as well as Nepali, Tibetan, Mongolian, Chinese, etc. Theodore Riccardi, *A Nepali Version of the Vetālapañcaviṁśati* 6, American Oriental Society, New Haven 1971

158 Such as the detailed account to be found in Bāṇa's *Harṣacarita*. English translation by E.B. Cowel & F.W. Thomas, MLB (reprint, 1961) 90-92

Varāhamihira mentions the rite several times in his *Bṛhatsaṁhitā* (English translation by Ramakrishna Bhat, 2 vols., MLB, 1981). At LXIX.37 he classifies it as *abhicāra* (black magic) and at XCVIII.7 he says that, for maximum success, the *vetālasādhana* should be performed under the *tīkṣṇa* (*dāruṇa,* dreadful) asterisms *Mūla, Ārdrā, Jyeṣṭhā* or *Āśleṣā*. Sorcerers who perform such rites (*vetālakarmajña)* are themselves persons under the stellar rulership of *Ārdrā*.

159 G. Roerich, *The Blue Annals* 757-8

restrained by means of four *khadirakīla*[160] and the *yogin* should sit upon it and perform a *homa* rite[161] in which he burns offerings of powdered gems. The second rite says that the corpse should be nailed down with *kīla* of jujube wood (*badara*). In both cases the *kīla* are presumably a precautionary measure against the *sādhaka* being overpowered by the monster when it arises.[162]

If offerings of *lohacūrṇa* (which could be either red copper filings or powdered red iron rust) are placed into the mouth of the corpse it will poke out its tongue which the *sādhaka* must immediately sever. This magical fetish will be "as useful to its owner as a retinue of one hundred retainers". The first version of the rite likens the tip of the tongue to a wish-fulfilling jewel (*cintāmaṇi*) obtained as a magical reward for the oblations of powdered gems. The owner of such a prize becomes 'an emperor among knowledge-holders' (*vidyādharacakravartin*) with the power to survive an 'intermediate aeon' (*antarakalpa*) and sport with the gods on the summit of Mount Meru. According to Tāranātha,[163] the severed tongue turns into a sword which bestows these powers[164] while the corpse itself turns to gold. The MMK says that the owner of the tongue may travel wherever he pleases and take possession of whatever he sees. After death he enters a pure realm or he becomes a king in the realm of men.

---

160 Acacia spikes. Acacia trees bear vicious barbs up to two or three inches in length and it may be these that are referred to here for, as written in the *Sādhanamālā* 171, *kaṇṭakena ... kīlayet*, "one should fasten (it) with a thorn". Later, however, the manufacture of ritual *kīla* demanded the wood of the tree itself. Cf. note 218, below.

161 The *homa* is to be performed in the mouth of the corpse.

162 Alexandra David-Neel, *Magic and Mystery in Tibet* 102-104 and Turrell Wylie, "Ro-Langs; the Tibetan Zombie" 74*ff*, provide graphic descriptions of the menace said to be caused by these uncontrolled "walking dead". Surprisingly, however, neither author mentions the role of the *kīla* in keeping them suppressed.

163 Chimpa & Chattopadyaya, *Tāranātha's History of Buddhism in India* 263
Tāranātha is said to have heard the biographies of many *siddhas* from his Indian teacher Buddhagupta "who was well travelled and a mine of stories". D. Templeman, *The Origin of the Tārā Tantra* 8

164 René de Nebesky-Wojkovitz, *Oracles and Demons of Tibet* 65, notes a green form of Mahākāla (mGon-po ljang-khu) who carries as an attribute a sword made out of *vetāla* tongue. Possibly *vetālasiddhi* is simply another term for *khaḍgasiddhi* ('attainment of the magic sword').

Almost identical accounts of these rites (including specifically the use of *kīla* to peg down the corpse) are to be found in Chinese translations of the *Vajrakumāra-tantra.*[165]

Bāṇa[166] and Somadeva[167] add colour to these descriptions by their observations that this *sādhana* is to be performed during the night of the dark moon (on the fourteenth night of the waning moon), within a *maṇḍala* illumined by the flames of lamps fed with human fat. The magic circle itself is to be drawn with powdered human bones and vessels of blood are placed in the corners. These authors confirm the view that the rite brings its successful practitioner to the state of a *vidyādhara,* warn of the dire consequences of failure, and make note of the tongue as a magical fetish that enables its bearer to travel without hindrance.

A connection between severed tongues and the risen dead is noted in the Pāli *Jātaka* tale of Padukusalamāṇava,[168] thus demonstrating the antiquity of the motif in Indian folklore but the actual significance of the connection is unclear.[169]

It is not the tongue gained from the *vetāla* which is of importance to us here, however, but the *kīla* as a means of keeping the animated corpse under control. With regard to this, Tāranātha recounts in his *sGrol ma'i rgyud kyi byung khung* the story of the slaying of a *vetāla* by Jñānadeva (a student of Śāntideva) who, "intoning Tārā's *mantra* and wielding his *kīla* ... caused the zombie to fall backwards and collapse with the crown of its head caved in".[170]

Japanese tradition has it that the words KĪLI KĪLI found in some of the *kīlamantra* are onomatopoeic for the creaking sounds made by the doors of the *maṇḍala* palace as they close, thus preventing the entry of obstruct-

---

165 T.1222. The significant contribution afforded by the Sino-Japanese tradition to a historical study of Vajrakīla is dealt with below. I am indebted, both here and below, to my colleagues Masahide Mori and Stephen Hodge for their invaluable assistance with all my enquiries into this field.

166 Cowell & Thomas, *Harṣacarita* 90-92

167 Tawney, *op.cit.* vol.1 31, & vol.2 138, 206, 207, 208, 232, 233, etc. Dozens of references are to be found within these two volumes.

168 V. Fausboll (ed.), *The Jātaka Together With its Commentary*, Trubner & Co., London (1883) III.511-512

169 The commentary furnishes no information on this point.

170 D. Templeman, *The Origin of the Tārā Tantra* 29

ing forces[171] but we return fully to the theme of the zombie and the *kīla* with the Nepalese tradition of architecture in which the threshold of a house is viewed as an actual or potential *vetāla*. In keeping with this view, every year the Nepali householder must drive a nail into the threshold of his dwelling in order to prevent this fearful monster from rising and it is particularly curious to note that this annual ritual is performed on *nāga-pañcamī,* the day dedicated by the Nepalese to the worship of serpents, thus maintaining the intimate connection between the *kīla* and the *nāga* noted earlier.[172] *Vetāla* are also to be observed lying across the threshold of hypaethral shrines in Nepal, such as the one to whom bloody oblations are presented at the entrance to the sacred site (*pīṭha*) of Pacali Bhairava on the banks of the Bagmati river.[173]

The sūtras

Within the early Buddhist *sūtras* in both Pāli and Sanskrit, the wooden stake is well known as a boundary-marker and so on but there is no discernible shift in emphasis in the direction of its apotheosis.[174] The single possible exception to this is the case of the *indrakīla* placed for protection outside the city gates in Śrī Laṅkā to which offerings of incense and flowers are made. But, in the words of de Silva, "this aspect of the *indrakīla* as an object worthy of honour is certainly an advancement made on the concept of *indrakīla* as revealed from Pāli and Sanskrit sources".[175]

The association of the *kīla* with doors, thresholds, boundaries and their protection being well attested, it is interesting to note the 63rd *sutta* of the *Sattaka-nipāta* in which the seven requisites for the protection of a

---

171 Y.Hatta, *Shingon Jiten (A Dictionary of Mantra)*

172 M. Slusser, *Nepal Maṇḍala* 362, 421. I am informed by a Nepali Hindu currently resident in London that this belief and its accompanying ritual are widespread throughout Nepal.

173 *ibidem* 335 and plate 369

174 A.K. Warder in his *Introduction to Pali,* PTS (1975) 363, defines *khīlo* as a stake for marking boundaries and *indakhīlo* as a "royal stake (marking the royal threshold, also as a symbol of firmness)". The *Pāli-English Dictionary* edited by T.W. Rhy-Davids & William Stede, PTS (1925) adds, "a large slab of stone let into the ground at the entrance of a house ... Threshold", to its definition of *indakhīla* and also lists the adjective *khīlaka* meaning "having stakes or stumps as obstacles".

175 Lily de Silva, "The Symbolism of the Indrakīla in the Paritta Maṇḍapa" 242

fortress are described. This *sutta* specifically states the pillar (*esikā* = *indakhīla*) to be the chief of these because, being unmovable, it is the very symbol of stability. The seven are then likened to 'seven forms of wealth' (*saptadhanāni*) that give proper security to the ascetic. According to this list, the pillar is like faith (*śraddhā*), the moat shame (*hrī*), the citadel modesty (*apatrāpya*), the armoury of swords and spears like learning (*śruta*), the well-armed troops are like valour (*vīrya*) or renunciation (*tyāga*), the wise gatekeeper who refuses entry to strangers is mindfulness (*smṛti*) or morality (*śīla*) and the tall, sturdy ramparts are like wisdom (*prajñā*).[176]

In a paper entitled "Buddhism, Taoism and the Rise of the City Gods",[177] Timothy Barrett highlighted a class of deity known as *nagara-devatā* ('gods in charge of cities') mentioned in the *Gaṇḍavyūha-sūtra.* In a certain passage of that *sūtra*[178] strongly reminiscent of the above citation from the *Sattaka-nipāta,* Ratnanetra (a god of this class) instructs the disciple Sudhana to guard and protect the city of the mind by strenuous endeavour in virtue. "Build strong walls about the city of mind by purification of mind in carrying out the vow of practice of universal good".[179] This passage, says Prof. Barrett whose paper has much to say about the cult of gods of walls, "attracted a considerable amount of Chinese commentary." It also says much about the Buddhist attitude to religion in which all practical matters in the mundane world are seen to have their metaphysical equivalents of practical value in the realm of the sacred. It is this attitude that lies at the heart of the apotheosis of the *kīla.*

A curious parallel process of apotheosis is to be observed in the iconography of the four goddesses who guard the doors of the *maṇḍala* of Viśvaḍāka, in which a white goddess in the east is the apotheosis of a lock or bolt (*tālaka*), a yellow goddess in the south is the apotheosis of keys (*kuñcikā*), a red goddess in the west is the apotheosis of a door panel (*kapāṭa*) and a black goddess in the north is the apotheosis of a dividing curtain (*kāṇḍapaṭa*).[180] Thus we should not be surprised to witness the

---

176 E. Hardy (ed.), *Aṅguttara Nikāya* IV, PTS (1899) 106

177 T. Skorupski (ed.), *The Buddhist Forum II*, SOAS (1991) 13-25

178 Ed. P.L. Vaidya, Darbhanga (1960) 339

179 Translation by T. Cleary, *The Flower Ornament Scripture* (Vol.3), Boston & Shaftesbury (1987) 306

180 Viśvaḍāka is the *ḍāka* of the *karmakula* in the group of five *ḍāka*. Abhayākaragupta, *Niṣpannayogāvalī* 77

eventual rise of the *kīla* as a deity, despite the absence of firm indications in the early Pāli sources.

Dawn of the kīlamantra (dhāraṇī)

Although very little in the earlier *sūtras* seemed to impinge directly upon the subject of our present enquiry, within the *dhāraṇī* that became increasingly prominent as a genre of later Mahāyāna literature are definite signs of the initial stages of a process through which the *kīla* came to be incorporated into the Buddhist fold as an instrument of magical power.

With regard to its function of stabilising the earth, there is the *Vasudhārā-dhāraṇī* for the goddess of the earth, which closes with the words TADYATHĀ KILI KILI AKṢA AKṢA (which may include the meaning of snake) BHAGAVATI. Even following the rise of the wrathful Vajrakīla *tantra,* the *kīla* retains its prior function of pacification of the earth and, in particular, the subjugation of the 'earth serpent'. The main purpose of the *Mahāmāyūrī-dhāraṇī,* cited above in connection with *vetāla,* is in fact to turn away snakes and to counteract the poison of snakebite. A phrase occurring several times within the *Māyūrī* charm runs ILI MILI KILI MILI.[181] This and similar phrases are also to be found elsewhere[182] and the important thing to note here is that, wherever they are met with, ILI and MILI refer to snakes[183] and KILI can be linked to the *kīla*. In this instance the *kīla* functions simply to create a magical barrier against snakes but it has an association also with the yogic skill of weather control, one of the earliest rites to demand the use of the hand-held *kīla*. This feat is thought to be achieved by overpowering those cloud-dwelling *nāga* held to be responsible for rainfall, itself reminiscent of the mythology of Indra.

The *Mahāmāyūrī-dhāraṇī,* even in its most primitive form, proclaims its usefulness as a magical means of protecting boundaries. By the early fourth century CE, however, this function had become so specifically marked that, in the appended notes to the text as translated into Chinese

---

181 A.F.R. Hoernle, *The Bower Manuscript* (reprint) Delhi (1987) 240e

182 *Vidyādharapiṭaka-aṣṭamahādhāraṇī;* OṀ KILI MILI and RU RU MI HE KILI MILI ACITTA. *Āryottamamahāvidyārāja-sūtra;* KILI (x9) followed by MILI (x9). *Mahāvajrameruśikharakūṭāgāra-dhāraṇī;* KILI KILI KILI MILI MILI MILI at one point and then KILI KILI MILI MILI LALALI at another. *Vajrajvālā-dhāraṇī;* MILI MILI (many times) and KILI MILI CAṆḌE ... Etc.

183 Cf. HT I.ii.32

by Śrīmitra (*circa* 340 CE), "there are instructions for the delimitation of the ritual area which is then to be decorated with five swords, five banners, five mirrors, twenty-one arrows and twenty-one lamps. The site is to be anointed with perfumes, and mustard seeds are to be burnt to expel obstructing demons".[184] This particular function of securing a protective boundary against evil (*sīmābandha*) gradually became almost the exclusive preserve of the *kīla*.

Among other very early references to the magical protective power of the *kīla* are those to be found in the *Mahābala-sūtra,*[185] a transitional text of the late Mahāyāna period displaying characteristics more commonly associated with *tantra* than *sūtra.*[186] It is said to have been taught by Śākyamuni Buddha to a large gathering of Vedic divinities (including the *daśadikpāla*) who had assembled on the peak of Mount Mucilinda. During the course of the *sūtra* the *bodhisattva* Vajrapāṇi[187] uttered the *dhāraṇī* of *vidyārāja* Mahābala and enumerated its virtues. The importance of the *kīla* is made evident within this text where it is stated that the *sūtra*'s very essence (*hṛdaya*) is contained in the word KĪLIKĪLA. Within the *dhāraṇī* itself occur the phrases NAMAŚ CAṆḌAVAJRAPĀṆAYE MAHĀYAKṢASENĀPATAYE OṀ KĪLIKĪLI VAJRAKĪLIKĪLĀYA SVĀHĀ... CAṆḌAKĪLIKĪLĀYA SVĀHĀ. BĀLAKĪLIKĪLĀYA SVĀHĀ.[188] RATNAKĪLIKĪLĀYA SVĀHĀ... VAJRAKĪLĀYA SVĀHĀ... OṀ MUNI MUNI MAHĀMUNI KĪLIKĪLA VEKI KAṬA KAṬA... etc.

Magic spells such as these Buddhist *dhāraṇī* played a significant role in the everyday life of the people of ancient India. From a very early date

---

184 S. Hodge, *The Mahāvairocana-tantra* Introduction

185 F.A. Bischoff, *Āryamahābalanāma-mahāyāna-sūtra,* Paris (1956). Mahābala is later to be found among the ten wrathful divinities in the primary entourage of Vajrakīla. His epithet used here, *mahāvidyārāja* (also noted in association with Amṛtakuṇḍalin), became in later texts freely interchangeable with the term *krodharāja*. Elementary characteristics of several of these *krodha* kings are clearly discernible in the *dhāraṇī* literature. To trace the evolution of each of them from such primitive sources, however, is a task outside the scope of the present work.

186 mKhas-grub-rje in fact, following the lead of "older authorities", classifies this text within the *kriyātantra*.
Lessing & Wayman, *Introduction to the Buddhist Tantric Systems* 133

187 Also called Caṇḍavajrapāṇi, whose role in the Vajrakīla *tantra* will be seen in Chapter Five, below.

188 In Chapter Three, below, Vajrakīla is styled 'Son of Heruka'.

the Buddhists utilised their sacred scriptures in the *paritta* ceremony[189] and, according to Hsuan Tsang,[190] the Mahāsāṅghikas compiled a *dhāraṇīpiṭaka* during the fourth century BCE. This was followed by a *vidyādharapiṭaka,* compiled in the north by the Dhammaguttas sometime during the third century BCE.[191]

From these sources may be surmised an evolutionary line of development of the rite of *sīmābandha* from the purely functional process of marking out a plot of ground by means of wooden pegs and lengths of string as outlined under the rubric of Architecture, above. During the course of this development, a religious element has been absorbed whereby the pegs have become imbued with magical power and almost transformed into gods. Such rites are then fully elaborated within the earliest historical strata of Buddhist *tantra* (*kriyā*), in which ritual activity predominates.

Sīmābandha in the lower Buddhist tantra

The *Susiddhi-tantra,* classified by Paṇ-chen bsod-nams grags-pa as a general *tantra* of the *kriyā* class dealing with the fierce rites of all three buddha families (*tathāgatakula, vajrakula, padmakula*),[192] "teaches in detail the rite of performing the *vidyā-dhāraṇī*" and "the protection according to *kriyātantra*".[193] Within this text the role of protection of the boundaries is allocated to Amṛtakuṇḍalin, a deity described as fierce guardian of the north and master of all *yakṣa.*[194] In the performance of his duty Amṛtakuṇḍlin manifests as Kīlikīla and, in association with his role as boundary protector, the *tantra* teaches the *kīlamudrā.*

---

189 Y. Matsunaga, "A History of Tantric Buddhism in India With Reference to Chinese Translations" 169

190 E. Lamotte, *History of Indian Buddhism* 286

191 Y. Matsunaga, *op.cit. ibidem.*

192 *rGyud sde spyi'i rnam par bzhag pa skal bzang gi yid 'phrog* LTWA (1975) 38

193 Lessing & Wayman, *op.cit.* 137

194 Later to become one of the *daśakrodha* deities in the primary retinue of Vajrakīla. The *yogatantra* SDPT states; "The wrathful Amṛtakuṇḍalin is common to the three families. Because he removes all obstacles he is said to be the lord of the *guhyakas* (*guhyakādhipa*)." SDPT 76

Throughout the sources referred to in this chapter, no distinction is made between Amṛtakuṇḍalin and Vajrāmṛta.

The procedures of this *tantra* as practised in Japan are described in a study of Shingon Buddhism by Adrian Snodgrass[195] who writes: "The sādhaka first performs the rituals of 'securing the boundaries' (*bandhaya sīman*) in which he defines the boundaries of the maṇḍala and expels the demonic influences that might hinder the performance of the ritual or harm the ritualist. The sādhaka secures the boundaries of the maṇḍala by wooden (or less usually iron or copper) vajra spikes (*vajrakīlakam*)[196] driven into the four corners of the *bodhimaṇḍa*. They not only delimit the borders of the maṇḍala but symbolise the firmness of the sādhaka's Bodhicitta, which harmful influences cannot move. The sādhaka symbolically drives the spikes into the corners of the *bodhimaṇḍa* by making a *mudrā* (thus)";

This procedure establishes and encloses the area into which the deities are subsequently to be invited and transforms the site into the indestructible *vajra* earth out as far as the *cakravāla*. Thus, according to the rite it becomes impossible for even the most powerful demons to enter and all evils within the ground are purified.

The Tibetan author Tsong-kha-pa, basing himself upon the same *tantra,* in his *Great Exposition of Secret Mantra* gives the *mantra* OṀ

195 A. Snodgrass, *The Matrix and Diamond World Maṇḍalas in Shingon Buddhism*. Quotation and *mudrā* drawing found on pp.58-61

196 The Japanese tradition generally equates this *vajrakīlaka* with a single-pronged *vajra,* but more details of the form of the *kīla* in Japan are given below.

KĪLIKĪLA VAJRI VAJRI BHŪR BANDHA BANDHA HŪṀ PHAṬ and says that the *yogin* should use it to empower scented water which is then sprinkled around the boundaries of his place of meditation in order to establish the *rakṣācakra*. He also explains the *kīlamudrā,* as in the diagram above, and uses it to implant an unspecified number of *kīla* in the form of fierce deities into the hearts of obstructors around the circumference of the meditation area. The above *mantra* is again recited as the trouble-making demons are thus being rendered powerless. Tsong-kha-pa also says that for *yogin*s in the *vajrakula,* self protection is afforded by the *mantra* OṀ KĪLI KĪLA VAJRA HŪṀ PHAṬ. According to him, Kuṇḍali and Kīlikīla (thought of as one in the Sino-Japanese tradition) are two separate deities always associated with the protective walls, protective canopy and the circle of *kīla* enclosing the ritually pure area.[197]

I quote from A. Snodgrass; "The vajra spikes (*vajrakīlakaṁ*) are variously referred to as the 'boundary spikes', the 'boundary vajra spikes', 'ground spikes', 'vajra spike boundaries', 'vajra flame boundaries', etc. The spikes are "twelve *shi*" long (about seven and a half inches) and are driven about one third of their length into the ground.... The *Darani shukyo* specifies not four but twenty-eight spikes: six on either side of the west gate, four at each of the other three gates, and one at each of the four corners. Annen's *Dainichikyo gishaku* calls for fifty-two spikes: twelve at each of the four gates, and one at each of the four corners".[198]

Furthermore; The *dhāraṇī* that accompanies the *mudrā* of the *vajra* spikes is OṀ KILI KILI VAJRA VAJRI BHŪRA BANDHA BANDHA HŪṀ PHAṬ in which KILI KILI is "spike, spike", referring both to the spike and to the action of spiking, VAJRA is 'unassailable wisdom' (*vajraprajñā*) and VAJRI is 'unshakeable meditation' (*vajradhyāna*). BHŪRA is 'firmness' and BANDHA BANDHA is "binding, binding". HŪṀ is the seed syllable of terror and also of *bodhicitta* and PHAṬ is the seed syllable of crushing and destroying. The *dhāraṇī* thus means that unassailable wisdom and unshakeable meditation spike down, firmly bind and terrify the demons,

---

197 J. Hopkins, *The Yoga of Tibet* 96-97. The Japanese Mantrayāna (Shingon) tradition follows this system exactly. The *kīlamudrā* given in Snodgrass (reproduced above) corresponds to that given in Hopkins and the *mantra* given in both Snodgrass and Hatta (*Dictionary of Mantra*) is OṀ KILI KILI VAJRA VAJRI BHŪRA BANDHA BANDHA HŪṀ PHAṬ which is little changed considering the amount of time and space that separates the two traditions.

198 A. Snodgrass, *op.cit.* 60-61, n.6

crushing and destroying their great power. As he makes the *mudrā* and recites the *dhāraṇī*, the *sādhaka* mentally strikes each corner of the *bodhimaṇḍa* three times with a single- or triple-pronged *vajra*(*kīla*).[199]

In a chapter called *Vighnakīlanavidhi* (rite of nailing down obstacles) in Kuladatta's *Kriyāsaṅgrahapañjikā* (*Detailed Compendium of Rituals*), instructions are given for the purification and protection of the earth prior to the building of a *vihāra*. According to this source, 32 *krodha* deities (an inner group of twelve and an outer group of twenty) are embodied in 28 *kīla*[200] which are arranged in two concentric squares enclosing the site designated for the construction. Each of the *kīla* located in the four corners of the inner square is to be thought of as being occupied by two deities. The master of the rite meditates upon himself as the deity Vajrahūṁkāra and utters the *sārvakarmika-mantra,* generally defined as the *mantra* of the deity presiding over the northern quarter of the *maṇḍala*. The *kīla* (which are said to be eight inches long, made of either acacia wood or gold) are then fixed into the ground and as each one is hammered in, in due order, the *mantra* of the residing deity is intoned and he is called upon

---

199 *ibidem* 64. This use of either a single-pronged or triple-pronged *vajrakīla* is understood in Japan to be authorised by the *Susiddhi-tantra*. Four *kīla* which were brought to Japan by Kobo Daishi, now preserved in the Yamato Muro Temple, are of the single-pronged variety and thus this type is favoured by the Shingon school. The Tendai school also uses single-pronged *kīla*. The tips of the Yamato Muro Temple *kīla* have an eight-petalled lotus design with a moon disc on top of that, and then a round jewel shape. The jewel, however, is the specific emblem of the *ratnakula* and as an alternative to this, in association with the various ritual functions of a *kīla,* the spike may bear a *cakra*, lotus or *vajra* upon its tip. (The Tibetan method of distinguishing *kīla* in association with the four or five *kula* of the higher *tantra* tends to be by material of manufacture.) Other *kīla* were taken to Japan by Engyo, Keiun and Chisho. According to these sources for the Sino-Japanese tradition, the main material to be used in the manufacture of *kīla* is *khadira* wood or else *nimba* wood (neem), iron or copper. According to T.889, translated by Tensokuzai of Kashmir (Sanskrit name uncertain) who arrived in China in 979 CE, sappy wood should be used to make the *kīla* for pacification, *śrīvṛkṣa* and *śirīṣa* for enriching, *khadira* for subduing and iron for destroying. *Kālacakra-tantra* III.12 lists eight materials without, however, any indication of their particular functions.

200 According to Stephen Hodge, Śubhakarasiṁha's commentary on the *Mahāvairocana-tantra* also specifies the use of 28 *kīla* but their arrangement on the ground is different. Six *kīla* are to be placed on either side of the western gate, four in front of the other three gates and one in each of the four corners, just as in the description given below taken from Bodhiruci's Japanese *Compendium of Dhāraṇī*.

to subdue a particular *vighna* ('obstacle') in the form of a Hindu deity. This being done, some of the *kīla* are then moved to new locations and details are given concerning the method of drawing lines for the plan of the *vihāra*, utilising lengths of string pulled taught between the pegs.[201]

An interesting story is told in the 'Prophecy of the Li Country' (*Li yul lung bstan pa*) in which a *kīla* made of juniper wood, which had been used in this way during the building of a *stūpa,* subsequently grew into a tree with five branches and began to preach the Buddhist Dharma, graphically illustrating the notion of the peg as the abode of a god.[202] The 'Li Country' (Khotan) is an area in which the Vajrayāna is known to have existed[203] and, thanks to discoveries made in Central Asia by Sir Aurel Stein, the use of *kīla* in the region is confirmed dating back to antiquity.[204] The configurations of those ancient *kīla* unearthed by Stein also readily confirms the view that they were conceived in some measure as the abodes of gods or spirits.

The chapter entitled *Parikramaṇavidhi* in Kuladatta's *Compendium of Rituals* outlines the method for establishing a protective circle around an area within which a tantric *maṇḍala* is to be constructed and this contains many additional elements derived from the later *yoganiruttara* class of *tantra*. To begin with, four assistants in the rite are assigned the role of 'masters of the gates' (*dvārācārya*). They fix one *kīla* into each of the four corners of a square as they recite the *mantra* OṀ GHA GHA GHĀTAYA ... etc.[205] and they are followed by the master of the rite (*karmācārya*) who, beginning in the northeast corner and moving clockwise, fixes eight *kīla* around the perimeter of the site while he recites OṀ VAJRAKĪLA KĪLAYA SARVAVIGHNĀN BANDHAYA HŪṀ. In this way 12 deities are arranged

---

201 Cf. E.W. Marasinghe, *The Vāstuvidyāśāstra Attributed to Mañjuśrī* 167
Also, a modern Newārī text on the rituals of *vāstuvidyā* (written in 1899 by Vajrācārya Jujumāna) describes the procedure of laying out the ground for the erection of a *stūpa* or other building using 38 pegs, measuring a span and four fingers in length, with 84 cubits of thread spun with strands of five colours.
S. Lienhard, *Nepalese Manuscripts* (Part 1) 107-108
For examples of similar rites in the Hindu tradition (where the pegs are called either *kīla* or *śaṅku*) see Alice Boner, *Śilpaprakāsa*; Bruno Dagens, *Māyāmata*; Tarapada Bhattacharyya, *A Study of Vāstuvidyā*; etc.

202 R.E. Emmerick, *Tibetan Texts Concerning Khotan* 46-47

203 H.W. Bailey, "Vajrayāna in Gostana-deśa"

204 R. Whitfield & A. Farrer, *Caves of the Thousand Buddhas* 174-175

205 Given in full below in the section dealing with *yoganiruttaratantra*.

around the square but, because the *ācārya* uses the four already fixed by his assistants, they are housed in only eight *kīla*. The rite ends with the worship of the 12 deities, who are presented with *bali* offerings and requested to subdue 12 *vighnān*.

Both Abhayākaragupta in his *Vajrāvalī* (see below) and Jagaddarpaṇa in his *Kriyāsamuccaya,* on the other hand, describe the wrathful *rakṣācakra* around the *maṇḍala* consisting of ten *kīla*. This configuration is the norm for such rites in Tibet, leaving the tradition of Kuladatta as something of an anomaly.

In his paper on "Monastic Initiation in Newar Buddhism", David Gellner describes an offering rite in which, one by one, ten Vedic gods are summoned and praised and then attacked by their counterparts from the set of *daśakrodha* deities. The attack is in each case instigated by the command KĪLAYA KĪLAYA HŪṀ PHAṬ, in which the denominative form of our word for 'nail', 'spike' or 'peg' is used.[206] The ten Vedic gods are a standard group known as the *daśadikpāla,* whose individual names have come to stand for the directions of the compass over which they hold sway. The Buddhist *tantra* are ambiguous in their attitude towards these ancient Indian deities. In the *yogatantra Sarvadurgatipariśodhana* (SDPT), for example, these gods bow down before the Buddha and each one offers his *mantra* "for the benefit and happiness of all living beings". Īśāna, 'the lord of spirits' (Śiva, Rudra, the guardian of the northeast), then assumes specific responsibility for the counteraction of poison, the stability of borders and the protective circle of *vajrakīla* and so on.[207] Within the SDP *maṇḍala* they occupy seats of honour, as they do in the entourage of many Buddhist deities.[208] In the *Hevajra-tantra* (HT) offerings are made to these gods in a fairly standard fashion but then they are abused and trampled on by low caste women. It is clear, however, that in the latter case their names are being used merely to designate the arrangement of the women (*ḍākinī*) into a circle around their lord.[209] In the *Vimalaprabhā,* on the

---

206 D. Gellner, "Monastic Initiation in Newar Buddhism" 89-93. This section of the rite seems to be derived from Abhayākaragupta's *Vajrāvalī* 36-37 but the placement of the deities accords with the Akṣobhya *maṇḍala*.
Cf. A. Wayman, *Yoga of the Guhyasamājatantra* 243

207 SDPT 51-53. Īśāna's vow in this source corresponds remarkably with the subsequent role of Vajrakīla.

208 Eg. Yogāmbara, Bhūtadāmara, Dharmadhātuvāgīśvara, etc., as described in Abhayākaragupta's *Niṣpannayogāvalī*.

209 HT II.iv.91*ff* and II.v.37

other hand, Indra (foremost of the group and lord of the east) takes on the role of the arch demon Māra, whose messengers seek to destroy the concentration of *yoga,*[210] and in the more wrathful *tantra* such as the *Vajrakīla* these deities are called *vighna* and described as being held captive and tormented by their Buddhist counterparts (the ten *krodharāja*) who mercilessly pin them to the ground.

In the majority of Vajrayāna rituals in which ten spikes are nailed around the periphery of the site to be protected, those spikes are meditated upon as the actual embodiments of the ten wrathful kings and they are driven into the hearts of the ten Vedic gods. The final 'canonical' word on the subject may be attributed to *Kālacakra-tantra* III.27; "... in order to protect the site, stabilising *kīla* of acacia wood are stuck into the ground with blows of a hammer in the positions of the ten *krodha* kings."[211]

Exceptions to this pattern have now fallen into disuse in Tibet although they are still to be encountered within the Japanese tradition as a legacy of archaic Indian praxis. According to the teachings of the *Vajrahṛdayālaṅkāra-tantra,* in order to qualify as a *vajraguru* with the competence to grant *abhiṣeka,* an *ācārya* must be skilled not only in the technique of drawing the *maṇḍala* but also in "the rite of accomplishing the fierce act of tying down the gods with the magic *kīla*".[212] A basic knowledge of *kīla* rites therefore appears to have been widely regarded as essential to the tantric adepts of India, an assumption that I believe to be confirmed by the legends and teachings of the early *mahāsiddha.*[213] Several centuries after the institution of these *kīla* rites in ancient India, it was stated in very matter of fact fashion by the Tibetan master mKhas-grub-rje that all tantric adepts, no matter to which school they belong nor the nature of the *maṇḍala* they are effecting, protect and bless the site by nailing the obstructing demons with *kīla.*[214]

---

210 Ed. J. Upadhyaya (1986) 10

211 B. Banerjee, *Śrī Kālacakra-tantrarāja* 96

212 Lessing & Wayman, *Introduction to the Buddhist Tantric Systems* 272

213 The rite of *kīlana* ('pegging down') is included among the magical activities mentioned by the *mahāsiddha* Matsyendranātha in Chapter IV of his *Kaulajñānanirṇaya.* Ed. P.C. Bagchi, Calcutta Sanskrit Series III (1934) 9

214 Lessing & Wayman, *op.cit.* 282

Sīmābandha in the yoganiruttaratantra

The final evolutionary phase of Buddhist *tantra* is marked by those texts in which all aspects of yogic praxis are internalised so as to be dealt with in the mind. This is not to say that adherents of these doctrines perform no outer rituals. On the contrary, the texts describe a great number of elaborate rites to be performed with meticulous observance of *minutiae.* Their theoretical premise, however, stresses the supremacy of mind to such an extent that all ritual activity is considered to be merely the play (*līlā*) of the god within.[215]

The *Guhyasamāja-tantra* (GST) describes the procedure for blessing the *yogin*'s meditation area thus; "(Imagine) Vajrakīla as an embodiment of the great king Vajrāmṛta and stab it, blazing with fire, into the circle of the ten directions."[216] This rite, called *jagadvinayaśāntivajra* (*vajra* which rules and pacifies the world), is apparently an abbreviated, almost entirely internalised version of the rite of ten *kīla* outlined above. This citation also seems to suggest that the implement employed in the rite is no longer the humble wooden peg or *kīla* of the earlier texts but a sophisticated and essential item of ritual paraphernalia now known as the *vajrakīla*. Note the continuing identification of Vajrakīla with Vajrāmṛta (Amṛtakuṇḍalin).

In the *Śrīcakrasaṁvara-tantra,* in order to place a protective circle around the *maṇḍala* the *sādhaka* is instructed to imagine a syllable HŪṀ in his heart from which he causes to emanate a multitude of *vajra* nails and *vajra* hammers. These hammers and nails are placed into the right and left hands of assistants (*dūta*) who then drag forth all obstructing forces, chief among whom are the Vedic *daśadikpāla*. Being summoned, those with virtuous minds take refuge in the *triratna* and are established in the mind of enlightenment, while those of an evil disposition are transfixed through the head with a *kīla* to the accompaniment of the *mantra* OṀ GHA GHA GHĀTAYA GHĀTAYA SARVADUṢṬĀN PHAṬ! KĪLAYA KĪLAYA SARVAPĀPAM HŪṀ PHAṬ! VAJRAKĪLAYA VAJRADHARA ĀJÑĀPAYATI SARVAVIGHNĀN KĀYA-VĀK-CITTA-KĪLAYA HŪṀ PHAṬ! (Oṁ begone, begone all evil ones! Phaṭ! Nail, nail all sins! Hūṁ phaṭ! Vajradhara instructs all obstacles to be nailed down with the *vajra* nail of body, speech and mind! Hūṁ phaṭ!) And they are pounded down to pulp

---

215 "The mind itself is the perfect Buddha and no Buddha is seen elsewhere." HT II.iv.75

216 GST XIII.75

with the hammers whilst reciting OṀ VAJRAMUDGARA VAJRAKĪLAYA ĀKOṬAYA HŪṀ PHAṬ! (Oṁ *vajra* hammer [you] must nail down, must beat! Hūṁ phaṭ!)[217]

Other kīla rituals

Thus far we have seen *kīla* chiefly in groups as boundary markers and (violent) protectors. They have been seen as magical pegs standing at the threshold preventing the intrusion of harm. As the guardians of order and stability they have served to destroy the power of *vetāla* and *nāga* at one extreme and to stabilise the *samādhi* of religious at the other. Indra, however, stabilised the earth by pinning it down with a single *kīla,* not with a circle of *kīla* around the boundary.

A single *kīla* of acacia wood (*khadira*)[218] is mentioned within a long ritual in the MMK.[219] The passage in question concerns solicitation of the beautiful Manojñā in order to gain her wealth and sexual favours. This charming nymph[220] bestows the elixir (*rasāyana*) granting long life to the *sādhaka* who may chose to live in a palace of the gods so long as he meditates upon the *kīla* stuck into the ground.[221]

The *kīla* as a ground-stabilising agent in the building of a temple has already been encountered above. Here, however, we have what is possi-

---

217 K. Dawa-Samdup, *Śrīcakrasaṁvara-tantra* 171. Variants of the GHA GHA *mantra* are to be found in a number of *yoganiruttaratantra*.

218 *Khadira* is *Acacia Catechu,* one of several varieties of acacia tree. Throughout the present work, however, the name 'acacia' is everywhere used to refer to *khadira* alone. Wood of this type is employed in many violent rites in a number of Buddhist *tantra* (eg. *Saṁvarodaya-tantra* X.22, etc.) and is considered by Indian doctors to cure obstinate skin diseases including leprosy (V.B. Dash, *Materia Medica of Indo-Tibetan Medicine* 181). Leprosy is held to be caused by vicious *nāga,* those troublesome subterranean spirits that are the prime targets in 'earth subjugating' rituals, and ritual *kīla* generally are to be found with *nāga* engraved upon them (see J. Huntingdon, *The Phur-pa, passim*). That the preferred material for their manufacture is acacia wood can be confirmed by the many references cited throughout this work including the passage from the GST quoted below (where I take the slightly ambiguous phrase *khadirāgrajam* to mean *khadirajam agram*, "the best is that made of acacia"). Cf. note 160, above.

219 MMK 570-571

220 F. Edgerton, *BHS Dictionary* 418, describes her as a *yakṣiṇī.* She also occurs in the retinue of Vajrāmṛta (*Niṣpannayogāvalī; maṇḍala* no.7)

221 *manasā dhyātvā khadirakīlakaṁ bhūmau nikhānayet. divyaṁ vimānam upapadyate. uddhṛte 'ntardhīyate.* MMK 571

bly the earliest reference to a single *kīla* as the stabilising force underpinning meditation upon a divine *maṇḍala* of residence. A later, but far more explicit source is the *Sarvatathāgatatattvasaṁgraha-tantra* (STTS). In the section concerning the delineation of the *maṇḍala* in Chapter XI it is written: "Having pierced the acacia wood spike in the centre of the *maṇḍala,* make a double-threaded string (and) with that, one should delineate (the circle). On that occasion, this is the 'heart essence' of the *kīla*; OṀ VAJRAKĪLA KĪLAYA SARVAVIGHNĀN BANDHAYA HŪṀ PHAṬ." (Oṁ Vajrakīla, spike! Transfix all obstructors! Hūṁ phaṭ!)[222]

The form of the *kīla* as we find it today may be derived in part from its erstwhile use as a wooden stake to which sacrificial animals were tethered prior to their ritual slaughter.[223] The above quotation from the STTS shows how the stake and tether are now employed as equipment for drawing circles, much as the hapless goats must have done whilst moving restlessly around the centres of their captivity. Such a procedure not only stabilises the centre but also links that centre directly to the circumference, thereby revealing the single *kīla* as the instrument through which the entire ground may be rendered firm.

Indra, however, did not confine his activities to the achievement of a firm and solid earth. Propping up the firmament he took the thunderbolt as his sceptre and ruled over the lesser gods of wind and rain.

In the MMK are found two short rites through which the *yogin* may seek to gain control over such atmospheric phenomena. In the first of these a "cloud-shaped *kīla*" (*kabandākārakīlaka*) is mentioned in connection with such dire omens as fiery comets, thunderbolts, darkness and disease. All untimely deaths are said to be pacified in the second rite by the simple expedient of burning incense, reciting *mantra*, flinging mustard seeds into the sky and the implantation of a *kīla* of acacia wood over

---

222 *maṇḍalasya tu madhye vai vidhvā khadirakīlakam, tatas tu sūtraṁ dviguṇaṁ kṛtvā tena prasūtrayet. tatredaṁ kīlakahṛdayam, oṁ vajrakīla kīlaya sarvavighnān bandhaya hūṁ phaṭ.* STTS 91. Note that, although the *kīla* is being used here in a very straightforward fashion (simply as a peg to hold down one end of a piece of string while a circle is being drawn around it), this citation evinces distinct features of a wrathful rite.

223 R. Mayer, *op.cit.* 170*ff*. The knots (*kanda*) of rope tied to the shaft of this stake are an important element in the later iconography of the sacred *kīla* (dealt with in the following chapter). These *kanda* along the shaft of the nail also have an association with the subtle centres of psychic energy (*cakra*) employed in *yoga* and imagined to be situated along the central *nāḍī* of the *vajra* body.

which *mantra* have been recited seven times. Thus the wind is held still and the clouds are fixed in their places.[224] The *Mahāvairocanābhisaṁbodhi-tantra* describes the rite for dispelling rainclouds by instructing the *yogin* to draw the image of such clouds upon the ground and mentally transform himself into the deity Vajrapāṇi. Arranging his fingers in the form of the *mudrā,* he should stab the point of the *vajrakīla* into the image and the rain will disperse.[225]

No longer employed purely for purposes of defence, then, the *kīla* is now a weapon of attack.

In his commentary on the SDPT, Vajravarman identifies the objects to be attacked as the various defilements (*kleśa*). Thus, in order to destroy sin, the *yogin* manufactures a '*kīla* of pacification' from white sandal wood, eight inches long with a large knot at the top and round at the tip. He imagines the buddhas and *bodhisattvas* to assemble upon that *kīla* and, as he nails down the defilements, he mutters OṀ VAJRAKĪLA KĪLA SARVAPĀPAŚĀNTIṀ KURU SVĀHĀ. Striking it with a hammer of silver having a handle of sandalwood he pronounces the curse OṀ ŚAPATHA.[226]

In the *Saṁvarodaya-tantra,* instructions are given for an act of malevolent sorcery (*abhicāra*) involving a six-inch *kīla* made of monkey bone (*vānarāsthimayaṁ kīlam*). Having empowered this *kīla* by reciting an unspecified *mantra* over it seven times, if it is burned at the enemy's door the enemy and his entire lineage will perish, or, if it is buried in a field where livestock is kept the animals will die.[227] A similar ritual is given in the GST where it is said that one should chant the *mantra* one hundred and eight times in order to empower an eight-inch *kīla* made of human bone (*mānuṣāsthimayaṁ kīlam*) which, if hidden near the enemy's door, will cause death within a fortnight.[228] The cycle of the *Vajrabhairava-tantra*, too, includes several short *vidhi* in similar vein. One such rite instructs the *sādhaka* to draw an effigy using charcoal from the funeral pyre upon a scrap of cloth taken from the shroud of a corpse. The effigy should be stabbed in five places with a *kīla* of human bone.[229] The same cycle also

---

224 MMK 274. The *kīla* on this occasion is unaccountably given a feminine form (*kīlakā*) in the published text.

225 S. Hodge, *The Mahāvairocana-tantra* III; "The Overcoming of Obstacles"

226 SDPT 85, n.28

227 S. Tsuda, *The Saṁvarodaya-tantra* XXVIII.21 & 22

228 GST XIV.55

229 P.105 *Śrīvajramahābhairavanāma-tantra* II, 136v

includes a *kīlamantra,* OṀ VAJRAKRODHA YAMARĀJA VAJRAKILI KILI HANA HANA MĀRAYA PHAṬ, which is to be recited as the *yogin* transfixes the object of his meditation with a bone *kīla,*[230] as well as instructions for stabbing an effigy in the groin as he presses down upon it with the sole of his left foot.[231]

Chronological summary

We are now in a position to assess the main stages through which the *kīla* developed into a hand-held ritual weapon in the armoury of the tantric Buddhists and attempt to reconstruct the path of apotheosis of Vajrakīla as a wrathful deity in the Vajrayāna pantheon.

Among the most ancient *kīla* in existence today are those discovered by Sir Aurel Stein in the vicinity of the frontier defence forts to the north of Dūnhuáng. A set of four such *kīla* (two of which are currently housed in the British Museum) have been dated as belonging to the first century BCE.[232] Approximately nine inches in length, they have been crudely fashioned from an unspecified species of wood into a shape that remains instantly recognisable after two thousand years as characteristic of the magical *kīla*. The upper part of each spike has been fashioned into the wide-eyed grimacing countenance of a wrathful deity, below which extends a tapering three-sided shaft culminating in a sharp point. If the experts at the British Museum are correct in their dating of these pegs then it would seem reasonable to assume that Buddhist *dhāraṇī* calculated to invoke and utilise the apotropaic power of the *kīla* may also have existed in the pre-Christian era. None of the currently available texts, however, can be dated prior to the third or fourth centuries CE although it is well-known that *dhāraṇī,* in general, had by then been long integrated into the vast corpus of Buddhist literature.

We have seen that the *Māyūrī* spell, in particular, was credited with the power of establishing a protective boundary against a range of hostile forces, especially snakes. The term *mayūra* means 'peacock' and the power of the spell is linked to the Indian belief that peacocks devour snakes in order to transform their poison into the shining colours of their iridescent plumage. In the final iconography of Vajrakīla, this legend is

---

230 P.106 *Śrīvajrabhairavakalpa-tantrarāja* II, 150r

231 *ibidem* 149r

232 R. Whitfield & A. Farrer, *Caves of the Thousand Buddhas* 174-5

recast into that of the mythical *garuḍa* which emanates from the belly of Vajrakīla and has a particular antipathy for *nāga*. We should also note the existence of a *kīla*-dart (*śūla*) topped with peacock feathers that is brandished as a weapon in the hands of several protector deities, including Śrīdevī.[233] At this stage, however, we simply have the notion of a ring of wooden stakes as (magical) weapons against snakes.

Within these early *dhāraṇī* it is also possible to discern primitive features[234] of the *krodharāja* which are later to become the companions of Vajrakīla within his wrathful *maṇḍala*. Indeed, it even seems feasible to trace the emergence of Hayagrīva from such early sources as the *Amitābhavyūha-sūtra*[235] but such a task is beyond the scope of the present work.

Concentrating our attention on Vajrakīla, therefore, we may add to the citations above by noting the occurrence of NAMA VAJRAKILI KILĀYA in the *Mahāvajrameruśikharakūṭāgāra-dhāraṇī*[236] before moving on to consider the next phase of Buddhist literature.

Studying the well-documented stream of translations that were made into Chinese from Sanskrit sources, Yukei Matsunaga has been able to show that a large number of tantric rituals were in vogue among Indian Buddhists from the early fourth century CE.[237] Within the *kriyātantra* that probably arose during the next two hundred years,[238] are to be found a large number of *kīla* rituals. The rite of *sīmābandha* is especially preva-

---

233 Lokesh Chandra, *Buddhist Iconography* 116

234 Specific epithets and *bījamantra*.

235 His *bījamantra* HULU HULU is abundant in that text.
Cf. R.H. van Gulik, *Hayagrīva* (*passim*)

236 In which text, also, Vajrapāṇi is praised for his great strength (*mahābala*), several *mantra* appropriate to the *krodha* kings are found and the words KAṄKAṬA JAYA VIJAYA (frequently encountered in Vajrakīla literature) occur.

237 J.W. de Jong, "A New History of Tantric Literature in India" 96

238 Texts cited above that belong in this category are the *Susiddhi-tantra* and the MMK. mKhas-grub-rje also includes the *Mahābala-dhāraṇī,* saying it pertains to the messengers (*pho nya*) and servants (*bka' nyan*) of the *vajrakula*. Lessing & Wayman, *op.cit.* 132-3

lent amongst these, but by no means exhaustive.[239] Other *kīla* rites in *kriyā* literature include those for animating corpses (*vetālavidhi*), controlling the weather, and the subjugation of local spirits. Throughout this period of tantric literature, the numinous essence of the *kīla* invoked in the earlier *dhāraṇī* has been supplemented by and absorbed into the hardware of ritual pegs. A marked change of emphasis has also taken place in that mundane objectives seem almost to have obliterated the quest for spiritual excellence. The *kīla* at this stage is employed in rites calculated to bring harm, satisfy erotic desires or procure slaves for necrophiles.[240] At one point the MMK uses the denominative form of the word *kīla* to indicate that which has been held down, broken or defiled. It then goes on to detail a method through which the situation can be revived and describes the outcome as "unpegged, set free" (*utkīlita*).[241]

The notion of Vajrakīla as a god also continued to evolve throughout this period and in the text known as the spell of *Vajravidāraṇā* both a deified hammer (Vajramudgara) and a deified nail (Vajrakīla) assume central roles in the *maṇḍala* of Vajrapāṇi. Here, the individual *mantra* of Vajrakīla is given as CURU CURU CAṆḌAKĪLI KĪLĀYA SVĀHĀ (Destroy! Destroy, fierce nail! Homage to the nail!) and the praise VAJRAKĪLIKĪLĀYA SVĀHĀ occurs repeatedly. We note also that the inner circle which includes both the hammer and the nail is surrounded by an outer circle consisting of ten *krodharāja*.[242]

---

239 The rite from the *Susiddhi-tantra* has been given above. The *homa* rite called *Acalapūjāvidhi* includes *mudrā* for a *bhūmikīla* (no.26), a *vajrakīla* (for erecting the *vajraprākāra* or indestructible fence, no.27), repelling demons after the invitation of the deities (no.38) and a wide *cakrakīla* for enclosing the world (*cakravāla*, no.44). MMK 693 instructs the *yogin* to prepare *kīla* of acacia wood and recite 108 *mantra* over them. By implanting those *kīla* in the four directions, the boundaries are made secure. Etc.

240 The hagiography of Kāṇha (Templeman, 1989) is replete with examples of *vetāla* slaves.

241 MMK 297

242 Lessing & Wayman, *op.cit.* 117

In the period of the *yogatantra* which followed (*circa* seventh century?),[243] the essential *mantra* [244] of Vajrakīla is noted in the STTS in a configuration which has remained virtually unchanged to the present[245] and it is applied to the Vajrakīla positioned in the very centre of the *maṇḍala*. STTS VI

---

243 The STTS and *Mahāvairocana-tantra* cited above belong to this group.

244 According to tantric theory the *mantra* is an aspect of the god. In discussing the procedures of *yoga* in the *kriyātantra,* for example, mKhas-grub-rje lists six gods. Among these are the 'sound-god' (*śabdadevatā*) and the 'letter-god' (*akṣaradevatā*) which are, respectively, the sound and the letters of the *mantra* to be recited. Lessing & Wayman, *op.cit.* 161. Thus we may postulate that the *hṛdaya* of Vajrakīla within the STTS attests at least a nominal existence of the deity at that time.

245 Apart from the general change of the vocative KĪLA to KĪLI, adherents of the Sa-skya school recite the *mantra* as it is found within the STTS while the rNying-ma-pa abbreviate the denominative imperative BANDHAYA (from the root *bandh*; fix, fasten, suppress or bind a victim) to BAṀ, a widespread technique in the formation of *mantra*. See; A. Wayman, "Imperatives in the Buddhist Tantra Mantras".

In the *Mahāvairocana-tantra,* for example, JAṀ stands for JAYA (be victorious!), TRAṀ for TRĀHI or TRĀYA (save!) and RAṀ for RAKṢA (protect!), all imperatives. C. Yamamoto, *Mahāvairocana Sūtra* X

Further *mantra* of interest deriving from this period are listed in Hatta, *A Dictionary of Mantra*. These include; OṀ VAJRAKĪLA KĪLAYA SARVA-VIGHNĀN BANDHA HŪṀ PHAṬ (said to occur only in the STTS passage cited above); OṀ VAJRA KILI KILI SARVAVIGHNĀN BANDHA HŪṀ PHAṬ (derived from the above? Found in the *Bussetsu daijyokanso maṇḍala-shojyo akushu kyo,* T.939); OṀ VAJRAKĪLA HŪṀ PHAṬ (from the **Vajrakrodha-samājavaipulya-vidhi* section of an **Avalokiteśvaravidyārāja-tantra*); OṀ KĪLI KILI VAJRA HŪṀ PHAṬ (given as the *mantra* of Vajra-kuṇḍalin in T.912–T.915); KĪLI KILI VAJRA MUḤ SVĀHĀ (related to Vajrakuṇḍalin and said to occur in the section dealing with *maṇḍala* construction for a *homavidhi* in T.912); OṀ KILI KILI VAJRA VAJRI BHŪR BANDHA BANDHA HŪṀ PHAṬ (dealt with above. Hatta explains it as the *mantra* required when four *kīla* are used to enclose a sacred area in order to strengthen the *sādhaka's bodhicitta* and remove all impediments. He cites its occurrence in five texts, *viz;* T.900, T.930, T.1085, T.1225, T.1226.)

The comprehensive index to the Taisho *Tripiṭaka* lists almost 100 entries for the *kīla,* most of which are to be found in sources having their roots in Indian traditions predating the *yoganiruttaratantra* of Vajrakīla that were supposed to have been transmitted to Tibet by Padmasambhava during the second half of the eighth century. Among them, the most significant citations are to be found in the translations prepared by Vajrabodhi and his disciple Amoghavajra (especially the *Vajrakumāra-tantra,* see note 252, below) during the first half of the eighth century. Another important source from which much information can be gleaned is the huge collection of *dhāraṇī* compiled by Bodhiruci before the end of the seventh century.

also introduces the myth of the overthrow of Rudra/Maheśvara through which a large number of Hindu deities become assimilated into the *maṇḍala* of the wrathful *heruka* Buddha. The overthrow of Rudra subsequently became central to the mythology of Vajrakīla.[246]

The iconographic forms of the *krodha* kings (ten of whom later comprise the primary retinue of Vajrakīla) also began to crystallise during this period. Buddhas with many faces and hands first appeared in Chinese translations from the early sixth century, with rituals and observances dedicated to Hayagrīva as a form of Avalokiteśvara from the late seventh century.[247] Wu-hsing, a Chinese traveller to India, obtained a copy of the *Mahāvairocana-tantra* in 685 CE and stated that "recently many people in India have vouchsafed the teachings of esoteric Buddhism". This *tantra* was the first of those translated into Chinese to teach the unity of *mudrā, mantra* and *samādhi* and explain them as yogic means to the attainment of the three mysteries of Buddha's Body, Speech and Mind.[248] Throughout this period of the *yogatantra,* the soteriological aspect of the Buddhist path was reasserted and the nefarious pursuits of the earlier *kriyā* period sublimated. Necrophiliac rites seem temporarily to have been abandoned whilst other activities are 'purified' and reinterpreted as skilful means (*upāya*) to the attainment of enlightenment.[249] Thus it is that literary references to the *kīla* throughout this period emphasise its value as a weapon in the struggle against evil, interpreting 'enemies' as those who bring harm to the doctrines of the Buddha. We also witness the emergence of a single *kīla* in the heart of the *maṇḍala* whilst retaining the earlier pattern of a protective circle of spikes around the *maṇḍala* periphery.

Early versions of the GST and the *Jñānasiddhi* of Indrabhūti (both of which feasibly arose around the close of the seventh century) list a circle

---

246 A detailed analysis of the earliest Buddhist versions of this myth has been made by Nobumi Iyanaga, "Recits de la soumission de Maheśvara par Trailokyavijaya". One of his early citations (p.681) links the hand symbol *vajraśūla (= vajrakīla)* to the *abhiṣeka* of *vajravidyottama.* The Hindus themselves incorporate this myth into their concept of the *vāstupuruṣa* in remarkably similar fashion (B. Baumer, *Kalātattvakośa* 36-37). Thus the correlation with architecture is maintained by the Brahmins, whilst for the Buddhists this aspect of the myth has particular associations with the eight great charnel grounds located around the periphery of the *herukamaṇḍala.*

247 Y. Matsunaga, *op.cit.* 173

248 *ibidem* 176-177

249 J.W. de Jong, *op.cit.* 93

of four *krodharāja*[250] whereas the later versions of the GST list ten. The earliest *Māyājāla-tantra* (as translated into Chinese), on the other hand, lists two groups of four *krodha* kings and thus would appear to represent a transitional stage between the *yogatantra* as represented by the STTS and the *yoganiruttaratantra* such as the later GST.[251] Those *krodha* kings are assigned *bījamantra* in the *Māyājāla* that are found unchanged in the Vajrakīla cycle today.

The Chinese Buddhist canon contains two *Vajrakumāra* (= *Vajrakīla*?) *tantra*,[252] said to be derived from the *Susiddhi-tantra*,[253] within which are

---

250 Yamāntaka (E), Prajñāntaka (S), Padmāntaka (W) and Vighnāntaka (N). The later *Sekoddeśaṭīkā* 36-37 also specifically equates Vighnāntaka with Amṛtakuṇḍalin.

251 J.W. de Jong, *op.cit.* 106. Vajravarman's commentary on the SDPT lists eight *krodharāja*. T. Skorupski, SDPT 313

252 Both catalogued together as T.1222 and said to have been brought to China from South India by Amoghavajra in 742 CE. This translator was a disciple of Vajrabodhi (born 689 CE) who composed T.1223, a shorter version "in accordance with the tradition of the west (India)". This *tantra,* manifestly of the utmost significance for a study of the *kīla*'s history, has been investigated by Stephen Hodge who concludes (in a private written communication) that the identification of Vajrakīla with Vajrakumāra is not clearly established here. In the later Tibetan tradition, however, the name Vajrakumāra uniquely and ubiquitously refers to the deity Vajrakīla.

With regard to the Vajrakumāra spoken of in the Chinese sources, he is often referred to as Kaṇikrodha, one of the major *kīla* deities employed in Kuladatta's rituals of nailing down the earth (*Kriyāsaṁgraha* III). In both Sanskrit and Chinese sources he is said to be blue in colour and T.1222 describes him as having six arms and three red eyes. He emerges from the ocean wearing a jewelled crown and garlanded with poisonous snakes. His eye teeth protrude and bite down upon his lower lip, whilst his brow is wrinkled with anger. His left foot rests upon a lotus that flowers on the summit of a jewelled mountain while his right foot remains half submerged in the water from which he arises. (Cf. R. Mayer, *op.cit.* 167, where it is argued that the crocodile snout halfway along the length of the Tibetan ritual nail marks the water-line, with the realm of the *nāga* below and the abode of the *deva* on Mount Meru above.) The *samaya* form of this deity is a single-pronged *vajra* (equated generally with the *kīla* in Sino-Japanese schools) which, however, he is nowhere stated to hold in his hand. T.1223 describes both yellow and red wrathful forms of this deity. T.1224 then repeats much of this material and may simply be a Chinese or Japanese reworking (by an unknown hand) of the earlier texts.

253 In Hodge's opinion (private communication), this is a false attribution.

to be found a collection of rites engaging both Kīla and Amṛta. Vajrakīla and Vajrāmṛta, later to emerge as quite distinct deities, are regarded as one in the Sino-Japanese traditions stemming from this period.

The subsequent rise of the *yoganiruttaratantra,* which Matsunaga places in the eighth century,[254] saw the highest flourishing of the Buddhist tantric doctrines in India and the rise of the *siddha* scholars. If, as we suppose, the *kīla* had by this time become an item of ritual equipment in the employ of Buddhist tantrics, such persons as the *siddha* would have been the very ones to carry them.

An incident in the life of Nāgārjuna is related by Marcotty[255] who, unfortunately, does not quote his source for the tale. Apparently, while Nāgārjuna was resident at the monastery of Nālandā he is reputed to have denied access to those holy precincts to a young woman who had been identified by him as the trouble-making demoness Caṇḍikā in disguise. Her path was effectively barred by the simple expedient of driving a wooden *kīla* into the ground within the monastery courtyard. This story is conceivably the earliest known anecdote relating to the magical prowess of the single ritual *kīla*.

The hagiographies of 84 prominent *mahāsiddha* of ancient India were gathered together in the 11th or 12th century by Abhayadattaśrī of Campārṇa. Among the stories he collected is that of the *siddha* Virūpa who is said to have transfixed the sun in the sky by stabbing his ritual *kīla* right on the line separating sunlight from shadow.[256] Virūpa came from the monastic academy of Somapurī in Bengal, thought to have been established at the end of the eighth century,[257] but whether the Kīla doctrines were taught there or not is unknown. On the other hand, however, we have noted above that minor *kīlasiddhi* are taught in at least three prominent cycles of tantric doctrines (Guhyasamāja, Cakrasaṁvara and Yamāntaka).[258] It would therefore seem reasonable to suppose that both Nāgārjuna and Virūpa learned magical techniques engaging the *kīla* from these sources, in the systems of which they were acknowledged experts.

---

254 Y. Matsunaga, *op.cit.* 179

255 T. Marcotty, *Dagger Blessing* 23-25

256 K. Dowman, *Masters of Mahāmudrā* 46. Note the way in which this legend modifies the paradigm of the *kīla* as an instrument for securing boundaries.

257 *ibidem* 50

258 It is possible, also, that *kīla* rites once formed part of the doctrines of Tārā, as evidenced by the incident of Jñānadeva cited above.

The most salient source from this period, however, is surely the GST within which we find half a chapter uttered by the apotheosised Vajrakīla himself.[259] This section teaches the GHA GHA *mantra* quoted above (here called the *sarvatraidhātukakāyavākcittakīlana-mantra*) within that fragment of the *tantra* devoted exclusively to an explanation of those *kīla* which transfix the Buddha's Body, Speech and Mind.

It begins with the *bhagavat* entering the *samādhi* called Binding *vajra* (*nibandhanavajra*) of the body, speech and mind of all *tathāgata*. The lord then utters this *mantra* for transfixing the body, speech and mind of all the three realms: OṀ GHA GHA GHĀTAYA GHĀTAYA SARVADUṢṬĀN PHAṬ! KĪLAYA KĪLAYA SARVAPĀPĀN PHAṬ! HŪṀ HŪṀ HŪṀ VAJRA-KĪLAYA VAJRADHARA ĀJÑĀPAYATI KĀYA-VĀK-CITTA-VAJRAṀ KĪLAYA HŪṀ PHAṬ! and, as soon as it was uttered, even those powerful beings possessed of great magic skill became fearful. Candrakīrti explains that "the ones possessed of great magic skill" (*maharddhikā*) are Śakra and the rest.[260] In the subsequent cycle of Vajrakīla literature these Vedic gods constitute the thrones of the *daśakrodha* kings but in this instance, terrified by Kīla's power they seek refuge in Mahāvajradhara.[261]

The root text goes on to say that *kīla* made of human bone, acacia wood or iron[262] are capable of destroying the threefold *vajrakāya,* to which Candrakīrti's commentary adds that, by striking those nails on the top with a *vajra* hammer, one extirpates all the sins of body, speech and mind. The three *kīla* themselves are said to have the nature of Vairocana, Yamāntaka and Amṛtakuṇḍalin.

With regard to the actual configuration (*vijṛmbhita*) of the *kīla,* it is said that the upper part has the aspect of the *samaya* deity whereas the lower section from the heart to the feet is in the form of a sharp spike.

---

259 GST XIV.58 to chapter end.

260 C. Chakravarti, *Pradīpodyotana* 158

261 It is regularly observed that those Hindu gods who are 'converted' by such wrathful displays soon become the Buddha's footstools; eg. Gaṇapati beneath the feet of Mahākāla, Śiva and Umā trampled underfoot by Śrīheruka, etc.

It is the normal practice of tantric initiates to meditate upon the *guru* on the crown of the head and the initiated gods are no exception to this rule. The iconography of the fierce deities in all respects, however, is typically extreme. Describing Vajrapāṇi as he tramples the prostrate Maheśvara, STTS 59 says that Mahādeva received *abhiṣeka* and experienced all the joys of liberation through his contact with the sole of Vajrapāṇi's foot.

262 Note the recurring correlation of the colours white (bone), red (wood) and black (iron).

The *Vajramālā-tantra,*[263] an early Indian commentary on the GST, adds that the ritual *kīla* should be made of acacia wood, thirteen inches (*aṅgula*) in length and three-sided in shape. It is to be marked with 'the three words' (OṀ ĀḤ HŪṀ), blessed with one hundred syllables[264] and purified by the rite of Amṛtakuṇḍalin. The *samayasattva* whose form comprises the upper half of the peg is, according to Candrakīrti, the triple-faced, six-armed Amṛtakuṇḍalin.[265]

A similar description is given by Nāgārjuna in his *Pañcakrama,* within which he judiciously rearranges the entire GST in order to teach the procedures of *yoga* in five steps. According to this new arrangement, the rites of the *vajrakīla* are to be performed as a preliminary to meditation upon the *maṇḍala* of Guhyasamāja and thus the *kīlanavidhi* is described in verses 8-17 of the *piṇḍīkramasādhana* which precedes even the first *krama:*

Generating the ten *krodha* kings,
  blazing with light and terrible like demons
Sprung forth from the syllable HŪṀ and
  standing resplendent in the *pratyālīḍa* attitude, (8)

(The *yogin*) should think of them in proper sequence
  upon the tips of the circle of ten directions.
In order to destroy all obstacles,
  visualising Sumbha[266] he should nail them down. (9)

---

263 P.82

264 The *mantra* of Vajrasattva.

265 Thus Amṛtakuṇḍalin's identification with Vajrakīla remains, notwithstanding the introduction of Vairocana and Yamāntaka.

266 A demon slain by Durgā (*Mārkaṇḍeya-purāṇa* LXXXV-XC), apotheosised by the Buddhists. The power of Sumbha (Śumbha) and his brother Nisumbha (Niśumbha) was invoked by Vajrapāṇi in the STTS prior to the defeat of Maheśvara. The *mantra* employed on that occasion, known as the *mantra* of four HŪṀs, has since become ubiquitous in rites of purifying the ground as a preliminary to any major *sādhana* practice. "In the Vajra family of Sumbha the Royal Formula has great magical power; endowed with the four HŪṀ syllables, it is active in all the rites." SDPT 76. Sumbha alone entered the ranks of the *daśakrodha* kings as Sumbharāja, guardian of the nadir. In the Vajrakīla cycle, however, his place is taken by Mahābala.

OṀ SUMBHA NISUMBHA HŪṀ GṚHNA GṚHNA HŪṀ GṚHNĀPAYA GṚHNĀPAYA HŪṀ ĀNAYA HO BHAGAVAN VIDYĀRĀJA HŪṀ PHAṬ.

Having thus summoned the misleaders by means of
this wrathful form,
The wise one should nail them all down
in accordance with the rite. (10)

The great king Vajrāṁṛta is to be manifest as Vajrakīla,
Dark like the petals of the blue lotus,
the glory of the *kula,* enveloped in flames. (11)

The portion below his waist should be generated
in the form of a spike *(śūla),*
Above which is the form of wrath
with three faces and six arms. (12)

Beneath him (the *yogin*) sees the multitude of hindrances.
Muttering the *mantra* he should stab the immovable *vajrakīla*
into the bodies of (those) obstructing demons. (13)

OṀ GHA GHA GHĀTAYA GHĀTAYA SARVADUṢṬĀN PHAṬ! KĪLAYA KĪLAYA SARVAPĀPĀN PHAṬ! HŪṀ HŪṀ VAJRAKĪLA VAJRADHARA ĀJÑĀPAYATI SARVAVIGHNĀNĀṀ KĀYA-VĀK-CITTAṀ KĪLAYA HŪṀ PHAṬ!

And he should contemplate Sumbharāja
with a hammer in his hand. (14)

Imagining the *vajra* fire that spreads everywhere,
(The *yogin*) should think that the wailing evils
are burned up (within it). (15)

Stabbing the *kīla* into the ten directions,
above, below and all around,
(The *yogin*) should meditate by means of the ultimate (truth)
upon the absence of self-nature in the triple world. (16)

Meditation concerning the non-truly-existent
is neither meditation nor non-meditation.
Thus, existence being not (truly) existent,
meditation may not be achieved. (17)[267]

These final verses denote the 'higher activities' (*stod las*) in which enlightenment is the chief aim, as opposed to the more widespread 'lower acts' (*smad las*) in which the *kīla* is employed predominantly for the destruction of demons.

All of this, I think, clearly indicates the importance of the *kīla* doctrines in their own right. Their independent status is further evidenced by the discovery in Nepal of a number of Sanskrit manuscripts, such as those in the library of the IASWR which include the *Kīlanacaryā* and *Kīlanavidhi* (each 24 folios in length), as well as a long text on the construction of *maṇḍala* and the bestowal of empowerment entitled *Kīlanadīkṣākrama* (65 folios).[268] Although these texts still await detailed investigation, they stand as eloquent testimony to the emergence of a *kīla* cult prior to its flourishing in Tibet.

The GST goes on to say that, "By means of *vajra* meditation even a buddha will certainly be stabbed (*kīlyate*). When Vajrasattva, the great king, strikes with the *kīla* he will quickly die."[269] And thus a paradigm of ritual *kīla* activity is ensconced.

This basic exemplar is amplified in the verses which follow where it is said that, in order to destroy the body, one recites the *mantra* OṀ CHINDA CHINDA HANA HANA DAHA DAHA DĪPTAVAJRACAKRA HŪṀ PHAṬ and strikes the *vajrakīla* into the head ('the dwelling of Vairocana') of (an effigy of) the victim. Death will occur as soon as he is struck.[270]

It is pertinent to note that the *mantra* given here corresponds in several particulars to that of Vajrakīla's consort Tṛptacakra or Dīptacakra, whose

267 L.de La Vallée Poussin, *Pañcakrama* 1-2

268 IASWR catalogue numbers MBB-II-68, MBB-II-185, 186 & MBB-I-59.
In *A Microfilm Catalogue of Buddhist Manuscripts from Nepal,* Nagoya University 1981, are found *Kīlanamantra* CH429, *Kīlanavidhi* A139F, CA48-2, CH250-B, *Kīlanapūjā* A151 and *Vighnakīlanavidhi* DH171, DH195

269 Fremantle's translation.

270 Employing either a substantial *kīla* or the *mudrā* noted above from the *Susiddhi-tantra*.

seed syllables in the rNying-ma school under consideration in this work are HANA HANA HŪṀ PHAṬ.[271]

In order to destroy the speech, one recites OṀ HRĪḤ BHUR BHUVAḤ and "inserts the *vajra* finger into the open (*vikasita*) lotus of wisdom". There one strikes with the *vajrakīla* and, once again, the victim is destroyed as soon as this is done.

The mind is destroyed with a *mudrā* of five prongs (*pañcaśūlāni*) and the *mantra* OṀ VAJRARĀJA HŪṀ. One imagines the *vajrakīla* to be filled with sparks of light as he plunges it into the heart of his enemy and thus his victim immediately dies.

"If the rite is correctly performed with the *yoga* of body, speech and mind, one can transfix the whole extent of the *vajra* realm of space, of this there is no doubt. Thus spoke the *bhagavan,* the Mahāvajrakīla."

(Fremantle's translation.)

According to Candrakīrti, the 'correct performance' of this rite involves the *sādhaka* entering the centre of a shining red *maṇḍala* where he arises in wrathful guise with his fangs slightly bared in a grimace (*īṣad-daṁṣṭrākarālavadana*). Surrounding him in their proper places are the ten *krodharāja* whose bodies have the nature of the triple *vajra* and who are described as exhibiting the form of Sumbha.

The passage in the *mūlatantra* closes with a eulogy delivered by the Buddha's retinue who thrill with joy at the boon just bestowed for the sake of living beings. Fremantle translates;

Oh best abode of secrets!
Oh gathering of essence!
Oh peaceful dwelling of Dharma!
Oh *vajra* vanquishing!
The transfixing of all the buddhas
and famous *bodhisattvas,*
The transfixing of *vajra* body, speech
and mind has been taught.
This is the transfixing of all *mantra,*

---

271 This *mantra* is to be found in the MMK (p.395) where it ends DĪPTACAKRA HŪṀ and is called the *mantra* of the *dharmacakra*. It is said to destroy all *kleśa* and so on and, most significantly, to fulfil the desires of the *yogin* by allowing him to "un-nail" them (*utkīlayati*) as he wishes.

born of truth,
Bestowing body, speech and mind,
The gathering of the truth of *mantra*s.

This particular half-chapter of the GST is evidently of considerable historical value to our study. Throughout the passage it is Mahāvajrakīla himself who propounds the ritual teachings, within which the emergence of his consort Tṛptacakra may also be clearly discerned. The *kīla* is placed within the *maṇḍala* and assigned quite a specific iconography: one half wrathful deity and one half nail. There is, furthermore, an elaborate advance in the ritual use of the *kīla* upon all previous citations, with instructions being given to stab the effigy in the head, throat and heart in order to subdue specifically the body, speech and mind. Despite its brevity, the text describes a highly sophisticated Vajrakīla rite in very clear terms. We must conclude, therefore, that the ritual technique of slaying with a *kīla* was already well established by the time of its redaction. The lamentable paucity of relevant literature in support of this view I suppose to result from the subsequent loss of much material including, perhaps, contemporaneous Vajrakīla *sādhana, tantra* and *āgama*. Sanskrit Buddhist literature, in general, has largely disappeared from the land of its origin and Indian history affords no shortage of examples of religious cults whose traces have all but vanished. Such an apparently tendentious hypothesis is supported by the Vajrakumāra texts translated into Chinese by Vajrabodhi and Amoghavajra in advance of the assumed date of the GST,[272] not to mention the many volumes dedicated to Vajrakīla in the *rNying ma'i rgyud 'bum* (NGB)[273] and other Tibetan collections. Nor is there anything odd in the fact of its intrusion here into the text of the GST. Kurukullā, for example, is an independent deity having no obvious connection with Hevajra and yet her *sādhana* is to be found at HT I.xi.12-15. On the other hand, of course, it is conceivable that this passage reflects a penultimate stage in the evolution of Vajrakīla as a deity, immediately prior to the formulation of *tantra* and other texts specifically dedicated to his name. On the testimony of both the Tibetan and Sino-Japanese traditions, however, I advocate the view proposed above. The rite of killing, demonstrated so succinctly in this extract, is

---

272 Although the problem of dating all such material is as yet unresolved, the general consensus supports this view.

273 Regarding the NGB see below, note 277.

raised almost to the level of an obsession in the Vajrakīla *tantra*. The entire genre of *yoganiruttara-tantra,* in fact, displays an atavistic predisposition towards the antinomian features of the earliest *kriyātantra* accompanied, however, by a marked change in philosophic outlook. Whereas we might suppose the earlier strata of tantric literature to reflect the mundane preoccupations of village sorcerers whose methodology it apparently incorporated without discrimination, it is clear that in the middle period (epitomised by the *yogatantra*) such wholesale perfidy of Buddhist ideals was abandoned[274] only to re-emerge as '*vajra* wrath' and so on in the *yoganiruttaratantra* of the final period.

An important feature noted in the *Guhyagarbha-tantra*[275] is the placement of a *kīla* within each of the four Families (*kula*) for the performance of 'the four magical rites' (*catvāri karmāni*). The 'orthodox' nature of these rites (and thus the establishment of the *kīla* as a part of that orthodoxy) is hinted at by relating them to the four syllables which ubiquitously serve as introductions to canonical literature: "*Evaṁ mayā* ..." ("Thus, by me ..."). *Guhyagarbha-tantra* XX (amplified by the commentary of kLong-chen-pa) specifies that an iron *vajrakīla* of indestructible reality is to be used with an attitude of wrath within a triangular (E) *maṇḍala* to destroy the body; a copper *padmakīla* of desire is to be used with an attitude of attachment within a semicircular (VAṀ) *maṇḍala* in order to subjugate all speech; a golden *ratnakīla* of pride is to be used with an attitude of joy within a square (MA) *maṇḍala* to increase one's indestructible brilliance and enlightened attributes; and a silver *buddhakīla* of lustrous radiance is to be used with an attitude of mental clarity within a circular (YĀ) *maṇḍala* to pacify all fury.[276]

The paradigm of a Vajrakīla *maṇḍala* is now complete. Vajrakīla as the *maṇḍalādhipati* has been joined by his four 'supreme sons' (as they become known in the Byang-gter literature discussed below), through whom he becomes lord of the five families with his own *karmakula* as the fifth. His retinue of *daśakrodha* kings has been established and to his original purely apotropaic role have been accrued all those activities appropriate to a *samyaksaṁbuddha*.

---

274 J.W. de Jong, *op.cit.* 93

275 G. Dorje, *The Guhyagarbha-tantra* 918

276 Cf. the Japanese tradition of single-pronged *vajra* bearing the various emblems of the *kula* upon their heads.

The collected tantric texts revered in Tibet as translations of works brought from India during the eighth century[277] include many volumes devoted to the worship of the *kīla* as just such a *samyaksaṁbuddha,* together with his retinue, although today, regrettably, no Indian redaction of any of these texts is known to western scholarship. Indian Buddhists, although aware of Vajrakīla, seem to have taken little interest in this deity at the centre of the *maṇḍala*, preferring to focus their attention instead upon his retinue of ten wrathful kings who may be called upon to surround and protect the sacred area occupied by any chosen deity.[278]

Thus, according to Abhayākaragupta's *vighnakīlanavidhi,* compiled in the 12th century from such sources as outlined above: In order to establish all beings on the stage of Vajradhara, the *yogin* should rise at dawn determined to destroy all obstacles. Following the contemplation of voidness he should visualise the syllable RAṀ and mentally transform it into the disc of the sun. Resting upon that sun disc is a syllable HŪṀ which, in turn, transforms into a *viśvavajra* upon which stands a HŪṀ. Blazing *vajra* born of the light rays of that syllable HŪṀ spread out in all directions to form a seamless wall and tent with a canopy composed of a network of arrows, above, and a blazing foundation of unbearably bright *viśvavajra,* below. Transforming himself in an instant into the quintessential *vajra* being (Vajrasattva) who is utterly victorious over the three worlds (*trailokyavijaya*) named Vajrahūṁkāra, the *yogin* stands in the centre of that area upon a sun and multicoloured lotus in the *ālīḍha* posture with right knee advanced and left leg drawn back. Very angry and blazing like the fire at the end of an aeon in a mass of rays of light, his two feet trample upon Bhairava and Kālarātrī and he takes as his food the entire multitude of interrupting worldly demons. He has three faces: yellow on the right, green on the left and his central face is dark blue. Each face has immense fangs and a lolling tongue, wrinkled eyebrows, a projecting forehead and three bulbous red eyes. Possessed of the six *mudrā,* across his brow is a row of five skulls and a garland of dripping heads oozing blood dangles from his neck. He wears a belt of human heads and is clothed in tiger skin. The flaming reddish brown hair of his head streams upwards encircled by the dark blue *nāga* king Ananta and he is adorned with Takṣaka

---

277 Eg. the NGB. Of the edition in 36 volumes published in Thimbu in 1973, vols.27-29 are devoted to Vajrakīla.

278 Cf. Lessing & Wayman, *Introduction to the Buddhist Tantric Systems* 283, where the nature of the central deity is explained.

and the rest of the *nāga* kings. With his two main hands holding *vajra* and bell he makes '*vajra* fists' pressed back to back, linked together with the two little fingers while the 'threatening' forefingers remain outstretched. Standing thus, with the gesture of conquering the triple world, he is established in self-radiant wisdom. His two hands on the right hold an iron hook and noose and those on the left, a skull and *khaṭvāṅga.* With his fanged face roaring the sound of HŪṂ, from the HŪṂ in his heart spread out rays of light that gather in all the hindering demons from the ten directions. The *yogin* should then consign those demons to the ten wrathful ones who have poured forth from the syllable HŪṂ.

In length those wrathful deities should be either eighteen or twelve or eight inches, in that order, and to be effective they should be six, four or three inches thick. Made of acacia wood or bone or iron, they should be placed in new containers and worshipped, smeared with white mustard seed and red sandalwood and wound with threads of five colours. Holding them in one's hands they should be empowered with the *mantra* of three syllables. Then, one at a time, those ten *kīla* should be bound with a garland of red flowers. Below the navel each *kīla* has the form of a single spike, above which they are to be contemplated in one's own (three-faced, six-armed) image, blazing like the fire at the end of an aeon.

Meditating thus and binding the *vajra* fist with his left hand, the *yogin* with his right hand takes the chief of all symbols, the averting hammer (*parāvṛtta-mudgara)* tied with a garland of flowers and, uttering a long drawn-out sound he strikes the ten HŪṂ-born *krodha* as they pierce the obstructors. OṂ VAJRAKĪLA KĪLAYA SARVAVIGHNĀN HŪṂ or else OṂ GHA GHA GHĀṬAYA GHĀṬAYA SARVADUṢṬĀN PHAṬ PHAṬ. KĪLAYA KĪLAYA SARVAPĀPĀN PHAṬ PHAṬ HŪṂ HŪṂ HŪṂ. VAJRAKĪLA VAJRADHARO ĀJÑĀPAYATI SARVAVIGHNĀNĀM KĀYA-VĀK-CITTAṂ KĪLAYA HŪṂ HŪṂ PHAṬ PHAṬ. With the first recitation he should fix the *kīla* on the head (of the victim) and then, muttering OṂ VAJRA-MUDGARA ĀKOṬAYA HŪṂ, he should beat it (with the hammer). In this way the *yogin* should begin in the northeast corner and, moving clockwise around the outside of the *maṇḍala,* should fix and strike the *kīla* of the eight directions within the 'circle of light' (*prabhāvalī*) that surrounds the circle of *vajra*. This should be done first of all by the *ācārya* and then, when the demons have been rendered powerless, by his assistants.[279] The *kīla* for the zenith should be pegged to the east of the eastern spike and

---

279 These are the four *dvārācārya* mentioned by Kuladatta, above.

that for the nadir to the west of the western one. Otherwise, as stated in the STTS and other sources,[280] "One should peg (those *kīla*) within the outer circle of light".

Abhayākaragupta then states that, in accordance with those (authoritative texts), *ācārya* of his day, having fixed the spikes around the outside of the *maṇḍala* house, make mounds of earth upon those ten places and there gratify the wrathful ones whose form is the *kīla* with flowers and so on and with parasols and gifts of food and the rest. By doing that, they say, all that is wished for is attained in the most excellent manner without any hindrance, even that pertaining to the gods. The *yogin* should meditate upon the host of obstructors attaining the blissful 'single taste of the natural condition' (*tathataikarasam*) due to being transfixed and hammered in that way, while the remaining hindering demons flee far away. Thus all beings above, below and across the world, everywhere out as far as the limit of the universe, are to be set free – firmly established in the absence of obstacles. This is the first method.

Alternatively, by reciting OṀ ĀḤ HŪṀ YAMĀNTAKṚT SARVADUṢṬENDROPENDRĀN SAPARIVĀRĀN KĪLAYA HŪṀ PHAṬ, OṀ ĀḤ HŪṀ PRAJÑĀNTAKṚT SARVADUṢṬAYAMĀN SAPARIVĀRĀN KĪLAYA HŪṀ PHAṬ, OṀ ĀḤ HŪṀ PADMĀNTAKṚT SARVADUṢṬANĀGĀN SAPARIVĀRĀN KĪLAYA HŪṀ PHAṬ, OṀ ĀḤ HŪṀ VIGHNĀNTAKṚT SARVADUṢṬAKUVERĀN SAPARIVĀRĀN KĪLAYA HŪṀ PHAṬ, OṀ ĀḤ HŪṀ ACALA SARVADUṢṬEŚĀNĀN SAPARIVĀRĀN KĪLAYA HŪṀ PHAṬ, OṀ ĀḤ HŪṀ ṬAKKIRĀJA SARVADUṢṬĀGNĪN SAPARIVĀRĀN KĪLAYA HŪṀ PHAṬ, OṀ ĀḤ HŪṀ NĪLADAṆḌA SARVADUṢṬANAIRṚTĪN SAPARIVĀRĀN KĪLAYA HŪṀ PHAṬ, OṀ ĀḤ HŪṀ MAHĀBALA SARVADUṢṬAVĀYŪN SAPARIVĀRĀN KĪLAYA HŪṀ PHAṬ, OṀ ĀḤ HŪṀ CAKRAVARTIN SARVADUṢṬĀRKACANDRAPITĀMAHĀN SAPARIVĀRĀN KĪLAYA HŪṀ PHAṬ, OṀ ĀḤ HŪṀ SUMBHA SARVADUṢṬAVEMACITRIPṚTHIVĪDEVATĀḤ SAPARIVĀRĀN KĪLAYA HŪṀ PHAṬ, all the obstructors in the guise of Indra and the rest who dwell in the east and other quarters are to be transfixed and beaten by means of those *mantra*, just as has been described above. This is the second method.

And if someone were to say that four *kīla* should be embedded in the four corners, (we reply) "Just in the (four) doorways!" Furthermore, the colours and forms and so on of the wrathful deities and of Indra and the rest may be known from established tradition. When it is the case that

280 I have been unable to trace this citation.

one wishes to meditate upon the vast circle of protection and yet possesses no spikes made of acacia wood and so on; during the performance of the ritual meditations of transfixing and hammering just described, the *yogin* should turn his hand over onto its back and, saying OṀ VAJRA HŪṀ, should wave it in the air and strike it on the ground thinking that by so doing he 'liberates' them.[281]

Coda

The foregoing aetiology of the divine nail has perhaps raised more questions than it has answered. The evolution of the *daśakrodha* kings within the literature of the tantric Buddhists, for example, is a topic worthy of a thorough investigation that must be neglected here for want of space. The myth of the subjugation of Rudra, barely touched upon in this chapter, is another. Thirdly there remains the whole question of the interaction between the Buddhist and Hindu *tantra* and, in particular, the role of the *kīla* in the rites of non-Buddhists.[282] That which I hope has been achieved here, however, is a fairly clear and comprehensive image of the magic nail as it evolved and became established within the Vajrayāna.

The next chapter explores the concept and iconography of the nail as expressed in the literature of Vajrakīla, an apotropaic god of supreme wrath. Although material for the present chapter has been consciously selected as far as possible from Indian sources, iconographic data and definitive evidence of a Vajrakīla cult are conspicuously absent from all such documents presently available. This situation, however, may be radically overthrown as Sanskrit material currently emerging from Nepal begins to be investigated. The literature of Tibet, on the other hand, is replete with such details. The magic peg evidently struck a sympathetic

---

281 *Vajrāvalī* 33-37. Abhayākaragupta in his final remark seems unaware of the *kīlamudrā* to be found in the *Susiddhi-tantra*.

282 For example, *kīla* are linked with the exorcism of evil influences in a rite of healing described by Eberhard Fischer & Haku Shah, "Treatment Against Ghosts and Spirits; the *bhagtai* ceremony of the Chodhri tribe in Gujarat." *German Scholars on India* Vol.II. Delhi, 1976, 51-60

chord deep in the Tibetan psyche[283] and I propose, therefore, to close this chapter by noting briefly the widespread prevalence of the *kīla* as an instrument of high religion and popular sorcery within the numerous traditions of that country.

Among the many legends that have accumulated around the earliest introductions of Buddhism to Tibet is a tale concerning two of the wives of emperor Srong-btsan sgam-po in the early seventh century. A princess from Nepal and another from China, both of whom were Buddhists in possession of sacred images, apparently rivalled each other in their determination to become the first in Tibet to have a temple erected in honour of her own particular Buddhist statue. No temple could successfully be built within that country, however, until the 'demoness of the soil' had been subdued. Through the geomantic expertise of the Chinese princess Kong-jo, the appropriate locations for the required subjugation were determined on the ground and then the spread-eagled form of the demoness was rendered immovable by transfixing her limbs. Thirteen shrines and *stūpa* were built in order to effect this. One of these pressed down upon her heart and then an inner circle of four transfixed her shoulders and hips, an intermediate group held firm her elbows and knees, and a final set pinned down her wrists and ankles. As a result of that subjugation, it is said, the land of Tibet was tamed in readiness for the introduction of the Buddhist Dharma.[284]

With regard to the building of the temple in the centre that pressed down upon the heart of the demoness, Erik Haarh[285] quotes the *rGyal rabs gsal ba'i me long* (160.149r) as saying; "The pillars were fashioned in the form of *kīla* and the *tantrics* rejoiced." Once more, therefore, we note the intimate association of the *kīla* with architecture in general and with pillars in particular.

---

283 R.A. Stein notes that the sacred mountains with which the country of Tibet abounds are popularly regarded as either *yul lha* ('deities of the country') or *gzhi bdag* (*sa bdag,* 'lords of the locality'). In particular they are thought of as the 'pillars of the sky' (*gnam gyi ka ba*) and '*kīla* of the earth' (*sa yi phur bu*), exactly the functions originally performed by the *Indrakīla*.
R.A. Stein, *Tibetan Civilisation* 203

284 M. Aris, *Bhutan* ch.1, offers an in-depth analysis (with variants, etc.) and historical appraisal of the fascinating legend so crudely outlined here.

285 Erik Haarh, *The Yar-lung Dynasty* 385

The scheme of subduing the land depicted in this tale has an obvious parallel in the system of fixing *kīla* into the four corners of the site, discussed at length above. Indeed, Kuladatta's system actually included both inner and outer concentric rings of nails. Compare this with the religious procedure involved in the seemingly simple act of erecting the tent which is to serve as dwelling for the *yogin* during periods of isolated retreat. According to a popular Tibetan tradition, the *yogin* should imagine all the dangerous demons of the area to be spread-eagled on the ground beneath his tent and, as he hammers in the tent pegs, he visualises *kīla* of meteoric iron (*gnam lcags*)[286] being driven through their limbs.[287] Such meditations are cast in specifically Buddhist terminology in these rites by calling upon the *ḍākinī* of the *pañcakula* to bring the *kīla* of the four *brahmavihāra*[288] from the four directions together with the *kīla* of *bodhicitta* which holds centre place.[289]

At a far social remove from the itinerant *yogin*s who must beg their way from one charnel ground to the next for the performance of such rites, is the powerful hierarch, the Dalai Lama. As mentioned above, the Great Fifth Dalai Lama experienced a series of ecstatic visions involving the ritual uses of *kīla* in more than a dozen rites, including not only rituals for the subjugation of demons but also rites for the promotion of long life and prosperity.[290]

Further examples can be found in Nebesky-Wojkowitz's *Oracles and Demons of Tibet,* a perusal of which quickly reveals the popularity of the hand-held *kīla* as a weapon of magic among minor Tibetan deities. The power of the *kīla,* however, may be iconographically incorporated in more ways than one. Amṛtakuṇḍalin, for example, became a '*kīla*-deity' not by

---

286 'Sky-iron', a ubiquitous tantric image thought to embody the paradox of *śūnya* (the empty sky) with functional manifestation (solid iron).

287 Cf. the poorly translated description given in the rite of *gcod* edited by W.Y. Evans-Wentz in *Tibetan Yoga and Secret Doctrines* 324.

It is also interesting to note that, within the barely disguised eroticism of the *kīla* transfixing the outstretched body of the demoness of the soil are discernible echoes of an ancient tale told (*circa* 900 BCE) in the *Jaiminīya-brāhmaṇa* in which a demoness whose body possessed a vagina on each limb was only finally overcome when seduced by a god whose own body had been especially equipped with a similar number of penises.

W.D. O'Flaherty, *Tales of Sex and Violence* 101-102

288 *maitrīkīla, karuṇākīla, muditākīla, upekṣākīla.*

289 W.Y. Evans-Wentz, *op.cit.* 306-7

290 S. Karmay, *Secret Visions,* plates 23, 42, 43, etc. and page 33, plate 4, etc.

the iconographer's gift of a spike to his hand but by the incorporation of the deity into the substance of the spike itself. Such a process resulted inevitably in some artistic modification of the form of the spike, usually vague but occasionally quite specific. Thus it is that a large number of ritual *kīla* show three faces at the top, for an overwhelming majority of the gods who are invoked to dwell within the *kīla* are of the three-faced variety. Other *kīla,* however, are clearly designed as the abode of a single, recognisable divinity. Hayagrīva with his horse's head, for example, is often to be found in the form of a spike and the list is surprisingly long.[291]

In the 16th century, the Tibetan polymath Tāranātha assembled a large collection of *sādhana* from various sources, among which, in a section devoted to Jñānamahākāla, is to be found a certain Garuḍapakṣavat Kīlapāda Pañjara Mahākāla (*sic.*) depicted in his published icon[292] as a single-faced, two-handed deity holding a *kartṛkā* and skull in front of his chest. Clothed and adorned with all the usual attributes of a *heruka* he has a pair of wings (an important element in the iconography of Vajrakīla) and his two (!) feet are implanted like nails into the heart of an enemy who lies supine within a fierce triangular prison (also an important element in the iconography of Vajrakīla). With the icon is his *karma-mantra*: OṀ MAHĀKĀLA HŪṀ PHAṬ! MAHĀKĪLA TRI YAṀ JAḤ JAḤ. MAHĀKĪLA TRI YAṀ *dgra bo* MĀRAYA. MAHĀKĪLA TRI YAṀ *thuṁ ril rbad.* KĪLAYA *sha rbad. dGra bo* NṚ MĀRAYA HŪṀ PHAṬ! SAMAYA HŪṀ PHAṬ! SARVAVIGHNĀN BAṀ HŪṀ PHAṬ! (I have replaced the syllable ṆĪ, written with reversed *gi gu* in the published text, by NṚ.) Note here especially the reduction of the word *bandhaya,* as found in the earlier *mantra,* to the seed syllable BAṀ, as found in all Vajrakīla *mantra* within the rNying-ma traditions.

These few examples of the *kīla* as an abiding concept in Tibetan thought are merely the tip of an iceberg. It is difficult, indeed, to find any general work on Tibetan religious art and culture that fails to mention the ubiquitous magic spike. The popularity of the *kīla* in Tibet, especially (but by no means exclusively) among the rNying-ma-pa, is an undoubted legacy of Padmasambhava, a charismatic figure who played a central role in the propagation of *kīla* rituals in that country. The history of the Vajrakīla

---

291 J. Huntingdon, *The Phur-ba; Tibetan Ritual Daggers,* depicts a number of nails that are also gods.

292 L. Chandra, *Buddhist Iconography of Tibet* vol.1, 324

doctrines, according to the view of its own sacred tradition, will be looked at as soon as the iconography of Vajrakīla has been dealt with in the following chapter.

Further reading of the Sanskrit sources are offered in Appendix II, below.

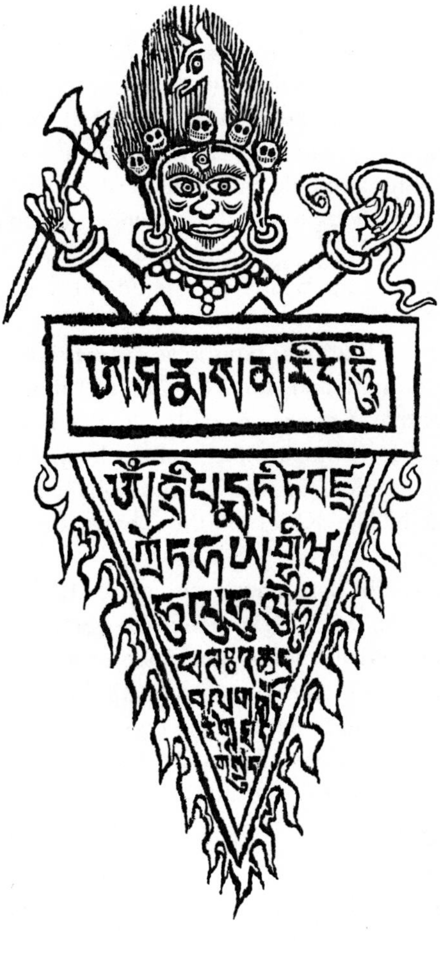

CHAPTER THREE

The iconographic form and function of ritual nails in the Byang-gter Kīla cult. The vajrakīla as a single implement of magic, multiple sets of kīla in the pattern of a maṇḍala, and Vajrakīla as the apotheosised chief of all nails, who both embodies and wields the impetuous spike.

High aspirations and low activities

Ultimately, the Vajrakīla is said to be the nail of essential meaning (*nītārtha*) and whoever takes hold of it is capable of destroying all dualistic grasping, thereby attaining the bliss of eternal *nirvāṇa*. Inwardly, this is achieved by meditating on the so-called *bhavakīla* in which the entire universe, with all of its confusing dualistic contradictions, is contemplatively united within the single image of a nail. This is symbolically expressed through the use of small ritual nails, some few inches long, made of metal or wood which are held in the hand of an 'exorcist' as he stabs at the 'demons' (dualistic thoughts) that are causing trouble to himself or his sponsor.

In Chapter Nine of the Byang-gter *mūlatantra* known as *The Black Razor* [293] it is said;

"With regard to meditational equipoise (*samāhita-samādhi*); the special activity is the enlightened mind (*bodhicitta*) that arises from the unmistaken and uncontrived *dharmatā* with the speed of a dreadful flashing thunderbolt in order to subjugate the vicious beings of the three realms. This *bodhicittakīla* which is fully accomplished in controlling the *traidhātuka* is called 'The Killer of the Three Realms Without Exception'."

And in Chapter Ten of the same *tantra* we read;

"By means of the *bodhicittakīla,* penetrate perfect knowledge for your own benefit (and then) destroy the ignorance of all sentient beings in the *traidhātuka* without exception by means of Vajrakīla!"

The *tantra* then goes on to explain the mystical significance of the nail, offering various interpretations of the term *kīla*;

"*Kī*" implies that all and everything is the mind of enlightenment.

"*La*" means that (the enlightened mind) pervades all things.

---

293 An edition and translation of this text (A2, etc., analysed below in Chapter Five) are to be found in *A Bolt of Lightning from the Blue*, Berlin 2002

"*Kī*" indicates the supreme lord of all phenomena.
"*La*" shows that all beings are within his retinue.
"*Kī*" indicates that all *dharmas* are unoriginated.
"*La*" shows the unceasing nature of playful creativity (*līlā*).
"*Kī*" indicates unity within the enlightened mind.
"*La*" shows the attainment of multiplicity within that.

Thus the magic nail, which in the previous chapter was employed to pin down *nāga, vetāla* and other demonic forces, is here called upon to serve its cultic initiates in the higher function of leading to enlightenment. The explanatory *Drag sngags zab pa'i lo rgyus*[294] describes the *kīla* from several points of view, presenting it as a multi-layered symbol capable of simultaneously sustaining a variety of interpretations.

"As for the real essence of the Vajrakīla, it is just the *dharmakāya* wisdom of natural awareness within which are the two *rūpakāya* having a similar meaning. Kīla's nature is the great bliss of *bodhicitta* and, as a focal point for living beings, all trees and forests arise as *kīla*. As for the words of truth of Vajrakīla, they are naturally abiding from the beginning in the *dharmakāya*. This is the *kīla* of secret skilful means (*guhyopāya*)."[295]

Here, then, the 'ultimate truth' of Kīla (the apotheosised *kīla*) is nothing less than the *trikāya* of buddhahood, having wisdom and bliss as the nature of Mind (the *dharmakāya*), 'naturally abiding words of truth' as the nature of Speech (*sambhogakāya*) and trees and forests as the manifestation of the Body (*nirmāṇakāya*).[296]

The artificial wooden stake that we have seen ritually employed as an instrument for stabilising the earth has its natural counterpart in the living tree which is everywhere known to protect the soil from erosion as well as to participate in the *kīla*'s function of weather control. Numerous citations from Buddhist scriptures could be called upon here to illustrate the popular motif of the tree as a stable, long-suffering and 'compassionate' refuge from the fierce heat of the sun (the *kleśa*) or a heavy downpour of rain,

---

294 B30, etc.

295 B30 140

296 The trees and forests of the macrocosm become the hairs on the skin in the microcosm. See the reference from the *Jñānodaya-tantra* in Appendix II, below.

which is less threatening than drought to the Indian mind.[297] Trees also serve as sources of the 'naturally abiding words of truth' in many a 'pure land' (*buddhakṣetra*) image. In the *Amitābhavyūha-sūtra,* for example, it is said that the sounds of the trees as their leaves rustle in the wind bring all beings to a state of mindful awareness of the Dharma.[298] Trees worldwide commonly serve as boundary markers and protectors of the border and in the previous chapter we noted a wooden *kīla* that, having grown into a living tree, proceeded to preach the Dharma.

The tree, with its roots piercing deep into the earth and its branches stretching up to the heavens, is often linked in mythological imagery to the cosmic Mount Meru. Also the column or pillar known as the *indra-kīla,* to which reference has been made above, is regularly associated with either Mount Meru, 'the tree of life' (*srog shing*), or the *bodhi* tree.[299] It is no surprise, then, to find in Byang-gter literature several descriptions of the *kīla* cast in terms of the macrocosmic imagery of Mount Meru. The Byang-gter text A33, for example, describes the sharp point of the *kīla* as a ferocious striker issuing from the jaws of a *makara,* above which *saṁsāra* and *nirvāṇa* are incorporated within the 'vast knots' (*mahākanda*) at either end of the handle. The eight-sided handle itself is said to radiate with the splendour of all creation.[300]

In a more elaborate description, the arising of this 'cosmic *kīla*' (*bhavakīla*) follows the traditional *abhidharma* paradigm for the unfolding of the universe.[301] Thus, on a foundation of the ferocious[302] elements of space, wind, fire, water and earth, the receptacle universe (*bhājanaloka*) emerges. The enclosing *cakravāla* has the form of a dark pair of interlock-

---

297 For a study of the popular motif of the tree in Indian thought, see Odette Viennot, *Le culte de l'arbre dans l'inde ancienne* Annales du Musée Guimet, Paris 1954

298 See Garma C.C. Chang (ed.), *A Treasury of Mahāyāna Sūtras* (Pennsylvania State University Press 1983) 349
Or *Buddhist Mahāyāna Texts* (SBE vol.49) 97

299 Lily de Silva, "The Symbolism of the Indrakīla" 249
W.D. O'Flaherty, *Asceticism and Eroticism in the Mythology of Śiva* 26

300 A33 235

301 A36 258-259

302 The five elements in the imagery of the wrathful *tantra* are terrifying space, a violent wind, the fire of doomsday, an ocean of blood, and an earthy foundation composed of flesh and bone.

ing triangles (*dharmodaya*), one red, the other blue,[303] within which swirls an ocean of blood. From the centre of the blood ocean arises the majestic Mount Sumeru in the form of a nail. The sharp tip of this nail presses down upon the hells and the *kāmadhātu* is enclosed within the great knot at the base of the shaft above. The lower half of the eight-sided shaft of this nail encompasses the *rūpadhātu* and its upper half comprises the realm of the *ārūpyadhātu.* The realm of the buddhas is symbolised by the great knot on the very top of the shaft. Thus the nail itself encompasses both the lowest depths of *saṁsāra* and the ultimate peaks of *nirvāṇa* and this is the nail which is rolled between the palms of the almighty deity Vajrakīla whose icon is to be described in this chapter.

"The great trichiliocosm resides within just such a *kīla* as this and any *kīla* manufactured in accordance with this design has great power."[304]

Thus the manifest *kīla* ranges in form from the naturally sharp thorn of the acacia tree, through the various man-made spikes of wood and metal, to the pillar, the tree, 'the tree of life', 'the tree of enlightenment' and, ultimately, to the *axis mundi* and the entire universe.

The *Drag sngags zab pa'i lo rgyus* continues with an explanation of how the three *kāya* of the *kīla* are brought into existence and how they function for the benefit of beings. Beginning with the *dharmakāya,* the text explains;

"The substance of the *kīla* of all-pervading wisdom (omniscient understanding) is the wisdom of natural awareness (*vidyājñāna*). The place in which it is implanted is the *dharmadhātu.* The extent of this understanding is infallible knowledge of the inseparability of wisdom and the *dharmadhātu.* The defect of not knowing this is that infallible wisdom is impossible to gain.

"The substance of the *kīla* of the secret mind of enlightenment is the *bodhicitta* of Mahāśrīheruka and the place of its implantation is the *bhaga* of his consort. When this has been fully understood, true sons and daugh-

303 Male and female are represented in peaceful tantric imagery by the white colour of semen and the red of menstruation, the very essences of life. In the wrathful *tantra,* however, the male colour is the blue or black of poison and that of the female is the red of blood spilled in slaughter, the very essences of death.

304 A33 236

ters can take birth from the Mother's *bhaga*. The defect of not understanding this is that such birth is not possible.[305]

"As for the substance of the *kīla* of limitless compassion, this is the arising of compassion within the *ālaya*. The place of its implantation is all living beings of the six realms. The measure of this realisation is the ability to benefit beings by means of unhesitating, unbiased compassion and the defect of not understanding this is the inability to benefit beings."[306]

Those three verses relate the three *kāya* to their corresponding moments: death, the intermediate state (*antarābhava*) and rebirth,[307] spoken of in terms of driving a spike into the appropriate 'ground'. Such meditations focus upon the *kīla* in its ultimate aspect (as *paramārthakīla*) and form part of the 'superior activities' (*stod las*) leading to enlightenment. They constitute the highest level of Vajrakīla praxis as stated in the texts themselves and are said to result in the morally praiseworthy 'achievement of the universal nail (*bhavakīla*)'. Initiates in the cult of Vajrakīla, however, also perform a large number of violent rites of a type akin to witchcraft or black magic (called *smad las,* 'lower activities')[308] and frequent references to such rites are found in the documents analysed in section three of the present work. The manufactured or 'conventional' nails (*saṁvṛtikīla*) pertaining to these lower activities of exorcism and destruction are described in the aforementioned text as follows;

"The substances of the material *kīla* with their signs and characteristics are silver, gold, copper and iron, together with the various woods that have an (occult) affinity with these metals. The places in which they are planted are the enemies, obstructors, trouble-makers and vicious ones. The measure of this understanding is the ability to destroy ('liberate') the

---

305 This verse is a typical example of the *sandhyābhāṣā* in which so many tantric teachings are expressed. Simultaneously it refers (a) to the union of wisdom and means with the resultant arising of buddhahood and (b) to the process of empowerment that purifies the *sambhogakāya*. For a discussion of this 'twilight language' see A. Wayman, *The Buddhist Tantras* 128-135

306 B30 140-141

307 For a full discussion of these correspondences, see Lati Rinbochay & Jeffrey Hopkins, *Death, Intermediate State and Rebirth.*

308 The 'lower' activities consist of the *catvāri karmāni;* the three 'gentle' (*mañju*) rites of pacification, increase and control, and the 'dreadful' (*raudra*) rite of slaying.

enemies and obstructors. The defect of not understanding this is that the enemies and obstructors are not disciplined or converted."[309]

The four kinds of metal mentioned here are considered characteristic of the *kīla* of the four families (*kula*) and the four rites (*karma*).

At the end of the *rTsa ba dril sgrub*, a *sādhana* said to have been taught to Padmasambhava by Śrīsiṁha, are mentioned three varieties of *kīla*. Those which are manufactured from either five or seven types of iron are praised as the best; those which are carved from acacia or other hard wood (*drag po'i shing,* which could also be translated 'ferocious wood'), cut when the stars and planets are calculated to be in favourable positions,[310] are said to be successful in any rite; and those which are not prepared in such ways are said to be ineffective.[311] The theme is further elaborated in another text in which the attributes of various *kīla* are outlined during the course of a conversation between Padmasambhava and King Khri Srong-lde'u-btsan. This text confirms that the *kīla* of the four *karma* and so on are characterised in their own individual ways, whereas the violent *kīla* that quells disturbances (*bar chad 'dul,* subdues interruptions) must be made of either wood or iron. If made of wood, then either red acacia or black rosewood should be used (although for the 'messenger' *kīla* any kind of thorny wood is recommended) and if made of iron then, again, the *kīla* made of five or seven types is praised as preeminent.[312]

The authors of these texts take it as axiomatic that the rite of slaying enemies by piercing their effigies with material *kīla* of metal or wood is merely the visible outer expression of a subtle inner meditation on the *trikāyakīla* directed towards enlightenment.

"That which makes the implantation of the *kīla* necessary is the requirement to subdue the interruptions of Māra. In so doing one spontaneously accomplishes the four rites and, as a result of this, the *trikāya* (ie. buddhahood). As for the manner in which these hindrances arise: in particular they become manifest for those vow-holders who are on the very verge of the attainment of *siddhi*. They do not arise for lesser beings. When obstacles really arise for a superior being, they may turn his mind away from his guru and his *vajra* brothers and sisters, away from the

---

309 B30 141

310 Acacia wood should be cut beneath the constellation Śravaṇa.
E.W. Marasinghe, *The Citrakarmaśāstra* 9

311 A32 228-229

312 A33 233-235

Dharma and his personal deity (*iṣṭadevatā*), away from the view (*darśana*) and his religious practice, away from the cultivation of *samādhi* and the performance of enlightened activity. Hindrances may also arise in the guise of enemies and thieves, the downfalls of broken vows, evil gossip, slander, disputes and all those things which destroy one's wealth and Dharma practice. All of these hindrances are obstructions due to Māra and, with regard to their subjugation, there is no method superior to that of Vajrakīla."[313]

Māra and Rudra: Embodiments of evil

The above reference to Māra, the standard epitome of evil in Buddhism, is rather unusual in the context of the Kīla literature where his place is everywhere taken by Rudra. I suppose this to be a conscious attempt on the part of the author of the text (said to be Padmasambhava) to represent the Kīla doctrines, which contain a large number of elements undoubtedly incorporated from a non-Buddhist milieu, in thoroughly orthodox manner.[314]

Traditional Buddhist cosmological theory supposes mental defilements (*kleśa*)[315] to be the fundamental cause of *saṁsāra,* the nature of which is distress (*duḥkha*). The 'Desire World' (*kāmaloka*), in which these *kleśa* are particularly prevalent, is considered to be populated by a vast range of gods and demons of all kinds (as well as men, animals, etc.) and yet, while Indian mythology in general tended to enlarge the list of demons and demonic types, Buddhism incorporated them all within the character of Māra. Later developments such as Māra's daughters and his demonic army and so forth, all derive their identity from this single figure, the sole demon of early canonical Buddhism.

---

313 B30 141-142

314 kLong-chen-pa, commenting on *Guhyagarbha-tantra* XV, asserts that Rudra, Māra, and even the primordial buddha Samantabhadra, are one.

With regard to such commentaries it has been suggested; "It is hard to avoid the conclusion that their primary intention is the 'buddhicizing' of the texts. The frequent warning given by lamas that tantric texts are meant to be read only with the accompaniment of their commentaries stems not from any intrinsic obscurity or ambiguity in the texts but from their essentially non-Buddhist or semi-Buddhist character."

B. Siklós, *The Vajrabhairava Tantra* 90

315 Chiefly ignorance (*moha*), lust (*rāga*) and hatred (*dveṣa*).

The Pāli *suttas* describe Māra as the Buddha's arch enemy. He is said to be the ruler of the *kāmadhātu* and thus to hold the human realm entirely under his sway. His powerful degenerative influence subtly pervades even the *rūpa-* and *ārūpya-dhātu* so that the sphere of buddhahood alone stands outside his reach. In an attempt to retain control of his subjects, then, Māra consistently opposes any religious endeavour that tends toward enlightenment, the sole means of escape from *saṁsāra*. He is the supporter of Vedic sacrifice through which the gods are nourished and sustained and a keen proponent of all false views. Continuously he seeks to disrupt meditation and to destroy insight. As the supreme obstacle to buddhahood he represents all that must be conquered before enlightenment is won and victory over Māra, the Evil One, is said to be the crucial event leading to *saṁbodhi*.[316]

Victory over Māra is traditionally attained through 'passive resistance' alone. The early Buddhist teachings present unwavering commitment to right view (*samyagdṛṣṭi*), right application of mindfulness (*samyaksmṛti*) and, above all, single-pointed absorption of the mind in *samādhi* as appropriate means of defence against his onslaughts. In the Vajrayāna, however, is developed the notion of 'wrathful compassion' as Buddhism adopted the stance exemplified by the doctrines of Vajrakīla and in the next chapter we will see how Padmasambhava is said to have overcome the obstacles to his own enlightenment as a result of his practice of Vajrakīla, emulating the paradigm of Indra *versus* Vṛtra.

Conquest of evil and the birth of Vajrakīla

The received mythology of Vajrakīla, however, describes the archetypal conquest of evil in terms of neither Māra nor Vṛtra. The epic struggle here is that of the buddhas *versus* Rudra. An early version of this myth is to be found in the fundamental text of the *yogatantra* class,[317] with more developed portrayals in the later texts of Cakrasaṁvara and other *heruka*

---

316 For further details, see T.O. Ling, *Buddhism and the Mythology of Evil*

317 STTS VI, quoted extensively in D. Snellgrove, *Indo-Tibetan Buddhism* 134*ff* and G. Tucci, *Indo-Tibetica Vol.I, The Stūpa* 135*ff*

manifestations.[318] The premier account, however, is given in the *mDo dgongs pa 'dus pa* XXII-XXXI.[319]

According to this myth; during a previous aeon of moral decline when Rudra, the arch demon of pride or egoism, held sway over the entire triple world, all the buddhas of the cosmos, unable through peaceful means to convince Rudra of the error of his ways, empowered a manifestation of great wrath in order to destroy him. At the time of his downfall, all of the males in the retinue of Rudra were killed and all of the females were raped. This is given a wholesome interpretation in the symbolic philosophy of the *tantra* where the masculine element is equated with creative imagination which, when perverted in the form of false views, must be destroyed. The feminine element is said to be the 'empty' (*śūnya*) nature of all manifestation and this is to be penetrated by the *vajra* mind (*vajra* = penis) in search of wisdom. The rape of Rudra's wife by the buddhas' wrathful manifestation resulted in the immediate birth of a son called Vajrakumāra (*Vajra* Youth), half *heruka* buddha and half *rākṣasī*. This 'Son of Heruka', also known as Vajrarākṣasa in remembrance of his maternal line, was the first earthly embodiment of Vajrakīla.[320] He was both ugly as a demon and beautiful as a buddha. Outwardly violent and inwardly tranquil, he was noble, base, arrogant and loving, a divine mystery as full of contradictions as his Vedic namesake.

The *Drag sngags zab pa'i lo rgyus*[321] states; "As for his name *Vajra,* this signifies the unborn *dharmatā*. His name *Kumāra* signifies freedom from old-age and decrepitude. That itself is the uncontrived and unmistaken truth which is impartial and does not fall to any side." And the BRT says; "This is the form of the wisdom manifestation of all the buddhas, the unbearable configuration of blazing wrath that emanates from the very nature of the *vajradharmadhātu.*"

When the monstrous body of the demon Rudra was conquered and hurled from the peak of Mount Malaya, it was scattered into the eight

---

318 The relevant chapters have, unfortunately, been omitted by S. Tsuda from his 1974 edition of the *Saṁvarodaya-tantra*

319 NGB 160. Accounts in English are to be found in Jacob Dalton, *The Taming of the Demons* Appendix A; Douglas & Bays, *The Life and Liberation of Padmasambhava* V-VI; and G. Dorje, *The Guhyagarbha-tantra* XV

320 *bKa' thang gser phreng* VI. The Tibetan text with an English translation is to be found in Lama and Low, *The Origin of Heruka and the Twenty-four Places,* published privately in Kalimpong (no date)

321 B30 139

directions. His head, heart, intestines and genitals (the four divisions of his trunk) landed in the cardinal quarters and his four limbs fell down in the intermediate directions. These areas are renowned in the myths as the eight great charnel grounds (*aṣṭamahāśmaśāna*) and in each one of these a special tree grew up. In the light of the above tradition in which all trees are viewed as living *kīla,* it is interesting to note that the eight types of *kīla* listed in the *Kālacakra-tantra* exhibit a remarkable similarity to the eight types of tree said to stand in these burning grounds.[322]

The nature of the conqueror

Thus Vajrakīla, whose methodology is declared the foremost means of overcoming Māra in the present aeon, is considered the son of the *heruka(s)* who slew Rudra in an aeon long gone. This paramount conqueror of the present age is now a full grown *samyaksaṁbuddha* in his own right having his own set of 'supreme sons' (see Part Three) and a lineage that includes the initiated *yogin* as the present 'son of *heruka'* on the throne of buddhahood.

The *Drag sngags zab pa'i lo rgyus* describes the nature of this deity in some detail, opening with an evocative picture of the successful practice of his rites as a preamble to the commentarial material. This preamble is calculated to inspire faith in the minds of cultic initiates and I include it here for the sake of the poetic glimpse that it affords us as observers of the Kīla cult. The motif of flying *kīla* to which we are introduced here is one that recurs repeatedly in the chronicles of the cult.

In Seng-ge-rdzong in Bhutan, Padmasambhava of Oḍḍiyāna and his consort Ye-shes mtsho-rgyal were practising the rite of rolling the Razor of fierce root *mantra,* which is the very essence of Vajrakīla. Signs of success having become manifest in vastness, the meditation *kīla* began to shake, tremble, fly up in the air and caper around. The painted images were laughing and the drums and cymbals played their own music. Natural awareness blazed forth as wisdom and vows of aspiration became attainments in reality. The eight classes of local gods and demons offered their own insignia and life essence and, making promises, they took oaths to act as protectors of the Kīla doctrines. The whole sky was filled with *vidyādhara* and *ḍākinī* and their hermitage was pervaded by sounds, bright

322 *Kālacakra-tantra* III.12 (See below, Appendix II)

lights and coloured rainbow rays. At that time, the Lotus Born guru of Oḍḍiyāna said to Ye-shes mtsho-rgyal:

"Varakīla is the manifestation of heroic power. The son of the non-dual union of the mother Samantabhadrī with the most mighty all-pervading excellent *heruka* whose form encompasses all the buddhas. During times of peace he manifests as Vajrasattva and his mind abides in tranquility. As for his family lineage: his is the Activity Family of Karma-heruka. During times of activity he manifests as *Ativināśanavajra (*Vajra* of Total Destruction) and, when manifesting as a *bodhisattva,* he is Vajrapāṇi. Thus he takes on whatever form is appropriate for the conversion of living beings. His manifestations are inconceivable and all buddhas are embodiments of Vajrakumāra. Within the *dharmakāya* which is the essential nature of all the buddhas are all the infinite possibilities that could be wished for. One should meditate unwaveringly upon that *dharmakāya,* viewing it as the assembly of buddhas. All deities are complete within the form of Vajrakumāra and the purpose or meaning of Vajrakumāra is complete within the solitary *bindu*[323] of the *dharmakāya*. Never at any time does he stray from the *dharmakāya*."[324]

And in Chapter Two of the *mūlatantra* BRT it is written;

In that place the *bhagavat* Mahāśrīvajrakumāra spoke these words: "Kyai! Pay attention to this, all you hosts here assembled! In the mighty charnel ground of the natural condition, reflected forms, like the images in a mirror or the moon in water, abide in the sphere of natural meaning without being covered by the stains of the afflictions. The teacher is like a miraculous display in the sky, teaching the Dharma of fierce *mantra* in the supreme charnel ground of the natural state." Thus he spoke.

And in Chapter Three;

(When it is said that) he is the supreme son of all *tathāgata,* the word 'son' means that he comes without birth from the *dharmatā* and 'supreme' means that he is the spontaneous fulfilment of enlightened activity. He is the son of all of them in order to destroy Rudra. The 'son' is the unborn *vajra* son.

Thus our Byang-gter sources present Vajrakīla as a numinous aspect of vibrant enlightenment, a potent force in the struggle against evil, imma-

---

323 In the terminology of *atiyoga,* with which the literature of Vajrakīla abounds, the fundamental nature of reality (*dharmakāya*) is likened to an all-encompassing non-dual ('single', 'unique') seminal point of light (*bindu*). See below, note 334

324 B30 138-139

nent in a variety of (essentially illusory) forms. As 'the son of the buddhas', he is a contrivance of enlightened wisdom (*prajñā*) specifically brought forth as a method (*upāya*) in opposition to the forces of darkness. Moreover; just as the Māra of the Pāli canon remains invisible to all but the Buddha and *arhats,*[325] and yet none can achieve that status without first recognising and routing the demon, so Vajrakīla embodies both the path and the goal of *saṁbodhi.* Successful meditation upon "the Kīla that destroys the enemies and obstructors" grants spontaneous liberation from *saṁsāra.*

Manifestation in the form of symbols

These numinous and powerful qualities of enlightenment are stated in the tantric texts to have appropriated the form and adornments of the conquered enemy. Thus Vajrakīla is invariably dressed in the 'spoils of war', those grisly clothes and ornaments of the charnel ground that were originally stripped from the body of the defeated Rudra and have subsequently been worn by all *heruka.* His clothing includes an upper garment of human skin, a cloak of elephant skin and a skirt of tiger skin (females wear leopard skin). Among his ornaments are the fivefold set made of bone (necklace, earrings, bracelets, apron and hairnet) associated with the five buddha families, numerous snakes encircling his limbs and body, a crown of five dry skulls, a necklace of fifty freshly severed heads, a belt of splintered bones, and so on. He is also characterised by the ten attributes of glory (*dpal gyi chas bcu*) which demonstrate his magnificent power and authority[326] and he paints his face with the three ointments (*byug pa'i rdzas gsum*): the dust of human ashes (*thal chen tshom bu*) on his forehead, drops of blood (*rakta'i thig le*) upon his cheeks and a smear of fat (*zhag gi zo ris*) across his chin. He is erotic and sensual. His

---

325 T.O. Ling, *Buddhism and the Mythology of Evil* 49-50

326 *Makara* heads worn as epaulets express his blazing glory, the sun and moon worn in his hair show the simultaneity of *prajñā* and *upāya,* his protruding fangs demonstrate the annihilation of birth and death, his *vajra* wings symbolise the fulfilment of all wishes, his upraised hair shows the reversal of *saṁsāric* tendencies, his coat of *vajra* indicates absolute authority, his military jacket of rhinoceros hide symbolises the invincibility of buddhahood, his aura of flames burns up malevolent forces, his girdle of knives cuts through any opposing tendency and the *vajra* worn on the crown of his head shows his own immutability. Gega Lama, *Principles of Tibetan Art* 390

captivating nine modes of dance (*navanāṭaka*)[327] are at once alluring and repulsive and his dwelling is a gruesome palace made of skulls.[328]

All the texts describe him as sporting in non-duality with his spouse, holding in his right hands a nine-pronged *vajra* indicating his mastery of the nine *yāna* and the ten *bhūmi,* and a five-pronged *vajra* showing his possession of the five *jñāna*. In his left hands he holds a blazing mass of (wisdom) fire and a *khaṭvāṅga,* proclaiming his mastery of all techniques of *yoga*. With his final pair of hands he rolls a *kīla* and the sky is filled with his *vajra* wings.

The body of the monster Rudra in his final birth had three faces, six arms and four legs and this, therefore, is the basic form of Vajrakīla.

Dark blue in colour, representing the spacious nature of his primordially pure mind, the deity Vajrakīla has a ferocious white face on the right side of his head that destroys the afflictions of anger. His left red face annihilates all impurities of desire and his central blue face vanquishes ignorance. Each face has an unblinking third eye in the centre of its forehead so that none of these mental defilements may pass by unnoticed.

According to the tradition of the *Guhyagarbha-tantra,*[329] his three faces indicate the destruction of the three poisons and the attainment of the three *kāya*. His six arms show the ability to liberate beings in the six realms and his four legs symbolise his four modes of activity (*catvāri karmāni*) as well as the liberation of beings from the four kinds of birth (egg, womb, moisture and miraculous). To this should be added that Vajrakīla simultaneously tramples down the four Māras: Skandha, Kleśa, Mṛtyu and Devaputra. It is also interesting to note that the eight kinds of garb associated with the charnel ground are listed in the *Guhyagarbha-tantra* (p.1167) as; raw hides, snakes, skull garlands, sunlight, moonlight, dry blood, grease and ashes, thereby combining into one list the several given above. Within the term 'skull garlands' are included a crown of dry skulls, shoulder ornaments of rotting heads and a necklace of 51 freshly

---

327 These nine modes, originating in ancient Indian treatises on dance and drama, are interpreted in A. Wayman, *Yoga of the GST* 327-328

328 Every element employed in the composition of the Buddha's celestial palace, the divine *maṇḍala* of jewelled light, finds its macabre counterpart in the Heruka's charnel dwelling, fabricated of mayhem, slaughter and pain.
See below, Chapter Seven, and also my *Maṇḍala Meaning and Method*

329 G. Dorje, *Guhyagarbha-tantra* 118

severed heads which indicate his total control of the past, present and future.[330]

This six-armed manifestation is widely known throughout the *bKa' ma* and *gTer ma* texts of the several rNying-ma canons. In the literature of the Byang-gter school, however, he is also recognised in the form of Mahottaradeva, an 18-armed variant rarely encountered elsewhere. This manifestation is also dark blue in colour and, according to B11 & C4, his three faces on the right are pale yellow, red and blue-green. His three central faces are white, yellow and dark blue, while those on the left are yellow-black, red and green. Otherwise, according to A4, one may view all the faces on the right as white, on the left as red and the central ones as blue.

Because I believe this particular form to be unique to the Byang-gter and therefore of intrinsic interest, I give here the full text of a hitherto unpublished hymn in his praise;[331]

ཧཱུྃ༔ དཔལ་ལྡན་ཆེ་བའི་ཆེ་མཆོག་ལྷ་ཡི་ལྷ༔
དུས་གསུམ་བདེ་བར་གཤེགས་པ་ཐམས་ཅད་ཀྱི༔
འཕྲིན་ལས་ཐམས་ཅད་རྫོགས་པའི་དཔལ་ཆེན་པོ༔
ཧེ་རུ་ཀ་དཔལ་ཁྱོད་ལ་ཕྱག་འཚལ་བསྟོད༔

HŪṀ The deity of the great and supreme gods of great splendour,
The great glorious one who has perfected all the activities of all the *sugata* of the past, present and future.
Salutation and praise to you, Śrīheruka!

འཇིགས་རྗེན་འདས་པའི་དུས་ན་སྨོན་བྱུང་བ༔
སྐུ་གསུམ་རྫོགས་པའི་ཁྲོ་རྒྱལ་ཕུར་པའི་ལྷ༔

330 Note that within the iconography of a peaceful deity such as the saviouress Tārā, the three times are indicated by lotus flowers – one still in bud, one currently blooming and another already withered.

331 From a ms in the private collection of C.R. Lama. The symbols stated in this hymn to be held in the deity's 18 hands are compared in Table 1, below, with those listed in two of the texts from our published collections.

སྲིད་རྩ་བདག་འཛིན་རུ་དྲ་སྡེ་གསུམ་འདུལ༔
རྩལ་ཆེན་འཕྲིན་ལས་རྫོགས་ལ་ཕྱག་འཚལ་བསྟོད༔

You who primordially arose in a time which transcends the world,
Kīladeva, ferocious king with the perfect three *kāya,*
Subduer of the three groups of ego-grasping Rudra,[332]
which are the very basis of saṁsāric existence.
Salutation and praise be to you,
the perfection of expressive power and enlightened activity!

གཏུམ་ཆེན་བརྗིད་པ་འགྱིང་ཞིང་སྙེག་པའི་སྐུ༔
བདུད་ཚོགས་སྡེ་བཅས་འདུལ་བའི་དཔའ་བོ་ཆེ༔
མི་སྲུན་སྲིན་པོ་ཁྲོས་འདྲའི་ཆ་ལུགས་ཀྱིས༔
སྲིད་གསུམ་གདུག་པ་འདུལ་མཛད་ཁྱོད་ལ་བསྟོད༔

Praise be to you with a graceful body, savage, splendid and proud,
The mighty hero in the guise of a ferocious, unruly *rākṣasa.*
You, who tames the hosts of Māras and their ilk,
Subjugator of noxious harm in the triple world![333]

བཞད་སྒྲ་འབྲུག་སྟོང་ལྡིར་འདྲའི་གད་རྒྱངས་ཅན༔
དྲག་ཤུལ་ཆེན་པོས་རི་རབ་ཐལ་བར་བརླག༔
འཇིགས་རུང་རྩལ་གྱིས་ཁམས་གསུམ་དུས་གཅིག་སྒྲོལ༔
དཔལ་ཆེན་ཁྲོ་བོའི་དབང་ཕྱུག་ཁྱོད་ལ་བསྟོད༔

Laughing a laugh with the sound of 1,000 rolling thunderclaps,
Your frightful appearance reduces Mount Meru to dust.
Liberating the *traidhātuka* in a single moment of terrifying style,
Praise be to you, Great Glorious Wrathful King
(*mahāśrīkrodheśvara*) !

---

332 These are the demons of pride related to body, speech and mind.

333 The *tribhava* (*tribhuvana*) are the three states of existence ruled by the *deva, nāga* and men. Svarga (the abode of gods), Martta (the abode of men) and Rasātala (the abode of *nāga* and demons) are situated above the earth, upon the earth and below the earth, respectively.

སྙིང་རྗེས་བསྒྲལ་བའི་དམ་ཚིག་ཆེན་པོ་ཡིས༔
འགྲོ་ཀུན་བྱང་ཆུབ་སྙིང་པོར་འདྲེན་མཛད་ཅིང༔
ཐུགས་རྗེའི་དབྱིངས་ནས་ཁྲོས་པའི་རྗམས་སྟབས་ཀྱིས༔
འཁོར་བ་གཏན་ནས་བརླག་བྱེད་ཁྱོད་ལ་བསྟོད༔

Through your great vow of 'liberating by compassion'
You lead all beings to the heart of enlightenment.
Through your fiercely violent method within compassion's sphere
You demolish *saṁsāra* completely. Praise be to you!

གདུག་ཅན་དྲག་པོ་འདུལ་བར་ཞེར་དགོངས་ནས༔
འབར་བའི་ཁྲོ་ཚུལ་དུ་མའི་གར་མཛད་ཀྱང༔
ཆོས་དབྱིངས་ཞི་བའི་ངང་ལས་མི་གཡོ་བ༔
དཔལ་ཆེན་མངོན་རྫོགས་རྒྱལ་པོ་ཁྱོད་ལ་བསྟོད༔

Intent upon subjugating the violent harmful ones,
You perform many dances in a blazing, wrathful manner
And yet you never stray from the peaceful disposition of
the *dharmadhātu*.
Praise be to you, glorious great king of manifest perfection!

ནམ་མཁའི་ཁམས་ཀུན་ཡོངས་སུ་ཁྱབ་པའི་སྐུ༔
གླིང་བཞི་རི་རབ་ཉི་ཟླ་གཟའ་སྐར་ཡང༔
སྐུ་ཡི་རྒྱན་དུ་ཆེ་བའི་དཔལ་ཆེན་པོ༔
ཆེ་བཙན་འགྲན་ཟླ་འབྲལ་བ་ཁྱོད་ལ་བསྟོད༔

You, whose form completely pervades the whole realm of space,
So that even Mount Meru, the four continents, the sun, moon,
planets and stars
Are the ornaments of your body. Oh, greatly splendid one,
Praise be to you whose majestic prowess is without rival!

གཉེན་པོ་ཡེ་ཤེས་གཞོམ་གཞིག་མི་མངའ་བས༔

ཉོན་མོངས་རྟོག་པའི་བདུད་ཚོགས་ཚར་གཅོད་ཕྱིར༔
བཅོ་བརྒྱད་ཕྱག་གི་གཡས་ཀྱི་དང་པོ་བཞིས༔
རྡོ་རྗེ་རྩེ་དགུ་འཁོར་ལོ་རྩིབ་བཅུ་དང་༔

You wisdom ally, manifesting as an unconquerable destroyer
In order to annihilate the demonic hosts of defiled thoughts,
You have 18 hands: With the first four on the right
You hold a nine-pronged *vajra* and a wheel with ten spokes,

རལ་གྲི་དབལ་ལྡན་བེ་ཅོན་འབར་བ་ཡིས༔
རི་རབ་ཆེན་པོ་ཀུན་ཀྱང་ཐལ་བར་རློག༔
བདུད་དང་འབྱུང་པོ་ཀུན་གྱི་ཀླད་པ་འགེམས༔
སྲིད་པའི་འགོང་པོ་སྤུན་དགུ་རྡུལ་དུ་རློག༔

A sharp-pointed sword and a blazing club, with which
Even the great mountain Sumeru is completely crushed to dust.
Confounding the brains of all *māra* and *bhūta,*
You grind to atoms the nine ’Gong-po brothers of phenomenal existence.

ཐ་མ་བཞི་ཡི་རྡོ་རྗེ་རྩེ་ལྔ་དང་༔
གྲི་གུག་ཐོ་བ་ཆོས་འབྱུང་འབར་བ་ཡིས༔
འགྲོ་རྣམས་ཐེག་པ་དགུ་ཡི་ལམ་ལ་འདྲེན༔
ཉོན་མོངས་དུག་ལྔ་གཏན་ནས་བརླག་བྱེད་ཅིང་༔
དོན་དམ་སྤྲོས་མེད་བྱང་སེམས་རྣམ་པ་ལྔས༔
རྒྱུད་ལྔའི་སེམས་ཅན་ཐར་པའི་ལམ་ལ་སྦྱོར༔

With the five-pronged *vajra,* curved knife, hammer and blazing *dharmodaya* of your lower four hands,
You guide beings on the path of the nine *yāna.*
Utterly demolishing the five poisonous afflictions,
You place the five families of sentient beings on the path of liberation

With the five *bodhi* minds of highest truth,
free of mental fabrication.

བཅོ་བརྒྱད་ཕྱག་གི་གཡོན་གྱི་དང་པོ་བཞིའི༔
ཐོད་ཁྲག་མེ་དཔུང་ཁ་ཊྭཱཾ་ཁྱུང་ཁྲ་ཡིས༔
བདུད་དང་དམ་སྲི་ནག་པོའི་ཕྱོགས་རྣམས་ཀུན༔
ཀུན་ཏུ་བསྡིགས་ཤིང་ཐལ་བར་བརླག་པར་མཛད༔

Of your 18 hands: With the upper four on the left you hold
A skull full of blood, a mass of fire, a *khaṭvāṅga* staff
and a falcon, which,
Aiming at the evil *māra* and *dam sri* demons,
completely pulverises them all!

ཐ་མ་བཞི་ཡིས་རྡོ་རྗེ་རྒྱ་གྲམ་དང་༔
ལྕགས་ཀྱུ་དགྲ་སྟ་བུམ་པར་གཙུ་ཡིས༔
སྲིད་གསུམ་གདུག་པ་མཐའ་དག་ཚར་བཅད་ནས༔
དུག་གསུམ་སྐུ་གསུང་ཐུགས་སུ་སྒྲོལ་བྱེད་ཅིང་༔
འཁོར་བའི་གཡུལ་ངོ་གཏན་ནས་བརླག་པར་མཛད༔

In your lower four hands you hold a *viśvavajra,* an iron hook,
a battle axe and a pot with an amulet on top.
Using these to completely eradicated the harmful extremes
of the threefold world,
You liberate the three poisons as enlightened body, speech
and mind
And utterly destroy the very army of *saṁsāra.*

དཔལ་ཆེན་ཆེ་བའི་ཆེ་མཆོག་ཀཱི་ལ་ཡ༔
ཁྲོ་རྒྱལ་མ་ལུས་འདུས་པའི་རྩལ་འཆིང་ཞིང་༔
མི་བཟད་སྟོང་ཁམས་བསྲེགས་པའི་མེ་སྟག་འཕྲོ༔
བཏབ་ན་ཡེ་ཤེས་ལྷ་ཡང་ཐལ་བར་རློག༔

The greatest of the great, Glorious Mahottarakīla,
Girding yourself with the energy of all *heruka* without exception,
Irresistible, as you radiate sparks of fire that burn up
a thousand worlds,
Touched by you, even the wisdom gods would be reduced
to ashes!

འབར་བའི་ཕྲེང་བ་འཁྲིག་པའི་འོད་ཟེར་ཅན༔
འོག་མ་གཉིས་ཀྱིས་རི་རབ་ཕུར་པ་འདྲིལ༔
ཁམས་གསུམ་ཡོངས་སྒྲོལ་དཔའ་བོ་ཆེ་ལ་བསྟོད༔

Enveloped in intermingling blazing chains of light,
You roll a *kīla* the size of Mount Meru in your two
lowest hands.
Praise be to you, great hero, by whom the three realms are
completely liberated!

གར་གྱི་དབང་ཕྱུག་རྣམ་པར་འགྱུར་བའི་སྐུ༔
དཔལ་དང་དུར་ཁྲོད་ཆས་རྣམས་ཡོངས་རྫོགས་ཤིང་༔
ཞབས་བརྒྱད་བརྐྱང་བསྐུམ་གྱད་ཀྱི་འདོར་སྟབས་ཀྱིས༔
དྲེགས་པ་ལྷ་ཆེན་གནོན་མཛད་ཁྱོད་ལ་བསྟོད༔

Lord of the dance with ever-changing form,
Fully adorned with the attributes of glory and those of the
charnel ground.
With the virile gesture of a champion, your eight legs
are drawn in and flung out.
Praise be to you who thus tramples down the arrogant great gods!

མཆེ་བ་ཟངས་ཡག་གཙིགས་པའི་ཟ་བྱེད་ཆེ༔
རབ་འབར་ཉི་མ་འབུམ་གྱི་འོད་ཟེར་འཕྲོ༔
ཁྲོ་གཉེར་གློག་སྟོང་འཁྱུང་འདྲའི་ཧམས་སྟབས་ཅན༔
མི་བཟད་སྐུ་ཡི་དངོས་པོ་ཤིན་ཏུ་འགྱུར༔

Great devourer, snarling with sharp-pointed fangs,
Blazing and radiating the light of a hundred thousand suns,
Your wrinkling brows rage in a terrifying manner
    with the speed of a thousand bolts of lightning
As you assume the guise of irresistible form!

རྔམས་པའི་ང་རོ་འབྲུག་སྟོང་ལྡིར་བ་བཞིན༔
ཐུག་འཚམས་རི་རབ་འབུམ་ཕྲག་བསྙིལ་བའི་སྐད༔
གད་རྒྱངས་དྲག་པོས་འཇིག་རྟེན་གཡོ་ཞིང་འདེབས༔
སྒྲུག་པའི་འཐོར་རླུང་ཀུན་ཏུ་གཡེང་ལ་བསྟོད༔

With an awesome roar like the rumble of a thousand thunderclaps,
The sound of your voice destroys a hundred thousand Mt Merus.
Your violent laughter sends the world into trembles –
A whirling, scattering wind that agitates everything.
    To you be praise!

ཁྲོ་བོ་ཤེས་རབ་ཡེ་ཤེས་མེ་བོ་ཆེ༔
ཡེ་ཤེས་ཆེན་པོའི་འོད་ཟེར་ཀུན་ཏུ་གསལ༔
འབར་བའི་ཡེ་ཤེས་མ་རིག་མུན་པ་འཇོམས༔
སྙིང་པོ་ཡེ་ཤེས་ཐིག་ལེ་རྣམས་ལ་བསྟོད༔

Your fierce great fire of *prajñā-jñāna* makes everything clear
    with rays of great wisdom light.
Your blazing wisdom destroys the darkness of ignorance.
Praise be to the *bindus*[334] of essential wisdom!

ཡེ་ཤེས་དཀྱིལ་འཁོར་ཁྲོ་བོའི་སྤྲིན་ཆེན་པོ༔
འཕྲོས་པས་དཀྱིལ་འཁོར་ཀུན་གྱི་ཆར་ཆེན་འབེབས༔

---

334 The solitary 'great *bindu*' (see next verse), which is an *atiyoga* term for the *dharmadhātu* within which the mind is primordially enlightened, is defined as having six aspects: the *bindu* of space (*dhātu*), the *bindu* of the utter purity of space, the *bindu* of the natural condition (*tathatā*), the *bindu* of wisdom (*prajñā*), the *bindu* of the 'all-good' (*samantabhadra*) and the *bindu* of spontaneous accomplishment. S. Karmay, *The Great Perfection* 118
See also T. Thondup, *Buddha Mind* 68 and note 323, above.

ཕྱོགས་བཅུའི་དཀྱིལ་འཁོར་ཡིད་བཞིན་འབྱུང་བའི་གཏེར༔
ཡེ་ཤེས་རྣམས་ཀྱི་ཐིག་ལེ་ཆེ་ལ་བསྟོད༔

As the great *heruka* clouds spread out from your wisdom *maṇḍala*,
There falls a mighty rain of all *maṇḍala*.[335]
You are the wish-fulfilling treasure of *maṇḍala* in the ten directions.
Praise be to you, great *bindu* of all wisdoms!

བདུད་རྣམས་ཀུན་གྱི་བདུད་སྟེ་བདུད་ཆེན་པོ༔
འཇིགས་བྱེད་འཇིགས་པའི་ཚོགས་ཀྱང་འཇིགས་པར་བྱེད༔
སྲིད་ཞིའི་ཆིང་བ་ཐམས་ཅད་འཇོམས་མཛད་པ༔
དུས་མཐའི་མེ་ལྟར་འབར་ལ་ཕྱག་འཚལ་བསྟོད༔

The demon of all demons, you are the great demon
And you terrify even the terrible hosts
of those who cause terror.
You are the one who breaks all the bonds of *saṁsāra* and *nirvāṇa*.
Salutation and praise be to you who blazes like the fire
at the end of time!

The consort Tṛptacakra; 'Circle of Satisfaction'

ཧཱུྃ འཇིགས་པའི་བཙུན་མོ་འཁོར་ལོ་རྒྱས་འདེབས་མ༔
ཀུན་ཏུ་བཟང་མོ་དཀྱིལ་འཁོར་ཀུན་གྱི་འཕྲུལ༔
གདུག་པ་འདུལ་ཕྱིར་སྲིན་མོ་ཁྲོས་པའི་གཟུགས༔
སྲིད་པའི་ཁོར་ལོ་ཡེ་ཤེས་རྒྱུ་ཡི་འདེབས༔

HŪṀ Fearful queen, Tṛptacakra!
Samantabhadrī, emanation of all *maṇḍala*!
In order to subdue noxious beings,

---

335 Cf. the *Sarvarahasya-tantra* (A. Wayman, 1984, verse 13) where the residents of the *maṇḍala* are called "a cloud of Dharma" and "rain" refers to the emanation of these deities from the heart.

you manifest in the form of a fierce *rākṣasī,*
Impressing the wheel of existence with the seal of your wisdom.

གཉིས་མེད་དོན་ལྡན་ཡབ་ལ་དགྱེས་པར་འཁྲིལ༔
ཕྱག་གཡས་ཁ་ཊྭཱཾ་བདུད་ཀྱི་མགོ་ལུས་གཞོམས༔
གཡོན་པས་ཐོད་ཁྲག་འཁོར་འདས་དབང་སུ་སྡུད༔
འཇིགས་པའི་སྐུ་ལ་ཕྱག་རྒྱ་ལྔ་ཡིས་སྤྲས༔

Rapturously embracing your consort, signifying non-duality,
In your right hand is a *khaṭvāṅga*,
with which Māra's head and body are ripped apart,
And in your left, in a skull full of blood,
you hold *saṁsāra* and *nirvāṇa* under your power.
Your terrifying body is adorned with the five *mudrā.*[336]

དྲག་པོའི་ང་རོས་འཇིག་རྟེན་གཡོ་ཞིང་འཁྲུགས༔
རྒྱུད་ལྔའི་སེམས་ཅན་ཐུགས་རྗེས་དབྱིངས་སུ་སྒྲོལ༔
སྲིད་གསུམ་གདུག་པའི་ཚོགས་རྣམས་ཐལ་བར་རློག༔
མཁའ་འགྲོ་ཡོངས་ཀྱི་གཙོ་མོ་ཁྱོད་ལ་བསྟོད༔

The world is convulsed and shaken by your violent roar
As you compassionately liberate the five families of beings
into the realm of space (*dharmadhātu*)
And grind to dust the hosts of noxious beings in the triple world.
Praise be to you, queen of all *ḍākinī* !

And thus we have the basic iconography of Vajrakumāra and his consort; a terrifying form with violent speech and blazing mind. Three *kāya* of horrendous power for the subjugation of all evils. In particular, the male is associated here with *upāya* (expressed in his epithet Karmakīla) while the female, as made clear in this description of her rapture, is the bliss ('satisfaction') inherent in *prajñā*. Less obvious is the manner in which Tṛptacakra complements her spouse's function of pegging down demons. In the previous chapter we noted her developing association with the

---

336 The fivefold set of bone ornaments.

notion of unpegging, freeing that which has been obstructed, and this theme comes to maturity here as she liberates all beings into the *dharmadhātu*. He performs the skilful function of nailing down obstacles while She simultaneously offers blissful release through wisdom.

Embodiments of paradox

The Dionysian dance in the flames of wisdom that consume the appearances of the world is to be taken here as symbolic of the *bodhisattva*'s passionate commitment to the vow of universal salvation. *Nirvāṇa* was thought of by the early Buddhists in terms of the individual extinction of a flame but the image employed here is that of the doomsday fire which brings an end to the system of *saṁsāra* altogether. "So singing and dancing the *yogin* always acts."[337] It is an incestuous image of the union of pleasure and pain which arise in mutual dependence. Vajrakīla and his erotic playmate are 'simultaneously born' (*sahaja*) brother and sister, a fact of some significance in the symbolic system of *tantra* where praxis aims to bring about the consolidation of complementary poles on the theoretical premise that "there is not the slightest difference between *saṁsāra* and *nirvāṇa*".[338] The passionate embrace of the couple, paradoxically, is to be read as a symbol of chastity. It is an image of desire fulfilled, not one of lustful yearning. Hinting at the yogic technique of *coitus reservatus,* Vajrakīla's perpetual union with 'The Circle of Satisfaction' marks the end of desire, just as their wild dance in the doomsday fire signifies the end of the tormenting heat of *kleśa*.[339] The most striking feature of the icon, however, is surely the fact that it purports to represent the life-enhancing qualities of wisdom, serenity, freedom of activity, long life and so on (yogic attainments to be met with in Part Three of the present work), in the ghastly guise of an utterly terrifying killer. The elemental interplay of sex and death is depicted here in an icon of extreme violence, the most powerfully destructive element of which is described in the BRT as the pounding thrust of their conjoined sexual organs.

---

337 HT I.vi.13, explained at II.iv *passim.*

338 HT I.x.32

339 W.D. O'Flaherty notes the use of ashes smeared on the bodies of a couple engaged in rites of tantric intercourse (as in the icon of Vajrakīla and his consort) as a remedy for the fever of love.
Asceticism and Eroticism in the Mythology of Śiva 246

This image of Vajrakīla incorporates traits of both god and demon. As an expression of the human psyche, then, it squarely addresses the problem of what Jung has called the 'shadow' side of the personality, consisting of those unpleasant aspects that elsewhere may receive only reluctant acknowledgement. The portrait is horrible in the extreme and yet is said to be alluring, magnetic, compulsively attractive. Vajrakīla is the embodiment of the absolute truth of the human condition, the unbiased, unflinching presenter of the best and the worst in a single icon accessible to the *yogin* through his meditative training. The demonic is here fully accepted as an aspect of the divine.

The divine retinue

Surrounding the central couple are the ten ferocious gods known as the *daśakrodharāja* (the ten *krodha*[340] kings): (Vajra)Hūṁkāra in the zenith, Krodhavijaya to the east, Nīladaṇḍa (SE), Yamāntaka (S), Ārya-Acala (SW), Hayagrīva (W), Aparājita (NW), Amṛtakuṇḍalin (N), Trailokyavijaya (NE) and Mahābala in the nadir.[341] Each of these wrathful kings is united with his queen and accompanied by a pair of particularly violent animal-headed, flesh-eating female spirits (*piśācī*), known as 'devourers' (*za byed*) and 'slayers' (*gsod byed*) because they are skilful predatory hunters and ravenous scavengers of carrion.[342] The names of neither the ten queens nor the twenty *piśācī* have so far been traced to any Sanskrit source so I am obliged here to tabulate the 40 deities of the primary Vajrakīla *parṣanmaṇḍala* employing an admixture of Sanskrit and Tibetan nomenclature. Such Sanskrit names as have been added in parenthesis are provisional equivalents culled from such sources as the *Niṣpannayogāvalī*.

---

340 The term *krodha* ('anger') is defined in the *Krodhabhairava-sūtra* as "that by virtue of which one becomes genuinely one-pointedly intent on removing whatever obstacles there may be to liberation".
Mark Dyczkowski, *The Canon of the Śaivāgama and the Kubjikā Tantras of the Western Kaula Tradition* 108

341 Similar groups are to be found in several *tantras*, their names and specific iconographies varying slightly from one tradition to another.
For further examples (taken from the GST, etc.), consult Abhayākaragupta's *Niṣpannayogāvalī* or the *Sādhanamālā*, etc.

342 Known variously as 'witches' or 'shape shifters' (*phra men ma*), 'speedy ones' (*mgyogs mo*), 'emissaries' or 'messengers' (*mngag mo*), such servants have been associated with the *krodha* kings since at least the period of the *Yogatantra* as evidenced by SDPT 313

In the zenith, on cushions of Brahmā and his consort is the dark blue[343] *krodharāja* Hūṁkāra in the embrace of sGra-'byin (Śabdavajrā). To their right and left stand the devourer with the head of a pig and the killer with that of a lizard.

In the east, on cushions of Indra, lord of the *gandharva,* and his consort is the white *krodharāja* Vijaya in the embrace of rNam-snyems (Śauṇḍinī). To their right and left stand the devourer with the head of a tiger and the killer with that of a vulture.

In the southeast on cushions of Agni, the great *ṛṣi,* and his consort is the pale (*skya,* 'tawny') *krodharāja* Nīladaṇḍa in the embrace of rDo-rje sder-mo (Vajranakhinī). To their right and left stand the devourer with the head of a yak and the killer with that of a raven.

In the south on cushions of Yama and his consort is the black *krodharāja* Yamāntaka in the embrace of Dur-khrod bdag-mo (Śmāśānikā). To their right and left stand the devourer with the head of a stag and the killer with that of an owl.

In the southwest on cushions of the king of the *rākṣasa* and his consort is the blue-green *krodharāja,* the noble Acala in the embrace of rDo-rje gtun-khung (Vajra Ulūkhalā). To their right and left stand the devourer with the head of a leopard and the killer with that of a crow.

In the west on cushions of Varuṇa, lord of the *nāga,* and his consort is the red *krodharāja* Hayagrīva in the embrace of rDo-rje gtum-mo (Vajra Caṇḍālī). To their right and left stand the devourer with the head of a cat and the killer with that of a hoopoe bird.

In the northwest on cushions of Vāyu and his consort is the tawny-red *krodharāja* Aparājita in the embrace of rDo-rje mda'-snyems (Śaragarvī).

---

343 The colours given here are those found in our text A6 50*ff.* Alternative schemes are depicted in A49 and B11. All of these *mahottarakīla* sources describe each *krodharāja* as having three faces and six arms: The upper pair of hands carry a *vajra* in the right and a skull full of blood in the left while between the palms of the lower pair of hands each deity rolls a *kīla.* Thus the specific attributes of each *krodha* king are held in the central pair of hands. According to A49; the dark blue Hūṁkāra carries a *vajra* and bell. The dark blue Vijaya carries an iron hook and fly whisk (*cāmara*). The (colour missing) Nīladaṇḍa carries a staff (*daṇḍa*) and heap of fire. The dark green Yamāntaka carries a staff and battle axe. The dark blue Acala carries a sword and noose. The dark red Hayagrīva carries a lotus and snake. The white Aparājita carries a *vajra* and discus (*cakra*). The dark green Amṛtakuṇḍalin carries a *viśvavajra* and club. The yellow Trailokyavijaya carries a *vajra* and trident and the smoke coloured Mahābala carries a hammer and wooden pestle. A49 518-529. See also below, Chapter Seven, Table 2.

To their right and left stand the devourer with the head of a wolf and the killer with that of a hawk.

In the north on cushions of the king of the *yakṣa* and his consort is the dark green *krodharāja* Amṛtakuṇḍalin in the embrace of rLung-'byin-ma (Vāyuvegā). To their right and left stand the devourer with the head of a lion and the killer with that of a bat.

In the northeast on cushions of the powerful Īśāna and his consort is the tawny-yellow *krodharāja* Trailokyavijaya in the embrace of gSod-byed-ma (Ghātukī). To their right and left stand the devourer with the head of a hyena and the killer with that of a weasel.

In the nadir on cushions of the *bhūmipati* and his consort is the smoke coloured *krodharāja* Mahābala in the embrace of rDo-rje bskul-byad (Vajrāveśī). To their right and left stand the devourer with the head of a tawny bear and the killer with that of a rat.

Variations on a theme

The Byang-gter scholar 'Phrin-las bdud-'joms, in his introduction to the Northern Treasures Kīla cult (B4), identifies three discrete systems of Vajrakīla as practised in this school: the Kīla as a multicoloured deity, the Kīla as a black deity and the combined deity Kīla system.

The system of the multicoloured deity was taken from the golden southern cache which contained the *mahottarakīla* teachings within which the main deity has nine faces and 18 hands and the *daśakrodha* deities each have three faces and six hands. All of the deities in this scheme are of different colours.[344]

The black deity system came from the northern cache of iron and this is the category of *mantrabhīrukīla*. The lord of the *maṇḍala* in this system has three faces and six hands and the *daśakrodha* deities each have one face and two hands. All of the deities have the same blue-black colour. As it says in the *mūlatantra* BRT; "The *daśakrodha* couples and all of the messengers have dark blue ferocious forms. They have single faces and roll *kīla* in their two hands.[345] The lower halves of their bodies are sharp-pointed, three-edged nails. They have *vajra* wings and (are adorned with) the artefacts of charnel grounds. With cries of HŪṀ and PHAṬ they terrify

344 B4 202

345 The twenty *piśācī* are to be imagined brandishing iron hooks in their right hands and *kīla* in their left.

the world and subjugate all vicious beings without exception." Vajrakīla himself may also be described in this system as having the shape of a nail below the waist. Whatever form he takes, however, beneath his unshakeable weight squirm the demons of ego, helplessly pinned to the primordial ground of being from which they erroneously arose.

The combined deity system is made up of teachings taken from both the northern and the central caches and goes by the name of *Phur pa dril sgrub* ('the *kīla* rolling *sādhana*'). This system generally takes all the deities to be black in colour, in accordance with the BRT, but it also includes a visualisation of the gods of the *maṇḍala* arranged within the body of the main deity, as described in the system of the *mahottarakīla*.[346]

The *maṇḍala* as it is described in the Kīla manuals, however, is generally far more complex than this simple paradigm of the emperor Kīla and his court of ten wrathful kings. Vajrakīla and Tṛptacakra in the centre may be accompanied by the one-eyed queen of the *mātaraḥ*, Ekajatī, and the king of the oath-bound protectors, Vajrasādhu. They, in turn, are surrounded by three, four or five *kulakīla* and then, around them, the *daśakrodharāja* with their queens and animal-headed assistants. Outside that circle stand the 21 supreme sons (an epithet regularly applied to any important subordinate of the chief Kīla) consisting of the groups of body, speech and mind manifestations (seven in each). In the four directions there are then the four guardians of the gates.[347] Around the *maṇḍala* perimeter stand the various oath-bound protectors of the Kīla doctrines, chief among whom are the twelve sister goddesses led by the dog-faced Śvanmukhā,[348] their twelve brothers[349] and the group of 28 fierce *ḍākinī* of the four classes. Countless minor protective deities may be added to the retinue and these are arranged in circles ever further from the *maṇḍala* epicentre.

'Phrin-las bdud-'joms goes on to add that "Nowadays empowerments should be given from these three cycles in such a way that the *mantrabhīru*

---

346 B4 203

347 In the east is the goddess Vajrayakṣā with the head of a hoopoe bird holding in her hand an iron hook. In the south is Vajrabhairavī with the head of a magpie, holding a noose. In the west is Vajrāmṛtā with the head of an owl, holding fetters in her hand, and in the north is Vajramāraṇī with the head of a hawk, holding in her hand a bell.

348 For descriptions of these twelve see below, Chapter Nine.

349 Comprising the three groups of Rosewood, Iron and Conch. (See below, Chapter Nine.)

maṇḍala is raised up to fill the sky by the addition of the Mahottarakīla. This is the manner in which the *vidyādhara* received those empowerments and the manner in which they should bestow them."[350]

A handful of nails

In order to assist the meditator in the daunting task of visualising such a vast and complicated pattern of nails, it is proper for him to lay out a ritual *maṇḍala* as a focal point for his devotions. This may be drawn in coloured sand or any suitable medium with pegs of wood or metal arranged upon it in the proper positions of the deities.[351] In a short text appended to the *Drag sngags zab pa'i lo rgyus* it is written;

"As for the measurements of Vajrakīla: The chief nail measures 18 inches. The great nails measure 12 inches. The speedily moving nails are 12 inches. The struck nails are eight inches and the nails of the four rites are also eight inches. The messenger nails are eight inches long and the protecting nails are six inches. The averting nails are four inches and the outer nails are just three inches long. The body of the chief peg is in *yuganaddha* form and the *daśakrodha* great nails are also in *yuganaddha* like the lord. The speedily moving nails are the twenty messengers that devour and slay. The struck nails are the sons and these are like weapons. The four nails at the gates are the pegs of the four activities. Then there are the circles of the 21 struck pegs and the 12 nails around the border.

"The supreme laying out of the Vajrakīla *maṇḍala* involves the use of a thousand nails. The middling is prepared with one hundred nails and the lowest form is set out with either five or eleven nails."[352]

Here; 'chief' refers to Vajrakīla and his consort, 'great' means the nails of the five families and the ten *krodha* kings and queens, the 'speedily moving' ones are their animal-headed assistants, the 'struck nails' are the 21 sons and the 'nails of the four rites' are the guardians of the four *maṇḍala* gates. The 'messengers' are the twelve major protectors while the 'protecting', 'averting' and 'outer' nails are the various (optional)

350 B4 203

351 Illustrated in T. Marcotty, *Dagger Blessing* 30-31

352 B30 143

groups of minor protectors.[353] In this way the *maṇḍala* of meditation is to be set out on the ground by means of coloured powder and a handful of wooden or metal spikes.

Five nails are the Kīla of the five families (*pañcakula*) and this is the most basic of all Vajrakīla *maṇḍala*. Eleven nails are the lord Vajrakīla together with his primary retinue of ten *krodha* kings. The expressions 'one hundred' and 'a thousand nails' indicate that the size and complexity of the Kīla *maṇḍala* is potentially without limit.

A number of *kīla* that were said to have been used by Padmasambhava in just such *maṇḍala* rituals were discovered among the artefacts in the Byang-gter cache. The powerful nature of these *kīla* as objects of religious awe places them firmly in the category of magical fetishes. We have seen above how success in the rite of invocation is thought to empower these ritual pegs with the actual presence of the deity, so that the pegs themselves become animated and extremely potent occult instruments. The motif of the living nail is repeatedly encountered in Tibetan literature dealing with the Kīla cult,[354] for every hand-held nail may be thought of as the embodiment not only of a specific deity (primarily, of course, Vajrakīla himself) but also of the entire *maṇḍala* of violent spikes.[355] As an occult weapon, then, the significance of the *kīla* is both more specific and more flexible than its rather abstract counterpart, the *vajra*.

Whenever a ritual *vajra* is taken up into the hand by man or god, it must be held in the right because the *vajra* symbolises the male energy of appropriate activity (*upāya*) or compassion (*karuṇā*) which, in the symbolic system of the Vajrayāna, is located primarily on the right hand side of the body. It is never held in the left (female, *prajñā*) hand. The *kīla,* however, may represent either the wrathful male activity of compassionate killing (in which case it is held in the right hand, perhaps with a skull full of Māra's blood as its feminine counterpart in the left), or it may be held in the left hand as a symbol of the perfection of wisdom (*prajñā-*

---

353 The *Phur pa drag sngags kyi 'phrin las,* for example, invokes 360 male and female messengers in six groups of 60: the Dung (conch) from the east, lCags (iron) from the south, Zangs (copper) from the west, gYu (turquoise) from the north, gSer (gold) from the nadir and bSe (rosewood) from the zenith. C24 264-265

354 Alexandra David-Neel, in her *Magic and Mystery in Tibet* 104*ff*, relates the way in which she came to possess "a fine piece of ancient Tibetan art" belonging to a deceased lama, a supposedly animated *kīla* that few Tibetans would willingly touch.

355 See A29 199-200, as detailed above in the Introduction.

pāramitā) which it demonstrates by annihilating all the confused appearances of ignorance. In the latter case its partner in the right hand may perhaps be a hammer (with which to pound down the nail), a *vajra* (emblematic of power) or an iron hook (with which to drag forth the victim to be impaled). Most often it is seen to be held in the right hand by male deities and in the left by females so that each may use it in accordance with his or her own nature, but this is not an invariable rule. As we have seen above, the ultimately non-dual power of the *kīla* is most effectively employed by solemnly rolling it between the palms of both hands (or the foremost pair of hands in the case of a multi-armed deity).[356]

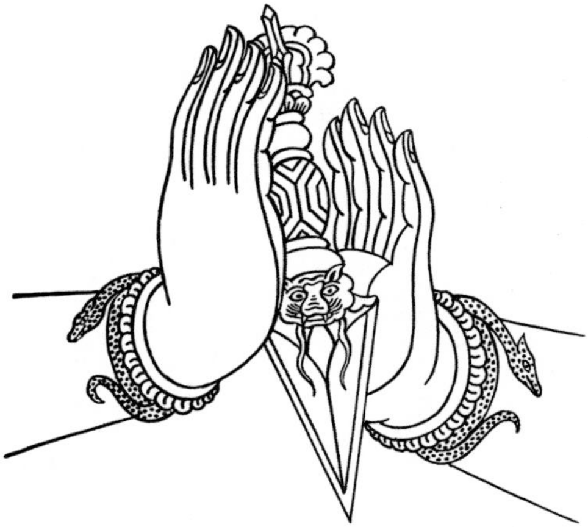

356 The solemn rolling of the *kīla* between the two palms accompanies the higher rites aimed at enlightenment. During the lower rites aimed at the subjugation of hostile forces, however, if a symbolic nail is employed it will most often be held in the left hand whilst being beaten into the ground with the aid of a *vajra* hammer held in the right (as is done in 'earth subduing' rituals which prepare the ground for the construction of a *maṇḍala,* etc.) or it will be held in either hand and used as a 'magic dagger' to stab and destroy an effigy of evil (as is done in countless rites of exorcism, etc.). A common partner to the *kīla* in such rites is the iron hook (held in the right hand), by which the 'demonic' is summoned and dragged down into form (an effigy) which is then destroyed by means of the *kīla* (held in the left). Icons of Vajrayāna *gurus* are also to be found in which these masters are depicted as wielding a *kīla* in each hand.

Table 1: The Eighteen Arms of Mahottarakīla

	Chapter Three		A28 184 & B11 535		A28 188-189 & B11 554-555	
	right	left	right	left	right	left
uppermost pair of hands	nine-pronged vajra	skull full of blood	nine-pronged vajra	skull full of Māra's blood	"anger must be destroyed by means of vajra wrath"	bindu in the sky
second pair	ten-spoked wheel	mass of fire	blazing wheel	mass of fire	"arousing the mind of supreme bodhicitta"[1]	"their hearts must be burned on the pinnacle of vajra fire"[2]
third pair	sword	khaṭvāṅga	sword	khaṭvāṅga	"blazing great blue weapon"	khaṭvāṅga of body, speech and mind
fourth pair	club	falcon	club	falcon	"must be seized! must be beaten!"	ABHICĀRA garuḍa
fifth pair	five-pronged vajra	viśvavajra	viśvavajra	kīla	viśvavajra of buddha activity	bhavakīla
sixth pair	kartṛkā	iron hook	amulet	vase	syllable HŪṀ, the abode of the lifespan[3]	vase of swirling nectar[4]
seventh pair	hammer	battle axe	iron hook	kartṛkā	iron hook of love and compassion	the kartṛkā that slays misleaders
eighth pair	dharmodaya	pot with amulet	hammer	A: secret sky B: blazing mortar	wind-creating hammer	A: secret sky B: blazing mortar
lowermost pair of hands	roll Mount Meru kīla		battle axe	blazing jewel	battle axe that smashes to fragments	wish-fulfilling jewel

Derived from the unpublished manuscript reproduced above in Chapter Three, the *Phur pa'i zur 'debs* (A28) and the *rDo rje phur pa che mchog gi 'phrin las* (B11)

[1 & 2] Verse missing in A28 [3] Personified as Hūṁkāra [4] Personified as Amṛtakuṇḍalin

CHAPTER FOUR

The Kīla chronicles: a *history of the Vajrakīla cycle from cultic sources*

The texts

Within the collections of Byang-gter Kīla treatises at our disposal are to be found five texts of the *lo rgyus* ('history') genre. Two of these, A26 (B51) & B30 (B55, C18), deal with the *mantrabhīru* (black deity) system and one, B13, deals with the origin of the *mahottara* (multicoloured deity) system. Then there is the *Gong khug ma*[357] (A27, etc.) and the useful commentary B4, written by 'Phrin-las bdud-'joms as an introduction to the history and doctrines of Vajrakīla for the benefit of his own disciples on the occasion of their ritual *abhiṣeka*. One further text is B40, which styles itself *nidāna* or introductory preamble outlining the circumstances in which the Vajrakīla cycle was initially revealed. Rather than historical records in the modern sense, these Kīla chronicles that inform the present chapter are accumulations of religious myth, products of an oral tradition of pious hagiography. Their view of the genesis and transmission of the Vajrakīla doctrines naturally diverges substantially from that outlined above in Chapter Two.

The revelations of mahāyoga

The Byang-gter commentator 'Phrin-las bdud-'joms, using as his sources the traditional *tantras* and *āgama,* describes the origin of *mahāyoga* doctrines in the symbolic language of Buddhist mysticism;

"In the *dharmadhātu* palace of Akaniṣṭha, the *dharmakāya* teacher Samantabhadra, acting within the unceasing state of the inseparable nature of form and wisdom transcending all words and syllables, emanated the circle of his own radiant awareness in the form of the five *jina* of the *saṁbhogakāya* shining clearly within his heart, stainless and naturally arisen. Having the spontaneous energy of great compassion, the various playful forms of peaceful and wrathful activity were made manifest. With an ocean of melodies of words, beyond speech or expression, these set into

---

357 A term of reference for the pith instruction lineage of Ye-shes mtsho-rgyal. A44 328, A46 416. According to 'Phrin-las bdud-'joms, the teachings thus transmitted concern the *mantrabhīru-kīla* . B4 196. Cf. above, note 75.

motion the wheel of the Dharma vehicle of the original meaning for the vast numbers of *vidyādhara* and *ḍākinī* and the male and female *bodhisattvas* established on the tenth *bhūmi.*"[358]

Such, then, is the cultic (emic) view of the origin of these doctrines which are regarded as the bearers of absolute truth, inseparably participating in a play (*līlā*) of divine reality. As such they remain essentially inexpressible, abiding forever in the natural condition of the *dharmadhātu* so as to be accessible only to those most spiritually advanced beings whose minds have already attained a cognition of highest truth. Their origin remains, therefore, permanently unoriginated and the sound of the *tantra* being promulgated is said to be the natural sound of the *dharmadhātu*.

In order to display these truths in a more relative way, however, some movement had to occur that broke away from the relentless self-absorption of the primordially enlightened state. 'Phrin-las bdud-'joms speaks of this outward movement in terms of a compassionate radiation from the heart of the supreme being;

"In particular the teacher Vajrasattva,[359] arising in the form of Vajraheruka, emanated from his heart the supreme son of all the buddhas by the name of Vajrarākṣasa or the heroic Vajrakumāra. This wrathful manifestation destroyed the great demon Matraṅgara Rudra and all the other *māra, rākṣasa* and unruly demons of pride. Having ground their bodies down to dust, he bound their consciousnesses under oath and established them as protectors of the doctrine.[360]

"Upon the peak of Mount Meru, which was the place of subjugation[361] of Māra (Rudra), having produced the mind of great wrath, he turned the wheel of the doctrine of fierce *mantra* for all the worldly arrogant ones and for the *mātaraḥ* and *ḍākinī* who had achieved *siddhi* by virtue of their wisdom and conduct. In this way, all of his disciples became matured into

---

358 B4 178

359 Vajrasattva is here to be understood as the *saṁbhogakāya* of Samantabhadra.

360 The *Phur pa gleng gzhi* says that Vajrarākṣasa arose as the wrathful embodi-ment of all the gods who had been unable to subdue Rudra by peaceful means. In this guise he overthrew Rudra and turned all the demons into his servants. B40 272

361 *bKa' thang shel brag ma* VI gives the place of subjugation as Mount Malaya.

buddhahood and this is known as the *rGyal ba'i dgongs rgyud,* the direct transmission of the Buddha's understanding."[362]

This myth is a close variant of the one outlined in the preceding chapter. Here, however, Vajrakīla is produced *in order to* subdue Rudra – not *as a result of* that subjugation. Thus is established the first lineage of Vajrakīla doctrines: 'the lineage of the Buddha's understanding'. The place is the peak of Mount Meru, the time follows the overthrow of Rudra, the teacher is Vajrakīla himself and the retinue consists of male and female 'arrogant worldly gods'.[363]

"After that the *yakṣa* Vajrapāṇi, keeper of the secret treasures of all *tathāgata,* gathered together the instructions in the great vehicle of secret *mantra* and, upon the blazing iron peak of Mount Malaya, he taught those doctrines again and again to the *vidyādhara* who had assembled there.[364] In particular he gave instructions to the five *vidyādhara* who were the leaders from the realms of *deva, nāga,* men, *yakṣa* and *rākṣasa.*[365] The *vidyādhara* of the *rākṣasa,* Matyaupāyika by name, having gathered together the words and syllables of the teachings, produced bound volumes of books in verse.

"Later, as a result of his beatitude, the fortunate king Indrabodhi of Avartamu in the country of Zahor, a monarch of much merit, saw seven special omens in his dreams: 1) Symbols of perfected Body, Speech and Mind melted into his body. 2) There was the gathering of a religious assembly. 3) Precious volumes of teachings fell down from the sky. 4) All

---

362 B4 178-179. According to the *Phur pa gleng gzhi,* the teachings were transmitted to the buddhas of the *pañcakula,* to the *bodhisattvas* known as 'the three lords' (Avalokiteśvara, Mañjuśrī and Vajrapāṇi), to 'the maroon *ḍākinī* with topknot' (which may refer to either Ekajaṭī or Karmendrāṇī) and to the three-faced Brahmā. They were then transmitted to the *vidyādhara* of the gods (Indra), *nāga* (Takṣaka) and men (King Indrabhūti who, having learned the 18 *tantra* of the *mahāyoga* from Vajrapāṇi, disseminated them widely in the human realm). B40 272-273

363 The place, teacher, time, doctrines and retinue are the 'five invariable features' (*pañcaniyata*) of all Buddhist teachings.

364 Other texts in the Byang-gter tradition, however, say that the one who gathered together all the teachings of the primordial buddha was Vajragarbha. bsKal-bzang padma dbang-phyug, *Autobiography* 373

365 "The god's name was Grags-ldan phyogs-skyong (Yaśasvī), the *yakṣa* was sKar-mda'-gdong (Ulkāmukha), the *rākṣasa* was bLo-gros thabs-ldan (Maty-aupāyika), the *nāga* was kLu-rgyal 'jog-po (Takṣaka) and the human was Dri-med grags-pa (Vimalakīrti)."
Thinley Norbu, *The Small Golden Key* 10

people upheld vows of religious discipline. 5) There was the celebration of a great religious offering ceremony. 6) Jewels and precious objects fell down like rain. 7) He received the prediction of his enlightenment.

"After that it really happened that some texts written in ink of beryl upon sheets of golden paper landed on the top of his house, perfectly in accordance with the oneiric indications. At that time the king was unable to understand even a single syllable of those volumes and so he offered up his prayers to Vajrapāṇi, the master of secret teachings. As a consequence of his devotion he met Vajrapāṇi face to face, receiving blessings and empowerments, and Vajrapāṇi taught to the king the general 18 classes of *mahāyogatantra*." [366]

This episode of the myth brings the teachings into the human realm. The name of Indrabodhi (or Indrabhūti) is deeply embedded in the early history of Buddhist *tantra* but, unfortunately, the man behind the name remains something of an enigma. So many legends are told about him that all scholars agree there must have been at least two (possibly three) persons so designated. Keith Dowman asserts that the king Indrabodhi who revealed the Vajrakīla doctrines and taught them to Dhanasaṁskṛta (who transmitted them to Padmasambhava) is not the same as the one mentioned here upon whose palace roof the texts were originally said to have fallen.[367] Clearly, however, our present author thinks otherwise.

What we may conjecture from the myth in its present form is that a certain wealthy man ('king', *kṣatriya*?) somehow or other came to possess manuscripts of an esoteric nature which he was unable to comprehend. The texts themselves could have come from anywhere, for magical teachings have enjoyed a wide circulation in India since prehistory. Perhaps his own interest in the mysterious contents of these manuscripts prompted him to copy the words (or have them copied) in gold and to ponder on their meaning. Eventually, no doubt, a wandering *yogin* would have been found who could assume the mantle of Vajrapāṇi[368] and instruct the king in their religious significance. 'Indrabodhi' is as much an epithet as a name and it is not difficult to imagine a wealthy patron of these doctrines, through whose help they were first propagated on any significant scale, being awarded such a title.

---

366 B4 179-180

367 See S. Karmay, "King Tsa/Dza and Vajrayāna", and K. Dowman, *Masters of Mahāmudrā* 232*ff*., for Indrabhūti's historiography.

368 Some sources cite Vajrasattva as the king's preceptor.

Whatever the historical veracity behind the legends, however, it is stated in all the religious chronicles that the 18 categories of *mahāyogatantra* were received simultaneously by the king Indrabodhi. These include the *mūlatantra Guhyagarbhamāyājāla* and the 17 explanatory *tantra* consisting of the five of Body, Speech, Mind, Good Qualities and Enlightened Activities, the five *tantra* of *sādhana,* the five concerning aspects of conduct plus two additional *tantra.*[369] Teachings of Vajrakīla are to be found within those 18 categories under the headings '*tantra* of Enlightened Activities'[370] and 'the five *tantra* of *sādhana*', the fifth of which is the *Phur pa bcu gnyis* (*Kīla-tantra* in twelve sections).[371]

In particular, the Kīla chronicles, such as the *Concise History*[372] written by gTsang mkhan-chen and the *gNam lcags spu gri lo rgyus chos 'byung* by bDud-'joms rinpoche,[373] say that these Vajrakīla doctrines were taught by Indrabodhi to Dhanasaṁskṛta who then passed them on to Padmasambhava, Vimalamitra and the Nepali Śīlamañju (see below) who extensively revised and commented upon them whilst in retreat at Yang-le-shod (present-day Pharping, Nepal).

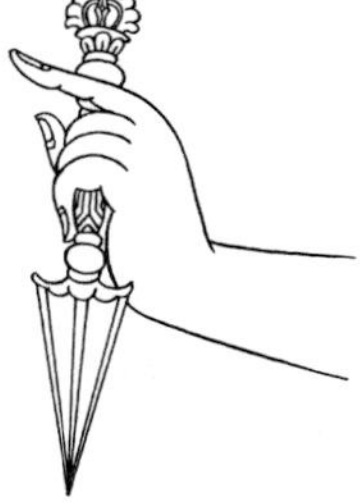

369 Tulku Thondup, *Buddha Mind* 30-31, lists the *Sangs rgyas mnyam sbyor* as the *tantra* of the Body, *Zla gsang thig le* as the *tantra* of Speech, *gSang ba 'dus pa* as the *tantra* of Mind, *dPal mchog dang po* as the *tantra* of Good Qualities and *Karmamālā* as the *tantra* of Enlightened Activities. The *Heruka rol ba, rTa mchog rol ba, sNying rje rol ba, bDud rtsi rol ba* and the *Phur pa rol ba (Phur pa bcu gnyis)* are the five *tantra* of *sādhana,* the *gLang chen rab 'bog, Ri bo brtsegs pa, Ye shes rngam glog, Dam tshig bkod pa* and the *Ting 'dzin rtse gcig* are the five *tantra* of *karma,* and the two supplementary *tantra* are the *rNam snang sgyu 'phrul drva ba* and the *Thabs kyi zhags pa.* All of these cycles of texts are to be found in the NGB.

370 NGB 325, the *Karmakīla-tantra,* attests in its colophon to an affinity with the *Karmamālā* of vol.17.

371 *Phur pa bcu gnyis.* NGB 220

372 The *Phur pa'i chos 'byung bsdus pa* is to be found in gTsang mkhan-chen, *rDo rje phur pa'i chos 'byung* 161-196.

373 K. Dowman, *Sky Dancer* 350, n.32

Apportionment of the sādhana

The *mahāyoga* treatises in general are divided into two sections: the 18 *tantra* (as above) and the eight classes of *sādhana.*[374]

Concerning this second division of the *mahāyoga,* our author 'Phrin-las bdud-'joms comments;[375]

"As for the very special eight great *heruka-sādhana,* the general *tantra* concerned with these as well as the very necessary oral instructions and so on, these were all entrusted to the hand of the *ḍākinī* queen, Mahā-karmendrāṇī. Having placed each one of these eight cycles of teachings into its own individual jewelled casket, she sealed them up as treasure within the body of the Śaṁkarakūṭa *stūpa* in the fearful charnel ground Śītavana. Later they were taken out and distributed amongst the eight great *vidyādhara,* themselves the emanations of supreme beings.

"With regard to this, it is written in the Vajrakīla text known as the *Cittaguhyakāya-tantra* ..." (he then cites a prophecy from the second chapter of our text A3, B10, C1 – see below, Chapter Five – concerning the eight great *vidyādhara* and goes on to say;)

"As it was prophesied in that quotation, eight incarnate *vidyādhara* came to be born in the world and each of them spent a considerable period of time engaged in strict ascetic discipline in the charnel grounds. After a while, when the time had come to bring forth those eight *tantra,* they gathered together at the great *stūpa* of Śaṁkarakūṭa and stood before the queen of the *ḍākinī.* "What is it that you want?" she demanded. "We want the *tantra*" they replied. And at that the *ḍākinī* queen entrusted one of the eight great cycles to each of the *ācārya* gathered before her and the sky was spontaneously filled with music."[376]

Despite the fairytale trappings of this episode I believe that here, too, we may profitably search an historically valid core. All traditions of the

---

374 The *tantra* section, however, includes many *sādhana* while the *sādhana* section also contains *tantra*. According to bDud-'joms rinpoche, the *sādhana* section has the two traditions of (a) the transmitted precepts and (b) the revealed treasures. He rationalises others' conflicting views by claiming Prabhahasti as the inheritor of the first tradition of Vajrakīla and Padma-sambhava as the inheritor of the second tradition, revealed from the Śaṁkarakūṭa *stūpa* by Karmendrāṇī. NSTB I.475-483

375 B4 180-181

376 B4 182

rNying-ma school in Tibet[377] assert this cycle of eight meditative practices to have been among the volumes of teachings compiled and arranged by the celestial *bodhisattva*[378] and subsequently entrusted to the *ḍākinī* queen Mahākarmendrāṇī. She is said to have divided the teachings into three groups under the headings 'General' (*phyi rgyud*), 'Special' (*dgos rgyud*) and 'Particular' (*bye brag gi rgyud*). In this regard, Yukei Matsunaga points out that the eighth century Indian commentator Buddhaguhya categorised tantric texts into the two divisions: *kriyā* and *yoga. Kriyātantra* were further subdivided into the 'General' (*spyi'i cho ga*) and 'Particular' (*bye brag*) classes.[379] Legend then says that the *ḍākinī* queen put the five General *tantra* together with the ten Special *tantra* of the *bDe gshegs 'dus pa* into a casket made of five precious jewels. The eight Particular *tantra* were placed into eight different caskets and all of these teachings were concealed in the Śaṁkarakūṭa *stūpa*.

Tarthang Tulku[380] says that, with regard to the Buddha's teachings, the *sūtra* were preserved by Ānanda and the outer *tantra* by Vajrapāṇi.[381] The inner *tantra*, which were taught by the *ādibuddha* Samantabhadra, were received by Caṇḍavajrapāṇi[382] who passed them on to Mahākarmendrāṇi who hid them away in the Śaṁkarakūṭa *stūpa* in Śītavana cemetery. In the base of the *stūpa* she hid all the texts belonging to the *sGyu 'phrul* cycle. In the middle she concealed the *bDe gshegs 'dus pa,* in which the *aṣṭa-mahāsādhana* (*sgrub chen bka' brgyad*) are taught within a single

---

377 See; Tulku Thondup, *The Tantric Tradition,* and Gyurme Dorje, *The Guhyagarbha-tantra.* Also K. Dowman, *Sky Dancer* 274*ff.*

378 T. Thondup, *op.cit.* 17, identifies this *bodhisattva* as Vajradharma. Other sources say either Vajrasattva or Vajrapāṇi. It is interesting to note here that Vajradharma is the foremost *bodhisattva* in the retinue of Amitābha, the buddha most adored by followers of the rNying-ma school because he is lord of the Lotus family (*padmakula*), whereas Vajrasattva (Vajrapāṇi) is the foremost of those in the circle of Akṣobhya. See the *Sarvarahasya-tantra* (A. Wayman, 1984), verses 83 & 91. The Byang-gter school also has a tradition of naming this *bodhisattva* Vajragarbha (see note 364, above, and also Chapter One).

379 J.W. de Jong, "A New History of Tantric Literature in India" 93
Cf. S. Tsuda, "Classification of Tantras"

380 *Crystal Mirror* V 272-274

381 For notes concerning the importance of Vajrapāṇi in the tantric tradition, see "Vajrapāṇi (alias Vajradhara) becomes preeminent" in D. Snellgrove, *Indo-Tibetan Buddhism* 134*ff.*

382 This distinction between Vajrapāṇi and Caṇḍavajrapāṇi is not apparent in other schools.

maṇḍala. The *bye brag sgos rgyud* texts were hidden in the entrance gates, the *gSang ba yongs rdzogs* in the flute, the *Rang byung rang shar* in the rim of the spire and the *Sangs rgyas mnyam sbyor* in the middle of the spire. All of these texts contain teachings pertaining to the practices of *mahāyoga* (*utpattikrama*) and *anuyoga* (*saṁpannakrama*). The *atiyoga* teachings of *Yang gsang bla med yang ti nag po* were hidden at the very top of the *stūpa* spire and then guardians were appointed to protect those precious texts until their appropriate time of withdrawal.

Tāranātha,[383] in a more general way, confirms the sealing up of the *tantra* "into eight great gold coffers which were put into silver vessels which, in turn, were put into vessels made of the seven precious gems" and concealed within a *stūpa* in the Śītavana charnel ground, a favourite meeting place of tantric *yogins.*

When, in later times, eight of the foremost *siddhācārya* of India gathered together at this *stūpa,* the *ḍākinī* queen appeared before them and distributed the *aṣṭamahāsādhana* teachings among them. The casket containing the *tantra* of Yamāntaka she entrusted to Mañjuśrīmitra and the casket of *tantra* pertaining to Hayagrīva she gave to Nāgārjunagarbha. The casket of Śrīheruka she entrusted to Hūṁkāra, Amṛtaguṇa to Vimalamitra, Vajrakīla to Prabhahasti,[384] Mātaraḥ to Dhanasaṁskṛta (holder of the earlier lineage of Vajrakīla), Lokastotrapūjā to Rambuguhya Devacandra, and the Mantrabhīru *tantra*[385] she gave to Śāntigarbha. Each of these eight *ācārya,* having successfully accomplished supreme *siddhi* by means of the particular doctrine that had been revealed to him, subsequently entrusted that teaching to his own disciples and in this way the *aṣṭamahāsādhana* became known in the world.

The Sino-Japanese tradition[386] tells of *tantra* being taught by Mahāvairocana (another name for the *ādibuddha*) to the *bodhisattva* Vajrasattva (whom David Snellgrove equates with Vajrapāṇi[387]) who kept them for

---

383 D. Templeman, *Origin of the Tārā Tantra* 32

384 The master Prabhahasti, from whom Padmasambhava received the Vajrakīla *tantra,* was a *bhikṣu* by the name of Śākyaprabhā before being initiated into the *tantra*. Several sources, however, (including our commentator 'Phrin-las bdud-'joms) cite Padmasambhava as the recipient of the Kīla doctrines on this particular occasion even though (see below) Prabhahasti is generally acclaimed to have been Padmasambhava's Vajrakīla preceptor.

385 Not to be confused with the *kīlamantrabhīru*.

386 A. Snodgrass, *The Matrix and Diamond World Maṇḍalas* 111

387 D. Snellgrove, *Indo-Tibetan Buddhism* 136

several hundred years before sealing them in an iron *stūpa* in South India. There they remained for several further centuries before being taken out by Nāgārjuna. This account, because it so clearly parallels the Tibetan version of events, raises several interesting issues. According to the Tibetan version, all eight cycles of *mahāyoga sādhana* arose in India simultaneously although it is quite clear from historical sources that only three of the cycles[388] were then widely spread in India by those who received them. The other five seem to have been largely lost in the subcontinent although all eight were transmitted to Tibet where their lines of transmission have remained unbroken to the present day. Whether the *stūpa* within which the doctrines had been concealed (i.e. the place of origin of the *tantra*) was in the north or the south of India is a question over which many scholars have been vexed. The esoteric school itself, of course, is not concerned with such problems and we find the equation *stūpa* = *caitya* = *citta*[389] which indicates that the place of origin is the *stūpa* (repository of buddhahood) in the mind. The Tibetan tradition of the *ḍākinī* queen can also be interpreted in this way if for '*ḍākinī* queen' we read 'muse'. Is the Tibetan account a later elaboration of a former tradition? Or has the legend of Nāgārjuna been abstracted from a fuller account by those who have a vested interest in that one person? If these two tales are mere fiction, how do we account for their similarity and for the fact that Nāgārjuna plays a prominent role in both?

The Tibetan tradition claims that, at the time when the eight great *sādhana* were first revealed, the moment was not opportune to open the casket containing the ten Special *tantra* of the *bDe gshegs 'dus pa* in which the eight are taught within a single *maṇḍala* and therefore that casket was replaced within the *stūpa*. It was later taken out when the *stūpa* was reopened by Padmasambhava who is also said to have received the *sādhana* in their individual forms directly from the eight *siddha* to whom they had originally been entrusted.[390] In the light of this rather confusing mass of conflicting details, all that may be said with any confidence is that, according to Tibetan sources, the Vajrakīla doctrines were taught in

388 Yamāntaka, Hayagrīva and Śrīheruka, the *sādhana* of Body, Speech and Mind.

389 A. Snodgrass, *op.cit.* 112. The Japanese tradition emphasises this 'inner interpretation' of the legend of the *stūpa,* for an elaboration of which see Taiko Yamasaki, *Shingon: Japanese Esoteric Buddhism* 88-89.

390 Some sources (see above, note 384) include Padmasambhava among the original eight.

India within the general context of the *yoganiruttaratantra* revealed in arcane fashion to a select group of prominent Buddhist *yogins* thought to have been active at some time during the eighth century CE. That particular transmission of *tantra, āgama* and *upadeśa* is known in Tibet by the name 'the *vidyādhara*'s lineage' or 'the lineage of symbols' (*rig 'dzin brda' brgyud*).

Although the chronicles distinguish clearly between the separate transmissions of the earlier corpus of Vajrakīla doctrines, said to have arisen at the time of the enigmatic king Indrabodhi, and this later tradition taken out from the *stūpa,* the transmitted precepts themselves are accorded no differentiating characteristics.

Another figure mentioned in several of the early chronicles is Mi-thod-pa-can, the *kāpālika* brahmin. gTsang mkhan-chen cites this mysterious personage as the originator of a line of Vajrakīla teachings and even goes so far as to say that it was he who gave the teachings to Karmendrāṇī which she then hid in the Śaṁkarakūṭa *stūpa.*[391] Such statements appear tacitly to admit the non-Buddhist origin of many of the *kīla* doctrines. More will be said about the *kāpālika* below when we come to deal with the provenance of the Mahottarakīla cycle but let us look first at two further historical puzzles: the teacher Padmasambhava and the huge cycle of Vajrakīla doctrines refered to in Tibetan chronicles as the '*Vidyottama-tantra* in one hundred thousand sections'.

Ācārya Padmasambhava

An important variant in the many biographies of Padmasambhava has been highlighted by Anne-Marie Blondeau,[392] on the basis of which they may be classified into two groups. The factor is mode of birth and the two categories of biography are those that propose a womb birth (*jarāyuja*) and those that speak of a miraculous birth (*upapāduka*) from the heart of a lotus. The miraculous birth stories, which are common in *gter ma* litera-

---

391 gTsang mkhan-chen, *rDo rje phur pa'i chos 'byung* 163
See also K. Dowman, *Sky Dancer* 350, n.32

392 A.M. Blondeau, "Analysis of the Biographies of Padmasambhava According to Tibetan Tradition"

ture, are the most widely known[393] but the *bka' ma* texts which are supposed to have come directly from India unanimously agree on a womb birth.[394] Of particular interest to us is the fact that the Vajrakīla chronicles support the notion of womb birth.[395]

'Phrin-las bdud-'joms[396] outlines the biography of Padmasambhava as it is told in the Kīla tradition by saying that king Manusiddhi[397] of Oḍḍiyāna, the son of gTsug-phud rigs-bzang,[398] had a son by the name of Śāntarakṣita.[399] "The boy had a red and white complexion and bore the marks of one who belonged to the *padmakula*. He was fully accomplished in all arts and sciences. Knots were to be seen at the top and bottom of his spine and his torso had eight sides to it (like the handle of a ritual *kīla*). The lower portion of his body was triangular in shape and his face and eyes were like half moons. With his red hair, abundant signs of Vajrakīla were evident at his birth.

---

393 Many of these *gter ma* accounts have been translated into English. Douglas & Bays, *The Life and Liberation;* Evans-Wentz, *Tibetan Book of the Great Liberation;* K. Dowman, *Legend of the Great Stūpa;* etc. Interestingly the womb birth story of Śāntarakṣita is found in the *Padma bka' thang* IX as a previous incarnation.

394 With regard to the *siddha*'s life in India, Tāranātha is said to have compiled his *rNam thar rgya gar lugs* relying "on Indian oral traditions inherited from his (Indian) masters". Blondeau, *op.cit.* 47

395 Although styled a *nidāna* for the Vajrakīla cycle, the *gter ma* text B40 (said to have been copied out three times and hidden in Mon-kha sprang-yag gi bag, sPa-gro stag-tshang and Zang-zang lha-brag) adopts the standard *gter ma* position of miraculous birth. *Viz:* Following the *nirvāṇa* of Śākyamuni, all the buddhas of the ten directions consulted together in order to prevent the decline of the doctrines and, from the paradise of Sukhāvatī in the west, the buddha Amitābha directed his thoughts towards Śākyamuni's *kṣetra,* the southern continent of Jambudvīpa. There, for the sake of all beings, Padmasambhava was spontaneously produced with neither cause (*hetu*) nor condition (*pratyaya*) in "the playful Sindhu ocean" (the Indus valley). He was endowed with the blessings of all the buddhas of the *dharmakāya,* the empowerments of all the buddhas of the *sambhogakāya* and the active instructions of all the buddhas of the *nirmāṇakāya*. B40 273-274

396 B4 183-188

397 The *bKa' thang shel brag ma* calls him prince Baddhaśikha, which is possibly the name of his father (cf. following note).
Douglas & Bays, *op.cit.* 64

398 *Śikhā Kulabhadra. bKra-shis stobs-rgyal, *Gu ru'i rnam thar ngo mtshar phun tshogs rgya mtsho* 174. (Blondeau, *op.cit.* 46)

399 Blondeau cites several variants of this name including Rakṣantara, Rakṣanta and Śāntarakṣi.

"When he grew up he went to India with his two best friends and became known by the name of Śākyasiṁha (one of the eight names of guru Padma) after being ordained as a monk by the teacher Śākyabodhi." This teacher is most likely to be Śākyaprabhā (= Prabhahasti), as will be confirmed below. Although our author is not specific on this point, it seems as if Padmasambhava's 'two best friends' (later identified as Vimalamitra and Śīlamañju) were also ordained at this time and given the religious names Śākyamitra and Śākya bshes-gnyen (really one name in two languages).

Louis de La Vallée Poussin, in his introduction to the *Pañcakrama,* places Śākyamitra in the eighth century as a pupil of Śākyaprabhā, an expert in the *vinaya.* Śākyamitra is said to have come from Kośala, to have written a commentary on the STTS and then travelled north to the Himalayan regions during the later period of his life where he worked extensively for the propagation of the Buddhist Dharma.[400] In *The Blue Annals* he is counted among the four most prominent recipients of the GST in the line of Saraha and Nāgārjuna, belonging to the fifth generation after King Indrabodhi.[401] Śākyamitra's historicity and awareness of *kīla* rites is therefore beyond doubt.

Following that, 'Phrin-las bdud-'joms tells of the meeting in Zahor[402] of Padmasambhava and the *ācārya* Prabhahasti, under whose guidance he is supposed to have received the secret *niruttara* empowerments of the *Māyājāla* cycle and heard in full the doctrines of the one hundred thousand sections of the Kīla *Vidyottama-tantra*. It must be presumed here that these were the Vajrakīla teachings obtained by Prabhahasti from the *stūpa* in Śītavana charnel ground. When speaking of the opening of that *stūpa,* however, our author claims Padmasambhava himself to have been the original recipient of the Kīla doctrines. Whatever their origin, the teachings of Vajrakīla have by this time supposedly grown in bulk (or metaphysical importance?) to the famous 'one hundred thousand sections of the *Vidyottama-tantra*'.

---

400 Louis de La Vallée Poussin, *Pañcakrama* ix

401 The lineage is given as; Indrabodhi to an unnamed *yoginī,* to Viśukalpa, to Saraha, to Nāgārjuna, to Śākyamitra. G. Roerich, *The Blue Annals* 359

402 Our text C36, in which the blessings of Vajrakīla are invoked from the various sites sanctified by their importance in the Kīla chronicles, invites Śākyaprabhā the *bhikṣu* (Prabhahasti the *vajrācārya*) from the land of Zahor.

In another, better known version of this legend, Padmasambhava is supposed to have received the Vajrakīla doctrines from Prabhahasti (a hierarch of Nālandā) in response to his plea for help in subduing the obstacles to his final enlightenment (referred to by the tantric term *mahāmudrā*) that had arisen during a period of meditative retreat in Nepal. In terms of religious mythology, this latter story is far more potent for it correlates the teacher Padmasambhava with the Buddha Śākyamuni who subdued the demon Māra on the eve of his own enlightenment. It also serves to highlight in dramatic fashion the chief value of the Vajrakīla doctrines in the eyes of its cult (to subdue all obstacles to omniscience) and to inspire faith in those doctrines as the supreme method for this task. Interestingly, also, the demonic force in this legend is embodied in the form of a gigantic serpent that "held back the waters of life" (rain) so that the process of creation (spring growth and reproduction) could not occur. Few of the cult initiates in Tibet, however, would be aware of the parallel between this legend and the earlier Vedic myth of Indra *versus* Vṛtra.

The earliest extant redaction of this episode from the life of Padmasambhava is in the document from Dūnhuáng classified as Pelliot tibétain 44. This small but historically significant text, scrutinised by F.A.Bischoff and Charles Hartman in 1971,[403] is "possibly the oldest document in existence referring to Padmasambhava" and was considered by G. Tucci[404] as "a major proof of the historicity of the *siddha*". It is also a major piece of evidence concerning Padmasambhava's transmission of the *kīla* doctrines from India.[405]

According to the later *gter ma* tradition,[406] Padmasambhava was accompanied on that occasion by the Nepalese maiden Śākyadevī whom he had met at the ancient *vihāra* of Śaṅkhu[407] in the northeast corner of the Kathmandu valley.[408] She apparently suffered from a slight physical de-

---

403 F.A. Bischoff & C.Hartman, "Padmasambhava's Invention of the Phur-bu"

404 TPS 88

405 In the opinion of Samten Karmay, the Kīla doctrines are the only teachings among the many said to have been transmitted by Padmasambhava for which there exists reliable historical evidence.
S. Karmay, *The Great Perfection* 6

406 Douglas & Bays, *The Life and Liberation* 315
K. Dowman, *Sky Dancer* 268. Etc.

407 Built in the second or third century CE. M. Slusser, *Nepal Maṇḍala* 271

408 For a description of Śaṅkhu Vihāra see K. Dowman, *A Buddhist Guide* 274-277, and M. Slusser, *op.cit. passim.*

formity (identified by the saint as omens of wisdom and virtue)[409] and had been abandoned by her father following the death of his wife in childbirth.[410] No mention is made of her in the early chronicles of the *bka' ma* tradition (such as the Pelliot 44 manuscript) but it is said by some today that she continues to emanate in the person of the Rāja Kumārī of Basantapur, one of the 'virgin goddesses' of Kathmandu.[411]

Our author 'Phrin-las bdud-'joms says that Padmasambhava made his journey to Nepal with the express intention of gaining the *siddhi* of a *mahāmudrā-vidyādhara*. This resolve on final enlightenment is clearly intended as a correlate to the Buddha's similar resolve as he made his seat beneath the *bodhi* tree. There, in a rock cave at Pharping (*yang le shod kyi brag phug*), Padmasambhava (and his tantric consort Śākyadevī?) engaged in the *sādhana* of the 'Nine Lamps of Heruka'.[412] In response to that, says 'Phrin-las bdud-'joms (again a clear allusion to Māra's response to Śākyamuni's resolve), "the vicious *nāga* of that vicinity known as Gyong-po (*Nāgakhara, 'Cruel Serpent') caused the earth to quake and no rain to fall from the sky for three years". All sources speak of this prolonged period of severe drought during which the crops were desiccated and large numbers of people died. The vicissitudes of drought and famine proving an insurmountable obstacle to his realisation of supreme *bodhi,* Padmasambhava dispatched two Nepalese messengers to India with a measure of powdered gold and a request for help to the *paṇḍits* and *siddhas* of Nālandā university, an institution renowned for the ritual expertise of its inmates. The Dūnhuáng manuscript names the two messengers as Shag-kya (Śākya?) Yur and I-So, whilst the *Lha 'dre bka' thang* identifies them as Ji-la ji-sa and Kun-la kun-sa-zhi.[413] The biography of Ye-shes mtsho-rgyal[414] confirms the association of Jila Jisad (Jila Jipha) with Śākyadevī and the cave at Yang-le-shod but makes no reference at all to Kun-la kun-sa-zhi. While the *Lha 'dre bka' thang* refers to Jila Jisad as "a practitioner of medicine", the biographer of Ye-shes

---

409 Her fingers and toes were webbed like the feet of a duck, a characteristic traditionally associated with a *mahāpuruṣa*.

410 Her story forms the subject matter of the *Padma bka' thang* LIII

411 K. Dowman, *Sky Dancer* 269

412 *Yang dag mar me dgu*. 'Yang-dag-thugs' being the rNying-ma-pa appellation of the *heruka* Cakrasaṁvara (Śrīheruka).

413 A.M. Blondeau, "Le Lha 'dre bka thang" 31. Keith Dowman's sources ("The Buddhist Guide" 251) calls them Jila Jisad and Kun-la ku-bzhi.

414 Tarthang Tulku, *Mother of Knowledge* 64. K.Dowman, *Sky Dancer* 54 & 317

mtsho-rgyal thought of him as "a king of Nepal", hardly a likely candidate for the post of messenger boy. Although not mentioned here by our author 'Phrin-las bdud-'joms, the Byang-gter tradition generally names one of the messengers as Jinamitra. This tradition believes, furthermore, that Jinamitra, having fulfilled his task in Nepal on behalf of Padmasambhava, promptly died and was reborn in Tibet as sNa-nam rdo-rje bdud-'joms in time to act as the messenger dispatched by king Khri Srong-lde'u-btsan to India to fetch Padmasambhava from Bodh Gayā.[415]

The Kīla Vidyottama-tantra

The assistance said to have been offered to Padmasambhava by those most knowledgeable Buddhist experts of his day took the form of 'the Kīla *Vidyottama-tantra* in one hundred thousand sections', a set of teachings so massive that his two messengers "could barely carry it".[416] A text by the name of *Vidyottama-tantra* (*Āryavidyottama-mahātantra*) is found in all editions of the *bKa' 'gyur* (P.402) but this is not the one referred to here. If there ever was in India such a text or collection of texts bearing this name and focussed on the doctrines of Vajrakīla, then it was lost long ago. More probably, however, the name is intended generally as *locus ascriptus* for the store of ideas pertaining to the deity without reference to a particular presentation of precepts. It may thus serve as a generic term for the vast conglomeration of individual treatises such as those currently found in Tibet (the title pages of many of which proclaim their descent from such a matrix) as well as to the oral tradition that accompanies them.[417] Also, it is not necessary to assume that this huge volume of teachings was ever written down on paper, for mystics the world over have always been capable of reading volumes into a few key words or sentences. The staggering weight of the doctrines conveyed at this time may simply be a metaphor for their great importance. The ambiguity of the various

---

415 Dalai Lama V, *Rig 'dzin ngag gi dbang po'i rnam thar* 431, and bsKal-bzang padma dbang-phyug, *Autobiography* 374

416 K. Dowman, "The Buddhist Guide" 251. Most sources stipulate Prabhahasti as the actual donor of the teachings at that time, thus confirming him as the personal preceptor of Padmasambhava. NSTB I.481 says that Padmasambhava studied the Kīla doctrines 18 times under Prabhahasti's tutelage.

417 Still to be analysed are the Sanskrit treatises of Buddhist *kīla* rituals noted above (Chapter Two) and the many minor texts of mixed Hindu/Buddhist ritual recently brought to light in Nepal by the NGMPP.

Kīla chronicles tends to confirm this hypothesis, for the title occurs as an article of faith in almost every Vajrakīla lineage, despite an acknowledgement of their discrete inceptions and the absence of any such named text.

Certainly it seems that Padmasambhava introduced a very large body of Vajrakīla teachings to Tibet, as practised to this day within both the rNying-ma and Sa-skya schools.[418] In the *rNying ma'i rgyud 'bum* (NGB) alone are more than 41 major treatises filling three entire volumes.[419] The popularity of these doctrines was such that countless *gter ma* have subsequently been brought forth by appointed 'revealers of hidden treasure' to supplement those originally taught, so that a recent project to gather together all of these teachings and texts resulted in a published compilation of 45 large volumes.[420]

The doctrines of Vajrakīla were at one time rejected as spurious by various teachers of the new schools (*gsar ma*) on the grounds that no original Sanskrit texts could be produced in evidence of their authenticity. All such opposition is said to have been crushed, however, when the Sa-skya Paṇḍita Kun-dga' rgyal-mtshan (1182-1252) discovered in Shangs sreg-zhing a Sanskrit text which was supposed to have belonged to Padmasambhava himself. The Sa-skya Paṇḍita's translation of this *Vajrakīla-mūlatantrakhaṇḍa* (VKMK, *rDo rje phur pa rtsa ba'i rgyud kyi dum bu*) is included in the *tantra* section of the Tibetan canon (P.78) and in our analysis of Byang-gter Vajrakīla literature in Part Three of the present work the contents of this short text will be shown to have tremendous relevance for the cult as a whole.[421]

In the light of the huge number of Vajrakīla texts held in great esteem by followers of the rNying-ma school in Tibet, it may be considered curious that no recension of the *bKa' 'gyur* includes any Kīla *tantra* other than

---

418 The large cycle of Vajrakīla doctrines adhered to by the Sa-skya school is said to have been taught by Padmasambhava to 'Khon klu-dbang srung and subsequently transmitted from generation to generation within the 'Khon family. 'Khon dKon-mchog rgyal-po (1034-1102) eventually abandoned the rNying-ma tradition in disgust at its later degeneracy, founding his own school at Sa-skya in 1073.

419 According to the catalogue of this collection prepared by E. Kaneko (Tokyo, 1982), vols. 27, 28 & 29 consist entirely of Kīla texts.

420 *dPal chen rdo rje gzhon nu'i chos skor phyogs bsgrigs* published by Bod-kyi shes-rig zhib-'jub-khang, Chengdu, 2002

421 Full text and English translation of the VKMK are to be found in my *Bolt of Lightning from the Blue* 79-90

the VKMK. This is despite the fact that Bu-ston (1290-1364) himself, one of the foremost compilers of the canon, informs us in his *Chos 'byung* (History of Religion) that his teacher, the *lo tsā ba* Nyi-ma rgyal-mtshan, had "seen parts of the *Vajrakīla-tantra* in Nepal"[422] and 'Brog-mi lo-tsā-ba Śākya ye-shes (born 992/993), an eminent scholar of the new translation period, claims to have seen the eight syllables of the *mantra* of Vajrakīla inscribed over one of the doorways in Bodhgayā. Also Śākyaśrībhadra (1127-1225), the great scholar of Kashmīr (*kha che paṇ chen*), confirmed that the practice of Vajrakīla as *iṣṭadevatā* was firmly established in India. The marked absence of such texts from the official collection of *Buddha-vacana,* then, cannot reasonably be attributed to hostility on the part of the compilers. The rNying-ma-pa explanation for their absence is that the initiated holders of these highly esoteric doctrines deliberately maintained their secrecy in accordance with tantric ordinance, never permitting them to become widely known.[423] Thus they have never been included in the published lists of canonical works, even the earliest catalogue of translations carried out at bSam-yas monastery.[424]

In the 15th century, fearing for the loss of these precious ancient teachings, Ratna gling-pa (1403-1478) gathered together all that he could find of the Vajrakīla *tantra*, *sādhana* and initiation manuals, transmitted as *bka' ma* from the time of Guru Rinpoche, and incorporated them in to the *rNying ma'i rgyud 'bum.* A hand written copy of this collection was prepared and preserved at his home, the mDo-mkhar lhun-grub pho-brang in gTam-shul, and eventually carved onto wooden printing blocks at sDe-dge monastery in the 18th century.

The existence of a Kīla cult among the Buddhists in eighth century India, however, must now surely be accepted as established, despite any uncertainty adhering to the title *Vidyottama-tantra*. Whatever texts were sent to Padmasambhava on that occasion and whether or not they actually came from the prestigious monastic university of Nālandā, all the chronicles proclaim that, as soon as the teachings arrived in Pharping, the hindrances and obstacles that had disturbed the guru's meditations were successfully overcome.

---

422 *Bu ston gsung 'bum,* vol.Ya, fol.179b Quoted by Roerich in *The Blue Annals* 102

423 G. Dorje, *The Guhyagarbha-tantra* 142

424 The *bKa' 'gyur dkar chag ldan dkar ma* compiled in the ninth century by sKa-ba dpal-brtsegs and Nam-mkha'i snying-po. See Marcelle Lalou, "Les textes bouddhiques au temps du roi Khri Srong-lde-btsan".

"Invoking Vajrakīla", says our commentator 'Phrin-las bdud-'joms, "Padmasambhava beheld a glorious vision of the *bhagavat* Vajrakumāra that filled the sky like the cosmic Mount Meru and he obtained from the deity unprecedented empowerments of wrathful activity. Then, rolling the ritual *kīla* between his palms, the *ācārya* sang this song;

དིཔྟ་ཙཀྲ་ཕུར་པའི་ལྷ་།
མཐིང་ནག་གཅེར་བུ་རལ་པ་ཅན་།
སྐུ་སྟོད་ཁྲོ་བོ་ཆེན་པོ་ལ་།
ཞལ་གསུམ་ཕྱག་ཀྱང་དྲུག་པ་སྟེ་།
ལྟེ་བ་མན་ཆད་ཕུར་པའི་དབལ་།།

Oh Circle of Light,[425] divine Kīla,
Dark blue in colour, naked and with long dishevelled hair.
The upper part of your body is a form of great wrath,
With three faces and six arms, and
Below the navel you are a sharp-pointed nail.

རབ་འབར་དྲག་པོར་གྱུར་པ་སྟེ་།
ཨུཏྤལ་སྔོན་པོའི་འདབ་འདྲ་བ་།
འབར་བའི་ཕྲེང་བ་འཁྲིགས་པའི་འོད་།
བཏབ་ན་ལྷ་ཡང་བརླག་འགྱུར་ན་།
གནོད་བྱེད་རྣམས་ལ་སྨོས་ཅི་དགོས་།།

Blazing brightly with great strength
Like the blue petals of an utpala flower,
With a radiant aura of intense light –
When touched by you, even the gods are destroyed!
What need is there to speak of those who cause trouble?

While the guru sat in meditation singing this song, there came to him in the evening the four Śvanmukhā goddesses and then, at midnight, the four

425 Dīptacakra ('Wheel of Light') is an alternative spelling for Tṛptacakra, the consort of Vajrakīla.

Mahātmādevī (bDag-nyid chen-mo). In the morning he was approached by the four Bhūmipati (Sa-bdag) sisters (called here bSe-mo mched-bzhi) and all twelve of these local spirits offered him their vital life essence. In accepting their gifts, the guru established each one of them as a protectress of the doctrines of Vajrakīla.[426]

These dozen goddesses have become very well known in the Kīla cult, with a large number of texts being devoted to their worship (dealt with in more detail in Chapter Nine, below).

The first group consists of goddesses in the guise of wild dogs. Throughout India dogs are thought of as the most unclean of all animals, polluted scavengers and the very epitome of evil. They are also regarded as the companions of the outcaste *kāpālika* Śiva during his wanderings as the god beyond the pale of orthodox Vedism.[427] The Hindu tantric text *Mahākāla-saṁhitā* instructs the *yogin* to worship such creatures as manifestations of Śiva's spouse by proceeding at midnight on the fourteenth (darkest) night of the waning moon, naked and with dishevelled hair, to a lonely, fearful spot such as a charnel ground. There, *bali* offerings should be scattered for the jackals who are then requested to slay the *yogin*'s foes.[428] Since this ritual is exactly as we find it in the Buddhist Kīla cult, it may be that this episode in the chronicles simply reflects the historical incorporation of *kāpālika* imagery and myth.

The second group corresponds to the Ṛtudevī, archaic 'goddesses of the four seasons', generally to be found as companions of Rematī. Details of their iconography are to be found, below, in Chapter Nine of the present work.

It is only to the final group of four sisters, the bSe'i lha-mo-bzhi (translated by Bischoff & Hartman as "the tetrademoness of Bse") that reference is made in the Dūnhuáng manuscript (folio 7a). The *Padma bka' thang shel brag ma* tells the story of their conversion in Nepal at the opening of Chapter LIV, and Nebesky-Wojkowitz suggests that this group may derive from the Bon demons of that name (also spelled bSve), noting that "numerous bSe are to be found among the *sa bdag*".[429] Our text B33 (C24)

---

426 B4 186. The song is from gTsang mkhan-chen, *rDo rje phur pa'i chos 'byung* 168

427 W.D. O'Flaherty, *The Origins of Evil in Hindu Mythology* 173 & 285

428 T. Goudriaan & S. Gupta, *Hindu Tantric and Śākta Literature* 80-81

429 René de Nebesky-Wojkowitz, *Oracles and Demons of Tibet* 15 & 310

invokes a group of sixty male and female bSe from the uppermost reaches of the sky.[430]

Interpreting this passage, then, as an allusion to the assimilation into the Kīla cult of minor deities from local traditions, an air of historical credibility is bestowed upon what would otherwise seem to be an episode of fantasy in the unfolding drama. Such an understanding is supported by gTsang mkhan-chen who says that the goddesses came seeking consecration on that occasion although they had long ago been bound under oath to serve the cause of living beings.[431]

All sources go on to say that the next task to be completed was the thorough revision of the texts of the collected doctrines. The translators of the Dūnhuáng manuscript describe this as the work of Padmasambhava alone but 'Phrin-las bdud-'joms and other sources make it clear that Padmasambhava, Vimalamitra and Śīlamañju conferred together. In fact, the Dūnhuáng manuscript (folio 6a) adds Prabhahasti (Pra-be-se) to the list and it is difficult to believe that his disciples would have "worked extensively on the *sādhana,* commentaries and 32 root *tantra* of Vajrakīla, such as the *Vajrakīla-guhyatantra* and the rest" in his absence.[432]

Although it is not possible to identify these "32 root *tantra* and the rest" with any certainty, the early chronicles at least make it clear that the accumulated wealth of Kīla doctrines incorporated inconsistencies and was therefore in need of revision and also that the first concerted attempt at rationalisation took place in Nepal on the basis of texts received from India during the first half of the eighth century CE.

Padmasambhava, Vimalamitra and Śīlamañju[433] are then said to have performed the rite of Vajrakīla in "the rock cave of the *asura*" (only a short walk from Yang-le-shod).[434] 'Phrin-las bdud-'joms, who actually places this event prior to the rationalisation of the *Vidyottama* texts, tells

---

430 See above, Chapter Three.

431 gTsang mkhan-chen, *rDo rje phur pa'i chos 'byung* 169

432 B4 186-187 and gTsang mkhan-chen, *op.cit.* 170. The revision of the Kīla doctrines by Padmasambhava, Vimalamitra and Śīlamañju are reported in the *Phur 'grel 'bum nag*, transmitted in Tibet by guru Padma to his consort Ye-shes mtsho-rgyal. For this text, see my *Bolt of Lightning from the Blue*.

433 The Dūnhuáng manuscript names them Ser-po (the Nepalese) and In-tra (Indra) Shu-gu-tu (or Śrī 'Gugs-ta, folio 8a). It also says that they were not alone but fails to identify their assistants (with the exception of Prabhahasti, mentioned above).

434 For a description of these sites see K. Dowman, "The Buddhist Guide" 249-254 & 255-258

us that "One of their *kīla* exhibited the supreme sign of flying through space. One *kīla* showed the middling sign of leaping and dancing above the *maṇḍala* and a third *kīla* showed the inferior sign of laughing and smiling." He then continues;

"The *ācārya* Padmasambhava took hold of that *kīla* that had flown through space and he stuck it into the ground in an area where there was a teacher of heretical doctrines who was causing trouble for the *buddha-dharma*. In so doing he utterly annihilated that area, including the teacher, his house and the surrounding forest. As soon as he had done so, however, a new forest arose even grander than the one that had previously been there.[435] The *ācārya* Vimalamitra took hold of that *kīla* that had danced upon the *maṇḍala* and he put it into the River Ganges. By this action he was able to destroy a certain *nāga* who had been supporting the lives of heretics. The Nepali master Śīlamañju took the *kīla* that had laughed and he thrust it into the mKhar-gong rock, reducing it to rubble and dust. In this way, as foretold in prophecy, he destroyed all heretics that were staying in that area, up as far as their leader. So the doctrines of the Buddha were enabled to flourish."[436]

This threefold theme, although encountered in all the chronicles, is variously recorded by the different authors. 'Jigs-bral ye-shes rdo-rje[437] confirms the events but omits many details while the Dūnhuáng manuscript, dealing with the matter very briefly on folio 8, exchanges the protagonists who overcame water and rock.

gTsang mkhan-chen in his *Concise History,* however, relates a parallel narrative set in India. According to his version, Padmasambhava, together with his consort and one assistant, performed the rite of Vajrakīla in Vajrāsana (modern Bodhgayā) until the signs of success became manifest as above. Padmasambhava is then said to have taken the *kīla* representing the wrathful Trailokyavijaya from the *maṇḍala* and to have caused the conflagration of a sandalwood forest near Triliṅga (Trimala) in south India where heretics who worshipped a *svayambhūliṅga* were "practising the evil art of black magic, bringing about a virulent infectious disease". The fire was started as he stabbed his *kīla* into the trunk of a tree near the *liṅga*. His consort (said to be "just like Vajrayoginī") took from the

---

435 This is the *kīla* called Srid-gsum bdud-'dul, about which, see above, p.35

436 B4 184-185

437 NSTB I.714

maṇḍala the *kīla* of Amṛtakuṇḍalin and travelled east to Bengal where an evil *nāga* who was well disposed towards heretics dwelt in a lake. "When those *tīrthika* made just so much as a simple *bali* offering to the serpent they were rewarded with many precious jewels and much harm was done to the followers of the Buddha through the miracle powers of the snake." The *nāga* and his retinue were destroyed when she plunged her *kīla* into that lake. "Within a week the lake was dry and all those heretics were dead." A *yogin* by the name of Ratnaśīla, who had acted as assistant in the rite, took one of the minor *kīla* from the *maṇḍala* and went to Rājagṛha in the country of Magadha. There, beside a huge boulder of crystal, a family of brahmin heretics had established their residence around a certain teacher who taught that the powers of clairvoyance and clairaudience were to be obtained without the necessity of undergoing ascetic privations. With a single thrust of his *kīla,* the boulder was reduced to fragments and their evil power destroyed.[438]

We may never know the personalities and local events that underlie such legends for, although the common themes are clearly discernible, the tales themselves present too many variants. Until the Sanskrit sources which have only recently come to light are analysed, however, these Tibetan texts remain the only testimonies we have of events surrounding the development and spread of a Kīla cult in India and Nepal prior to the transmission of the Vajrakīla doctrines to Tibet.

Having established a consistent body of knowledge relating to the worship and ritual praxis of Vajrakīla on the basis of the *Vidyottama* collection, Padmasambhava is said to have transferred to the rock cave at gYa'-ri-gong in the border area between India and Nepal in order to continue his meditations. All sources speak of this as a 12 year period of retreat focussing on the 100,000 sections of the *Vidyottama-tantra*,[439] and the meditations in which Padmasambhava was engaged at that time are said to be encapsulated in a number of the Byang-gter *sādhana* to be analysed, below, in Part Three of this study.

Thus far we have looked at two lines of Vajrakīla doctrine; one stemming from Indrabodhi and the other said to have been received by Prabhahasti

---

438 gTsang mkhan-chen, *rDo rje phur pa'i chos 'byung* 164-166

439 Our text C23, for example, begins with the oft quoted verse; *O rgyan padma 'byung gnas kyis, phur pa bi to ta ma la, 'bum sde'i rgyud la blo sbyang nas, gYa' ri gong gi brag phug tu, mi lo bcu gnyis bar du bsgrub.*

at the opening of the *stūpa* in Śītavana. Both teach procedures for meditation upon Vajrakīla in his three-faced, six-armed form, known in the Byang-gter school as 'the black deity system'.[440] We have seen above, however, that the Byang-gter also recognises the Kīla with nine faces and 18 arms, a 'multicoloured deity system' having a separate genesis.

The mahottarakīla cycle

In the biographies of Padmasambhava known as the *bKa' thang gser phreng* and the *bKa' thang shel brag ma,* the story is told of the 'scorpion guru' who imparts to Padmasambhava the doctrines of Vajrakīla. The *bKa' thang gser phreng* places this incident in the Śītavana charnel ground near Bodhgayā, while the *bKa' thang shel brag ma* speaks of its occurrence in a great charnel ground to the west of Rājagṛha.

The *Concise History* of Vajrakīla by gTsang mkhan-chen places the episode, not in a great charnel ground in line with the other sources, but in Yang-le-shod following the successful performance of the Kīla rites by Padmasambhava, Vimalamitra and Śīlamañju. According to this text, a gigantic iron scorpion fell down upon the roof of the cave in which the three were meditating and appeared before them, mocking and jeering. The *ācārya* (Padmasambhava) transformed himself into a pig in order to eat that scorpion which promptly metamorphosed into the deity Vajrakumāra, from whom they all received "the unassailable empowerments for the ferocious rites".[441]

The Byang-gter cycle includes an entire text, the *Phur pa che mchog gi lo rgyus* (B13), devoted to the episode of the scorpion. As betokened by its title, the scorpion is herein said to be the source of the *mahottarakīla* teachings which nowadays appear to be known only within this tradition. According to the text, Padmasambhava went to visit the guru Dhanasaṁskṛta in order to request Dharma instruction and, having received from him all the various teachings on the path of secret *mantra,* became

---

440 A similar 'black deity system' is said to have been devised by Ya-'brog-pa gu-rub yang-dag on the basis of the *rDo rje phur bu chos thams cad mya ngan las 'das pa'i rgyud chen po* (NGB 336, a text cited several times in the Byang-gter commentaries of Padma 'phrin-las, eg. A46 418).
G. Roerich, *The Blue Annals* 156

441 gTsang mkhan-chen, *rDo rje phur pa'i chos 'byung* 168 The author states that the deity chose to manifest in this way "in order to examine the attainments (of the three practitioners)."

victorious over debaters and followers of heretical doctrines. He was henceforth renowned as Siṁhanāda, 'He who roars with the voice of a lion'.[442] After giving these teachings, the guru Dhanasaṁskṛta announced to his disciples, "We all, master and retinue, should go to the lake island *Jalendradvīpa in order to perfect the rite of producing *amṛta* nectar", and having said this, they all departed. They made their home on that island in a cave of blue rock and this angered the *bhūmipati, nāga* and pestilential local spirits who then caused the great lake to overflow. The planets and constellations of stars above also became furious and threw down repeated storms of hail and lightning, violent winds and blizzards of snow. Because of all this, the *yogins* were achieving no results from their *sādhana* practice and so they went off in search of a doctrine that could put a stop to the interferences.[443]

Arriving at the great charnel ground of Śītavana they found a black iron scorpion with nine heads living there in a cave, holding aloft a golden sword in his right hand and expounding the Dharma to himself. "I am the lord of all those in the world who have no lord. I am the defender and friend of all those who have no protector" he said. Because this iron scorpion was very angry, the teachings on that occasion consisted of instructions on bringing anger onto the path. His having nine heads was a sign of his having reached the highest peak of the nine *yāna* and his sword was a sign of his having cut through the *kleśa* with his perfect wisdom (*samyakprajñā*). A great light like the glow of the setting sun was always shining at the place where he stayed.

The guru said, "In this place there will arise either a jewel of Brahmā or a great demon of destruction." After he had spoken, they dug down and unearthed a casket of maroon leather within which was this fundamental commentary on the root *tantra,* inscribed in letters of gold upon dark blue paper. At that time neither the *ācārya* Dhanasaṁskṛta nor the teacher Padmasambhava was able to comprehend it and, even though it was shown to 500 other scholars, it could not be understood. They therefore

442 Another of the famous 'eight names of the guru'.

443 Note that once again the motif of harassment to meditation is cited as the reason for seeking the Kīla doctrines.

attached it to the tip of a victorious banner and, circumambulating it, they worshipped it with offerings.[444]

Then Padmasambhava said, "If we ask the iron scorpion for the meaning, he will either refuse to explain or he will speak." So they prepared for the scorpion a six-legged throne of jewels and, inviting him to sit upon it, they circumambulated him, presented him with offerings and prayed to him fervently with devoted minds. In an instant that scorpion of iron transformed himself into the *bhagavat,* the glorious Vajrakumāra with nine heads and 18 hands pronouncing in his own language the sounds KĪLAYA HŪṀ PHAṬ from the *dGongs rgyud* (*Tantra* of the Ultimate Intention).[445] It was by means of this utterance that the miraculous transformation with nine heads and 18 hands arose from the sphere of non-arising, so it is said. Then he taught the *tantra* known as **Svayambhūsvodaya* (Spontaneously Generated, Self-Arising) from the section "Anger is destroyed by means of *vajra* wrath" up as far as the words "KATHAṀ KATHAṀ", together with instructions concerning its means of attainment. "This was the manner in which the *mūlatantra* of *vajra* wrath arose as authoritative, generally indestructible adamantine speech."

As far as can be judged from the few words cited here, this '*mūlatantra* of *vajra* wrath' exhibits a remarkable similarity to the VKMK. Indeed, the entire text of the VKMK is probably to be found scattered among the various works that style themselves 'root *tantra* of Vajrakīla'. Many of its verses, for example, are to be found in the Byang-gter BRT analysed in the following chapter, thus lending weight to the idea that perhaps there never were large numbers of Vajrakīla texts in Sanskrit, despite persistent references to the fabulous 'one hundred thousand sections' of the *Vidyottama-tantra*. Our chronicle, in fact, goes on to state that the *Vidyottama-tantra* was taught in order to elucidate the meaning of the *mūlatantra,* which suggests that the bulk of Vajrakīla texts may have been redactions of an oral tradition centred on only a few root texts.

---

444 Both the *gSer phreng ba* and the *Shel brag ma* say that the scorpion withdrew the teachings from beneath a triangular stone and as soon as they were seen they were immediately understood. gTsang mkhan-chen also says that by showing these *śāstra* to the 500 *paṇḍita,* "the borderland between Nepal and India became like a wellspring of *bodhi*".

445 Possibly the *rDo rje phur pa gsang ba'i dgongs rgyud chen po,* said to be derived from the *Vidyottama-tantra*. NGB 353

In the words of the chronicle;

"In order to make that clear, the teacher (presumably the scorpion) taught the continuation *tantra* called *Vidyottama* in one hundred thousand sections. At that place he propounded the introduction (*nidāna*) in which the five 'invariable features'[446] are set forth and then he taught the 100,000 verses. In order to clarify the meaning of the fundamental *Vajrakrodha-tantra* ('the *mūlatantra* of *vajra* wrath'), five explanatory *tantra* were taught which are the *tantra* of the Body, Speech, Mind, Good Qualities and Perfect Activities. The mother *tantra* is the *Heruka-mūlatantra* (from which are derived?) the five *tantra* of the five supreme sons, ten *tantra* of the ten wrathful kings and 12 *tantra* of the 12 oath-bound guardians. The *nidāna* itself is a *tantra* called the Rasp Razor of Life (*Srog gi spu gri se brdar*) and for all of the *samaya* deities there is a **Samayasamāja-tantra*. In that way, 27 *tantra* have been taught.[447]

"In the cycle of treatises there are the eight treatises in the eight directions and there are six classes of *āgama* in the cycle of *āgama*. The philosophical viewpoint of the authoritative *Vidyottama-tantra* in one hundred thousand sections is complete and perfect in every respect. The small heart text is a clear guide to the perfect activities of the deity Vajrakumāra and for higher activities there is the *Guhyakīla-tantra* (? our text A3) which is an accomplished *yātudhāna* or demonic means for the complete eradication of all trouble-makers."[448]

The chronicle concludes with the proclamation that, having successfully attained all of these teachings, Dhanasaṁskṛta and Padmasambhava contemplated the instructions and took them fully to heart. Then, when they thrust a *kīla* into the lake they were able to subdue all vicious

---

446 See above, note 363

447 If the *tantra* of Body, Speech, Mind and the rest are identified as 'the five supreme sons', I suppose the 27 referred to here comprise the listed groups of five, ten and twelve. This leaves the *Vajrakrodha-mūlatantra,* the *nidāna* and the *Samayasamāja-tantra* excluded from the reckoning. NGB 338-347 are Vajrakīla *tantra* concerning the ten wrathful kings but the firm identification of any text is problematic.

448 Normally the 'higher activities' are the meditations that lead to buddhahood (the supreme *siddhi)* while the 'demonic means for the complete eradication of all trouble-makers' are considered to be lower activities. The meaning of this entire paragraph is obscure. In a ritual of the *Yajurveda* we read; *yātudhānebhyaḥ kaṇṭakakāraṁ,* "to the *yātudhāna* demons (should be sacrificed) trouble-makers". R. Mitra, "On Human Sacrifice in Ancient India" JASB XLV,1 (1876) 76-118. See also H.G. Türstig, "The Indian Sorcery Called Abhicāra" 78-81, on *yātudhāna* rites.

trouble-makers from among the eight classes of gods and demons and they gained the two types of *siddhi* of Vajrakīla.

Thus, according to this source, doctrines relating to Mahottarakīla were initially divulged in India to both Padmasambhava and Dhana-saṁskṛta. Considered chronologically, they are among the final revelations of Vajrakīla and if these teachings then went straight to Tibet in the hands of Padmasambhava, *tantra* relating to the deity in this guise may never have circulated in the land of their origin. Sceptics, of course, would question their supposed Indian provenance and their doubts may be increased when it is noted that such doctrines did not appear in Tibet either until much later, for I have been unable to locate any citation of the 18-armed Mahottarakīla in the *bka' ma* material translated in the eighth century. Paradoxically, however, the Byang-gter Mahottarakīla texts (dealt with below, Part Three) exhibit primitive features that would seem to indicate their greater antiquity.

None of the known Kīla chronicles deals further with the aetiology or dissemination of the Kīla cult in India, a knowledge of which may perhaps be derived in the future from sources in Sanskrit. All Tibetan authors dealing with subsequent events, now turn their attention towards Tibet.

The invitation of Padmasambhava to Tibet during the reign of Khri Srong-lde'u-btsan is too well known to be elaborated here. There are just two points in this episode of specific interest to the present study. The first of these is that the leader of the messengers dispatched by the king to escort the guru from India was the king's uncle and life-long companion, sNa-nam rdo-rje bdud-'joms, whom the chroniclers call "preeminent among the practitioners of Vajrakīla".[449] Revered as the founder of the Byang-gter tradition, he is said to have mastered the teachings under the guidance of Padmasambhava in the eighth century and subsequently revealed them to the world as a Dharma treasure in 1366 when reincarnated as Rig-'dzin rgod-ldem. This has been dealt with above, in Chapter One.

The second point upon which the Kīla chroniclers insist is that the rites employed by Padmasambhava on his journey to Tibet for the subjugation of the local 'gods and demons', and his subsequent conversion of the Tibetan landscape, were specifically the rites of Vajrakīla. Buddhist tantric praxis, moreover, posits the identity of the *sādhaka* with the

---

449 E. Schmidt, *The Great Gate* 26

presiding deity of his chosen *sādhana* and thus whenever Padmasambhava ritually invoked the presence of Vajrakīla he was himself transfigured as 'the lord of the nails'.

Iconic scorpions and kīla

The wealth of legends accruing to the (largely mythological) figure of Padmasambhava has led to his renown in Tibet as the *aṣṭanāmaguru* (*gu ru mtshan brgyad*) 'the teacher with eight names'. These eight names are taken from the hagiography of the guru and relate to the various episodes in his life and the ways in which he was regarded by different people at different times, mainly in India.[450]

Raised as the adopted crown prince of king Indrabhūti, he was known first of all as the royal Padmarāja (Padma rgyal-po). Committing murder, he was banished to the wilderness where he underwent the *mahāvrata* penance of a *kāpālika* and became known as the *yogin* Sūryaraśmi (Nyi-ma 'od-zer).[451] As a lay Buddhist scholar of great learning he is said to have been acclaimed as Mativat Vararuci (bLo-ldan mchog-sred) and, being ordained as a *bhikṣu,* was revered as an actual buddha and celebrated as Śākyasiṁha (Shākya seng-ge). As a tantric priest he was renowned as the *ācārya* Padmasambhava (Padma 'byung-gnas) and glorified as Siṁhanāda (Seng-ge sgra-sgrog), the ferocious debater who defeated all heresy. During the bestowal of *abhiṣeka* he was honoured as the lord of the

---

450 The miraculous birth, royal upbringing, renunciation of the palace, years of asceticism and study, etc., are all motifs through which hagiographers of Padmasambhava sought to identify him as 'the second Buddha'.

451 Hindu law codes teach a penance known as *mahāvrata* (great vow) involving voluntary exile to the forests or cremation grounds, etc., for a period of 12 years to be observed by the slayer of a brahmin. There the penitent must dress in animal skins and carry a skull bowl for food and a skull staff (*khaṭvāṅga*) as the emblems of his crime, entering villages only during the day for the purpose of begging alms. The tantric *kāpālika* of a later period took up these practices, smearing their bodies with ashes and adorning themselves with bones. They devoted themselves to ritual sacrifice of a more or less scatological type and the worship of Śiva in his wrathful guise as Bhairava through which they sought to attain mundane *siddhi* and ultimate union with the deity. They also practised *yoga* involving the *nāḍī* and *cakra.*

D. Lorenzen, *The Kāpālikas and Kālāmukhas* 73-95

Similar practices were performed by itinerant Buddhist *yogins* known as *vajrakāpālika* and the *Saṁpuṭa-tantra* refers to the vow as either *vīracaryā-vrata* (vow of heroic conduct) or *yauvarājavrata* (the vow of a crown prince).

Abhayākaragupta, *Vajrāvalī* 219

maṇḍala, the divine Saroruha Vajradhara (mTsho-skyes rdo-rje-'chang) and being invited to Tibet he became the wrathful rDo-rje gro-bo-lod, subjugator of Himalayan *genii loci.*

His Indian names are included in the *mantra* through which he is invoked in religious ceremonial[452] and the episodes from his life are recounted in detail in his many biographies. The sole exclusively Himalayan form of the guru, then, is the one known as rDo-rje gro-lod, and this is the form in which he wields the ritual *kīla.* According to the religious traditions of Tibet, he is said to have appeared in this guise specifically in order to "bind under oath all the high and low non-human spirits of the land and thus convert the whole country to the Dharma". Mounted upon a pregnant tigress capable of flight, Padmasambhava in the guise of rDo-rje gro-lod visited 13 separate locations throughout the Himalaya, each of which subsequently became known by the appellation 'Tiger's Nest' (sTag-tshang).[453]

Tibetan icons depicting this form of the guru show him in the conventional robes of a Buddhist *bhikṣu* but with the long hair and bone ornaments of a *kāpālika yogin.*[454] This image may well provide another clue to the non-Buddhist origin of many *kīla* doctrines as it seems to suggest that the precepts of the Buddha as upheld by *bhikṣu*s became somehow overlaid with the cult of the *kīla*. Indeed, the demon upon whom the guru in this guise is seen to trample has the form of a Buddhist monk!

The icon exists in several well-known variants and of particular interest to us here is the fact that the *hastacihna* held in Padmasambhava's left hand may be either an iron scorpion or a *kīla,* indicative of an iconic equivalence. The guru himself is often depicted from the waist down in the form of a *kīla*[455] and in the biography of Ye-shes mtsho-rgyal he is said to have manifested as rDo-rje gro-lod at the end of a session of ritual practices focussed on Vajrakīla. The passage in question is remarkable for the graphic account it contains of a Vajrakīla *abhiṣeka* in which, it should

---

452 Such as those found in the *Yang gsang rig 'dzin yongs rdzogs kyi bla ma gu ru mtshan brgyad bye brag du sgrub pa ye shes bdud rtsi'i sbrang char zhe bya ba,* a manuscript of which was brought to India from east Tibet by C.R. Lama in 1985.

453 T. Thondup, *The Tantric Tradition of the Nyingmapa* 144, in which he also states that *gter ma* were later recovered from several of these sites.

454 Pema Thaye, *Concise Tibetan Art Book* fig.26

455 Gega Lama, *Principles of Tibetan Art* 241

be noted, the participation of sNa-nam rdo-rje bdud-'joms is also recorded.[456]

Two initiation rituals published in 1961 by Muses & Chang[457] through which the empowerments of 'the fierce guru' are to be bestowed, point specifically to the identical nature of the guru and 'the Buddha Vajrakumāra'. Both texts list a nine-headed iron scorpion among the symbols of the deity while the second text alone describes the lower part of the guru's body in the form of a *kīla,* "the weapon that kills the evils, agonising and tormenting them". In the *maṇḍala* of the deified rDo-rje gro-lod, iron scorpions stand guard in the four gateways and innumerable scorpions encircle the *maṇḍala* periphery, forming the protective enclosure typically associated with *kīla.* All of this makes it clear that, iconographically, the scorpion and the *kīla* are readily interchangeable. Did this situation arise as a result of legends concerning the scorpion as a teacher of the Vajrakīla *tantra*? Or were the legends derived in order to explain an iconic convention of uncertain origin?[458]

In the *kāyamaṇḍala* of the combined *aṣṭamahāsādhana,* the deity to be contemplated within the secret (genital) centre (*guhyacakra*) is Vajrakīla. Here, however, within the *kāyamaṇḍala* of the canonised Padmasambhava in his *kīla*-wielding form, the *guhyacakra* is said to be the abode of Yakṣa Me-dbal in the form of a demonic blacksmith. This *yakṣa* has a wrathful, snarling face with all the usual attributes of a terrifying deity and in his two hands he holds a *vajra* hammer and a lasso of fire (*me yi shags*). In Tibet, blacksmiths are thought of with fear and awe. Their work is seen to be akin to magic and, naturally, they are the ones whose task it is to fash-

---

456 K. Dowman, *Sky Dancer* 90. It is also interesting to note that the purpose of the ceremony was to be the subjugation of the gods and demons of the "barbarian borderlands and beyond" which brings us back to the *sīmābandha* rites noted above in Chapter Two as the single most important element in the evolutionary history of the *kīla.*

457 C.A. Muses (ed.), *Esoteric Teachings of the Tibetan Tantra,* translated by Chen Chi Chang 3-47. On pp. 19-20 the scorpion is said to have nine heads, nine mouths, nine eyes and nine stings. "The right sting (pincer?) touches the top of the universe, the left one touches the bottom of the earth. The body flames with the fire of hell." It is then said that all demons, obstacles and enemies of the past are hungrily devoured by the scorpion while those of the future will all be subdued through its power.

458 Perhaps a clue to this may be found in the belief that the bites and stings of serpents and scorpions have their origin in Rudra, for in Chapter Three (above) we have shown that the iconography of Vajrakīla derives from the form of Rudra. J.L. Shastri (ed.), *Garuḍa-purāṇa* II.XXXII 121

ion the iron *kīla.* The hammering of white hot metal on an anvil in the groin is a powerful meditative image and the sharp, non-dual spike that is forged in this secret place when hammer and fire are brought together is the impetuous and powerful nail that can pin down all demonic urges in a moment. Is it mere coincidence that the *kīla* once used to slay the coiled serpent Vṛtra is now found in just that place where the coiled serpent Kuṇḍalinī[459] resides? Even more curious is the fact that, in esoteric astrology, the dominion of the constellation Scorpio in the human body is the groin.

Scorpio, a fixed water sign, is associated in western mythology with the river Styx that separates the living from the dead (echoes of the *vetāla* at the threshold?) which is guarded by the three-headed Cerberus (highly suggestive of images associated with Śvanmukhā as well as with the two-headed dogs of Yama), ruled by Pluto (lord of the underworld, the special domain of *nāga*) and the astrological domain of all that pertains to death and its mysteries. An accepted alternative image for the scorpion in astrological symbolism is the eagle and we note that from the navel of Vajrakīla shoots forth a mighty *garuḍa* eagle. Garuḍa is the sworn enemy of all serpents[460] and serpents are regularly depicted entwined along the lower parts of ritual *kīla.* It is also pertinent to note here the mention of a protective circle of eight *khadirakīla* in the *Garuḍa-purāṇa.*[461] Further investigation is clearly required in order to determine the debt owed by the Buddhist system of Vajrakīla to ancient Indian myths of the scorpion and Garuḍa (Pakṣirāja).[462] The Kīla doctrines having been compiled, however, they were then transmitted to Tibet.

---

459 Kuṇḍalinī is thought of by Hindu *tāntrikas* as a coiled serpent that lies sleeping at the base of the spine. A. Avalon, *The Serpent Power* 347, verses 10-11

460 The emanation of Garuḍa from Vajrakīla's navel is described in the deity's *sādhana* (eg. A32 226) but in Vajrakīla icons this fabulous bird is usually depicted as flying over his head.

With the beat of his wings, Garuḍa is said to be capable of forcing the entire triple world to a standstill. V. Fausboll, *Indian Mythology* 79

461 J.L. Shastri (ed.), *Garuḍa-purāṇa* I.XX 8-10

462 Unfortunately it seems as if all the original *Gāruḍa-tantras* (the primary concern of which was the magical production of counteragents to poison and snakebite) as well as the *Bhūta-tantras* to which they were closely affiliated (primarily dealing with the exorcism of malevolent ghosts and spirits) have long since been lost to posterity. Mark Dyczkowski, *The Canon of the Śaivāgama and the Kubjikā Tantras of the Western Kaula Tradition* 41

The transmission to Tibet

Our chronicler 'Phrin-las bdud-'joms sums up the well-known amalgam of religious myth and history concerning this period by telling us that, while Padmasambhava himself was active in India and Nepal, "an incarnation of the *ārya* Mañjuśrī had taken birth in Tibet in the person of the *dharmarāja* Khri Srong-lde'u-btsan who held in his mind the wish to establish there the doctrines of the Buddha. He therefore invited the *bodhisattva* abbot (Śāntarakṣita) from the land of Zahor and, having determined the site and drawn up plans for a temple, in the year of the female fire ox (797 CE) the foundation stones were laid and the walls were built up of wood and stones. All that was built up by the workers during the day, however, was destroyed during the night by the wild unruly gods and demons of Tibet. When the king asked the abbot just why that should be so, the abbot instructed the king to invite the *ācārya* Padmasambhava."[463]

The king therefore "dispatched sNa-nam rdo-rje bdud-'joms and his three companions to India, each endowed with a measure of gold pieces and a golden bowl." These messengers met Padmasambhava in Vajrāsana where he is said to have been acting as preceptor to king Sūryasiṁha and they presented him with their invitation.

'Phrin-las bdud-'joms makes no mention of the journey from India to Tibet but all other chroniclers stress the *guru*'s role in subjugating a large number of local gods and demons *en route,* converting all of them to Buddhism and binding them under oath to protect the Buddhist Dharma.[464] gTsang mkhan-chen, having given the details of several major battles with local demonic forces, winds up by saying that "in general, all of the harmful *'dre* and *srin* were subdued by means of Vajrakīla".[465]

Upon his arrival in Tibet, Padmasambhava is said to have performed the earth rituals (*bhūmividhi*) for the temple of bSam-yas in accordance with the *tantra* of Vajrakīla so that all obstacles to its construction were dispelled. Thereafter, the assembled scholars of India and Tibet began their programme of translating the various *sūtra* and *śāstra* into Tibetan

---

463 B4 187

464 A long list of these subjugations is to be found in K. Dowman, *The Legend of the Great Stūpa* 82-86

465 gTsang mkhan-chen, *rDo rje phur pa'i chos 'byung* 175

and, in particular, "special teachings were given by Padmasambhava in the retreat house at mChims-phu."[466]

When he taught the *maṇḍalas* of the *aṣṭamahāsādhana,* Padmasambhava granted empowerments to 'the king and the twenty-four subjects'[467] and it is said that "the lady Ye-shes mtsho-rgyal, having cast her flower onto the deity Vajrakīla, was given all the individual teachings of the Vajrakīla *tantra, āgama* and *upadeśa* and, having put them into practice, she beheld the *deva*'s face. She then had the ability to raise a human corpse to life again, the powers of mystic union (*sbyor ba*) and liberation (*sgrol ba*), the capacity to nourish the dead and care for their welfare and so on. She attained powers that reached to the limits of the extreme".[468]

"Furthermore", continues 'Phrin-las bdud-'joms, "from the ruling king Khri Srong-lde'u-btsan, from the lady Ye-shes mtsho-rgyal, from sNa-nam rdo-rje bdud-'joms, from Shud-pu dpal-gyi seng-ge, mChims Śākyaprabhā, lCog-ro gza', 'Khon klu-dbang srung, and from Rong-ban yon-tan arose the various lineages of teachings known as 'the king's tradition', 'the tradition of the lady', 'the sNa-nam tradition', 'the Shud-pu tradition', 'the mChims tradition', 'the lCam tradition', 'the 'Khon tradition' and 'the Rong-zom tradition'. All of these are lineages of Vajrakīla teachings and each one of them has demonstrated its miraculous powers."[469]

Our earliest record of the propagation of the Vajrakīla lineages (the Dūnhuáng manuscript) exhibits almost no obvious relationship to this account by 'Phrin-las bdud-'joms. The first in Tibet to be instructed in the Kīla doctrines are there said to be Ba-bor be-ro-ca (Ba-gor Vairocana),[470] the Kashmirian Nya-na si-ga, Dre Tathāgata (could this be Dre rgyal-ba blo-gros, a minister of the king and one of the first Tibetans to receive ordination as a Buddhist monk?[471]), 'Bu-na a-nas, mChims Śākyaprabhā (as above), rDo-rje gnyan (a place name?), sNa-nam (presumably our sNa-nam rdo-rje bdud-'joms), Byin ye-shes-brtsegs, gNyan rNyi-ma btsan-ba-dpal, lDe-sman rgyal-mtshan and the abbot (*upādhyāya*) 'Bum-tang-kyis.

---

466 B4 188

467 See Douglas & Bays, *The Life and Liberation* 544-593 for list.

468 For the events of mTsho-rgyal's life see K. Dowman, *Sky Dancer.*

469 B4 188

470 Vairocana is also held to have learned the doctrines of Vajrakīla in India from Śrīsiṁha. S. Karmay, *The Great Perfection* 25

471 K. Dowman, *Sky Dancer* 283

Later commentators, however, agree more closely with 'Phrin-las bdud-'joms' list. 'Jigs-bral ye-shes rdo-rje, for example, repeats it almost verbatim with the curious exception that, in his view, the sNa-nam tradition and the Rong tradition are identical.[472] gTsang mkhan-chen simply asserts that the chief lineages founded at that time were those of the King, Ye-shes mtsho-rgyal, sNa-nam rdo-rje bdud-'joms and his messenger companions. He also asserts that an entirely separate lineage of Vajrakīla doctrines was introduced to Tibet by Vimalamitra.[473] All chroniclers make much of the miracle powers said to have been demonstrated thereafter by the recipients of these Kīla doctrines. 'Phrin-las bdud-'joms continues;

"The *ḍākinī* Ye-shes mtsho-rgyal, for example, thrust her *kīla* into a raging forest fire that had gone out of control at mChims-phu and put a stop to it. Immediately after that a new forest grew up even bigger than the one before it. On another occasion she made the *tarjanī-mudrā* with her *kīla* towards crows that were flying high overhead and they fell down upon the ground. As for sNa-nam rdo-rje bdud-'joms, he quelled a raging fire at Has-po-ri with his *kīla* and showed miraculous *kīla* in the sky. Shud-pu dpal-gyi seng-ge thrust his *kīla* into the green faced mountain of 'On and buried it in the rock as if he had sunk it into mud and mChims Śākyaprabhā, with the recitation of only a few *kīlamantra,* caused the heart of a ferocious blue wolf to become separated from its skin and ejected from its body."[474]

Later lineages of practice

"From among those lineages of practice listed above, the Kīla tradition of the lady was given by the *ḍākinī* Ye-shes mtsho-rgyal to Ngam-'dre, otherwise known as *ācārya* gSal-le. He lived for a thousand years before going to the sky realm of Khecara. From him the tradition passed to the great *kīlavidyādhara* Lang-lab byang-chub rdo-rje. While Lang-lab was still a youth, his uncle and other relatives rose up against him as enemies and he asked Ngam-'dre to present a petition on his behalf to the local ruler. Seeing this as an opportunity for great compassion, Ngam-'dre gave him the doctrines of Vajrakīla. As a result of having put them into practice, Lang-

---

472 NSTB I.710, 712. Some of the ritual *kīla* mentioned here were concealed among the treasures that were unearthed by Rig-'dzin rgod-ldem in 1366.

473 gTsang mkhan-chen, *rDo rje phur pa'i chos 'byung* 176, 189

474 B4 188-189

lab saw the face of the *deva* and put a stop to all his enemies. Although he became widely renowned as a man of great power, he never abandoned poverty.

"At one time while Lang-lab was working as a shepherd, Rva lo-tsā-ba rDo-rje grags-pa together with a large retinue of his followers came to the place where Lang-lab sat with his disciples. Now, Rva lo-tsā-ba was very famous on account of his great powers and, wherever he went, all the important people of Tibet felt that they had to offer him their salutations and respect for they feared that those who failed to show him reverence would be killed by his *samādhi* of Yamāntaka. If it is asked, What kind of things were said about him?, it was said that he had killed 13 *bodhisattva* who were established on the *bhūmi,* including the venerable Marpa's son Darma mdo-sde, as well as translators who were related to him and others who were their equals. Even so, Lang-lab did not bow down in reverence before Rva lo-tsā-ba. Upon seeing this the people all thought, "Is this a really stupid man, or what?" And then the people began to wonder whether he was also a man of (occult) power due to his knowledge of Vajrakīla. "Perhaps he is the most powerful man of all! And yet, although he knows the doctrines of Vajrakīla, he has no wealth and is forced to act as the guardian of others' sheep." So they discussed the matter among themselves.

"As for Rva lo-tsā-ba, he thought to himself, "Ah ha! Well if this fellow is so swollen up inside with pride that he fails to prostrate himself to me then just wait! He will not live beyond this evening!" And that evening Rva lo-tsā-ba sat absorbed in meditation on Vajrabhairava and, summoning Lang-lab in his imagination, he performed the rituals for the fourfold *yoga* of slaying while the venerable Lang-lab stayed taking care of sheep in the fields.

"In the place where Rva lo-tsā-ba sat performing his invocations, at first there fell down from the sky like rain all the *kīla* of thorny wood from the outer edges of the Vajrakīla *maṇḍala* so that his disciples all fled in terror. Secondly, the forty *heruka* consisting of the devourers, slayers and the *daśakrodhakīla* all rained down as iron spikes causing his disciples to huddle together in panic. Thirdly, the sky became filled with a mass of fire and the sound of roaring and above the head of Rva lo-tsā-ba appeared the *karmasiddhi* ('accomplishment of activity') manifestation of Vajrakumāra made of meteoric iron. The upper part of his body was in the form of a wrathful deity and the lower part terminated in a sharp spike which rested on the crown of Rva lo-tsā-ba's head. Terrified out of his mind, Rva lo-tsā-ba prayed for forgiveness and prostrated himself on the ground with ever increasing faith. When he promised to behave himself, the miraculous apparition disappeared and the next day he sent an invitation to Lang-lab and offered him enormous veneration and praise.[475]

"Due to that the people have a saying; "He who knows Yamāntaka must bow down before Vajrakīla." And this has become a very well known expression.

"Thus it was that the *ācārya* Lang-lab byang-chub rdo-rje gained his four most important disciples, chief among whom was the man from Mon-dgu known as sKyi-nag gyang-'gyel, 'The One Who Caused the Wall of sKyi-nag to Tumble'.[476] Because the people of his district had robbed him of his wealth, livestock, dwellings and lands, that man of Mon-dgu went to Lang-lab and requested the teachings of Vajrakīla. Having accepted him as a disciple, Lang-lab bestowed upon him the empowerments and taught him the *tantra* and *upadeśa* and instructed him to invoke the deity for nine months. "After that you must practise the *sādhana* of the protectors of Rosewood, Iron and Conch (Crystal) for a further two months" he told him and gave him the necessary instructions.[477] Due to practising in that way, the disciple experienced a measure of success ('gained the stage of heat') and then he went away.

"While he was walking along a steep narrow path one day, he came across a number of people who were strolling nearby, warming themselves in the sunshine. Suddenly, without exception, they all turned upon him in hostility. Taking a *kīla* from his breast pocket, he threw it down upon the rock which exploded into fragments like house bricks, killing all those who had risen up against him. Because of this feat, that disciple subsequently become known as 'The One Who Caused the Wall of sKyi-nag to Tumble' and the succession of lineage holders through which his tradition of Kīla teachings have been transmitted remains famous to this day.

---

475 B4 189-191. Despite this apparent conversion, however, gZhon-nu dpal says that Rwa lo-tsā-ba eventually murdered his hated enemy Lang-lab byang-chub rdo-rje. G. Roerich, *The Blue Annals* 156

476 The other three are identified by 'Jigs-bral ye-shes rdo-rje as sNa-nam shes-rab tshul-khrims, sKrang phur-bu-mgo of Rong and Nyang-nag of 'U-yug rol-po. NSTB I.714

477 Our text B28, etc. The protectors of Rosewood, Iron and Conch include three groups of four brothers that accompany the twelve 'sisters' (Śvanmukhā and the rest) introduced above. See below, Chapter Nine.

"Now, with regard to the 'Khon tradition: This passed from 'Khon klu-dbang srung-ba to his younger brother rDo-rje rin-chen and then it continued to be passed down within the family which produced an unbroken succession of fully accomplished practitioners for eight generations. This lineage continues up until today and it is now known as Sa-phur or Sa-lugs (the Sa-skya-pa Kīla or the Sa-skya-pa lineage).

"The lCam tradition originated within the family of the lCogs-ro queen (one of the consorts of king Khri Srong-lde'u-btsan). Within this family was born a princess of fierce *mantra* known as 'The One With the Dark Red Face' and from her the lineage was passed on to lHa-rje gnub-chung. This lCam tradition is also said to be the cycle of teachings that gave the venerable Mi-la ras-pa his magical power.

"It is impossible to relate the whole story because, apart from the ones already mentioned, there are records and accounts of an inconceivable number of *vidyādhara* from the three countries of India, Nepal and Tibet who have gained *siddhi* through practising the *sādhana* of this god of gods."[478]

With this remark 'Phrin-las bdud-'joms lightly dismisses a problematic area of Vajrakīla historiography. Tibetan chroniclers are unanimous in declaring the Vajrakīla doctrines to have been widespread in both India and Nepal but, unfortunately, the proclaimed 'records and accounts' of the early practitioners are meagre.

Having thus outlined the various lineages of Vajrakīla teachings in the *bka' ma* tradition, 'Phrin-las bdud-'joms goes on to explain how these doctrines became integrated into the lines of *gter ma*. He illustrates his chronicle with numerous citations of prophetic utterances from Byang-gter canonical works in order to show the supreme importance of the Northern Treasures as an authentic source of Vajrakīla empowerment. In one of the texts that he quotes (our document A33), king Khri Srong-lde'u-btsan interrogates Padmasambhava concerning the *kīla* made of iron that he perpetually kept about his person. Padmasambhava replied;

"Listen to me well, your royal majesty. This is a very important matter and if I were to explain it to you at length it would be beyond all comprehension. I will therefore say that, in a nutshell, its purpose is simply to quell all disturbances. Although I myself have no fear of the four *māra*, in

478 B4 191-193. The transmission of the doctrines in the human realm is known as *Gang zag snyan khung brgyud tsul*, 'the ear-whispered tradition of mundane individuals'.

order to bring my disciples up to final liberation in the *buddhakṣetra* it is necessary to display the skilful methods of overcoming all hindrances as they arise. If the teachings of these skilful methods are not made available to the *yogin*s of the future who wish to engage in the practice of secret *mantra* and to the royal patrons such as yourself who protect the Dharma, they will be overpowered by the obstructions of Māra. Therefore you must earnestly apply yourself to these doctrines for the sake of your children and future generations."[479]

Again the king asked him; "Oh, *mahācārya*! In accordance with what you have said about the great importance to all beings of practising the path of Vajrakīla, I pray that you will grant the blessings of the *Vajrakīla-tantra* and full cycle of teachings for the benefit of people of the future."

Padmasambhava replied; "Just as you have requested, oh king. I, Padmasambhava, having collected together many weapons in the form of *kīla* have blessed them all through *sādhana* practice and hidden them as treasures for the future in a multitude of different places. In particular, in the country of Tibet I have had 108 iron *kīla* prepared by Tibetan blacksmiths, another 108 iron *kīla* crafted by the most excellent blacksmiths of Nepal, 100 meditation *kīla* of acacia wood made by outcaste artisans amidst the terrible screams in the charnel grounds and 100 *kīla* of black rosewood fashioned by Chinese craftsmen. Then, having absorbed myself in meditation at bSam-yas mchims-phu, the blue hermitage at Lho-brag, the tiger's nest at sPa-gro, the lion's fortress at 'Bum-thang, the crystal cave at Yar-lung, the great fortress of sGrags and at the white rock in gLo-bo, I blessed all of those places and hid important treasures within them. In particular I concealed 300 consecrated *kīla* in the most important places: bSam-yas mchims-phu, the white rock mountain at mKhar-chen and at Zam-bu-lung in Shangs. Each one of those *kīla* is destined to be of benefit to future generations of your royal family and to all those people who are holders of the doctrines of secret *mantra*". Thus he spoke.[480]

The guru then added, "During the final five hundred year period of the Buddha's doctrines, future members of your royal line will be born in upper Mang-yul in the district of Gung-thang for whom many demonic ob-

---

479 A33 232-233. At this point the original text discusses in detail the absolute & relative natures of the *kīla* (233-236) along lines similar to those followed in our previous chapter. Omitted in B4.

480 B4 194-195. At this point in A33, the king, disturbed to hear of his family's future decline, requests knowledge of that period when the *kīla* would be required and wishes to know how the *kīla* will help. A33 238

structions will arise and, as a direct result of your dynasty being cut, a time of great trouble will come upon the people of Tibet. Therefore, in order to save that situation and rescue people from those troubles, there is a special treasure for the protection of the kings of Gung-thang. This has been hidden inside a mountain of rock that looks like a heap of poisonous snakes which is situated in the land of the black stone cairn to the north. Contained within this treasure there is a *kīla* the length of my handspan, forged of iron by the most skilful of Nepalese blacksmiths. It has been consecrated as a *karmakīla* and so, merely by brandishing it in the air, all the mischief of enemies and obstructors will immediately be averted. The name of that *kīla* is *Tribhuvanamāravinaya, 'The Controller of Demons in the Three Worlds', and its activity is such as to quell all demonic interferences. There is also a *kīla* which has the blessings of Krodha-mañjuśrī (Yamāntaka) which was carved by Chinese experts from black rosewood. It is eight of my finger-widths in length and is for use in meditation. The name of this *kīla* is *Jvalanuttara, 'Supreme Radiance', and whoever continues to hold it will very quickly see the face of the deity Vajrakumāra. There is yet another *kīla* in that treasure which was made by an Indian expert from five different kinds of iron. The length of it is five of my finger-widths and it goes by the name of *Putragaṇasūrya, 'The Sunshine of a Host of Sons'. Its activity is such that the family lineage of its owner will run for many generations." So spoke the guru.[481]

According to the *Gong khug ma* (A27, etc.), three master craftsmen from the border regions, working together in 'Bum-thang (Bhutan), fashioned three boxes of black leather and four of maroon within which were placed eight sets of 21 *kīla* made from seven kinds of iron. Later, having spent three months practising the *sādhana* of Vajrakīla in Seng-ge-rdzong, Padmasambhava is said to have included those boxes of *kīla* among the treasures secreted for the welfare of future generations in seven different places: the 'places of virtue[482] and auspiciousness' in 'Bum-thang, the lion's fortress of Bhutan (Mon-kha Seng-ge-rdzong), the 'place of the iron *kīla*' in Lho-brag, the tiger's nest of sPa-gro, the white rock of mKhar-chen

481 B4 195-196. The three *kīla* mentioned here are those found wrapped in maroon silk in the central compartment of the Byang-gter treasure chest. B4 hereafter cites no more of A33 which continues stressing the immense value of the Byang-gter to the royal lineage of Tibet.

482 "The Precious Place of Virtue" (Rin-chen dge-gnas) in Bum-thang is a temple in the village of Zung-nge in the Chu-smad valley. Regarding this and the other Bhutanese locations, see M. Aris, *Bhutan* 7 & *passim*.

and Zang-zang lha-brag. In all, 78 Vajrakīla *tantra,* 23 *sādhana* and 321 *upadeśa* were hidden in those places together with eight *niṣevanakīla,* ten *kīla* for the attainments and 100 *kīla* for striking. Having been sorted out into various groups they were hidden away in their separate locations.[483]

As for the particular treasure hidden away in Zang-zang lha-brag, this was stored in one of the maroon leather boxes secreted deep within a rock cavern of triangular shape like a wrathful *homakuṇḍa* on the eastern face of the mountain. It contained everything that a future king would need in general and, in particular, it contained the instructions known as *Gong khug ma.*[484]

"Of equal importance", said Padmasambhava, "are the *niṣevanakīla, sādhanakīla* and the *karmakīla* that I myself concealed within that treasure after having gained in full the signs of *siddhi* through my practice in the lion's fortress."[485]

The Byang-gter cache is also said to have contained "the *niṣevanakīla* made of acacia wood that was used by the lady Ye-shes mtsho-rgyal in the rock cavern of Chu-bo-ri when she killed the seven demons of the extremities as they flew overhead in their magical transformations as crows." Also, "the *niṣevanakīla* made from the thorny wood of king Gesar's land of Khrom that had been used by rDo-rje bdud-'joms in putting a stop to the raging fire on the mountain at Has-po-ri." Of particularly great importance, however, are said to be "the *upadeśa* for the protection of the king and subjects of Tibet during the future age of degeneration and strife".[486]

"As for the one who would be born in accordance with the predictions, having the empowerments and authorisation to take out the heart of this treasure of Lha-brag, it was written in the prophetic treasure of Myang-ral; "Nearby the black rocks to the north of this place, the blessed incarnation of the wonderful deeds of rDo-rje bdud-'joms will arise to protect the kings of mNga'-ris."

"And also in the *Svayambhūsvodaya-tantra;* "The noble being, the *tāntrika* rDo-rje bdud-'joms, having fully taken to heart the three *abhiṣeka,* the three *tantra* and the three *upadeśa* will conceal them as treasure in front of the mountain called bKra-bzang which is to the north

483 B4 196-197

484 See notes 75 & 357, above.

485 B4 197. The entire text of A27 is included at B4 196-197

486 B4 197-198

of the direction in which the sun sets from here. There they will rest upon a rock in the shape of a tortoise for a period of 700 years from now. Then, 620 years after my departure from Tibet, there will come a *yogin* of good *karma* by the name of Rig-'dzin rgod-kyi ldem-'phru-can who will be like my own heart's son. He has been fully entrusted with the profound empowerments of that treasure and he will engage it before he reaches twice twenty years of age.""'[487]

All of that, however, has been dealt with above in Chapter One.

Having been born in fulfilment of these prophecies, then, the *gter ston* Rig-'dzin rgod-ldem unearthed the casket of Byang-gter treasures, within which the texts concerning Vajrakīla were found principally in the compartments made of gold and iron, and, "having taken out the material *kīla,* he blessed them as deities".[488]

Our commentator then proceeds to narrate the way in which these sacred treasures came to be transmitted to the present day.

In brief: the son of the *gter ston* was rNam-rgyal mgon-po and the writings on the scrolls of yellow paper that had been entrusted to him by his father were subsequently transmitted to the *mantradhara* rDo-rje mgon-po. From him they were passed on to Nga-dbang grags-pa and then to the incarnation of the *gter ston*'s son, Sangs-rgyas dpal-bzang, from whom they went to the great teacher of Se, Nam-mkha' rgyal-mtshan. Thence to the Grang-so *gter ston* Śākya bzang-po, from whom they were transmitted to bDud-'joms' own incarnation Legs-ldan bdud-'joms rdo-rje. Next in line were 'the incarnation of the Dharma king Khri-sde', bKra-shis stobs-rgyal dbang-po'i sde, and Legs-ldan-rje's further incarnation, Rig-'dzin ngag gi dbang-po. Then came the incarnation of Gung-btsan called Rig-'dzin stobs-ldan dpa'-bo, followed by Zur-chen chos-dbyings rang-grol who was himself recognised as the incarnation of gNyags Jñānakumāra. He then transmitted the lineage to 'the omniscient lord of all Tibet', the Great Fifth Dalai Lama, rDo-rje thog-med-rtsal whose own disciple, Rig-'dzin padma 'phrin-las, was the reincarnation of the original vulture-feathered *gter ston*. From him the line was passed to 'the most

487 B4 198
488 B4 200

excellent incarnation of Khams', Rig-'dzin padma gsang-sngags, the teacher from gNyags.[489]

The doctrines of Vajrakīla that were transmitted along this line, said originally to have come from India in the eighth century and to have been revealed as the Northern Treasures in 1366, are now to be looked at in Section Three.

489 B4 200-201

Part Three

THE NORTHERN TREASURES KĪLA

CHAPTER FIVE
The Byang-gter Vajrakīla tantras

When Rig-'dzin rgod-ldem opened the casket of Northern Treasures he found within it only two small *tantra* relating to Vajrakīla.[490] From the golden southern chamber of the casket he took out the *Cittaguhyakāya-tantra* in ten chapters (A3, B10, C1, E3), which opens with a description of Māra Kālarudra. This evil being is said to have arisen in the world during the period of darkness between the appearances of the buddhas Dīpaṅkara and Śākyamuni and to have become lord and master over all creatures. Because his reign was causing havoc throughout the three realms of living beings, the compassionate minds of all the buddhas were moved to act in accordance with the sacred power of their former vows. From the heart of the supreme buddha Samantabhadra in non-dual union with his consort arose the buddha Vajrasattva and his spouse. While the heart of this non-dual Vajrasattva couple remained at peace within the *dharmadhātu,* their form arose as Mahāśrīvajraheruka and his consort Krodheśvarī and from their union was born a son, Vajrarākṣasa by name, emanation of the heroic majesty of Vajrakumāra.

At that time, the Māra Kālarudra and his entire retinue of male and female *rākṣasa, māra* and arrogant ones were all destroyed. Their flesh was eaten, their blood was drunk and their bodies reduced to dust.[491] Their consciousnesses were bound under oath and they were established as protectors of the Dharma.[492]

Then (Chapter Two), on the summit of Mount Meru which was the place of subjugation, the uncompromising intention (*drag po'i dgongs pa*) of all those buddhas brought forth a son from the heart of Vajraheruka called Caṇḍavajrapāṇi[493] who was praised as the buddhas' representative and entrusted with the secret doctrines. From the mouth of the mother

---

490 He also discovered the 21st chapter of the Kīla *Garland of Flames Tantra* (A31, C13, E15) which is discussed below, Chapter Eleven.

491 This is the basis of the fierce rites of slaying which seek to re-enact that primal deed. It is also remembered during the celebration of the community feasts which are dealt with below, Chapter Twelve.

492 A3 20-21

493 The rNying-ma-pa regard this deity as a previous incarnation of Guru Padma. The Byang-gter school in particular devotes an entire cycle of teachings to the guru in this form (*Thugs sgrub drag po rtsal*).

Tṛptacakra was emanated Krodhakālī[494] and she was consecrated as his consort. From the mother's nose issued forth the consciousness of Māra Kālarudra and he was bound as a guardian of the teachings and blessed with the name Mahākāla.

Thus the scene is set and the lineage of the Vajrakīla doctrines established. The son Vajrapāṇi now begins to question his father the *mahāśrīheruka* Vajrakumāra with regard to those doctrines.

The first instruction he receives is to carry the knowledge of the destruction of Rudra into the world after the coming teacher Śākyamuni has passed into *parinirvāṇa*. He is told to set up a series of eight teachings and to manifest eight teachers[495] who will master those doctrines and practise them in the eight sacred places.[496] These eight supreme and eight secondary emanations are to be produced from Vajrapāṇi's Body, Speech, Mind, Good Qualities, Enlightened Activities, Ferocity (*raudra*), Manifestation (*nirmita*) and supreme Awareness (*vidyā*). The appearance of these manifestations in the world of Jambudvīpa is said to be Vajrapāṇi's method of converting all beings to the doctrine of the secret Mantrayāna. His form as the ferocious Caṇḍavajrapāṇi, totally free of all fear and apprehension, is the emanation of the heart of Vajrakumāra which subdues all that is to be subdued in the body. All that is to be subdued in the speech is to be controlled by the *samādhi* of fierce HŪṀ[497] and by the repetition of HŪṀ, which is the miraculous power of the Speech of all *tathāgata* without exception. All that is to be subdued within the mind is tamed by the innermost essence of the Mind of Samantabhadra, which is shown to be naturally arising and spontaneously present (*svayambhūsvodaya*).

For those who delight in emanation, the root *maṇḍala* of *heruka* is shown. For those who possess mind and intelligence (*blo dang mig ldan*), the *mahottara* Vajrakumāra is shown. For those who delight in extreme

---

494 Another name for the well-known Vajravārāhī.

495 The *aṣṭamahāsādhana* and the eight *ācārya* who are said to have been the original disseminators of those doctrines are discussed above, Chapter Four.

496 The charnel grounds that arose in the eight directions marking the sites where Rudra's scattered body fell.

497 According to STTS VI, HŪṀ is the '*vajra* syllable' of Vajrapāṇi by means of which Rudra himself was first subjugated.

brevity, the heart practice of the supreme son[498] is shown. For the holders of the awareness of fierce *mantra,* 13 *upadeśa* of attainment are shown. For those who delight in the practice of *nāḍī* and *prāṇa* within the body, the method of Krodhakālī is taught and, in order to protect the teachings, the invocation of Mahākāla is shown.[499]

These six topics then form the subject matter of the next five chapters of the *tantra.*[500] First of all Vajrapāṇi asks for an explanation of the method through which one generates the *herukamaṇḍala* and Chapter Three is entirely devoted to answering this question.

The *yogin* is instructed to retreat to an isolated forest grove in the mountains. There he should make offerings to the peaceful local spirits (*bhūmipati*) and generate the four Great Kings (*caturmahārāja*) in the cardinal directions around his chosen site. He should then draw the *maṇḍala,* square and with four doors, by carefully laying down the lines and colours.[501] A sanctified *kīla* (*tshangs pa'i phur bu*) is placed in the centre as the abode of the *devatā,* with an encircling retinue of 21 triangles around this, and then all the lesser gods are established in their proper places.

The *yogin* then sets out the essential inner offerings of nectar, blood and sacrificial *bali* cake (*sman rak gtor gsum*) and, with his face turned towards the north, he should gradually absorb his mind into the *samādhi* of the rite, performing the activities in a state of non-agitation.

---

498 This is a vague honorific title which, in the present instance, refers to Caṇḍavajrapāṇi, the son of Vajrasattva. Elsewhere the term is generally used to denote either Vajrakīla himself (as the supreme son of *heruka*) or his own supreme sons (*nirmāṇakāya* emanations) who may be either the four known as Buddhakīla, Ratnakīla, Padmakīla and Karmakīla (Viśvakīla) or the 21 known as the seven supreme sons of the Body, seven of Speech and seven of Mind. We have also met with the term used to denote the three deities Amṛtakuṇḍalin, Hayagrīva and either Yamāntaka or Mahābala.

499 A3 21-23

500 Exactly which texts are being referred to here as "the 13 *upadeśa* of attainment" is unknown.

501 A general explanation of these techniques is to be found in my *Maṇḍala Meaning and Method.*

Four times per day the *yogin* should make offerings and recite the deity's *mantra*.[502] He should visualise himself in the form of the six-armed Vajrakīla, just as has been described above, and recite the *mantra* until this form is stable and clear. He should then recite it while meditating upon the sphere of the deity's mind, after which he should abide in the state beyond conception. In that way, during the cycle of day and night, he performs the recitations in proper succession until six thousand million recitations have been completed. When success in the practice has been achieved the *yogin* will directly perceive the face of the deity, the ritual *kīla* in the *maṇḍala* will jump up and dance around, and the offerings of blood and semen will come to the boil.[503]

In Chapter Four, Vajrapāṇi is taught the method of meditating upon Mahottarakīla, which is a practice to be engaged in by those who have gained the signs of success in the six-armed Vajrakīla outlined above.

---

502 Our text C32 explains the intention of this Vajrakīla *mantra* in terms of the enlightened perception of *dharmatā*. Thus, OṀ is said to be the supreme foundation or primary cause (*gzhi rtsa*), the instigator of all *tathāgata*. It is the syllable that manifests all *jina*. It stands for the underlying reality (*dharmatā*) of *nirvāṇa* beyond suffering and the mind of enlightenment itself. By VAJRA is indicated the *mudrā* that seals the body, speech and mind of the countless sentient beings that arise from within the sphere which is not limited by either depth or circumference. Those beings are recognised as not abiding anywhere and this is the truth of the *nirvāṇa* of the enlightened mind. As the *yogin* recites KĪLIKĪLA, all beings are 'liberated' (i.e. killed) by means of the rays of light that emanate from his body, speech and mind and yet they are not cut off within the truth of the *nirvāṇa* of enlightenment. YA indicates the great passion of the enlightened mind of *dharmatā* and the compassion that remains until both heaven and hell are emptied. In this way all beings are established in the non-abiding *dharmatā* of the enlightened mind. SARVA indicates the vast number of forms of living beings that arise from the womb of the Mother on account of *bodhicitta*. They are known as non-abiding by the wisdom of the utterly pure enlightened mind. By means of the *bodhicitta* arising from the aperture of the Father, the enlightened mind manifests limitless skilful means as a cause for all births and this is signified by the word VIGHNĀN. In that way, by BAṀ, the enlightened mind of *dharmatā* beyond all sorrow is the non-dual union of wisdom and means. HŪṀ is the enlightened mind of *dharmatā* beyond all suffering, the pure offspring of the five *kula,* the spontaneously accomplished five *kāya* that reach to the limit of the absolute. By PHAṬ, the spontaneously accomplished perfect activities that are achieved entirely without effort are the enlightened mind of the ultimate truth of *nirvāṇa*. The single-pointed *kīla* of such understanding is known as the *svabhāva* vehicle of the past and future.

C32 341, taken out as a treasure from the black iron cache in the north.

503 A3 23-26

Going to a terrifying spot where both sky and earth have ferocious forms, the *yogin* draws the complete *maṇḍala* adorned with courtyards, doors, gateways and so on, in the centre of which is the triangular abode of the deity with a half-moon at each of its three corners. He should close the boundaries to obstructing forces[504] and implant the deity's *niṣevaṇakīla* in the centre, surrounded by the three *kīla* of Body, Speech and Mind. The *kīla* of Body is to be implanted on the half-moon in the east, with those of the Speech and Mind on the moons to the south and north respectively. In the courtyards are placed 12 *kīla* for the three red and black groups[505] and the four *kīla* of the activities are arranged in the four doorways. The threefold offerings of nectar, blood and cake are set out together with the other fierce offerings,[506] and in the inner courtyard of the *maṇḍala* are placed four kinds of milk, black blood and melted butter.

---

504 A36 (A48) describes three stages of *sīmābandha*. In the first ('outer') stage, with himself clearly visualised as the deity Vajrakīla, the *yogin* summons all the obstructors and misleaders and warns them to depart. He then recites the well-known *mantra* of four HŪṀs which is said to have great magical power, effective in all rites (SDPT 76 & 91-92). The 'inner' boundary is closed by the *daśakrodha* kings who emanate from the heart of the *yogin* and immediately proceed to annihilate the ten non-virtues, thus closing the border to all impurities. The 'secret' boundary consists of an awning (*vitāna*) of *kīla* above, from which rain down *kīla* missiles, descending like thunderbolts, a foundation (*bhūmi*) of *kīla* below, from which *kīla* dart out, rising and falling like flames in a blazing fire, and an encircling latticework (*jālaka*) of *kīla* from which more *kīla* spark out like shooting stars. In this way, the site is protected on all sides by an impassable barrier of violently active nails. The entire area, furthermore, is patrolled by an army of ferocious deities who kill all enemies and obstructors with a variety of weapons. A36 254-255

505 The term *dmar nag sde gsum* occurs frequently in the Byang-gter Kīla literature as a referent for the male (black) and female (red) protectors. In the present case, however, it clearly refers to the 12 females, Śvanmukhā and the rest. Precedents are to be found in Indian literature where *kṛṣṇarakta* is taken to mean 'delighting in darkness' and to refer to those who roam abroad at night (*rātrau caramāṇā*). Such a term (which could also be taken to mean 'delighting in evil') is entirely appropriate to this class of subjugated protectors but the play on word-meanings is not carried over in the literal Tibetan translation. Alexis Sanderson, "Evidence of the Textual Dependence of the Buddhist Yogānuttaratantras on the Tantric Śaiva Canon" 24

506 All the regular peaceful tantric offerings have their wrathful equivalents. Thus; *arghya* and *pādya* are bowls of blood, *puṣpa* is a flower-like arrangement of sense-organs, *dhūpa* is the stench of smouldering flesh, *dīpa* is a lamp with wick of human hair fed by human fat, *gandha* is bile, *naivedya* is a plate of human meat and *śabda* is provided by thigh-bone trumpets and skull drums.

When all is ready, in an instant of thought the *yogin* transforms himself into the supreme form of the deity with nine heads, 18 hands and eight legs that trample the arrogant worldly gods. At his head, throat and heart he should imagine *jñānasattva* like himself in form but white, red and blue respectively in colour. All should be seen as a unified appearance of clarity and emptiness (*bhāsvaraśūnyasaṁbheda*). Around him are the three supreme sons: the white Mahābala in the east, red Hayagrīva in the south and dark green Amṛtakuṇḍalin in the north. The red and black *mātaraḥ* in the courtyard are thought of as messengers that listen attentively to one's orders and immediately carry them out. Four wrathful goddesses stand as guardians in the gates. With the divine pride of himself as the deity, the *yogin* recites the various *mantra* of accomplishment while he sees himself standing between the sun and moon, encircling Mount Meru with his arms and trampling the great trichiliocosm (*trisāhasramahāsāhasralokadhātu*) beneath his feet. In a single gulp he drains the great ocean of existence.

The signs of success are that the *yogin* truly sees the *maṇḍala* deities and that they carry out his orders, either in reality, in visions or in dream. After that, by the recitation of the activity *mantra,* he will have the ability to summon people[507] and wild animals from afar to act as his servants and the sacramental articles become empowered. His *kīla* will then truly slay demons as it is stabbed into an effigy made of parched barley flour.

When practising the rite in order to gain the supreme *siddhi* of buddhahood, the *yogin* performs these activities in the guise of the deity himself.[508] If, however, he simply desires to perform the fierce activities in an ordinary way, he should incite the three classes of red and black protectors to act.[509]

Chapter Five explains the practice of Caṇḍavajrapāṇi, 'the supreme heart son' (*thugs sras mchog*), for which the external supports of a *maṇḍala* and ritual articles are not required. The *yogin,* remaining established in the unwavering bliss of spontaneous *samādhi,* is instructed to transform himself into the deity in a single instant of mindful awareness. The form of the deity is described in some detail in the text and it is said that his mind abides in a fearless equanimity of naturally-arising ferocity. When his awareness moves from that state, then, like a thunderbolt falling

---

507 Specifically, women (*bud med*) are mentioned.

508 Curiously, the deity named in the text is Caṇḍavajrapāṇi.

509 A3 26-29

from the centre of the sky, the *yogin* should build up a wall of sound by reciting the ferocious syllable HŪṀ.

A single HŪṀ is explained as the intentionality of *dharmatā,* two are said to include skilful means, three are the heart sound of the *trikāya,*[510] four are the four immeasurables for the benefit of living beings, five symbolise the five *jñāna,* six possess the six letters,[511] seven are speech with the melodies of Brahmā,[512] eight are the harmonious sounds of the wrathful ones,[513] nine bring the *tribhava* under control[514] and ten grind to dust those who mislead the world.[515]

These HŪṀs are to be imagined springing forth from the *yogin*'s body of divine pride like sparks from a fire, pervading the entire *bhājanaloka* so that all appearances are purified. The *yogin* should contemplate with clarity all phenomena as HŪṀ,[516] bright like the stars and planets in the sky. One thousand million world systems reverberate with the sound of HŪṀ like the thundering roar of a turquoise dragon and he should abide in the sphere of awareness which is the union of clarity and emptiness, as if watching the sun rise brightly in the sky.

Without wavering from that *samādhi,* the *yogin* should recite the ten HŪṀs either three, seven or 21 times. The signs of success for the *yogin* are that he becomes free of desire and loses all mundane attachments, the world appears as if filled with the light of the sun and moon rising simultaneously in the sky, the *yogin*'s own inherent wisdom shines forth in all its nakedness and whatever accomplishments he thinks of ('the *siddhi* of the heart') will be attained.[517]

In Chapter Six, the *sādhana* of Vajravārāhī is explained for the benefit of one who desires to experience the reality of voidness.

Such a *yogin* should go to an extremely isolated place and meditate upon his body as having neither flesh, blood, bones nor internal organs. Like an illusion, it is a body made only of light and he should meditate

---

510 Text B. A says they are the sound of Body, Speech and Mind.

511 The *ṣaḍakṣari* are OṀ MAṆIPADME HŪṀ.

512 Seven kinds of harmonic pitch or musical tone (*glu dbyangs kyi nges pa bdun*) are listed in the *Mahāvyutpatti*.

513 The eight great deities of *mahāyogatantra*.

514 Presumably the *tribhava* are controlled throughout the three times in order to bring the total to nine.

515 The *daśadikpāla*.

516 Text B says that all appearances arise as the luminous clarity of the mind.

517 A3 29-31

upon it as being red, shining and clear. Then, on a sun disc situated below his navel, the *yogin* should visualise the body of Vārāhī arising from the syllable MA, red in colour and as small as a grain of mustard. She is said to be the embodiment of the *yogin*'s own inherent wisdom and thus the *yogin* generates an awareness of emptiness and form.[518]

The seventh chapter of the *tantra* is devoted to an exposition of the sanguinary wrathful rites to be carried out in an isolated and terrifying charnel ground on the edge of a precipitous ravine. There the *yogin* should build up a triangular *maṇḍala* in three tiers,[519] which he smears with the blood of vultures or wild beasts containing an admixture of powdered iron, copper and bell-metal. The *maṇḍala* is then encircled by a series of 21 *rākṣasī,* small triangles made of poisonous wood.

An effigy is prepared, into which the consciousness of the enemy is to be summoned, and it is bound with green and red threads and placed in the centre of the *maṇḍala.* Then, maintaining the *samādhi* of himself as the *mahottaradeva,* the *yogin* recites the *mantra* which summons the three groups of oath-bound protectors and puts them to work: OṀ VAJRAKĪLI KĪLAYA DHADDHI MAMA KARMA ŚĪGHRAM KĀRAYE SARVA VIGHNĀN BAṀ HŪṀ PHAṬ. After three thousand recitations, the oath-bound ones should really appear and then the *yogin* should perform the ritual of dragging forth the enemy. This he does by imagining 21 ferocious beings[520] to emanate from the depths of dark blue triangles,[521] which themselves are thought of as having arisen from the syllable E. These violent gods are then imagined to truly drag forth the consciousness of the enemy to be subdued. Reciting NṚ and TRI as many times as necessary, the *yogin* adds VAJRĀṄKUŚA JAḤ at the end and it is by means of this wild *mantra* of five heroic syllables that the enemy is truly held captive in the effigy. This will certainly be achieved if the *mantra* are recited for three whole days. The *yogin* slays (the living effigy) by saying "*So-and-so* TRIG NAN" and piercing the *kīla* into the centre of the skull. "*So-and-so* NYAGS THUM RIL" at the base of the neck. "HUR THUM rBAD" on the life vein. "NĀŚAYA rBAD" on the navel and "MĀRAYA rBAD" on the four limbs.[522]

---

518 This symbolic meditation thus aims to achieve a result identical in nature to that of the more prosaic *Prajñāpāramitāhṛdaya-sūtra.* A3 31-34

519 B & C. A3 says that the *maṇḍala* should be square.

520 Unnamed but most likely to be the 21 supreme sons of Vajrakīla.

521 Presumably the previously laid out circle of 21 triangles.

522 The text instructs the *yogin* to dissolve the *mantra* into those specified parts of the effigy.

Signs of success in the rite are (the appearances in a dream) of living beings dying of disease or being slain in a hunt, or the destruction of a town from fire or the *yogin* hearing the sound of laughter. Following the arising of these signs, the effigy should be cut up and divided into three pieces:[523] one of which is burned in a fire of poisonous wood, one of which is entrusted to the black *nāga* and one of which is to be cast out and trampled underfoot.[524] Finally the *yogin* should present offerings of thanksgiving to the *dharmapāla.*[525]

Chapter Eight is very short and merely confirms that the demon Rudra, following his defeat by the buddhas, was instructed in the doctrines of secret *mantra* and initiated as a powerful protector of the Vajrakīla teachings. He is worshipped as Legs-ldan-bdud (*Sādhumāra, 'the Good Demon') by waving a black silk tassel and reciting his *mantra,* thus causing him to be present in the *samaya* article of shaggy yak's blood.[526] During the time of his invocation he should be generated in wrathful guise, wearing a long black gown and standing in the posture of a champion. During the time of the attainment of *siddhi* he is generated as one of great energy, like a king mounted upon a lion. When he is being summoned to carry out the magical deeds he is generated as a hero, mounted upon a tiger in the manner of a messenger. He is a deity through whom all activities may be realised. Due to the fact that in the ancient past this protector was once the direct adversary of Vajradhara himself, his *sādhana* is said to be very profound.[527]

The non-dual unity of the teacher and the doctrine is presented in Chapter Nine as the special characteristic (*lakṣaṇa*) of *tantra*. Mahāśrīvajrakumāra announces that he himself is the body of Vajrakīla and that this is the *tantra* of his mind (*citta-tantra*) which must be kept secret from those of no merit. Outwardly it is due to the existence of his body (called the *kāya-tantra*) that this secret *tantra* of his mind can exist. What it teaches as *sādhana* is the spontaneous self-arising of all the wrathful ones from the *vajra* HŪṀs (reverberating in his own heart). Because it is a

---

523 Text B, in common with all recensions of the BRT and the *sādhana* A44 etc., says that a single effigy should be divided into three pieces but A & C say that three effigies are required.

524 These three activities are discussed below, Chapter Ten.

525 A3 34-35

526 This means that a bowl of yak's blood is to be placed upon the altar as the life support of the deity and he is imagined to be present within that.

527 A3 35-36

doctrine of ferocious self arising, this Vajrakīla *tantra* is known as *Svayambhūsvodaya.*[528]

Chapter Ten is merely a brief colophon. It tells us that this secret *tantra* of the *kīlakāya* was taught by the *bhagavat* to Vajrapāṇi for the purpose of subduing all those who are to be converted. It names the special protector of the doctrine as Mahākāla and tells us that he will subdue all enemies and obstructors who cause interference to this *tantra,* wherever a copy of the text is to be found. By entrusting the doctrine to Mahākāla in this way, its stability is ensured so that it may remain in the world for a long time to come.[529]

The second *tantra* to be included within several of the collections is the BRT (*Śrīvajrakīlapotrihala-tantra,* sic),[530] discovered by Rig-'dzin rgod-ldem in the black iron compartment in the northern section of the treasure chest. Its internal structure is much better organised than that of the previous *tantra* and I take it to be a later composition. The former text seems to me to be a very early Vajrakīla *tantra* indeed, or at least to include primitive elements.[531] We have seen that it was delivered as a discourse by the main deity to his interlocutor Caṇḍavajrapāṇi and this is the normal pattern in the earliest texts for the pronouncement of both *sūtra* and *tantra*. The following *tantra,* however, claims to have been 'self proclaimed' in a manner that is typical of the eighth century texts followed by the rNying-ma-pa school. That is to say, it was taught by the lord of the *maṇḍala* to a retinue of his own emanations and, instead of being taught in a 'recognisable' place[532] it was taught in the Akaniṣṭha heaven (here em-

---

528 A3 36-37. Curiously, this appellation is the one given in the chronicle looked at, above, in Chapter Four dealing with the mythical origin of the *tantra*. What is strange is that the words quoted therein come not from this *tantra* but from that belonging to the black deity cycle (scrutinised below).

529 A3 37

530 A2, B31, C19, E21. An edition and translation of this *tantra* are to be found in my *A Bolt of Lightning from the Blue* 93-106.

531 According to this *mahottarakīla* cycle, Rudra was subdued by Vajrapāṇi which accords with the earlier teachings of the STTS etc. but is at variance with the later doctrines of *mahāyoga* in which the credit is given to Hayagrīva. This cycle also maintains the early very close association of Vajrakīla with Amṛtakuṇḍalin, an identity that was gradually resolved in the later *tantra* such as the BRT where the two deities are separated entirely.

532 The summit of Mount Meru may be far away but in Buddhist cosmology it is still reckoned to be a physical abode.

ployed as a synonym for *dharmadhātu*) that has neither centre nor circumference. In other words, its locality is not to be located anywhere.

Furthermore, while this second *tantra* displays a clear and well established Vajrakīla *maṇḍala,* the first was abbreviated and vague. The retinue of 21 ferocious deities described in the previous *tantra* is rarely encountered in the Northern Treasures Kīla literature and the fierce rituals taught therein, as shown above in Chapter Two, can be historically established as forerunners of the deified nail.

Finally, the contents of the first *tantra* are not all of relevance to the cult of Vajrakīla. The *sādhana* of Vajrapāṇi and Vārāhī, for example, although still popular as *yoganiruttara* practices, no longer form a part of this cult. The teachings of the second *tantra,* on the other hand, are all of prime significance and this leads me to conclude that the text was written down at a time when the cult doctrines themselves had already become well ordered and systematised.

The *nidāna* (Chapter One) of this second *tantra* describes a ferocious charnel ground within which is situated the *maṇḍala* of deities having Mahāśrīvajrakumāra and his consort Tṛptacakra in the centre. Around them are arranged the *daśakrodha* kings with their consorts, the twenty *piśācī* who are their emanated messengers, the supreme sons who fully accomplish all *karma,*[533] and the further emanations and countless tertiary emanations of which their retinue is comprised. All of these deities are said to abide there "in their natural state" and this is explained by likening them to reflected forms, like images in a mirror or the moon in water, which rest in the sphere of natural meaning without ever being covered by the stains of emotional afflictions. The teacher is said to be like a miraculous display in the sky, teaching the Dharma of fierce *mantra* without ever straying from this natural condition.

The second chapter emphasises the importance of practising the *sādhana* of unsurpassed enlightenment and the lord of the *maṇḍala* urges his retinue to arise from the profundity of their rapture in order to demonstrate it for the sake of those to be converted. "The chief of families is the *vajrakula*. The light of wisdom is the destroyer of darkness which overcomes the afflictions of *saṁsāra*. The Conqueror (Buddha) is the sole complete friend of sentient beings. For the sake of all beings, the throne of the teacher must be magnificently displayed!" Thus he spoke.

---

533 I.e. the four Kīla of the activities (*catvāri karmāni*).

In Chapter Three it is specified that the Akaniṣṭha palace within which these deities abide is really the *dharmadhātu,* an association already made evident by the way in which it had been described but not one endorsed by earlier Buddhist teachings on cosmology.[534] The lord of the *maṇḍala* then arose there in bodily form. He is described as having three faces, six arms and four legs spread wide apart. His right face is white, the left red and his central face is blue. In his right hands he holds a nine-pronged *vajra* and a five-pronged *vajra.* In his left, a blazing mass of fire and a *khaṭvāṅga.* With his final pair of hands he rolls a *kīla* and the sky is filled with his *vajra* wings. His body is adorned with the articles of the charnel ground and he remains sporting in non-duality with his spouse.

"HŪṀ Anger must be destroyed by means of *vajra* wrath! A great blue blazing weapon arises as a drop from the centre of the sky. It enters the door of the life force and one should meditate upon it in the centre of the heart." Thus he spoke.

This establishment of the *mahābindu* within the *yogin*'s heart is highly reminiscent of Hindu teachings concerning the *puruṣa* or 'inner man'. The *Śāradātilaka* XXV.58 says that the *puruṣa* residing in the heart is pure consciousness (*caitanyamātra*) and that it abides upon a sun disc (*ravimaṇḍalastha*) as 'the primordial seed' (*ādibīja* = *mahābindu* in Buddhist terminology). Other texts indicate the *puruṣa* as all-pervading like the sky and composed of radiant light.

The *Vāstusūtra-Upaniṣad* IV.1 describes this inner man as standing "like the post of a *yūpa*" (*yūpasya daṇḍa iva*) which, as noted above, may be identified with our *kīla*. The *Brahmasaṁhitā* V.3 places a *vajrakīla* in the heart as the *mahāyantra* ('great device') which is the only non-Buddhist reference to a *vajrakīla* that I have encountered. That great device, situated in the pericarp of a lotus in the heart, is surrounded by a protective circle of ten spikes (*śūla*) situated in the ten directions and thus corresponds to the teachings given herein of the Vajrakīla *maṇḍala* in the

---

534 Akaniṣṭha heaven is described in early *abhidharma* works as the most subtle ('highest') of abodes within the *rūpadhātu*. The *dharmadhātu,* on the other hand, is an all-encompassing concept that is beyond the defining limitations of any of the three 'worldly' *dhātu*. *Yogatantra* texts cite Akaniṣṭhaghanavyūha, here associated with the *dharmadhātu,* as the site of Śākyamuni's enlightenment.

heart.[535] That this is the intended meaning is made explicit in the *abhiṣeka* text outlined in the following chapter of the present work.

This same verse opens the VKMK. It also occurs in Chapter Seven of the *Phur pa bcu gnyis*[536] and in many other places, thus confirming my thesis that this *tantra* was compiled at a time when the doctrines of Vajrakīla had already become fully formulated. Furthermore, these words are said to have been spoken by the nine-headed scorpion when he taught the Vajrakīla *tantra* in the Śītavana charnel ground, as recounted in our text B13.

The *tantra* then goes on to explain the etymology of the epithet 'supreme son' (this time applied to Vajrakīla as the supreme son of all *tathāgata*): the word 'son' being said to mean that he comes without birth from the *dharmatā* and 'supreme' means that he is the spontaneous fulfilment of enlightened activity. He is the son of all the buddhas in order to destroy Rudra, where 'son' means the unborn *vajra* son.

The *daśakrodha* couples and all of the messengers are then described as having dark blue ferocious forms. They have single faces and roll *kīla* in their two hands. The lower halves of their bodies are sharp-pointed, three-edged nails. They have *vajra* wings and are adorned with the artefacts of charnel grounds. With cries of HŪṀ and PHAṬ they terrify the world and subjugate all vicious beings without exception.

Now follows the second verse of the VKMK: "HŪṀ The sacred oath of killing by compassion is neither murder nor aggression. Having established the aggregates (*pañcaskandha*) as *vajra*,[537] one should meditate upon consciousness as [the] *vajra* [deity]."

The next three verses (with minor variations in wording) are also to be found in the VKMK, but the order of the first and second verses is reversed in the Peking edition.

"HŪṀ Meditating upon oneself as the wisdom embodiment of all the buddhas, one should arise in the unbearable form of blazing wrath that emanates from the essential nature of the *vajradharmadhātu*.

---

535 B. Baumer, "Puruṣa" in K. Vatsyayan (ed.), *Kalātattvakośa* 23-40 See also note 545, below.

536 NGB vol.19

537 This line in the VKMK reads; *phung po rdo rje'i bdag nyid de.*

"HŪṀ All those who hold the awareness of Vajrakumāra must bring into effect the universal *vajra*.[538] The deities of the *bhavakīla* must fulfil wisdom's wrath!

"HŪṀ Through the practice of skilful means[539] for the benefit of sentient beings, disciplining those suitable to be converted by means of love and compassion, having completed the activities of buddhahood, please bestow empowerments and blessings in this place."

The VKMK then calls forth all the deities of the *maṇḍala* by means of their individual *mantra* before continuing with the following six-line verse of general invocation which, in our *tantra,* follows immediately:

"HŪṀ In order that the empowerments, realisations and successful accomplishment (*siddhi*) of the universal *kīla* may be attained, you deities of wisdom wrath must please come here! When the gods of great wrath have arrived, the signs and symbols of success must be shown and the *siddhi* of the Kīla be bestowed!"

As this is said, the exceedingly ferocious ones are imagined to come forth from the depths of the charnel ground and to pulverise all the enemies and obstructors in the ten directions.

Then, in Chapter Four, all the arrogant worldly demons who have become terrified at the wrathful might of the *heruka* buddhas, together with the *mātaraḥ* who have developed power through wisdom, speak to the *maṇḍala* deities and offer their essential life force, pledging themselves to act as servants. Having taken the pledge, they are given a stern warning by the lord of the *maṇḍala* never to transgress their oaths. These words of warning are found in the VKMK immediately after they are summoned[540] to take their places around the periphery of the *maṇḍala*.

"HŪṀ Whichever evil being shall transgress these secret *vajra* oaths shall have his skull drawn out in one hundred splinters by the *mahāheruka*s of great power. Listen here, you hosts of trouble-makers and misleaders, do not deviate from my instructions!"

---

538 The VKMK reads *'khor ba rdo rje* instead of *srid pa'i rdo rje* throughout.

539 This verse occurs many times in the various Vajrakīla texts at our disposal, usually with the phrase given here (*thabs kyi spyad pas*) but sometimes reading *thugs spyod pas* ("through the heart practice").

540 They are summoned by means of the *mantra* that they originally offered as their 'essential life forces'. The holder of these 'life forces', the one who knows their *mantra,* can then summon these oath bound ones at will.

The *tantra* now goes on to describe the occasion on which these fierce spirits originally took their oaths, and the conversation continues with the frightened worldly gods submitting fully to the authority of the *maṇḍala* deities and affirming the sincerity of their pledge. They seek refuge in the compassionate deities of the *maṇḍala* and offer their help in the fulfilment of any activity that the *yogin* may request of them.

In Chapter Five these oath-bound ones are taken at their word and put to work. The pattern of calling their names in order to invoke their presence is almost identical to the pattern found in the VKMK: "HŪṀ The time has come for the *mahāsamaya*! The time has come for the great emanation! The time of the mighty messengers has come! The time has come for the Śvanmukhā[541] (sisters)! The time of the Mahātmādevī has come! The time has come for the great Bhūmipati! The time to fulfil your sacred oaths has come![542] The time has come to bring forth your powerful skill!"[543]

They are then ordered to catch, beat and securely bind all those hindering demons who interrupt the attainment of *siddhi*. They are told to identify the interrupters by their vicious, angry minds and not to confuse them with friends.[544] Finally they are instructed to pull them in forthwith, cast them down and drive them mad (or make them silent) so that they become utterly subdued.

The deity Vajrakīla then turns his attention to the captives brought in by his speedy messengers and warns them to pay careful heed to his admonitions. All of this has its parallel in the VKMK, where the same sentiments are found expressed in different words. With the closing verses of this chapter, however, we return to a more exact correspondence:

"HŪṀ All you vicious ones with angry minds, whether you be gods or demons, any that obstruct me must be deprived of their magic power and witchcraft. You must be thrashed! Such is the diligence of the blazing *vajra*.

"All evil ones who transgress my orders will have their hearts burnt up on the peak of *vajra* fire and their body and speech will be reduced to

---

541 This name is translated into Tibetan in the VKMK.

542 Line omitted here in the VKMK but inserted much further on, at the end of the section, in slightly different wording.

543 The VKMK reads; "The time to liberate has come!"

544 The *yogin*'s task is to recognise his own emotional defilements as the true enemy and not follow them as if they were his friends.

ashes. In the blazing mortars of the wrathful mothers, when pounded by the *vajra* hammers, even the gods are destroyed!" And that brings us to the close of Chapter Five.

In Chapter Six the method of becoming one with the deity (*āsevana*) is shown: Arranging the ritual *bali* in an isolated place, the *yogin* should clearly visualise himself in the form of the great glorious deity. In his heart he should imagine the *jñānasattva,* unadorned and similar in appearance to the main deity, and he should meditate upon him as being the size of his thumb tip.[545] In his heart is his emblem, a nine-pronged *vajra,* the size of a grain of barley. In the centre of that is a blue syllable HŪṀ, the symbol of speech, as fine as if drawn by a single hair. Around the outside of that revolves the Kīla *mantra,* golden in colour and extremely fine.

When the *yogin* has perfected that visualisation within his heart, he should imagine rays of light spreading out from the *mantra,* pervading the whole trichiliocosm and filling it with with radiance. By that light the vicious beings of the three realms are subdued. The *mantra* itself should be recited thirty million times in the state of clarity and emptiness, until the signs of success have arisen.

Now, in Chapters Seven and Eight, the method of propitiating the deity is shown in a manner that is almost identical to the fierce rite described in Chapter Seven of the *Cittaguhyakāya-tantra* above. Whereas, however, the former *tantra* described those whose task it is to drag forth the enemies and obstructors as a series of 21 ferocious beings radiating from dark blue triangles, the present text says that these ferocious helpers are innumerable. Also, while the above *tantra* instructs the *yogin* to place various syllables of the 'destructive activity *mantra*'[546] upon the four main *cakra* and the four limbs of the effigy to be destroyed, the present *tantra* gives no such instructions and the *mantra* itself is much longer. Finally, the present *tantra* naturally enough does not instruct the *yogin* to visualise himself in the 18-armed *mahottara* form of the deity whilst engaged in the rite.

Following that, Chapter Nine teaches a meditational equipoise (*samāhitasamādhi*) that clearly emphasises the essentially compassionate nature of the wrathful rite. In order to subjugate the vicious beings of the three realms, it explains the special activity of *samādhi* to be the arising of

---

545 This description of the *jñānasattva* corresponds to the description in the *Upaniṣads* of the *puruṣa* or inner spirit of man. The *Kaṭhopaniṣad* IV.13 says *aṅguṣṭhamātraḥ puruṣo jyotir ivādhūmakaḥ;* "(Shining) like a light without smoke, the *puruṣa* is the size of one's thumb tip." See also above, note 535.

546 The DHADDHI *mantra*.

the enlightened mind from the unmistaken and uncontrived *dharmatā* with the speed of a dreadful flashing thunderbolt. This is the *bodhicittakīla* which is fully accomplished in controlling the *traidhātuka* and it is called 'The Killer of the Three Realms Without Exception'. Having ground the bodies of the demons down to mincemeat, the *yogin* should imagine the triple world filled with flesh and blood. This is the secret requisite, the vital juice of the oral commentaries that slays the lustful ones by means of compassion. In a single moment of enlightenment exists *nirvāṇa* beyond comprehension, *nirvāṇa* that transcends the world. This enlightened mind that cuts through doubt is the unchanging *bodhicitta*. Free of sin it is perfectly liberated, free of exertion it is spontaneously fulfilled.

The exegesis of the wrathful rites in terms of an inner meditative experience which does not contradict the essential tenets of *buddhadharma* is continued in Chapter Ten where the *samādhi* of secret *mantra* is explained under four headings:

The first thing to be shown is the non-dual mind of enlightenment. Secondly, the various awarenesses (*vidyā*) are taught. Third is the intentionality of violent *mantra* recitation, and fourthly, body, speech and mind are explained.

(1) Upon the production of a thought one should meditate upon it as the utter purity within the very nature of perfect purity and, in this way, if a pure thought arises great happiness is attained. If the *mantra* is recited many times, anything can be attained and, if the *samaya* vows are protected, *siddhi* will quickly result.

(2) Employing the *bodhicittakīla* the *yogin* should penetrate perfect knowledge for his own benefit. Then, for the benefit of others, he should destroy the ignorance of all sentient beings in the *traidhātuka* without exception by means of Vajrakīla.

(3) For the sake of beings who are lacking in awareness, the skilful *yogin* should bring about the results of pacification (*śāntika*), increasing prosperity (*pauṣṭika*), overpowering (*vaśya*) and destroying (*abhicāra*), as required, by means of the appropriate rites.

(4) To the mind of enlightenment, oneself as well as all gods and demons are free of both birth and death. Cutting the vital breath of the afflictions, death is cast aside and one's span of life is prolonged.

(We shall have occasion to return to these four overarching themes during the course of our continuing study of Northern Treasures Vajrakīla literature.)

This tenth chapter then continues with a religious etymology of the word '*kīla*', as outlined above in our Chapter Three:

"*Kī*" means that all and everything is the mind of enlightenment.

"*La*" means that the enlightened mind pervades all things.

And so on ... These are indications of the nature of the deity and therefore, it is said, it is exceedingly important for the *yogin* to engage himself in the praxis of Vajrakīla.

Chapter Eleven is really just a colophon. Within it we learn that this 'supremely secret blazing *Black Razor Tantra*' is taught by all *sugata* of the four times and ten directions within the unborn sphere of the *dharmatā* in order to slay those sentient beings with perverse views. It is to be entrusted in its entirety to one whose thoughts have been purified, who has sharp (penetrating) wisdom, is diligent in perseverance, who has attained a realisation of the Mahāyāna, who possesses an excellent mind and is of good *karma*. Finally, we are told, this *tantra* is protected by the oath-bound *dharmapāla*s.

Thus we note that this particular *tantra* exhibits a very clear and well ordered structure. The *maṇḍala* of deities is clearly defined at the beginning and then the rites associated with them are set out in a logical manner. We are reminded, however, that these appearances and activities are no more than the illusory play of compassionate wisdom that arise merely in order to counteract delusion. The ultimate nature of the entire 'wrathful' display, then, is actually not other than the blissful peace of *nirvāṇa*.

In subsequent chapters we shall see how the fundamental teachings of these two *tantra* form the basis for the entire cycle of Vajrakīla texts at our disposal.

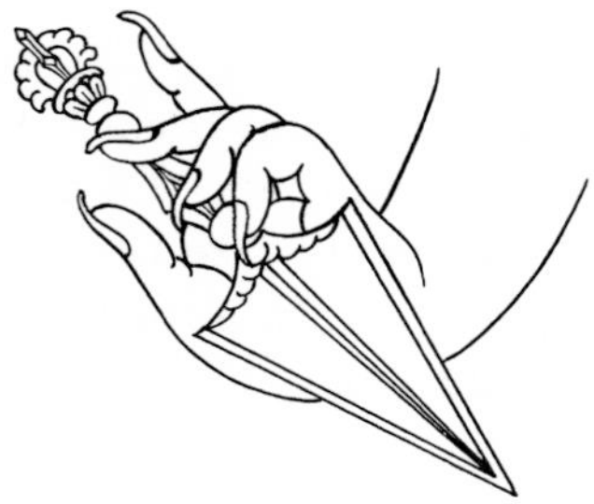

CHAPTER SIX
Rites of empowerment

In his general introduction to the Byang-gter Kīla cycle (B4), 'Phrin-las bdud-'joms mentions five topics to be discussed with regard to empowerment: 1) The characteristics of the *ācārya* who is to bestow the empowerment, 2) The nature of the disciple who is to receive it, 3) The benefits to be derived from the bestowal of empowerment, 4) The disadvantages of not being initiated, and 5) The reason why it is necessary.

He then deals with each of these topics in turn by citing pertinent passages from various *mahāyogatantra* to be found in the NGB and elsewhere. Thus, with regard to the characteristics of the *ācārya* who is to bestow the empowerment, he quotes a verse from the *Māyājāla-tantra* (NGB 222) thus;

> The teacher (is like) a copious river
> abundant with treasure.
> Having heard all the oral commentaries
> and being skilled in the performance of ritual,
> He keeps warm the vital secrets.
> Upon a *yogin* of such ability one should rely wholeheartedly.

As for the nature of the disciples who are to be initiated, they are described in the same *tantra* as being;

> Fully purified through the trainings of listening,
> contemplation and absorption,
> Those who have acquired the wisdom eye
> are said to be acceptable recipients,
> Having dedicated themselves completely
> together with all they possess.

The benefits to be derived from the empowerment itself are described in the *dBang rin po che'i rgyud* (unidentified) as follows;

> If the complete ritual of empowerment is bestowed
> in proper stages in accordance with tradition,
> In this very life one will become equal to the mighty Vajradhara.

The disadvantages of not being initiated are described in the *Guhya-garbha-tantra* X.8 (NGB 190);

> Failing to satisfy the teacher and thus
> failing to receive the empowerments,
> Even though one studies hard with diligence,
> no result will arise and destruction will come.

And also, in the *rDzogs pa rang 'byung* (unidentified) it is said;

> Lacking the support of empowerment in secret *mantra,*
> no *siddhi* will ever arise.
> Just as one cannot prevent wild unmarked sheep
> from escaping across the river.

And why is empowerment necessary? As it says in the *Nyi ma 'khor lo'i rgyud* (unidentified);

> Just as on a good field of fertile land that has not been
> carefully cultivated, no harvest will grow to mature.
> Just so, on (the fertile ground of) *dharmatā*,
> without the ripening empowerments,
> How will the *siddhi* of *yoga* arise?[547]

We have already noted above that the Northern Treasures Vajrakīla teachings include rites pertaining both to a black deity (*mantrabhīru* and *kṣura* cycles) and a multicoloured deity (the *mahottara* cycle). According to 'Phrin-las bdud-'joms,[548] these various systems were united into one by Rig-'dzin padma 'phrin-las, whose method of empowerment within a single *maṇḍala* subsequently became the standard for this school. Padma 'phrin-las' own 70-folio text is to be found in collection B immediately following 'Phrin-las bdud-'joms' introduction to it (and also as E57) but is included in neither A nor C. 'Phrin-las bdud-'joms' slightly shorter reworking of that text, dated 1766, is found as C40. With regard to the original *gter ma* material that is of primary concern to us here, however,

547 B4 203-204

548 B4 203

there are two important texts included in four of our collections and these deal with the black and multicoloured deities separately.

From the golden southern section of the treasure cache, Rig-'dzin rgod-ldem is said to have taken out the *Che mchog gi dbang chu* (A8, B12, C5, E8) pertaining to the 'water consecrations' (*udakābhiṣeka*) of the eighteen-armed *mahottara* form of the deity. These rites, said to have arisen spontaneously, "were written down for the benefit of *vidyādhara* on the path of secret *mantra* in order that their inner strength (*ātman*) may become fully developed, and to enable them to bestow the blessings of the empowerments on others". Although this ritual is designed to bestow the consecrations of the *mahottarakīla* cycle, the internal structure of its contents conforms to the paradigm of the BRT and VKMK and it includes in its liturgy many verses from those two texts. This is surprising because those texts belong to the *kṣura* cycle of the black deity and thus we have, once again, an overlapping of the traditions for which it is difficult to account. It is possible that the different iconic forms of the deity were not originally associated with distinct bodies of religious doctrine or it may be that the separate traditions of Vajrakīla were conflated long ago, either in India or Tibet.

Other than the fact that it seems to quote from texts of the wrong tradition, however, the general scheme of the rite is perfectly logical in its methodology. It utilises the root *tantra* as a basic framework for generating the outer and inner *maṇḍala* of the deity and, as the ritual proceeds, the guru explains to the neophyte the significance of the various meditations involved. In this way the neophyte is 'initiated' and, by the blessings of his teacher, 'empowered' to perform those meditations on his own. Subsequent to his empowerment, the disciple is expected to devote his time and energy to mastering meditation on the Vajrakīla *maṇḍala* in order to achieve the *bhavakīla* for the benefit of all living beings. He commits himself to maintain the tantric vows in general and to enter a covenant (*samaya*) with the major and minor deities associated with the Vajrakīla doctrines. In short, he becomes responsible for maintaining the purity of the Vajrakīla lineage and for its enrichment.

Of the four redactions at our disposal, B is most helpful thanks to the inclusion within it of interlinear notes at various points (A also includes a few notes towards the end of the text) and C is particularly corrupt with several lacunae and a wealth of misreadings.

As for the rite itself; the text begins by stating that one within whom great love and compassion have been born and who possesses a knowledge of the weapons that protect against harmful enemies and obstructors, should gather up 'the three essential articles'[549] for the practice of the *bhavakīla* and go to an auspicious and isolated place of ritual power (*gnas chen*). Taking all the ingredients for the medicine that conquers disease and generous quantities of offering articles,[550] the *vajra* master should carefully perform the rites of purifying the chosen site. Having received permission for the *maṇḍala* from the local *bhūmipati* and having presented a *bali* offering to unfriendly trouble-makers, the master should then take possession of the site and mark out its boundaries by placing piles of stones in the four corners (*tho bzhi brtsigs*). He then performs the ritual that protects the site in exactly the same way as it was performed above.[551] The master now lays out the great blue-black *maṇḍala,* in the centre of which is placed a drawing of the demon Rudra. This effigy is to be transfixed with a spike that is meditated upon as being the actual deity Vajrakīla himself.[552]

While the *maṇḍala* is being drawn, with a ferocious voice the *vajrācārya* should recite words (partly culled from the two *tantra* noted above) to the effect that; "Having given birth to the supreme mind of enlightenment, we *vidyādhara* are the representatives of the buddhas of the three times and now, for the sake of perfecting the *bhavakīla,* we contemplate that a shining *bindu* arises in the centre of the sky and enters the door of life in our hearts." Thus the drawing of the *maṇḍala* is undertaken by the *ācārya* whose mind is absorbed in the ferocious *samādhi* of the blazing great blue weapon in his heart.

As the *ācārya* mutters OṀ LAṀ HŪṀ LAṀ STAMBHAYA NAN VAJRA-STAMBHAYA NAN KATHAM, from the 21 fierce gods in union[553] radiate rays of light of the five wisdoms[554] that melt into the world and into the

---

549 *sMan rak gtor gsum.*

550 Text A says; "articles that support life".

551 See above, Chapter Five, where the *sīmābandha* rite is given in note 504.

552 A8 68

553 It would seem logical to associate this figure with the 21 supreme sons of body, speech and mind but the text makes it clear (below) that the reference is to the central *yuganaddha* deity (counted as one) and his retinue of ten *yuganaddha* wrathful kings (counted as 20).

554 Blue, white, yellow, red and green.

hearts of all sentient beings so that all phenomena, both animate and inanimate, are blessed as wisdom.[555]

Then, on a piece of cloth taken from a corpse in the cemetery, the *ācārya* should draw the arrogant figure of Rudra and, separating him from the gods who would assist him,[556] he summons the consciousness of that demon and causes it to dwell within the drawing. That drawing is then placed in the very centre of the *maṇḍala* and around it are arranged four stones (or skulls) which are visualised as four buddhas. The buddhas are invited to abide in those stones and they are presented with offerings and so on. Then, in a powerful voice, the *ācārya* warns all who would attempt to obstruct the work of the *vidyādhara* within whom has been born the mind of supreme enlightenment that they are about to be rendered powerless even if they be gods, let alone demons. OṀ VAJRAKĪLI KĪLAYA SARVA ANAYA HŪṀ.[557]

Then the body of that proud Rudra should be slain by means of the fierce ritual. On the place of consciousness (the heart), which should be marked on the drawing with a syllable HŪṀ, the *ācārya* stabs the nail at the very junction of good and evil (*dkar nag mtshams su*). During the performance of that action he should contemplate the truth of *dharmatā* and the power of buddhahood, for it is the very essence of the wrathful rite. Muttering, "Now is the time for the great act of sorcery (ABHICĀRA)," the *ācārya* abides in the sphere of the *dharmakāya,* free of mental fictions.

As the external (symbolic) *maṇḍala* is being drawn upon the ground, the *ācārya* is instructed to open his heart and guard the door of his life by placing upon it the seed-syllable of Hayagrīva. This is said to be the true meaning of the words found in the Vajrakīla *Svayambhūmūlatantra,*[558] "One should meditate upon it arising in the portal of life (*srog gi sgo ru shar*) and being present in the door of the heart (*snying gi sgo ru*)." Thus the *ācārya* meditates upon the eight-petalled *cakra* of his heart, which is the naturally present *maṇḍala,* as he draws upon the ground the eight-petalled lotus of the symbolic *maṇḍala* for the empowerment.

---

555 The *bhājanaloka* is transformed by this blessing into the wisdom *maṇḍala* of residence, and the *sattvaloka* into the resident wisdom deities.

556 See below, Chapter Nine.

557 A8 69-70

558 Our text A3, within which, however, the quoted words (from a verse found in several Vajrakīla *tantra,* including the BRT) are not to be found. See above, Chapter Five.

Contemplating this drawn *maṇḍala* as composed of the five nectars and so on,[559] the *ācārya* should bless the lines and colours as they are put down with melodious prayers. Having sprinkled (the earth) with blood from the heart (*citta khrag,* sic),[560] the four shining lines (of the *maṇḍala* border) are marked in place.

Then the deity Hayagrīva is generated in the centre, surrounded in the primary directions by his retinue of four wives (*gsang yum*), HAYAGRĪVA HULU HULU GṚHṆA GṚHṆA HŪṀ PHAṬ. In the four intermediate directions, from the syllables KAṬAṄKAṬE, are generated the goddesses of the earth[561] riding upon yellow sows. Inviting the deities to abide within the *maṇḍala,* the *ācārya* should present them with offerings. They are then reminded of the former occasion when the bodies of those who obstructed the Dharma were ground to dust and of the promises that they themselves made at that time. The protectors are instructed to listen carefully to the orders of the present *vajra* master and faithfully to carry out their duties of rendering his enemies powerless. When these orders have been successfully accomplished, the *ācārya* should present the deities with a further series of offerings.

Following that, a skull and a vase are purified with the smoke of black frankincense (*gugguladhūpa*) and a sprinkling of nectar. The two vessels are then filled with 'ambrosial water', the essential nature of which is blessed as wisdom by the recitation of the *mantra* of Amṛtakuṇḍalin, and the skull is placed on top of the vase. Muttering BHRŪṀ, the vase and skull are transformed into the *maṇḍala* palace of the gods and, by reciting the *mantra* of the deities over seeds of white mustard, each grain is transformed into a deity and these are poured into the vase. In this way the *ācārya* fills the palace with its divine residents, generating all the wrathful gods down to the four goddesses who guard the gates.[562]

A drawing of the *maṇḍala* with all of these gods is then to be placed over the top of the skull and sealed with a symbolic blazing *vajra.* The neck of the vase should be tied with rags from the charnel ground and, as

---

559 The nectars (semen, blood, excrement, urine and flesh) stand for the five naturally-arising buddhas within the physical body. Meditating in this way, the *ācārya* harmonises the outer *maṇḍala* that he draws upon the earth with the inner *maṇḍala* spontaneously present in his heart.

560 Replacing the perfumed water employed for sprinkling the earth when the peaceful *maṇḍala* is to be drawn.

561 Called here *bse yi lha mo.* See above, Chapter Four.

562 A8 70-72

the *ācārya* recites ŚIKRIN VIKRIN HŪṀ, a twig from a cemetery tree should be inserted into its mouth. The vase should then be entwined with intestines.

Following that, the *vajrācārya* holds the vase aloft in his hand and, loudly beating on the great drum, he calls the deities to be present in order to bestow the empowerments upon his disciples and to bless them. They are then offered the five kinds of spontaneously arising nectars, the sacrificial *bali* cake possessing six varieties of taste, and the flesh, blood and bones of the liberated enemies and obstructors.[563] The purificatory *mantra* of one hundred syllables (the *mantra* of Vajrasattva) is then recited, after which the deities are once again urged to be present in the vase. The words to be recited at this juncture have already been noted above as occurring in both the VKMK and the BRT; "HŪṀ Empowerments and blessings must be bestowed in this place ..." etc. and as they are recited now, the deities melt into the centre of the vase. In that way the preliminary rites establishing the *maṇḍala* of deities within the vase are completed[564] and this is immediately followed by the establishment of the deities within the body of the disciple.

This section begins with a verse in which the *krodharāja* Hūṁkāra together with his consort Śabdavajrā and their assistant emanations with the heads of a pig and a lizard are invited to be present in order to bestow blessings and empowerments upon the assembled disciples who are to be the Kīla *vidyādhara* of the future. These four deities are all urged to perform the great deeds of skilful means for the sake of the world. The text then instructs the reader to repeat the verse ten times, changing just the names of the deities, so that all the gods of the *maṇḍala* may be summoned from the ten directions in their groups of four. The deities are then established within the body of the disciple as he is purified with nectar. As the *vajrācārya* pours water from the vase (on to the head of the disciple), the disciple salutes both his master and the deities of the *maṇḍala* and makes this plea; "HŪṀ Gods of the Universal *kīla*, please

---

563 These offerings stand for the five *skandha*, the six spheres of sensory experience and the three primary *kleśa* respectively, all of which are henceforth to be recognised by the initiate in their own true nature and dedicated for the sake of all sentient beings to the wrathful *maṇḍala* of Vajrakīla deities.

Further details regarding the nature of these offering articles are to be found below, Chapter Twelve.

564 A8 72-73. Cf. the peaceful rite for the preparation of the vase to be found in *Illuminating Sunshine* 23-38.

turn your minds of supreme enlightenment towards we *vidyādhara* who must act as representatives for the buddhas of the three times." In that way the disciple takes refuge in the deities and binds himself under oath.

The *ācārya* then enters the *samādhi* of Amṛtakuṇḍalin and recites his *mantra* whilst tying a protective cord as an amulet around the disciple's left arm. (This ritually purifies all the defilements of the disciple's body. The purification of his speech and mind then follow:) As the disciple takes refuge in the deities, he makes a vow to adhere firmly to the mind of enlightenment[565] and then, meditating upon the fierce king Hayagrīva, he purifies all the defilements of his speech and promises never to commit them again. Finally, sipping a little of the sacred nectar water and meditating upon the the deity Aparājita, he purifies all the past defilements of his mind. In that way the rites for the preparation of the disciple are completed[566] and there now follows the ritual of the *maṇḍala* which is the main part of the empowerment ceremony, likened in the text to "a storehouse of precious jewels".

At first, the *sādhana* which calls forth the deities should be performed (see next chapter) until the signs of success have arisen and then the stages of empowerment should proceed, beginning with a nectar water ablution. The disciple should be blindfolded with red cloth and the guru should ask,[567] "Oh, fortunate son of a noble family. You who wish to enter the door of the *maṇḍala* of profound empowerment, how much faith and diligence do you possess? How much wealth and merit do you have as gifts to offer?" To which the disciple replies, "In order to stand close to the *vajra* master I offer this, my body, and even my very life. As a fee for the empowerment I offer all my wealth and merit."

---

565 Line missing in both B & C.

566 A8 73-74. There is often a break at this point, the *adhivāsana* ceremonies being performed on the evening of the first day and the main empowerment rituals throughout the following day, determined to some extent by the nature of the disciple's dreams during the intervening night.

567 There are large gaps in the text of C during this conversation between guru and disciple.

The next section concerns the oath-water.[568] As the master stirs the nectar in the skull with a *vajra* he says, "May your life force and body remain firm! HŪṀ Now is the time to take the great vow. From today onwards you are the son of myself, Vajrapāṇi, and you must do just exactly as I say in every detail. You must never act disrespectfully towards me, for if you should ever abuse me then the elements of your life will decay and you will fall into the *vajra* hell. Oh, fortunate son of a noble family, if you guard well these vows and do not abandon your guru or the gods of the *maṇḍala* or your *vajra* brothers and sisters, if you do not sever the continuity of the *mantra* and *mudrā* and do not disclose the secrets to outsiders, then, if you are able to maintain your root vows of body, speech and mind[569] this water of sacred oaths will definitely cause you to become Vajrasattva himself!" And as the *vajrācārya* recites the *mantra* of Amṛtakuṇḍalin he places some of the nectar upon the tongue of the disciple.[570]

Then the *maṇḍala* deities are caused to descend into the heart with the words, "HŪṀ Anger must be destroyed by means of *vajra* wrath!" and so on (noted above as occurring within both the BRT and the VKMK). The guru should explain the importance of this to his disciple by saying, "Oh, son of good family. Due to this absorption of the *jñānasattva* within your heart, you will at all times remain in the state of unshakeable *samādhi.*"

The guru then opens the eastern door of the *maṇḍala* and, standing within it, he prays to all those who maintain the awareness of Vajrakumāra to reveal the universe as the ferocious wisdom *maṇḍala* of Vajrakīla, thereby manifesting the Universal *kīla*. He summons the actual visible form of unbearable blazing wrath, the deity Vajrakīla who is the embodiment of the wisdom of all the buddhas, to arise from the *dharmadhātu.* Then from the body, speech and mind of the guru and *devatā,*[571] fierce rays of light shine out which burn up the residual karmic body of the disciple,

---

568 Varuṇa, the god of water whose name is etymologically linked to the word *vrata* (vow, solemn oath), is represented in the *Ṛgveda* as the deity whose function is to preside over such oaths. He separates truth from falsehood and watches over all oaths and promises (traditionally solemnised with water), protecting and rewarding the faithful and punishing the perfidious (often by infecting them with the watery disease, dropsy). Paul Thieme, "King Varuṇa." *German Scholars on India* Vol.1 (Varanasi, 1973) 333-349

569 To see all appearances as the *maṇḍala,* to hear all sounds as *mantra* and to recognise all thoughts as the play of divine wisdom.

570 A8 74-75

571 The guru is considered to be inseparable from the *devatā* throughout the rite.

causing the consciousness abiding within it to melt down and flow out like pure liquid gold. The disciple is instructed to imagine that the pure liquid of his consciousness is absorbed into the heart of the guru from where it descends to the guru's *vajra*. It is then ejected into the womb of the guru's consort so that he may be reborn from there as a true son of the buddha. Completing the stages of entry in that way, the disciple is born into the *maṇḍala* and he should imagine himself in the form of an eight-year old youth.[572]

Now, inside the *maṇḍala,* he receives the consecrations. Taking up the vase, the guru repeats the verse cited above from the BRT and VKMK, "HŪṀ Empowerments and blessings must be bestowed in this place ..." and he recites the heart *mantra* of all the deities, adding to the end of each the words, "The consecration that purifies the ten non-virtues is bestowed!"

Imagining himself to be Hayagrīva, the guru binds the *mudrā* of 'the Assembly of Precious Jewels' (*rin chen 'dus pa*)[573] on a level with his disciple's ears and says, "TRAṀ The supreme secret empowerment that transcends suffering ..." etc. With such words as these the guru explains the meaning of the secret teachings to his disciple and the disciple, having heard them, should not proclaim them abroad. As he recites the *mantra* at the end of this section, the *ācārya* pours out some water from the vase which his disciple should drink.

Binding the *mudrā* of 'the Assembly of Lotuses' (*padma 'dus pa*) on the tongue of his disciple, the master says, "HRĪḤ By the eighty melodies of clear discrimination, all the wishes of living beings are satisfied. The object of wisdom (*shes rab don*) is beyond imagination and yet it abides in the signification (*don*) of all things great and small."

Then, as both guru and disciple meditate upon themselves as the deity Amṛtakuṇḍalin, the master places into the hands of his disciple a *vajra* and bell held together in the form of a cross and says, "HŪṀ For the sake of all beings you must perform the skilful deeds of disciplining them by means of love and compassion. Fully perform the deeds of a buddha!"[574]

---

572 A8 75-76

573 Notes describing these *mudrā* are given in B.

574 These lines are part of a verse already noted above in both the BRT and VKMK, beginning; "Empowerments and blessings must be bestowed in this place ..."

Absorbing himself into the *jñānasattva* in his heart, the guru recites the deity's *mantra* of invocation 21 times followed by the closing lines of the oft-quoted verse that opens the VKMK; "It enters the door of the life force and one should meditate upon it in the centre of the heart." The guru then holds aloft the vase[575] and, placing it upon the crown of his disciple's head he proclaims, "HŪṀ The blessings and empowerments of all those who hold the awareness of Vajrakumāra, the representatives of the *jinas* of the three times, are now bestowed upon you!" The entire lineage of those who hold the awareness of Vajrakīla are then called forth from their natural abodes, beginning with the buddhas of the three *kāya* headed by the *dharmakāya* Samantabhadra; "HŪṀ Supreme *heruka* Samantabhadra! For the sake of all beings arise now from the *dharmadhātu* and, speaking with the naturally ferocious sound of the *dharmatā,* bestow the *vidyādhara* blessings!"

Then the five wisdom buddhas of the *sambhogakāya* are exhorted to arise from their spontaneously perfected pure *kṣetra* and the *nirmāṇakāya* Vajrapāṇi is called from Alakāvatī. His consort, the *ḍākinī* Karmedrāṇī[576] is summoned from "the great abode of *bodhisattva*" which is identified by a note in text A as "the spontaneously arising great charnel ground of the *dharmatā*". Then the three-faced Brahmā, the first of the gods to have heard these teachings, is summoned from his abode above the peak of Mount Meru. He is followed by the *vidyādhara* teachers from the realms of gods, *nāga* and men: Indra Śatakratu from his excellent palace of Vijaya, the *nāgarāja* Takṣaka from his refuge in the depths of the Sindhu Ocean and the meritorious king Indrabhūti from his abode on the summit of Mount Malaya. Then the learned Śākyaprabhā is called forth from Zahor and Padmasambhava is invoked from his rocky cave at Pharping. Vimalamitra is summoned from the banks of the River Ganges and the Nepali Śīlamañju from his retreat hut in the forest of Mandāra (Coral trees). The princess Ye-shes mtsho-rgyal is summoned from the lion's fortress of Bhutan and sNa-nam rdo-rje bdud-'joms is called forth from the red rock 'treasury' cave in Rong.[577]

In this way the lineage holders of the Vajrakīla doctrines up until the time of their concealment in the eighth century are called forth from the various locations with which they are especially associated. As their

---

575 An interlinear note in text A adds the word *gtor ma* here.

576 Equated by a note in text A with Vajravārāhī.

577 A8 76-79

blessings and empowerments are received, they are all urged to "speak with the naturally ferocious sound of the *dharmatā*". Our texts A & C say that this completes the series of five outer empowerments but text B continues to invoke the holders of the lineage by calling forth the *gter ston* Rig-'dzin rgod-ldem from the peak of Mount bKra-bzang, his son rDo-rje mtshan-can from the household of great blessings, Gang-chen sangs-rgyas bstan-pa from the sacred place of Mount dPal-'bar, the kind master Sangs-rgyas dpal-bzang from the abode of impartial activity for the benefit of others, the *tāntrika* Chos-rGyal sems-dpa' from his hermitage in Nge-lung, the *vidyādhara* Sangs-rgyas bstan-pa from the pure display of the *dharmadhātu* and the holder of secret *mantra,* Śākya bzang-po, from the sun and moon throne on the crown of the (author's own) head.[578]

As for the inner empowerments which follow, the first essential is for the disciple to enter the three *samādhi*. Thus he first of all absorbs his mind in the state of *tathatā,* within which he generates great compassion for all beings. Projecting this compassion in the form of 'the causal seed-syllable' (*rgyu'i yi ge*), the disciple proceeds through the stages of building up the divine *maṇḍala* palace. Having generated the palace complete with all adornments, he meditates upon himself in its centre upon a lotus throne with cushions of piled up Rudras, the sun and moon. Reciting, "HŪṀ Anger must be destroyed by means of *vajra* wrath ..." and so on, he imagines himself truly to be the deity Vajrakīla.

He is then consecrated with the deity's crown of skulls as the *ācārya* recites, "HŪṀ This is the precious jewel of all the buddhas, shining with immeasurable light. It bears upon it the symbols of the five supreme *kula* and with it you are crowned master of the *traidhātuka*. HŪṀ OṀ SVA AṀ HĀ. HŪṀ In this realm where birth and decay are the natural conditions applying to sentient beings and all phenomena, you, oh son of noble family, are consecrated today with the spontaneously arising ineffable empowerment. A A A VAJRAKĪLI KĪLAYA HŪṀ You yourself are the *vidyādhara* king with the *jñānasattva* abiding in your heart. The portal of your life vein is guarded by the wrathful king Hayagrīva who enforces his commands with *vajra* sparks. Now you must arise as that very king, for you are invested with power as the master of the *traidhātuka*. HAYAGRĪVA HŪṀ JAḤ NAN."

---

578 Text B, then, is updated to the 16th century by a disciple of Śākya bzang-po who places the latter on the crown of his head. B12 575

Then the consecration of non-dual *bodhicitta* is bestowed by the *yuganaddha* deity in the secret *yoni* of the mother with the words; "HŪṀ The sacred oaths of killing by compassion ..." and so on, as noted above in the BRT and VKMK. And, by that recitation alone, the secret inner consecration is bestowed.[579]

Following that, the ten beneficial consecrations[580] are bestowed: Due to the placing of the five-lobed crown upon the top of his head, the disciple receives the empowerment of five wisdoms. Due to the consecration at the place of the heart,[581] the empowerment of the seed syllable is obtained. Due to being entrusted with the *vajra* and bell, the fundamental empowerment of the hand symbols (*hastacihna*) is gained. Due to the generation of the *jñānasattva* within, the power of the body of Mahāśrī-heruka is gained. Due to being consecrated with dangling earrings, the power of the speech of Hayagrīva is obtained. Due to being consecrated with a beautiful umbrella (*chattra*), the wrathful empowerment of the body is gained. Due to being consecrated with a garland of flowers, the wrathful empowerment of speech is gained. Due to the consecration of all the hairs on his body, the power of *vajra* armour is gained and, due to being consecrated with food and drink, the power of wealth and enjoyment is obtained.[582]

Now follows the empowerment of 21 *jñānakīla*[583] in the heart. Having anointed the disciple and purified the temple with incense and so on, the guru recites the eight-line prayer, "HŪṀ All those who hold the awareness of Vajrakumāra ..." and so on, thus bestowing the empowerment of the lord of the *maṇḍala*.[584] Then he holds his *kīla* up in the air and invokes the lord of the zenith Hūṁkāra and his consort Śabdavajrā together with their pig- and lizard-headed assistants. "The activities of buddhahood must be fulfilled and, through this skilful method for the sake of sentient beings, all must be disciplined by means of love and compassion. The consecra-

579 A8 79-81

580 All manuscripts list only nine consecrations.

581 The texts do not specify what is used to empower the disciple's heart. Some gurus touch the spot with a *vajra* or a *kīla* while others choose to anoint it with either drops of nectar water or powdered vermillion, etc.

582 A8 81

583 Actually 42 deities including the animal-headed emanations. (See above, note 553)

584 B notes that the *ācārya* should roll a ritual *kīla* between the palms of his hands as he recites this prayer, after which he uses it to bless the crown of the disciple's head.

tion of mastery of phenomena (*dharmavaśitā*) is bestowed! OṀ VAJRAKRODHA HŪṀKĀRA HŪṀ! GARJA GARJA PHAṬ! OṀ ĀḤ HŪṀ SVĀHĀ. VAJRAHŪṀKĀRA A Ā ĀVEŚAYA!"

The master then holds his *kīla* towards the eastern direction and invokes Krodhavijaya and his group, who are urged to bestow upon the disciple the empowerment of superior intelligence (*cetovaśitā*).

In like manner, he turns to face the southeast, the south, southwest and so on, invoking in turn all the *krodharāja* of the ten directions together with their consorts and animal-headed emanations and he establishes them all within the body of the disciple.[585] Due to their blessings the disciple receives, in due order, the consecrations of supremacy (*vaśitā*): in knowledge (*jñāna*), life span (*āyus*), pure birth (*upapatti*), joyful aspiration (*adhimukti*),[586] material possessions (*pariṣkāra*), deeds (*karma*), prayer (*praṇidhāna*) and miracle power (*ṛddhi*).[587] Thus those secret consecrations are bestowed.[588]

Now the empowerments for the fierce rites of slaying are bestowed. As the *ācārya* entrusts into the hands of his disciple all the various wrathful substances and weapons that cause death, the discus (*cakra*) and the fiery pit (*agnikuṇḍa*),[589] he recites the next verse from the BRT ending with the words, "... the signs and symbols of success must be shown and the *siddhi* of the *kīla* be bestowed!" He then adds, "JAḤ HŪṀ VAṀ HOḤ. NṚ TRI ŚATRŪN MĀRAYA rBAD!" and summons the speedily-moving

---

585 Text B specifies the points of the body to be touched with the ritual *kīla* during the consecrations. The gods from the zenith enter via the crown of the head, those from the east enter the heart (centre of the chest), those from the southeast via the right breast, south through the upper right arm, southwest the right shoulder blade, west between the shoulder blades, northwest the left shoulder blade, north the upper left arm, northeast the left breast and those from the nadir enter the disciple's body via the base of the spine.

586 All manuscripts repeat *dharma* here.

587 Definitions of these ten *vaśitā* are to be found in the *Daśabhūmika-sūtra* 70.8-18, where they are said to be acquired by a *bodhisattva* on the eighth stage. They are listed again, below, within the present text and once more in the text that follows but, despite their evident status as a category of sacred *dharma,* their presentation here is neither consistent nor complete. Apotheosised in feminine forms, the ten are joined by Tathatā and Buddhabodhiprabhā to form a retinue of 12 goddesses in the *Dharmadhātu-maṇḍala* as described by Abhayākaragupta, *Niṣpannayogāvalī* 19.

588 Only text C makes this point, the line is missing in the other two mss. A8 81-84

589 In Tibetan ritual this pit does not necessarily contain a lighted fire but may simply be a triangular iron box regarded as an inescapable prison.

messengers with the words, "HŪṀ The time has come for the *mahā-samaya* ..." etc., as in Chapter Five of the BRT.

These speedy messengers are incited by means of the DHADDHI *mantra* to drag forth the enemies and obstructors so that they may be slaughtered. The *ācārya* holds aloft the 'transfixing nail' (*gdab phur*) and addresses the demons thus; "HŪṀ Because the supreme mind of enlightenment has arisen within us, we *vidyādhara* are the representatives of the *jina* of the three times. All you arrogant, trouble-making enemies and obstructors who interrupt us, steal our *siddhi,* persecute us and shorten our life-spans, are now dragged forth here in an instant due to the blessings of the *mahākrodha* Vajrakīla. Now you must really be killed and experience the pain of your bodies being ground down to dust! OṀ LAṀ HŪṀ LAṀ STAMBHAYA NAN. MOHA GHAYA BHAGAVAN. ŚIKRIN VIKRIN VAJRAHŪṀKĀRA HŪṀ HŪṀ PHAṬ PHAṬ. OṀ VAJRAKĪLI KĪLAYA JAḤ HŪṀ VAṀ HOḤ SARVAVIGHNĀN VAJRAKĪLI KĪLAYA HŪṀ HŪṀ PHAṬ PHAṬ. VAJRAHŪṀKĀRA HŪṀ A." Thus the empowerment for the fierce rite of destruction is bestowed upon the disciple.[590]

As the *ācārya* flings a mixture of white, red and black mustard seeds, iron and copper filings and the ashes of a corpse towards that poisonous effigy (*dug gi ngar glud*) he recites the long *mantra* of incitement and instructs the ferocious deities thus; "HŪṀ Those obstructors who interrupt our *siddhi,* those vicious beings with vindictive minds, must be seized, beaten and securely bound! They must be recognised and separated from their friends! Drag them forth immediately and make them silent! They must be thrown down and oppressed! Having come under my power, they must listen to my commands!"

Then, taking up the *kīla* of the oath-bound ones, the *ācārya* says, "HŪṀ You host of servants and messengers who are obedient to our orders! You who took your oaths in former times should come here now in fulfilment of those vows and quickly demonstrate the accomplishment of your tasks!"[591]

Then the disciple is entrusted with the curved flaying knife (*kartṛkā*) of the 'killers' (*ghātakara*);[592] "HŪṀ Whatever evil being there may be

---

590 A8 84-86

591 A8 86-87

592 The *kartṛkā* is not a weapon normally associated with these animal-headed emanations of the *daśakrodha* kings, generally described in the texts and depicted in art as wielding *aṇkuśa* and *kīla*.

who violates the secret orders of Vajra(dhara), that one will have his skull smashed to a hundred splinters by the powerful might of the *mahākrodha-rāja!* Listen well, you hosts of obstructors and misleaders, and do not transgress my orders!"

Then the effigy is smeared with blood and poison and the enemy is warned that, whether he be god or demon, any arrogant being with vicious mind who causes trouble for the Dharma will immediately be deprived of his power and skill. "SARVA ANAYA HŪṀ PHAṬ ..." etc.[593]

There then follows the empowerment of the *vajra* hammer and ladles for the sacrificial fire (*homadarvī*). As those implements are placed into the hands of the disciple the *ācārya* recites, "Beat! You blazing *vajras,* beat! Having had their hearts burnt up on the pinnacle of *vajra* fire, all those evil-minded ones who transgress my orders must have their bodies beaten down to pulp! HŪṀ HŪṀ HŪṀ PHAṬ PHAṬ PHAṬ!"

Then the empowerment of union. The disciple should go through the stages of self generation, as outlined in the *adhivāsana* section above, until he arises as the ferocious *vajra* couple (*rdo rje drag po'i zung*).[594] He should complete the essential part of the ritual activities, performing the *sādhana* until he comes to the section of the general offerings (*gaṇacakra*) and the presentation of *bali.*[595] He should generate the *daśakrodha* kings clearly within his own body and their ten wrathful queens within the body of his consort Tṛptacakra. Outwardly he should meditate upon the visible forms of the deities whilst inwardly he concentrates either upon the subtle nervous system of the *nāḍī* or upon the *mantra* in their hearts.[596] In that way the disciple generates the *maṇḍala* of union (*sbyor ba'i dkyil 'khor*) and he purifies the outer world and all living beings with the radiant rays of light that emanate from his body as he recites the *mantra.*[597]

Now, in order to receive the empowerments within that *maṇḍala,* the disciple should visualise himself very clearly as the *yuganaddha* deity Vajrakīla. Then, as (the *ācārya*) murmurs BHAGAVAN, the disciple should imagine the syllable OṀ at the base of the father's five-pronged *vajra,* HŪṀ at its midsection and PHAṬ at the tip. In the centre of the mother's eight-petalled lotus, the red syllable A should clearly be seen. Muttering

593 A8 87

594 All manuscripts read *rdo rje drag po'i zungs ma.*

595 Text B says, "up as far as the section of praising the deity".

596 Called here *citta'i dbus,* 'the centre of the mind'.

597 A8 88

ŚIKRIN causes the union of the father to expand and VIKRIN, the bliss of the mother to increase.[598] As (the *ācārya*) says ŚIKRIN ANAYA, the couple engage in the non-dual play of great enjoyment and from the sound of that union arise the syllables JAḤ HŪṀ VAṀ HOḤ. Saying KATHAṀ, the 21 deities all unite and thus the disciple experiences bliss. "As the heart burns up on the pinnacle of *vajra* fire, from the centre of the sky arises the *bindu* which enters the door of life and one should meditate upon it in the centre of the heart. May the achievement of the Universal *vajra* be attained! By means of the blazing great blue weapon, great wisdom spontaneously arises." With these words (derived from three separate verses of the BRT), *bodhicitta* is brought forth and implanted.[599] "HŪṀ In the blazing *yonis* of the wrathful mothers, the pounding of *vajra* hammers destroys even those who are gods! KATHAṀ KATHAṀ KATHAṀ HŪṀ HŪṀ HŪṀ PHAṬ PHAṬ PHAṬ ..." etc. Reciting thus, *bodhicitta* is increased.[600] Eventually the seminal fluid is reabsorbed from the secret *yoni* of the consort. Being drawn back into the father's *vajra,* it ascends the central *nāḍī* to the skull. Finally the mother herself dissolves into light and is absorbed into the *mūlacakra* of her lord.[601]

The disciple is then instructed to meditate upon the whole assembly of gods in the *maṇḍala* of Vajrakīla who are such that the reality of their forms can never be expressed (*anabhilāpya*), shining with brilliant light. Their speech is the spontaneous sound of the *dharmatā* beyond the limits of expression and their minds are settled in the natural sphere which cannot be described, free of all objectifying thoughts (*'dzin rtogs*). As he abides in this contemplation, he should recite this prayer of ultimate truth (*yang dag don kyi bden pa*); "I invoke the truth of *dharmatā*, the blessings of secret *mantra* and the power of the buddhas! Now is the time for a display of violent sorcery, for those are the very actions which are necessary!"

---

598 Could these be corruptions of *śīkarin* (spurting water) and *vikārin* (feeling emotion, falling in love)?

599 Thus, as the disciple implants semen (relative *bodhicitta*) within the *yoni* of his consort, enlightenment (absolute *bodhicitta*) is implanted within his own heart.

600 By means of this verse from the root *tantra* and the pounding *mantra,* the disciple is urged to experience such bliss that he will no longer incline toward lower *yānas*. H.H. Sa-skya khri-'dzin, oral communication.

601 A8 88-89

The master then dispatches the offerings to their natural place and dissolves the created *maṇḍala* to its pure state.[602] Finally the guru sprinkles the disciple with water from the vase and thus he is consecrated as a representative of the *jina* (*rgyal tshab*).

This empowerment of self-arising spontaneous appearance which is an initiation into the uncreate, a treasury of precious consecrations taken from the wrathful *Svayambhūsvodaya-tantra,* is completed.[603]

Text C finished several pages ago and A finishes here. Text B, however, goes on to rejoice in the great virtues of this series of consecrations and to explain that, through the power thus bestowed upon the disciple, his body, speech and mind are purified so that he will arise as a buddha in the pure land of Vajrasattva. A benedictory prayer (*praṇidhāna*) is appended which is said to have been spoken by the great guru Padmasambhava for the benefit of his disciple Ye-shes mtsho-rgyal at the time when she herself first received this very empowerment. Later, in the lion's fortress of Bhutan, it was repeated for the king and 24 subjects on the occasion of their empowerment, after which it was written down and hidden away in Ri-bo bKra-bzang in the white treasury of conch within the triangular rock cave that is shaped like a fire pit.

Due to receiving the empowerments of Hūṁkāra, his consort, and their assistant *piśācī,* the faults of sexual misconduct[604] are abandoned and one gains mastery of the process of birth. May the pure understanding of the perfection of knowledge (*jñāna*)[605] arise! Due to receiving the empowerments of Krodhavijaya and his retinue, the faults of taking what was not given are abandoned and power over material possessions is gained. May the perfection of wisdom (*prajñā*) arise! Due to receiving the empowerments of Nīladaṇḍa and his retinue, the faults of wrong view are abandoned and mastery of wisdom is gained. May the perfection of skill in means (*upāya*) arise! Due to receiving the empowerments of Yamāntaka and his retinue, the faults of taking life are abandoned and the power to prolong one's lifespan is gained. May the perfection of meditation

---

602 By which is meant *śūnyatā* in both cases. The *bali* are placed upon the temple rooftop for the birds to eat and the coloured powders of which the *maṇḍala* was composed are swept up and entrusted to the care of the *nāga* inhabiting the nearest river or lake.

603 A8 89-90

604 The standard list of ten wrong deeds (*daśaduścaritāni*) begins here.

605 The standard list of the ten perfections (*daśapāramitā*) begins here, although the order in which they are presented is unusual.

(*dhyāna*) arise! Due to receiving the empowerments of Ārya Acala and his retinue, the faults of speaking lies are abandoned and the power of prayer is gained. May the perfection of patience (*kṣānti*) arise! Due to receiving the empowerments of Hayagrīva and his retinue, the faults of slander are abandoned and mastery of phenomena is gained. May the perfection of enthusiastic perseverance (*vīrya*) arise! Due to receiving the empowerments of Aparājita and his retinue, the faults of foolish prattle are abandoned and the supremacy of mental ability is gained. May the perfection of generosity (*dāna*) arise! Due to receiving the empowerments of Amṛtakuṇḍalin and his retinue, the faults of abusive speech are abandoned and mastery of ritual activity is achieved. May the perfection of prayer (*praṇidhāna*) arise! Due to receiving the empowerments of Trailokyavijaya and his retinue, the faults of malice are abandoned and mastery of miracle power is gained. May the perfection of strength (*bala*) arise! Due to receiving the empowerments of Mahābala and his retinue, the faults of conceit[606] are abandoned and the power of joyful aspiration is gained. May the perfection of morality (*śīla*) arise![607]

Due to the empowerment of the body as a deity, all the sins of the body are purified. May the power of meditation upon the body as a *maṇḍala* of gods arise! Due to the empowerment of speech as *mantra,* all the sins of speech are purified. May the power of the full potential of speech arise! Due to the empowerment of mind with the symbolic *kīla,* all evils of thought are overcome. May the understanding of one's own mind as the *dharmakāya* arise!

Due to this empowerment within the *maṇḍala* of the profound Vajrayāna, may all virtues be blessed with the power of the wish-fulfilling jewel! Due to these consecrations with the symbolic articles of the gods, may the power to slay all the haughty enemies and obstructors be gained! Due to the empowerments of the three supreme sons,[608] the three root *kleśa* are abandoned. May the *siddhi* of body, speech and mind arise! Due to the empowerments of the 12 oath-bound protectors (in three groups of four), may the power to annihilate the four *māra,* the *tīrthika* and the groups of misleaders, enemies and obstructors arise! Due to the empow-

---

606 The text reads *rlom sems* (conceit) but, according to the list in the *Mahāvyutpatti,* it should read *brnab sems* (covetousness).

607 All manuscripts repeat *praṇidhāna* and *kṣānti* here, the power and perfection already allocated to Ārya Acala.

608 In this text; Aparājita, Hayagrīva & Amṛtakuṇḍalin.

erments of the four goddesses who guard the gates, mental habit patterns (*vāsanā*) are purified as the four boundless minds. May the four rites be achieved without limit!

Oh, you fortunate disciples, you *vajra* brothers and sisters who have today received all these empowerments of secret *mantra* within the profound *maṇḍala* of Vajrasattva, as a result of these empowerments the ten non-virtues which act as causes for rebirth in the states of woe are all purified. You must therefore perfect the nature of Vajrasattva and reach the stage of a *samyaksaṁbuddha*. May you protect the oaths and commitments with your life! Thus the ten *pāramitā* are attained. Through the complete attainment of this *maṇḍala* of the Vajrayāna, may you quickly ascend to the 13th stage (*bhūmi*) of Vajradhara!

The text finishes here with a final note to the effect that, as he makes this prayer for the benefit of his disciples, the guru should scatter flowers upon their heads.[609]

Now, with regard to the rite of empowerment into the black *kṣura* cycle of Vajrakīla, Rig-'dzin rgod-ldem found the considerably shorter text known simply as the *sPu gri nag po'i bdang chog* (A14, B63, C20, E30) in the black iron cache to the north. According to this text, the empowerment itself serves three primary functions. The first of these is the consecration of the mind as awareness, the second is the consecration of the symbols as personal emblems, and the third is the consecration of the *yogin*'s own emanated form as the resultant fruit of buddhahood.

With regard to the first consecration; the self empowerment (*sva-adhiṣṭhāna*) through which the mind becomes known as 'the king of awareness' (*vidyārāja*) is established by means of the *maṇḍala* of 11 *kīla* embedded in the ground of all-pervading light.

The consecration of the *mudrā* as personal tokens has three parts: the consecration of symbolic articles, the consecration of the hand symbols (*hastacihna*) and the consecration of the five qualities of desire. The text goes on to explain that the symbolic articles are white mustard seeds, *amṛta* nectar, the sacred crown, the *vajra* & bell, the vase, and the eight articles of the charnel ground. The hand symbols are eleven *kīla*.[610] Nothing further is stated at this point with regard to the consecration of the five qualities of desire, nor are any comments made at any stage with

609 B12 586-589

610 A14 124-125

regard to the third purpose of the rite, the consecration of the *yogin*'s own body as the resultant fruit.

The rite itself is said to consist of five main stages: 1) Drawing the *maṇḍala,* 2) Gathering the requisite articles, 3) Invoking the deities through the various steps of *sādhana,* 4) Actual bestowal of the empowerment and, 5) Prayers of benediction when all else has been completed.

1) Firstly, as for the drawing of the *maṇḍala*: Within a square, one armspan across, should be drawn a circle and, within that, a triangle. Around the edge of the circle should be drawn a wheel with eight spokes (*cakra,* but usually drawn as an eight-petalled lotus), which should then be adorned with eight semicircular moons. Within each moon should be placed a triangle. Then the courtyards and doorways and so on of the enclosing palace should be drawn on all sides.

2) The indispensable articles required for the rite are said to be 11 *kīla,* a skull with auspicious markings, some white mustard seed, a *vajra* & bell, and a five-lobed crown.

3) The rite begins with the purification of a ritual vase and its transformation into the divine palace of the gods by means of the syllable BHRŪṀ, just as in the rite above. Then the individual grains of white mustard are transformed into deities and so on, as before, until the *maṇḍala* of residence and residents are established within the vase and offerings have been presented to them. Almost the same words are used to describe this process in both ritual texts but the *mantra* given are different. In this case, however, atop the vase is placed neither skull nor drawing of the *maṇḍala.*

The text then discusses the procedure through which the major deities of the *maṇḍala* are to be established within symbolic *kīla* arranged upon the diagram on the ground. Each of those eleven *kīla* should be blessed eight times by performing the ritual of inviting the god to be present within it. Each invited deity should then be presented with offerings and praise and so on in the manner explained in the *sādhana* texts (looked at in our next chapter). It is said that the power of the *kīla* to bestow the blessings of empowerment upon the disciple arises during that period while the *mantra* that cause the deity to approach are being recited.[611]

Then there follows the ritual of the disciple's entry into the *maṇḍala.* First of all the disciple should bathe. (A sprinkle of water on the head from a ritual vase is all that is generally deemed necessary by Tibetans

---

611 A14 125-126

with respect to this injunction.) Then, reciting the *mantra* of the *daśa-krodha* kings, the *ācārya* should expel the *vighna* and meditate upon the *rakṣācakra*. The disciple should then offer the fee for his empowerment and the '*maṇḍala* of offering' in which he renounces all attachment to this world.[612]

A note in the margin of text A says that the eyes of the disciple should be blindfolded at this point (symbolic of his current unenlightened state). Nowhere in the subsequent text, however, does it ever say that the blind-fold should be removed.

The disciple then takes refuge in the Vajrakīla *maṇḍala,* generates *bodhicitta* and promises to adhere to the general pledges of the five families.[613] After that he makes this plea to his guru in words taken from the BRT; "Kyai! *Vajrācārya,* please listen to me! I pray that the deities of the Universal *kīla* and you *vidyādhara* who are the representatives of the buddhas of the three times will bestow upon me the empowerments and *siddhi.*"

There then follows exactly the same conversation between guru and disciple as found in the previous rite except that, in this case, the guru explains to his disciple that, if he is able to keep his vows pure, sipping the water of sacred oaths will cause him to become the *jñānasattva* (instead of Vajrasattva, as said above). An interlinear note in text A adds that, as the disciple swallows the drops of nectar placed upon his tongue at that time, the blessings of all the *maṇḍala* deities descend into his body.[614]

Then the disciple, in a state of perfect mindfulness, should recite the *mantra* of the deity and instantaneously arise in the form of the glorious Vajrakīla with three faces, six arms and four legs spread wide, etc. Texts B & C describe him as standing in non-dual union with his consort but text A has two lines in which Tṛptacakra is mentioned by name and in which she is described as the great consort whose right arm embraces her lord and whose left hand presses a skull full of blood to his lips.

The great *bindu* from the depths of the sky then enters the door of the disciple's life force and so on, and the text goes on to describe the deity's ferocious retinue in verses taken from Chapter Three of the BRT, as above.

---

612 See Sangpo & Hopkins, *Tantric Practice in Nying-ma* 154-160

613 See S. Beyer, *The Cult of Tārā* 406 or SDPT 102 for the pledges of the five families.

614 A14 126-128

Then, from the OṀ, ĀḤ and HŪṀ in the forehead, throat and heart of himself clearly visualised in the form of Vajrakīla, rays of light radiate out to invite the *maṇḍala* of *jñānasattva* and the disciple says, "HŪṀ In order to receive the *siddhi* and empowerments ..." and so on, as before.

Summoning the wisdom deities, the disciple should contemplate that his ordinary body, speech and mind truly become the actual Body, Speech and Mind of the *bhagavat* Śrīvajrakumāra.[615]

4) In the guise of the deity, the disciple then receives from his guru the various cult articles, beginning with the grains of white mustard. As the preceptor hands these over he says, "HŪṀ These grains of white mustard are the most potent of magical substances. They grow in the land of the heroes (*vīra*), their aspect is that of the *bhagavat,* their *mantra* is that of Vajrapāṇi (HŪṀ), and their activity is the subjugation of enemies and obstructors. Due to the empowerment of this potent article, oh fortunate disciple, you yourself gain the strength to overthrow all enemies and obstructors."

Then, as the disciple accepts from him a few drops of nectar, the *ācārya* recites; "HŪṀ This sacred substance of swirling nectar is greatly enjoyed by those who have gathered the three worlds under their sway. This fivefold powerful nectar arising from desire annihilates the five families and renders them free of birth and death. The empowerment of this swirling nectar is now bestowed upon you. OṀ ĀḤ HŪṀ VAJRA-AMṚTA-ABHIŚIÑCA AṀ OṀ ĀḤ HŪṀ SVĀHĀ."

Next is the consecration of the five-lobed crown, which is bestowed with the same verse as found in the empowerment rite of the *mahottara* cycle above but for which the *mantra* given here is RATNAMUKUṬA-ABHIŚIÑCA MAṀ TRAṀ TRAṀ TRAṀ TRAṀ TRAṀ.

Then the disciple is entrusted with the *vajra* and bell as the master explains to him that it is the great empowerment of wisdom and means (*prajñopāya*) and that, whoever maintains the awareness of *vajra* and bell, transforms *saṁsāra* into *nirvāṇa* by purifying it of all faults. OṀ VAJRA-PRAJÑĀBHAVA-ABHIŚIÑCA HŪṀ.[616]

Following that, as the disciple is given sips of water to drink from the vase, the guru recites the verse cited in the previous ritual, "The activities of buddhahood must be fulfilled ... etc." and, as he recites the combined *hṛdaya* of all the *maṇḍala* deities, he bestows the various powers of those

---

615 A14 128-129

616 A14 129-130

deities upon the disciple. The difference here is that, whereas in the previous ritual the consecrations were bestowed by a touch of the *kīla* at various points on the disciple's body, here the deities enter with the drops of vase water through the mouth.

Then the disciple is consecrated with the hand symbols which are the insignia of the gods, beginning with the *kīla* of Vajrakumāra and his consort. The guru takes it from the centre of the *maṇḍala* before him and as he places it between the palms of his disciple's hands he says, "HŪṀ From the centre, this is the spontaneously accomplished great deity, the *bhagavat* Vajrakumāra with his supreme consort Tṛptacakra. He has three faces, six arms and stands in a posture of pride. At the midpoint of this *kīla* is a great knot containing the entire *maṇḍala*[617] and its three-sided blade tapers to a sharp pointed tip. With this very *kīla* of *yuganaddha* buddhas I empower you, oh fortunate one!" He then recites the root *mantra* of Vajrakīla, adding KĀYA-VĀK-CITTA-ABHIŚIÑCA HŪṀ ĀḤ, and thus the empowerment of the lord of the *maṇḍala* is bestowed.

Then, one by one, the *kīla* standing in the ten directions are taken up from the *maṇḍala* and entrusted to the hands of the disciple. As he does this, the guru explains the nature of the gods that reside within that particular nail and the nature of the empowerment that is bestowed by means of it. As in the previous ritual, these ten deities are associated with the ten *vaśitā* but once again their order is jumbled. At the conclusion of each empowerment, the disciple is urged to use it as a skilful method to promote the welfare of all living beings and the *mantra* of the individual deities are recited to invoke their presence.

Following the empowerments of the *maṇḍalādhipati* and the *daśakrodha* deities, the text goes on to say that the empowerments of the four gate-guarding goddesses are to be bestowed, although the ritual manner of achieving this remains unspecified. By means of these empowerments of the goddesses from the east, south, west and north, the faculties of love (*maitrī*), compassion (*karuṇā*), sympathetic joy (*pramuditā*) and equanimity (*upekṣā*) are said to be bestowed.[618]

Now the disciple is consecrated with the eight articles of the charnel ground in order to adorn those *heruka* of the ten directions abiding within his body. The first adornment is a cloak of freshly flayed wet elephant

---

617 In the meditation of the *bhavakīla*, it is the knot at the top of the *kīla* that contains the *maṇḍala* of the gods.

618 A14 131-134

skin, through which the empowerment of the *dharmadhātu* is gained. A skirt of tiger skin is said to provoke terror. Dangling bunches of snakes are the revolving ornaments.[619] An upper garment of full human hide bestows the power to brighten the darkness of ignorance (by removing the veil of the five *skandha*). A necklace of severed human heads bestows the power of control over the *traidhātuka* (severing all past and future rebirths. Text C says that it bestows the power of controlling the three poisons.) Spots of blood on the cheeks bestow the empowerment of passionate compassion. A smear of grease under the chin bestows the empowerment of the essence of truth, and lines of cemetery ash upon the forehead empower the *yogin* to subjugate enemies and obstructors.[620]

Then there is the consecration of the five qualities of desire: "HŪṀ All that is required in the way of food and drink and all that could be desired of the objects of the five senses, these are the articles which are offered to the hosts of gods of the Vajrakīla *maṇḍala* (which now reside within the body of the practitioner) and thus the empowerment of the five qualities of desire is gained!"

Then the consecration of the offerings of food and drink is bestowed: "HŪṀ This meat has the qualities of the five *jñāna* and, through the power of its blessings, your own body, speech and mind are consecrated with those five wisdoms, and the power of *vajra* life (*vajrāyus*) is gained!" Then all the foodstuffs that have been set out as offerings upon the altar are blessed so that they become divine food (*naivedya*) and, as it is distributed among all those present (*gaṇacakra*) in accordance with the method outlined in the *sādhana* texts, the disciple should once more present an offering *maṇḍala* and extensive gifts to his teacher.

5) As the *maṇḍala* is dismantled and the various ritual objects are gathered up and put away, elaborate prayers dedicating the merit of the ceremony to the welfare of all beings (*puṇyapariṇāmana*) should be offered as the final stage of the ritual.[621]

---

619 A play on the word *āvartana*, in which the winding motion (*āvartana*) of a snake is likened to the turning away (*āvartana*) of the enemies and obstructors as soon as they see these fearful ornaments. Text C, however, says that this consecration gives one the power of coiling with the consort in a mutual embrace.

620 A14 134-136

621 A14 136-137

CHAPTER SEVEN
Rituals of the creation stage (*utpattikrama*)

Being received into the cult as a member through the foregoing rites of empowerment, devotees of Vajrakīla are expected to assist in the work of manifesting the universal *bhavakīla* by regularly engaging themselves in sessions of invocation, propitiation and meditation upon the deity, the importance of which is reflected by the large number of *sādhana* to be found within the text collections.[622] Indeed, the *sādhana* is a paradigm for almost all subsequent cultic activities, the various aims of which are put forward by shifts in emphasis of its different parts and/or by the addition of new parts.

In the *Byang gter phur pa'i 'phrin las rgyas pa,* a lengthy manual in 110 folios by 'Phrin-las bdud-'joms, the main ritual is prefaced by prayers of a general Buddhist nature (the taking of refuge and generation of *bodhicitta,* etc.) as well as liturgy for the invocation of the lineage holders of the Byang-gter Kīla tradition and verses of self-consecration for the *yogin*'s own speech, his rosary, *vajra,* skull-*ḍamaru, kīla* and the various offering articles collected for worship of the deity. 'Phrin-las bdud-'joms evidently based his work upon several of the short *gter ma* documents to be found within the collections currently under consideration and it exemplifies the manner in which the ritual performance of a *sādhana* may be elaborated at will.

Among the *gter ma* documents themselves are to be found both *mahāyoga* and *atiyoga* texts, those of the *mahāyoga* being devoted either to the multi-coloured *maṇḍala* or to the *maṇḍala* of black deities. Later liturgical works included within the collections tend to a synthesis of these various approaches.

We may take as example the *Phur pa thugs kyi 'phrin las,* 'ritual activities that pertain to the heart of the Kīla' (A45, B42, C35), in which the stages of meditation for the performance of the black deity's *sādhana* are briefly summarised. This rite is considered to be of such fundamental sig-

---

622 At least 21 texts may be thus categorised, the majority of which are to be found in more than one collection. Outside the published collections, of course, there also exist many such *sādhana* in the possession of initiates who require no other text for their purposes.

nificance to the cult that, of all the texts in the published collections, it is unique in having been carved onto xylographic blocks for printing and wide distribution.[623] Unfortunately the printed edition bears no colophon to indicate when, where or by whom the blocks were carved.

The *sādhana* revealed in this text conforms to a standard ritual pattern: 1) *Sīmābandha* (outer purification), 2) Confession of sins (inner purification), 3) Blessing the offerings (secret purification), 4) Contemplation of the three *samādhi* (commencement of the main practice), 5) Generation of the *maṇḍala,* 6) Invitation of the deities, 7) Welcoming the deities as they arrive, 8) Uniting the *jñānasattva* with their *samaya* counterparts, 9) Praising the divine qualities, 10) Recitation of the *mantra* in order to stabilise the *bhavakīla,* 11) Presentation of offerings to the *maṇḍala* deities in three parts: a) the presentation of primordial purity represented by the upper portion of the *bali,* b) the presentation of that which has been purified, in which a second portion of the *bali* is offered with a confession of sins, and, c) the presentation of impure flesh, blood and bones of slain demons. Following this, 12) The left-overs are taken outside and given to the lesser gods and spirits to whom they were promised in ages past and from whom oaths of fealty may be demanded. 13) The deities are then dismissed and the merit of the rite is dedicated to the future enlightenment of all sentient beings.

The actual wording of the text is very simple. Each meditative stage is listed in due order and, for most of the stages, one or two verses are given in which the meditation is described. These verses may be recited by the *yogin* as they are found in the text or they may be amplified from other sources and elaborated as desired. Most sections conclude with a *mantra* through which the meditation is supposed actually to be put into effect.[624] The ultimate success of the rite is entirely dependent upon the *yogin*'s ability to effectuate these magic spells and therefore the text states at the outset that it is to be practised only by those who have formerly com-

---

623 It seems, however, that the distribution of printed copies did not reach the compilers of collections B & C, for they include the text in manuscript form only. Full text & English translation are to be found in my *A Roll of Thunder From the Void* 101*ff.*

624 These *mantra* are for the most part omitted here as they add nothing to our understanding of the ritual.

pleted their preliminary tantric training (*sngon 'gro, pūrvayoga*).[625] Only the *atiyoga* texts (A32 & 35, etc.) stress the worship of the guru as the essential factor in the rite that quickly leads to the attainment of *siddhi*.[626]

At the beginning of the rite, the *yogin* should turn his face toward the north and meditate upon himself with unwavering concentration as the actual deity Śrīvajrakumāra. He then establishes a protective circle around himself by imagining the ten *krodharāja* issuing forth from his heart and spreading out into the ten directions. These ferocious deities completely bar the way to all impurity and annihilate the ten wrong deeds in order to establish living beings on the path of liberation. While engaged in such contemplation, the *yogin* recites their *bījamantra*.[627]

In order to confess his failings and bless the offerings, the *yogin* recites, "HŪṀ Mahāśrīheruka and your retinue, please listen to me! Previously, throughout beginningless *saṁsāra* I have accumulated causes for rebirth in the states of woe due to falling under the power of the five *kleśa*. This I confess in the presence of the host of wisdom deities. Please grant the *siddhi* of purifying appearances! Be present here in this *maṇḍala*. Bless the offerings and bestow the empowerments!"[628]

In the *Che mchog gi 'phrin las* (B11, C4, D5), a parallel text from the *mahottarakīla* cycle, blessings and empowerments are received in the form of light rays originating from the foreheads, throats and hearts of all the *maṇḍala* deities. As these rays enter the *yogin*'s body, speech and mind he imagines that all the vows of the three *kāya* are fulfilled and his sins are purified.[629]

The *mahottarakīla* text then deals at length with the establishment of the 'natural' foundation of the *maṇḍala* within the body of the practitioner. This is composed of a central area of faeces with swirling white semen to the east, a heap of flesh like a mountain to the south, foaming red blood to

---

625 The *pūrvayoga* practices of the Byang-gter tradition are elaborated in a text known as *gZer lnga*, 'Five Nails', an edition of which was published in 1970 from blocks preserved in the mTho-mthong Monastery, Solu Khumbu, Nepal (no further publication data given). It is also to be found with an English translation as vol.16 in the Byang-gter series by C.R. Lama and James Low, and a commentary is available from www.wandel-verlag.de/en

626 A32 222, A35 248

627 The VKMK specifies exactly which seed-syllable corresponds to which deity but in the present text the *mantra* are simply presented as a group at the end of the instructions for meditation. A45 404-405

628 A45 405-406

629 B11 526

the west and a lake of urine to the north. Above this the *yogin* should mentally construct an awning as he binds the tent *mudrā* and around the outside he should visualise an encircling lotus wall.

Placing his hands together, the *yogin* should imagine Vajrakīla between his palms and the *daśakrodha* kings upon his fingers. Seated with his consort upon his lap, the *yogin* should concentrate upon her *yoni*, in the centre of which he visualises the syllable ĀḤ, red and shining brightly. He then imagines rays of white light streaming forth from the OṀ at the base of his *vajra,* bright red light shining from the HŪṀ at its midsection and blue light radiating from the PHAṬ at its tip. His ardent desire for the bliss of her 'secret cavity' is said to annihilate all worldly attachments.[630]

Gradually the *yogin* extends this contemplation until he is able to visualise the entire *traidhātuka* united in non-dual bliss. Then the white *bodhicitta* of that union falls down like rain and he imagines the *maṇḍala* base to become a great lake of nectar. Muttering ACITTA APARACITTA HŪṀ, the *yogin* imagines all the *mudrā* deities to shimmer and dissolve into light which is then absorbed into the centre of the nectar and, as he recites the *mantra* of Amṛtakuṇḍalin, the *yogin* imagines that lake of nectar to seethe and swirl. In the centre of the lake stands a lotus throne with the corpses of demons heaped upon it as cushions. Reciting HAYAGRĪVA HŪṀ, the *yogin* imagines the snarling red-black figure of Hayagrīva holding sword and *kīla* and around him in the four directions, from HULU HULU HŪṀ PHAṬ, arise his four wives. In the east is the white rGyas-'debs (Mudritā), wielding an iron hook. In the south is the yellow Za-byed (Grasanī), holding aloft a noose. In the west is the red rMongs-byed, (Mohanī) wielding fetters and in the north is the green Tshe-'phel (Āyurvardhanī) who holds a bell.[631] As these four goddesses embrace their lord, the nectar drops of their union fall slowly downwards causing the goddesses to dissolve into light from the feet upwards. As this light is absorbed into the lake of nectar, Hayagrīva himself descends and melts into it until only his upper half remains there as its guardian.

Reciting PHAṬ PHAṬ PHAṬ, the *yogin* should flick a little of the nectar with his finger. As it touches his own body it is absorbed into himself so

---

630 B11 527-528

631 The four wives spring forth from *huluhulu,* explained in the lexicons as the inarticulate sound of pleasure uttered by women. A red-black Hayagrīva holding lotus and *viśvavajra* is depicted with four goddesses conforming to this description in L. Chandra, *Buddhist Iconography of Tibet* vol.1 132-133. Their names, however, are not those given here.

that he gains the *siddhi* of body, speech and mind. Touching the offering articles, it is absorbed into them so that they become free of blemish and any defect in their preparation is purified and made good. Touching the bodies of the obstructors and demons, they crumble to dust so that victory over them is won.

The carcasses of those slain enemies and obstructors are imagined to have the outer form of a dish of precious offerings whilst inwardly they have the nature of a corpse full of nectar. Placing a great heart in the centre of that dish of precious offerings, as the *yogin* recites a binding *mantra* he winds a length of wool around the heart, reminding himself of the *samaya* that binds his own heart to the deity. The heart is then adorned with the flesh of ignorance and the bones of anger, sprinkled with the bile of pride and immersed in a pool of the seething blood of desire. Imagining the whole of phenomenal existence to be incorporated within that offering, the *yogin* raises it up as a gift to the deities. Outwardly, the text says, he imagines his gift to be presented by the six goddesses of all sensual pleasure while inwardly meditating upon it as consisting of the five wisdoms derived from the purification of the five poisons. Thus all grasping desire, which is the single cause for transmigration throughout the six *gati,* is utterly destroyed. Binding the *mudrā* called 'blazing', the *yogin* as Vajrakīla gathers together the eightfold consciousness of the slaughtered universe which he establishes within the *nāḍī* of his heart, from where he then radiates a *mantra* causing the world to become flooded beneath a tidal wave of blood. That which is visualised outwardly as an ocean of blood, it is explained, is inwardly the truth of no-birth and secretly the fecund drops of the mother.[632]

The *yogin* then immerses himself in the three *samādhi* of the *utpattikrama* which rid his mind of mundane conceptions concerning the material world and serve as a basis for the arising of the divine *maṇḍala.* The first *samādhi* is the contemplation of *tathatā,* epitomised here as the *dharmakāya* (*dharmatā*), the second is the arising of an all-pervading compassion, and the third is the production of the causal syllable HŪṀ.[633] Thus, from the sky-like *dharmakāya* which encompasses all sentient beings with its compassion, the *yogin* should imagine the spontaneous appearance of the syllable HŪṀ. From this HŪṀ spring forth the five elements which pile up, one above another, and upon this foundation rests a

---

632 B11 528-530

633 Cf. T. Thondup, *Buddha Mind* 38

Mount Meru made of bones, with the *maṇḍala* palace of the gods upon its summit.

This 'ferocious palace' is briefly described in the Black Deity text as dark blue in colour, square, with four doors and festooned with ornaments. Encircling the *maṇḍala* perimeter are a *vajra* fence and a mass of fire that blazes like the conflagration at the end of an aeon.[634] In the *mahottarakīla* text, however, the entire process is described in a manner that emphasises both the inner nature of the *maṇḍala* (as composed of the *yogin's* own body) and the identification of the *yogin* with the cosmos. Furthermore, it specifically structures the universe in the form of a *kīla*. According to this text, five lights radiate out from a blue syllable HŪṀ and as they gather back together they cause that great HŪṀ to shine as bright as the sun and moon.[635] As the *yogin* recites PHAṬ PHAṬ PHAṬ HŪṀ LAṀ, the HŪṀ spontaneously explodes into the five directions so that within the sphere of non-dual appearance and emptiness it is as if five syllables had suddenly landed upon an open plain in the formation of a *maṇḍala*. Deep space is born from the dark blue PHAṬ and in the centre of that, from a dark green PHAṬ, arises a churning mass of crossed wind. From a dark red PHAṬ arises a blazing great fire like that at the end of an aeon, and from a bright red HŪṀ comes a swirling seething ocean of blood. Rising up from the centre of the ocean is a shining Mount Meru of bones, metamorphosed from a white syllable LAṀ. Then, as dark maroon light shines forth from the syllable OṀ upon the summit of that mountain, the whole universe of phenomenal appearance is transformed into the three-sided *bhavakīla,* the sharp tip of which pierces the very depths of hell. Its lower great knot envelops the *kāmadhātu* of gods and men. The lower half of its octagonal handle encompasses the *rūpadhātu,* comprising the 17 heavens of the *brahmaloka,* while the upper half comprises the formless realms of the gods of the four infinities. Within its upper knot is the palace of the *tathāgata,* around which is established the great circle of the *maṇḍala*. Thus the universe assumes the clear appearance of a *kīla*.

---

634   A45 406

635   Buddhist thought in general, and especially Vajrayāna thought, posits radiance as a fundamental quality of mind. *Pañcakrama* I.43, for example, defines consciousness as luminosity (*vijñānaṁ ca prabhāsvaram*) and thus the creative syllable HŪṀ which is the compassionate energy of the enlightened mind produces, maintains and manipulates all phenomena by means of radiance. Equating this radiance with the lights of sun and moon symbolises its nature as the indivisible unity of wisdom and means.

The ferocious palace of the *tathāgata* within the upper great knot consists of nine blue-black triangles, around the central one of which stand three semicircles of control and a circular border of skulls. The eight pillars inside the palace are composed of purplish human corpses set upon pedestals of tortoise with the planets as their capitals. The great gods Brahmā and the rest are laid across the tops of these pillars to form the 16 golden beams of the ceiling. Large numbers of corpses of adults and children are spread over the beams to form the rafters and these are plastered over with a mixture of faeces and urine. Wings of birds are then laid across that to form the roof. Looking up, one sees awnings and decorative projecting mouldings, parasols fashioned from corpses, dangling flags of human skin and a 13-tiered spire with the heart of Rudra himself upon its peak. Small golden bells hanging from every corner resound with the sound of the Mahāyāna Dharma. Looking down upon the ground, one sees that the four sides of the outer perimeter of the central palace are painted green as a sign of the total accomplishment of the four classes of magical activity. Outside this stand the remaining eight dark blue triangles and everything is enclosed within a courtyard, the whole area of which is filled with a swirling agitated ocean of blood.

The walls of the palace are built up of tightly packed dry human skulls with projecting ornaments of freshly severed heads. From the mouth of each skull blazes fire, from each nostril issues smoke and rivulets of blood gurgle down from the eyes. The projecting end of every beam is fashioned in the form of a lion's face, from the great jaws of which dangle tangled bunches of writhing poisonous snakes. All around the walls are hung garlands of intestines with pendant hearts, livers, lungs, eyeballs and so on. From the open windows shine the lights of sun and moon and the inside of the palace is filled with goddesses offering all manner of red articles gratifying to the senses.

Around the outside of the palace runs a decorative golden frieze hung with dark blue chains and green half-chains. It has an upper apartment that glitters white and a triumphal archway is situated at the approach to each of its four doors. The four doorways in the four directions are each enclosed within a vestibule and each has a threshold made of tortoise and a lintel of *makara*. The individual doorways are distinguished by the caste of snakes whose corpses are employed in their manufacture,[636] fixed at the feet with nails of meteoric iron and at the head with vicious nails of the eight great planets. Rays of light spread out from the glorious *maṇḍala* to a radius of ten million *yojana* and it is enveloped in wreaths of powerful incense from piles of smouldering corpses. The entire edifice is without distinction of outer and inner.[637]

Both texts go on to explain that in the centre of the palace there is a great *vajra* rock and a lotus throne supporting the discs of the sun and moon with the eight classes of demons piled up like cushions, upon which rests the syllable HŪṀ. Upon the transformation of this syllable into a *vajra,* rays of light radiate out. When the lights return to the *vajra*, the *yogin* himself arises in its place in the form of the deity Vajrakumāra with three faces, six arms and four legs spread wide. Standard iconographic descriptions of the deity follow, the essential difference between the black and the multicoloured systems being that in the latter tradition the deity is said to reside in the *yogin*'s heart and to be no bigger than his thumb tip.[638]

The *mahottarakīla* text then goes on to describe the actual body of the *yogin*, which here assumes the 18-armed form described above in Chapter Three. Within the head, throat and heart of this vast body reside *jñāna-sattva* of his body, speech and mind. United with his consort, the *yogin* makes the sacred oath of 'killing by compassion'.[639]

The *daśakrodha* kings that comprise the deity's retinue are described as single-faced in the black deity text and as triple-faced in that of the *mahottarakīla*.[640] The rest of the *maṇḍala* comprises the supreme sons, the four goddesses who guard the gates and the circles of the twelve oath-bound protectors, the *kiṁkara* servants and the countless messengers and

---

636 The door to the east is made of white snakes of the *kṣatriya* caste, that to the south of yellow *vaiśya* snakes, the western door of red *brāhmaṇa* and the northern of black *śūdra*.
Cf. Gega Lama, *Principles of Tibetan Art* 389-390

637 B11 531-534

638 A45 406-407, B11 534

639 B11 535-537

640 A45 407, B11 538-542. The latter text provides a separate description for each *krodha* king, delineating the colours of the three faces and the attributes held in the six hands. The *piśācī* emanations are also described and the unique feature of this text is that each emanation is said to wield the very weapons carried by her *krodha* lord in his central pair of hands.
(See below, Table 2)

assistants. By visualising them all clearly just as they are described, the *yogin* is instructed to cause them actually to be present before him.[641]

The next two verses in which the intention of the rite is declared, beginning with the words "HŪṀ All those who hold the awareness of Vajrakumāra must bring into effect the universal *vajra* ..." have been noted above in Chapter Five as occurring in both the BRT and the VKMK. They are followed here by a *mantra* not found in those texts that serves to bestow the consecrations of Vajrakīla's enlightened body, speech and mind; OṀ VAJRAKĪLI KĪLAYA KĀYA-VĀK-CITTA-ABHIṢIÑCA HŪṀ ĀḤ.[642]

With a verse that continues to follow the wording of the *tantras* very closely, the wisdom deities are invited to approach the *samayamaṇḍala;* "HŪṀ JAḤ In order that we may accomplish the *bhavakīla* and receive the empowerments and *siddhi,* you unchanging host of wrathful *jñānasattva* please come here! And, having arrived, may you great gods of wrath please accept these outer, inner and secret offerings. Please bestow on us the Kīla *siddhi* and may the signs and symbols of success appear!"

The *mahottarakīla* text states that this verse should be recited in a most plaintive tone with a voice like thunder.[643]

As before, the descent of blessings is accomplished by means of *mantra* and then the *jñānadeva* are honoured with salutations; "With single pointed mind we salute Vajrarākṣasa and his retinue in order to maintain divine pride and to subdue the violent conduct of the three classes of beings".[644] The *jñānadeva* then merge as one into the *samayamaṇḍala* and in this way the *yogin* becomes united with the body, speech, mind, good qualities and enlightened activities of all the buddhas.

---

641 A45 407

642 A45 407-408. The *mahottarakīla* text says that by KAṬAṄKAṬE YETA KARA OṀ the blessings of the body melt into the crown of the head. JAYE VIJAYE ĀḤ the blessings of the speech melt into the throat. ACITTA APARACITTA HŪṀ the blessings of the mind melt into the heart. The ability to slay the three realms simultaneously is the *siddhi* of the body. The sound of the *dharmatā* Vajrakīla is the *siddhi* of speech. Self-clarifying meditation on spontaneously arising wisdom is the *siddhi* of mind. B11 545

643 B11 546 which then goes on to describe the minor deities of the *maṇḍala* in some detail. B11 547-548

644 A45 408. The *mahottarakīla* text reads; "ŚRĪVAJRA NAMAḤ In truth all *dharma* and oneself are free of duality. In the state of absolute truth we salute the *maṇḍala* of deities and present these offerings." B11 548

Offerings of cooling water for the feet, flowers, incense, lamps, perfume, food and music are then presented, together with all objects of the six senses and the essential medicine, blood and ornamented *bali* cake. Flesh, blood, bones, the inner organs and gall bladder are offered, together with a continuous stream of nectar which is the non-dual mind of enlightenment. In that way, the text explains, all the outer, inner and secret offering articles without exception are presented to the *maṇḍala* deities who are requested to accept them and bestow empowerments and *siddhi.*[645]

The black deity *sādhana* continues by honouring the body of the lord Vajrakīla, praising him as the quintessential splendour of all *tathāgata* of the three times without exception,[646] and his consort is honoured as the glorious clarity of unoriginated pure consciousness. The ten *krodharāja* are praised as the ones who bestow liberation through mastery of the ten *bhūmi,* while their ten consorts are honoured as possessing the ultimate meaning of the ten *pāramitā* which purify the ten non-virtues. The assembled host of supreme sons are praised as those who, through the strength of their compassion, 'liberate' all vicious trouble-makers and the 20 animal-headed emanations are honoured as the ones who liberate the 20 *kleśa* in their own place. The four fierce goddesses who guard the gates are praised for their enthusiasm in protecting against outer and inner obstacles. Finally, respects are paid to the hosts of minor protectors around the *maṇḍala* periphery who have taken solemn pledges in the presence of the *jina*. The instruction in the text at this point is to recite the *hṛdaya* of all these deities as much as possible.[647]

---

645 A45 408-409. The *mahottarakīla* text reduces the long list of offering articles mentioned here to the three essentials of medicine, blood and *bali*. These, however, are presented in elaborate fashion with their symbolism fully examined. B11 548-549. Cf. below, Chapter Twelve.

646 The *mahottarakīla* text equates the nine heads of the deity with nine wisdoms of the radiantly clear *dharmatā*. The upper three heads are said to gaze with love and compassion upon all those who are to be converted. The middle three are said to bestow the blessings of empowerment and *siddhi,* while the three lower faces purify the body, speech and mind. The text then goes on to identify the symbols held in his 18 hands, equating many of them with lines from the *mūlatantra*. B11 554-555. See above, Table 1.

647 A45 409-410

Following that, offerings are presented to the entire assembly (*gaṇa-cakra*)[648] from the highest gods to the lowest. To begin with, the offerings are purified by fire, air and water[649] and blessed by the syllables OṀ ĀḤ HŪṀ, symbolic of enlightened body, speech and mind. Incited by the sound of HŪṀ, the wisdom *maṇḍala* of wrathful deities is invited to be present at the feast in order that the *bhavakīla* may be accomplished and empowerments and *siddhi* received. The offerings that they are asked to accept are as before but on this occasion they are referred to in Sanskrit with the prefix *vajra* (*vajrārghya, vajrapuṣpa,* etc.). They are described as consisting of the purest ingredients, "an unsurpassed array of offerings from which rays of light of the *pañcajñāna* radiate out, adorned with the excellent sensual qualities of all that could be desired," and the bliss that they bestow is said to fulfil all broken vows.

The actual presentation of these marvellous offerings is in three parts. The first part[650] is offered to all the *maṇḍala* deities with the request that, upon accepting it, they avert all disruptions of enemies and obstructors and bestow both supreme and ordinary *siddhi*.

The second part[651] is offered with a confession of any breaches of sacred obligation that may have been committed by the *yogin* with either body, speech or mind due to carelessness and ignorance, and the forgiveness of the 'lords of great compassion' is requested for all such errors; "HŪṀ The confused minds of all ignorant sentient beings sink under the power of the delusions of discursive thought. Vows are transgressed even when standing at the very door of the great *maṇḍala* of secret *mantra*. Therefore, whatever confusions, errors, lapses and breaches have been committed with regard to either the primary or secondary *samaya* are now

---

648 Time permitting, Tibetan lamas generally begin the *gaṇacakra* section with often extremely lengthy liturgies inviting large numbers of *dharmapāla* to the feast.

The *mahottarakīla* texts B11 and C4 diverge at this point. Although both texts cover the same ground, their wording is completely different from here on.

649 The outer appearance of the offerings is dissolved into emptiness by burning etc., just as the universe is destroyed at the end of an aeon.

650 In the performance of the ritual, the *karmācārya* would at this point divide the main *bali* cake horizontally into three parts, the uppermost portion of which is now presented to the chief deities of the *maṇḍala*.

651 The first half of the lower portion of the cake.

confessed in the presence of the *trikāya-guru* and any impurities in the presentation of the assembled offerings and sacred *bali* are confessed in the presence of the *ḍākinī* and Dharma-protectors." Calling out to attract the attention of Vajrakumāra and his retinue, the *yogin* confesses to those 'embodiments of the *kīla* whose nature is divine activity' all the mistakes he has made due to grasping at (illusory) objects as real. Having failed to perceive the fundamentally pure wisdom nature of the five *kleśa* and having thus been overpowered by confusion, the *yogin* confesses that he has created for himself a dualistic nightmare in which phenomena are either accepted or rejected on the purely arbitrary basis of personal desire. All this is confessed.

For the offering of the third part,[652] having prepared an effigy of the enemies and obstructors, the *yogin* should contemplate the truth very carefully[653] and separate the victim from his protector gods.[654] He then dispatches messengers to summon the minds of the demons and forcibly install them within the effigy. While the messengers spread out in all directions in pursuit of their quarry, the *yogin* should continuously recite E RAṀ PHAṬ RAṀ JVALA RAṀ TRI YAṀ JAḤ NṚ TRI VAJRĀṄKUṢA JAḤ VAJRAPĀŚA HŪṀ VAJRASPHOṬA VAṀ VAJRAGHAṆṬĀ HOḤ PRAVEŚAYA A TRI YAṀ JAḤ HUR THUM JAḤ MĀRAYA PHAṬ. When the effigy has truly become the embodiment of demons, it is pierced with the ritual *kīla* and the demons liberated. Then the slain effigy is offered to the wisdom deities with the words, "HŪṀ Mahāśrīvajrakīla and your retinue, open your mouths! Your mouths are like the blazing pit of a sacrificial fire, with teeth arranged like firewood and tongues like sacrificial ladles. This corpse of the liberated enemies and obstructors is pressed to your mouths. May you reduce every atom of it to dust! OṀ VAJRAYAKṢA KRODHAVIJAYA KHĀHI!"[655]

---

652 The remaining portion of the *bali* is offered here, together with an effigy of the sacrificial victim.

Jan Gonda notes that grain offerings have been used to represent animal sacrifices since the Vedic period, with the various parts of the grain standing for flesh, blood and bone.

Jan Gonda, *Rice and Barley Offerings in the Veda* 23

653 That is, one should begin this section with the prayer called 'a declaration of truth' (*satyavākya*), which Edgerton (*BHS Dictionary*) describes as "a solemn statement of truth as a means of magic control of events".

654 See below, Chapter Nine.

655 A45 410-412

The offerings are then shared out for the enjoyment of the gathered assembly. After they have been distributed, the remnants are collected together, sprinkled with nectar and offered to the servants and assistants from the *maṇḍala* periphery who are reminded of their former vows and instructed to act upon them immediately, fulfilling the tasks that they promised to perform of protecting the doctrine and the doctrine holders.[656] The liturgy for this section of the rite is particularly interesting in our text B11 in which many new iconographic details of the minor deities are to be found. There we read that the *yogin* should imagine the offering dish to be a ferocious *maṇḍala* containing an ocean of blood, a mountain of bones and a great heap of human flesh. The deities are then invited as follows;

"HŪṀ From the *maṇḍala* of human flesh piled up like a mountain, you 32 wrathful *ḍākinī* please come here! From the palace with walls built of skeletons, you 28 *īśvarī* please come here! From the charnel ground of piled-up hearts old and new, you seven mothers and four sisters all bound under oath please come here! From the *maṇḍala* composed of fresh and decaying bones, you 360 messengers please come here! ḌĀKINĪ HŪṀ HŪṀ JAḤ SARVAPAÑCĀMṚTA KHĀHI.

"HŪṀ Why was the first portion of the offering not given to you? That was presented to the wisdom deities from whom empowerments were received for the benefit of beings. Why was the middle portion of the offering not given to you? That was presented to the mother goddesses and *ḍākinī* of high rank from whom the *siddhi* of the four magical activities were requested. Why have these remains not been touched by our mouths? They are presented to you servants and obedient messengers as reminders of your former vows. Without mixing everything up into one, you must each perform your duties in accordance with your rank. In the sphere of the *dharmatā,* however, all things are equal!

"HŪṀ In the red semicircular *maṇḍala* of control, the remainder of the offerings are piled up like Mount Meru and the four continents. Waves of the blood of lust and desire are bubbling, heaps of the bones of anger rattle and chunks of the flesh of ignorance quiver. The sensuous delight of the fivefold nectar is beyond imagination. You 32 oath-bound worldly *ḍākinī,* receive this offering of Mahāśrī's orders and perform your tasks as promised on behalf of us *yogins*.

"You *vajrakiṁkara* of great wrath, you wrathful *vajra* mothers whose ferocious breath pervades the three realms, *vajrayakṣa, vajrarākṣasa,*

---

656 A45 412-413

vajrabhūta, vajraśvāna, vajrayama, vajravetāla, vajra lords of death, *vajrakālarātri,* you great ones who catch the breath with an iron hook, obedient ones who carry away calumny, you who move like the formless wind, you who push back trouble as if moving in a dance, you who delight in the acquisition of a thousand skulls, who cast beckoning gestures to the triple world, great ones who liberate the threefold world with compassion, you great *mudrā* of the assembly and so on, together with all your retinue of *vajra* sons and daughters, the 18 great *kiṁkara* who liberate the triple world – the sensuous delight of the fivefold nectar is beyond imagination. Receive this offering of Mahāśrī's orders and perform your tasks as promised on behalf of us *yogins*.

"Displaying demonic forms utterly impossible to bear, you 28 powerful *īśvarī* – the sensuous delight of the fivefold nectar ... etc.

"Daughter of Indra,[657] shining goddess whose noose is composed of rays of sunlight; daughter of the *ṛṣi* Agni, shining goddess with the lustre of fire whose garland is composed of lightning; daughter of Yamarāja, blazing ferocious daughter, she of the *vajra* mortar; daughter of the *rākṣasa* king, shining goddess of death wielding a sword; daughter of king Varuṇa, great blazing one attached to scent; daughter of Vāyu, king of the wind, you shining goddess with an eagle overhead; daughter of the *yakṣa* king, all-pervading shining goddess whose face is a shooting star; daughter of the king of obstructors, great shining goddess with the ears of an ox (elephant?), to all you eight great blazing goddesses – the sensuous delight of the fivefold nectar ... etc.

"She who desiccates the triple world in an instant, she who brandishes a sword and she who wields a net, she with a corpse, she who summons and she who bestows sensual experience, to all you *mātaraḥ*[658] – the sensuous delight of the fivefold nectar ... etc.

"In the east is the swiftly moving one, princess of the *gandharva*; in the south is she who hurries, princess from the realm of Yama; in the west is the swiftly moving one, princess of the *nāga*; and in the north is she who hurries, princess of the *yakṣa*. To you four great sisters who have taken oaths with deep sincerity – the sensuous delight of the fivefold nectar ... etc.

---

657 Textual hiatus omits Indra's daughter. This group are known as the eight blazing goddesses (*'bar ma brgyad*).

658 One mother goddess appears to have been omitted, for there should be seven in this group.

"Messengers in the eastern direction, you 60 women in the family of Conch moving faster than the wind, you must perform your task of slaying the enemies and obstructors! Messengers in the southern direction, you 60 women in the family of Iron moving faster than the wind, you must perform your task of slaying the enemies and obstructors! Messengers in the western direction, you 60 women in the family of Copper moving faster than the wind, you must perform your task of slaying the enemies and obstructors! Messengers in the northern direction, you 60 women in the family of (there appears to be a hiatus here. According to C24 the family of the north is called Turquoise. This should be followed by Gold from the nadir and then, from the zenith, those in the family of) Rosewood moving faster than the wind, you must perform your task of slaying the enemies and obstructors! Each of you 360 messengers has four faces and four arms, wings, fangs and claws. You grasp at the life force and slay the enemies; to all of you – the sensuous delight of the fivefold ... etc.

"MAHĀMĀṀSA-RAKTA-CITTA-BASUTA-GOROCANA-SARVAPŪJĀ KHĀHI. Thus they are entrusted with their duties."[659]

The last group to be called are the 12 bsTan-ma whose sacrificial *bali* is described as excessive and powerful (*lhag la dbang ba*). In accepting this cake they reaffirm their oaths and are instructed to fulfil their appointed tasks.[660]

Going outside and scattering the offerings, the *yogin* takes the dish upon which they were gathered and, turning it upside down, he suppresses beneath it the vow-breaking demons. Invoking Vajrakīla and all the deities of the *maṇḍala* by calling upon their former vows, the gods are asked to trample these demons down to dust; "The dance of pleasure of the glorious great *heruka* stomps upon the hearts of vow-breaking demons. The dance of pleasure of their ferocious consorts stomps upon the hearts of enemies and obstructors. By the pounding thrusts of the wrathful males, their ferocious consorts are filled with pleasure."

Finally, returning inside the temple or place of meditation, the *yogin*s gather up the sacrificial articles and recite auspicious prayers as a general benediction for all beings.[661]

---

659 B11 558-562

660 The *mahottarakīla* text adds here that, after the 12 bsTan-ma who dwell on the periphery of the *maṇḍala* have received their offerings, the *maṇḍala* itself gradually dissolves from the edges until all surrounding deities are absorbed into the central figure. B11 562, C4 61

661 A45 413

The *atiyoga* rites said to have been taught to Padmasambhava in India by Śrīsiṁha[662] dispense with the bulk of those things discussed above. The emphasis in these short texts is placed upon the mind of the *yogin* who is instructed to abandon mental weariness and contemplate the purity of all *dharma*s that by nature lack any objectivity. Having generated an all-pervading compassion that reaches to the limits of space, in a state of blissful awareness that is free of discursive thoughts he should meditate upon the *maṇḍala* of black deities (described in these texts in orthodox manner) and thus all demons are overthrown.

The *rTsa ba dril sgrub* (A32), however, also presents interesting side-lights on the nature of the Kīla cult. It includes, for example, a detailed description of the magical *kavaca* that may contemplatively be 'worn' as a protective charm. Arising in the vast form of the deity, the *yogin* should imagine each pore of his body to be protected by a miniature wrathful guardian brandishing aloft a fearsome weapon and that, all together, these tiny emanations cover him completely as a protective suit of armour. On his navel stands the ferocious Vajragaruḍa who takes as his food all dangerous beings. Conch shell white in colour, this eagle has iron wings, rolling yellow eyes, an indestructible body and should be clearly visualised grasping a serpent in his iron beak and claws.[663] This text is also unique in offering guidance to the *yogin* with regard to the problem of demonic possession. All other texts scrutinised in the current study treat demons as (symbolic) outer phenomena, teaching methods for their subjugation requiring the meditator to reach out into the ten directions in order to "drag them forth and slay" them. The present text, however, also considers the necessity of dealing with an offending demon that has taken residence within the *yogin*'s own body. In that case, it is said, one should meditate very deeply upon fire and, with the demon held clearly in mind, burn him up where he stays.

---

662 A32 & 35, etc., found in three collections. Vairocana, also, is said to have studied the doctrines of Vajrakīla in India under Śrīsiṁha.
S. Karmay, *The Great Perfection* 25

663 A32 226-227

Table 2: Iconography of the Daśakrodha Kings

	colours				attributes[1]	
	body	**right face**	**left face**	**central face**	**right hand**	**left hand**
Hūṁkāra (zenith)	sky (deep blue)	white	blue	vajra-conch	bow	arrow
Krodhavijaya (east)	white	red	green	vajra-conch	trident	discus
Nīladaṇḍa (southeast)	blue	white	red	vajra-conch	club (*dbyug tho*)	mass of fire
Yamāntaka (south)	blue-black	black	blue	vajra-conch	club (*be com*)	club (*dbyug tho*)
Ārya Acala (southwest)	blue-green	red	maroon	vajra-conch	razor	noose
Hayagrīva (west)	red	blue	white	vajra-conch	sword	noose
Aparājita (northwest)	red	yellow	green	vajra-conch	ensign	fan
Amṛtakuṇḍalin (north)	green	white	yellow	vajra-conch	viśvavajra	bell
Trailokyavijaya (northeast)	yellow-green	yellow	red	vajra-conch	(?) *khra dong*[2]	discus
Mahābala (nadir)	smoke	green	yellow	vajra-conch	hammer	pestle

Derived from the *rDo rje phur pa che mchog gi 'phrin las* (B11), 538-542

[1] These columns refer to the central pair of hands. Each deity wields a vajra & skull in his upper pair of hands and rolls a kīla between the palms of the lower. Note that in this text, the animal-headed emanations to the right and left of each krodha king are also said to carry the attributes listed here.

[2] Also found as *kha trom, kha dong & kha tong.*

CHAPTER EIGHT
The attainment of unsurpassed enlightenment

Having mastered the stages of *utpattikrama* and accomplished the mental transformation of the universe into the vast *maṇḍala* of Kīla deities (*bhavakīla*), the *yogin*'s next task is to manifest perfect enlightenment within that ideal theatre through the process of *saṁpannakrama.*

The Northern Treasures Kīla text presented as the ultimate guide "to the attainment of unsurpassed enlightenment" is the *dKar po lam gyi sgron ma,* 'The Lamp of the White Path' (A9, B15, C6, E9), which is said to be like a lamp illuminating the procedures through which the power of Vajrakīla may be gained. The colophon of the text claims it to be a quintessential instruction derived from *tantra,* taught to Ye-shes mtsho-rgyal by Padmasambhava, and within it are found details of the three *cakra* of body, speech and mind. Certainly the basic structure of the meditation, based upon the three *vajra* syllables (OṀ ĀḤ HŪṀ) residing in the *yogin*'s forehead, throat and heart, is fundamental to tantric methodology but its special application here in combination with the condensed DHADDHI *mantra* of the Vajrakīla cycle is most unusual. Innumerable variants of the DHADDHI *mantra* are taught in the texts of the black deity cycle, with the sole purpose of inciting the servants of the Vajrakīla doctrines to set about their violent tasks of attacking the enemy. Within this *mahottarakīla* text, however, the *mantra* is internalised and applied directly to the goal of enlightenment. In the absence of any parallel or similar instruction for meditation to be found within the root *tantra* of Mahottarakīla (A3) analysed above, we are unable to determine whether this commentary derives from the personal insight of the teacher[664] or from some other, as yet unnoticed, traditional source.

The text begins with a salutation "to the wisdom embodiment of spontaneously arisen great *vajra* wrath" and the statement that this teaching is the quintessence of all the combined *upadeśa* of Vajrakīla within a single succinct explanation. The *yogin* who wishes to practise this meditation, it is said, may either engage the assistance of a *samaya* partner or perform the task alone 'in the manner of a lion'. Collecting together the requisite

---

664 A similar teaching is to be found in brief in the Mahottarakīla *sādhana* B11 536-537, also said to have been taught by Padmasambhava.

ritual articles he should retire to an auspicious place, blessing and purifying the site in the usual manner. Setting out the *maṇḍala* in its elaborate form, he should arrange upon it the necessities of worship. He should meditate upon the *rakṣācakra* and purify all the sins of his body and speech. He should bless the three essential offerings of medicine, blood and *bali*, and generate the *bīja* of the elements from the sphere of appearance and emptiness. Then, constructing in his mind the divine residence of the gods, he should visualise himself clearly as the deity Vajrakīla seated upon a throne in the non-dual embrace of his consort. Around him he should see the *daśakrodha* kings and their queens, together with their retinues of assistants and so on, all generated in accordance with the procedures outlined above. Before him and to his left and right stand the three supreme sons of his body, speech and mind, said here to be the life force of the essential purity of 'liberation'. Having thus established the *samayamaṇḍala,* this should be blessed as wisdom by the descent of the *jñānadeva* and the *yogin,* his own nature perfected as skilful means, should present all the deities with offerings and praise. In this way, applying himself assiduously to the *yoga* of approaching and becoming one with the deity, the *yogin* establishes his mind in divine pride and accomplishes through *mantra* an attitude of supreme *bodhicitta,* utterly free of all worldly hopes and fears.[665]

Clearly visualising himself in the form of the great glorious Vajrakīla, the *yogin* should see upon the crown of his head a white wheel with nine spokes upon which is arranged the body *mantra* consisting of nine syllables which bar the doors of nine moral downfalls. In the centre of the wheel stands the syllable OṀ and around its rim are arranged the letters of Vajrakīla's *hṛdaya*, here referred to as 'the *mantra* of violent suppression and repulsion', and the whole wheel blazes with light.

The combined *mantra* to be arrayed upon the crown of his head is given in the text as OṀ VAJRAKĪLI KĪLAYA KĀYAVAJRA KAṬAṄKAṬE YA YETA KARA IMĀN SARVAVIGHNĀN BAṀ HŪṀ PHAṬ, explained as follows: The eight seeds of violent suppression (OṀ VAJRAKĪLI KĪLAYA) are the luminous body (KĀYA) marked with the triple VAJRA. By KAṬAṄKAṬE, sins are purified and, by many repetitions of YA, the *nirmāṇakāya* is attained. All other beings are purified by YETA KARA (? *yeṣṭhakāra*). Moral downfalls of the body are purified in their own place by IMĀN and all sins of the body are gathered together by SARVA. The

665 A9 92-93

heads (of the demons of sin) are crushed by the *yoga* of VIGHNĀN, and by BAṀ the manifestation of *dharmatā* is accomplished. By HŪṀ, indivisible reality is contemplated, and by PHAṬ the *yogin*'s body is liberated as the *nirmāṇakāya*. This is the ultimate goal (*abhiprāya*) of the body on the path of secret *mantra*.

Remaining in a state of ecstatic fixation upon this wheel, the *yogin* recites the *mantra* and imagines the wheel to revolve in an anticlockwise direction as rays of white light stream out to pervade the entire trichiliocosm. As they rise upwards, the light rays summon the hearts of all *tathāgata* and present them with offerings. Spreading out in every direction, they strike the bodies of all beings in the six classes, purging them of sin and, gathering back together again, those rays of light are absorbed into the wheel which then becomes exceedingly bright. As it revolves, each and every defilement within the *yogin*'s body is drawn into the light and burned up like feathers in a bonfire.

At the completion of the *mantra* recitation, the wheel melts into the all-pervading *mahābindu* until it remains like a solitary white pearl, the emblem of the *yogin*'s natural purity, upon the crown of his head. The notion of a material body made of flesh and blood is turned aside and the *yogin*'s clearly visible appearance is known to be devoid of inherent nature (*svabhāva*). This is the attainment of *bodhi,* the great secret of the secret Mantrayāna.[666]

The wheel at the throat is red in colour and also has nine spokes. At its centre is the syllable ĀḤ, which has the blissful nature of the enjoyment of six tastes, and the *mantra* of violent suppression is arrayed around its rim. Upon its spokes are the nine syllables that are the essential means of accumulating *siddhi,* which, the text explains, become ineffective if seen by those who have no vows.

The *mantra* of this wheel is given as OṀ VAJRAKĪLI KĪLAYA VĀKVAJRA JAYE VIJAYE KURU KARA IMĀN SARVAVIGHNĀN BAṀ HŪṀ PHAṬ, about which it is said that the unstoppable eight seeds (as above) arise as the *mantra* of divine speech (VĀK) which is the second VAJRA. JAYE is the speech of utter purity. VIJA indicates victory over mundane speech and YE purifies all defilements of the speech of others. By KURU KARA wisdom arises, and by IMĀN is shown the ultimate truth[667] of the natural condition. SARVAVIGHNĀN purifies sin. BAṀ is

---

666 A9 93-95

667 C says it shows the two truths.

the sphere of speech that pervades the *dharmatā*. HŪṀ contains within itself the nature of unstoppability and PHAṬ is the liberation of speech as the *saṁbhogakāya*. Such is the ultimate goal of speech on the path of secret *mantra*.

As the *yogin* begins his recitation of the *mantra,* the wheel flares up in a bright blaze of light which completely envelops his body and purifies him of sin. Radiating outwards, the rays of light delight the *tathāgata* of the ten directions who purge away all defilements of speech of the six classes of living beings. Returning to the wheel, the red light is absorbed within it and all defilements of the *yogin*'s speech are washed clean as if by water, so that both outwardly and inwardly he becomes radiantly pure as if permeated by the light of sun and moon.[668]

The *cakra* of light at the heart is blue in colour and has either nine spokes and rim, as before, or else it may be visualised in the form of a *śrīvatsa* with eight corners.[669] In the centre of that diagram in the heart is located the syllable HŪṀ which is the *bindu* of the indestructible life force itself, the very essence of the wisdom mind. By just this syllable are all worlds emptied and *śūnyatā* made manifest. The eighteen *bījamantra* are said to abide in purity and around them is arrayed the *mantra* of violent suppression.

The secret *mantra* for that profound state is OṀ VAJRAKĪLI KĪLAYA CITTAVAJRA ACITTA APARACITTA MAMA VAŚAṀ HŪṀ MATAṀ MYAK KARA IMĀN SARVAVIGHNĀN BAṀ HŪṀ PHAṬ, about which it is said that the eight seeds of violent suppression are the self-secret of the mind (CITTA) which is the third VAJRA. ACITTA (inconceivable) is the mind free of faults. The five syllables APARACITTA (unsurpassed mind) is the *vajra* mind which cannot be overthrown by another and the five syllables MAMA VAŚAṀ HŪṀ are the five *jñāna* which spontaneously arise when all mental fabrications of ignorance are abandoned. MATAṀ blocks the door to becoming and rebirth. By MYAK KARA, consciousness is purified

---

668 A9 95-96

669 Although Sir Monier-Williams in his *Sanskrit-English Dictionary* says that this emblem looks like "a cruciform flower", in Tibetan art it is always depicted as an endless knot (usually having ten loops) and it is very difficult to see how it could be arranged "with eight corners". B11 536 speaks of an eight-faceted jewel in the heart with a three-pronged *vajra* in its centre. *dPal be'u* may therefore stand here for some kind of gem. In any case, the *mantra* given here has ten divisions (also called "eighteen" by a curious process of reckoning) and yet the wheel that contains it is still said to have nine spokes.

and by IMĀN the door to the lower realms is closed. SARVAVIGHNĀN purifies all defilements of mind, and BAṀ is the mind's self-luminous wisdom. HŪṀ is the uncontrived understanding of reality, and by PHAṬ the mind is liberated as the *dharmakāya*. This is the ultimate goal of the mind on the path of secret *mantra*.

As he performs the recitation, the *yogin* imagines the wheel to blaze with light so that as it revolves it burns away all the defilements of mind. The rays of light that spread out from that wheel make offerings to the hearts of all *tathāgata* and as they return they purify all sins of the six classes of living beings. They then gather together and melt back into the wheel. All sins of mind everywhere are cleansed so that the mind becomes like a highly polished mirror within which the *yogin* confidently views all appearances as the natural clarity of wisdom spontaneously arising from the *dharmatā* sphere of emptiness.[670]

The *yogin* should practise the three goals in that way until the stage of 'heat' (*ūṣman*)[671] is attained in body, speech and mind. Until then, the text insists, the *yogin* should keep these three wheels as his inexhaustible ornaments and thus purify the habitual patterns (*vāsanā*) of holding to the duality of appearances in terms of subject and object. Ignorance will thereby become illuminated as a state of wisdom and he will attain the perfect three *kāya*. By means of these meditations, the wisdom mind will become clearly manifest and the state of omniscience quickly gained.

This *upadeśa* is a 'tree of life' (*srog shing*) composed of unchanging crystal and the *yogin* should know that by putting these instructions into practice, all obstacles will be cleared away so long as he recites these syllables of the condensed DHADDHI *mantra*.

670 A9 96-97

671 Heat or warmth is a stage associated in the *sūtras* with the path of *yoga*, the second of the five paths (*mārga*). In this context, however, the term refers to the attainment of a satisfactory climax in meditation.

CHAPTER NINE
Gaining control of the mischievous spirits

Having attained the highest degree of occult power through total identification with the deity, the *yogin* is now in a position to demonstrate his mastery of the phenomenal world in the fulfilment of his Mahāyāna pledge to liberate all beings from *saṁsāra*. The way in which he honours that commitment forms the subject matter of both this and the following chapters.

In particular, the *yogin* at this stage should be capable of bringing under his control those mischievous spirits who formerly swore an oath of allegiance to support and protect the Vajrakīla Dharma and its practitioners and which, if properly coerced, may greatly assist the *yogin* in the execution of his religious duties. Although such occult mastery is often much admired by a largely superstitious public, Buddhist hierophants since the sage of the Śākyas himself have denounced these practices as improper and unsuitable for those whose minds are seriously set on enlightenment. Tāranātha, for example, says that the attainment of power over worldly *ḍākinī* is really a hindrance to spiritual progress[672] and bDud-'joms rinpoche warns that the practice of black magic is like playing with a sharp weapon that may easily cut off the practitioner's own life.[673] The popularity of such rites with both *yogins* and laymen alike, however, is evident throughout Tibetan culture at large and amply testified to by the number of treatises dealing with the subject to be found among the material presently under consideration.

The *bKa' nyan lcags kyi ber ka,* 'Iron Cloak of Obedient Servants' (A10, B19, C7, E10), is one of the rites specifically mentioned in our *them byang* through which the *yogin* may seek to gain control over those 'elemental spirits'. Referred to in its colophon as 'the central heart of *yoga*', it is said to have been taught by Padmasambhava to Ye-shes mtsho-rgyal in the lion's cave at sPa-gro stag-tshang before being hidden away as treasure for the benefit of future generations. The *bSe lcags dung gsum srog gi citta* (B28) indicates it as the means through which Lang-lab byang-chub rdo-rje gained his remarkable occult power although, it may be remembered,

672 D. Templeman, *Tāranātha's Life of Kṛṣṇācārya* 88

673 Terry Clifford, *The Lamp of Liberation* 50-51

the service rendered him by the protectors proved ultimately insufficient to prevent his untimely demise by black magic.[674] B28, in which the pith teachings described here are much elaborated, proved invaluable in determining the meaning of the present text.

A drawing of the three concentric *maṇḍala* circles[675] and so on and the arranging of ritual articles is said to be unnecessary for the practice of this rite[676] but the *yogin* must have a clear recollection of enlightened intention (*abhiprāya,* the subject of our previous chapter) and be established in the state of *tathatā*. Thus mentally prepared, the *yogin* summons all the servants (*bran*), messengers (*pho nya*) and obedient ones (*bka' nyan*) and tells them that the time has come for the fulfilment of their oaths. Maintaining his position of authority over them through mindfulness of the *sādhana* of Vajrakīla (referred to throughout this text as Vajrayakṣa), the *yogin* recites the *hṛdaya* of the deity ('the *mantra* of suppression and control') and the individual *mantra*s of his wrathful entourage. He then recites "the *mantra* of 2 x 18 syllables that pertain to the *mātaraḥ*"[677] and thus the oath-bound ones are summoned by hooking their hearts with their *hṛdaya*. Overpowering them with the fierce *sādhana* of HŪṀ, the *yogin* should recite the vital *bīja* of the messengers on the day of the full moon and, when they have come, he should remind them of their former vows.

Keeping them suppressed, the *yogin* should recite seven times the *mantra* of the fierce kings Yamāntaka, Hayagrīva and Amṛtakuṇḍalin, followed by the words which entrust them with their sacred duties, twice. Those deities then seize the servants by the life force of body, speech and

---

674 An account of Lang-lab rdo-rje is to be found above, Chapter Four.

675 The inner circle consists of the *maṇḍalādhipati* and his consort, the intermediate circle is that of the *daśakrodha* kings, and the outer circle is the assembly of oath-bound protectors. C32 340

676 B28, however, describes in detail a *maṇḍala* which may be drawn specifically in order to accomplish this rite. At the heart of the diagram is a six-pointed star, the points and intermediate spaces of which serve as seats for the 12 chief protectors. B28 124

677 The division of the DHADDHI *mantra* (referred to here) into groups of nine, nine and 18 has already been noted (Chapter Eight, above). We will meet with it again in this chapter, below.

mind and place them before the *yogin* like standing statues.[678] With himself clearly visualised as the god, the *yogin* should fix his gaze upon the oath-bound ones and strike them with rays of light emanating from the *mantra* revolving in his heart.[679] As the rays turn around and gather back together, those spirits let out wailing cries of misery. Tormented by suffering, they are guided to the *samaya* and, being thus affirmed in their oaths, they are given their instructions. The signs of success that arise in the awakened mind are like the experience of carnal pleasure with a woman, the appearance of ferocious carnivores, treasure, or the miracle powers of leprosy *nāga* (*mdze can klu*).[680] All defilements vanish as quickly as shadows on the sky but until then the *mantra* should each be recited hundreds of times.[681]

The nectar on the altar should be replenished with a mixture of the finest ingredients, and the offerings of nectar, blood and *bali* should be presented. The *yogin* should recite the *mantra* that invoke and incite the helpers and then enjoy the assembled offerings. The secret *mantra* themselves may either be recited separately on that occasion, piling them up like weapons as each one is recited a hundred times, or else all three may be amalgamated into a single long *mantra*. OṀ VAJRAKĪLI KĪLAYA ACITTA APARACITTA MAMA VAŚAṀ TRAG MATAṀ MYAG KARA A IMĀN ŚĪGHRAṀ STAMBHAYA NAN CHINDA CHINDA HŪṀ PHAṬ. OṀ VAJRAKĪLI KĪLAYA JAYE VIJAYE KURU KARA IMĀN JA JA VAŚAṀ JA

---

678 The text at this point offers a short alternative to the full invocation of those three deities in which it is said that, in order to incite them to act, the *yogin* should recite BANDHA JVALA CHINDA and with a crazed mind (*yid snyo ba*) he should imagine a blazing weapon upon his tongue and three times he should cast a violent curse against his enemy so that the enemy's head is burst asunder.

679 B28 describes this meditation as follows: Whenever those oath-bound goddesses become rebellious or angry and refuse to obey their orders, the *yogin* should clearly visualise himself as the glorious Vajrakīla with those twelve protectors imprisoned in front of him within a triangular box of iron. Then, from the deity's heart, countless red-black JAḤ syllables should be sent out to strike those mischievous *ḍākinī* on the syllables MA in each of their own hearts. Those MA syllables are attracted to the JAḤs like iron needles to a magnet and thus the *ḍākinī* are robbed of all self control and summoned helplessly before the *yogin*. Only after they have submitted to his authority and offered up their life essence (*srog snying*) should the *yogin* re-empower them and bind them under oath. B28 126

680 Oneiric indications listed in B28 include the appearance of a well-dressed noble lady, a black yak, black birds and carnivorous beasts.

681 A10 100

NAN ŚĪGHRAṀ STAMBHAYA NAN JVALA JVALA HŪṀ PHAṬ. OṀ VAJRAKĪLI KĪLAYA KAṬAṄKAṬE YA YETA KARA IMĀN KA KA VAŚAṀ KA NAN ŚĪGHRAṀ STAMBHAYA NAN BANDHA BANDHA HŪṀ PHAṬ. All this is to be recited seven times. Then the abbreviated version, IMĀN VIGHNĀN STAMBHAYA NAN, with which one focusses upon the body, speech and mind of all of them, followed by DHADDHI MAMA KARMA ŚĪGHRAM KAṄKA KĀRAYE OṀ LAM LAM HŪṀ LAM LAM IMĀN VIGHNĀN STAMBHAYA NAN.[682]

The text then gives a *mantra*, the purpose of which is to effectuate the stages of nourishment and healing (*gso ba*); OṀ VAJRĀMṚTAKUṆḌALI HŪṀ VAJRASAMAYAM IDAM TENA RAKṢAM KĀYA-VĀK-CITTA-VAJRA-SVABHĀVĀTMAKO 'HAṀ SAMAYA IMĀN *beat on the life force of So-and-so* BHYO. Thus the *yogin* refreshes his vows with nectar and unites himself fully with divine body, speech and mind. So doing, the oath-bound ones are deprived of their personal power and put to work as his servants.

This concise, cryptic text ends with an apologia in which it is stated that the true purpose (*artha*) of the way of secret *mantra*, clarified at length in other teachings, is here condensed into 'the triple essence of Vajrayakṣa'. Thus, his white face on the right is said to be the real Yamāntaka, who stirs up the brain blood in the skulls of the four bSe-mo goddesses. His red face on the left is the powerful Hayagrīva, who cuts to pieces the base of the tongues of the four Śvanmukhā sisters. His blue central face is Amṛtakuṇḍalin, who confounds the heart *cakra* of the black *ḍākinī*. This triple essence is a curse through which the oath-bound servants may be kept under control. Calling them hither with force, they may be incited to attack the enemy and the *yogin* should lavishly offer them the assembled foodstuffs and *bali*. Other than this there is no secret instruction that can act as an iron cloak of obedient servants.[683]

With regard to these three groups of protective goddesses, said above (Chapter Four) to have offered their services to Padmasambhava in Nepal as he meditated upon the Vajrakīla doctrines sent to him from Nālandā: B28 informs us that the white group (called the family of Rosewood) consists of those who have transcended *saṁsāra* and who move like wild animals in the evening twilight. They are the life force of speech (more usually associated with the colour red) and their correspondence in the

682 A10 101

683 A10 102

body is a white syllable MA in the centre of an eight-petalled lotus on the tongue. There they dwell supported upon a white wind (*prāṇa*), going in and out like the repeated attraction of iron to a magnet. The black goddesses (the Iron family) with hair of matted blood locks hover between the transcendent and the mundane and move like *rākṣasa* demons in the dead of night. They abide in the heart as the life force of the mind upon a black syllable MA in the centre of an eight-sided sun and they are attracted to anything black just as bees are attracted to flowers. The worldly class of red goddesses (the Conch family) are most potent just before dawn, a characteristic they hold in common with medicine. They are the life force of the body (more usually associated with the colour white) and abide in the 'conch ocean' (skull) upon a red syllable MA in the centre of an eight-spoked wheel between the eyebrows ('upon the *ūrṇā*'). They depend upon blood in the way that children depend on mother's milk.[684]

These three groups of goddesses, hitherto called Śvanmukhā and the rest, are internalised here in a manner typical of doctrines from the *mahottarakīla* cycle. Clearer descriptions of the 12 goddesses are to be found in our texts A7 (60-66), A28 (193-195), A44 (356-358), A53 (677-681 & 704-706), B36 (230-234), etc. and in a lengthy commentary by Padma 'phrin-las not found within the published collections.[685]

Śvanmukhā herself is described in these texts as being dark blue in colour with the head of a wolf (*spyang*). Her mount is a female nine-headed wolf of iron and she wields in her hands a skull-topped staff and a *kīla* of iron. Her sister Sri-ra (the meaning of which is unclear) is yellow in colour and has the head of a wild dog. She wields an iron hook and a golden *kīla* and rides upon a wild yellow bitch with eight tongues. Stretching out her tongues in the eight directions, this mount is said to bring the eight classes of local demons under control. Sṛgāla[686] is red in colour and has the head of a fox. Her weapons are a *vajra* and a *kīla* of copper, and her mount is a three-legged vixen. Kukkura (Ku-ku) is green in colour and has the head of a dog. She waves a banner made from the skin of a child and has a *kīla* of turquoise. She rides upon a turquoise-

---

684 B28 128-129

685 I have in my possession the relevant pages of a third generation photocopy of this text (lacking the title page) which I obtained from Prof. C.R. Lama in 1989 who informed me that it is known as the *bKa' 'brgyad rnam nges*.

686 Orthographic variants of this name include Śana, Sriṅga and Srila.

coloured bitch with long hair. These are the four Śvanmukhā sisters in the Rosewood family, also known as 'the goddesses of evening'.

The next group are the four Mahātmādevī (bDag-nyid-ma):[687] Rematī (Re-tī)[688] is dark blue in colour and her long black hair pervades the *traidhātuka*. She carries "the supreme *kīla* fashioned from a human leg"[689] and a *khaṭvāṅga,* wears a cloak of human skin and rides upon a three-legged mule. Remajā (Re-dza) is dark yellow, carries a golden sickle and a turquoise box, wears a rainbow cloak of peacock feathers and rides upon a doe. Remajū (Re-dzu) is dark red, carries an iron hook and a skull cup full of blood, wears a belted cloak (*re lde'i lwa ba*) and rides upon a blue water buffalo. Remajī (Re-dzi) is dark green, carries a notched stick (*khram shing*)[690] and a ball of thread (*gru gu*), wears a water-patterned cloak of black silk (*chu dar lwa ba*) and rides upon a camel with a white flash on its forehead. These are the four 'goddesses of midnight' in the family of Iron, also known as queens of the four seasons (Ṛturājñī, some-

---

687 The term *mahātma* (*bdag nyid chen po*) is employed within *atiyoga* to indicate the spontaneity and freedom of natural enlightenment.
S. Karmay, *The Great Perfection* 130. Cf. NSTB II 13, n.152

688 A goddess Revatī is described in the *Yoginī-tantra* XIII as the consort of Śiva who is forced to remain in exile in the barbarian (*mleccha*) borderlands where her children are appointed to be the guardians of local shrines to the goddess Kāmākhyā. Schoterman's comments about her seem pertinent here in the light of our findings above (Chapter Four) when he says; "The story of Revatī in the *Yoginī-tantra* can be regarded as an illustration of a common phenomenon ... the embedding of a foreign/local deity into an established religious system." J.A. Schoterman, *The Yonitantra* 7 (New Delhi, 1980)

Revatī is also the name of a constellation of stars (*nakṣatra*) said to be inauspicious. *Garuḍa-purāṇa* II.IV 176

689 According to the *bDud 'joms phur pa* cycle, this goddess carries a mirror.

690 The notched stick has been shown to be an incised wooden record of sin and thus a tally of punishment due. A. Rona Tas, "Tally-stick and Divination Dice in the Iconography of Lha-Mo", *Acta Orientalia Hungarica* VI,1-2 (1956) 163-179

In his article, Tas points to the association of the four goddesses currently under discussion (in their guise as queens of the four seasons) with midnight but he does not account for it (pp.174 & 177). The appellation 'goddesses of midnight' may therefore already have been current prior to their subjugation by Padmasambhava.

times with Rematī as their chief and fifth member of the group)[691] and occasionally as 'the Śrīdevī group'.

The final group of four consists of the Conch family Bhūmipati sisters (Sa-bdag-ma), also known as 'the bSe-mo goddesses' and 'the goddesses of morning'. Of these; Ya-byin, the daughter of the *bdud*, is dark blue in colour and she carries an iron hook and a *kīla* for striking (*gdab phur*). She wears a long-sleeved gown of blue silk and rides upon a horse of Māra (*bdud rta*) or turquoise dragon. De-byin, the daughter of the planets (*gza'*), is yellow in colour and carries a golden *kīla* (or lasso) and a porcupine. She wears a gown of black silk and rides upon a horse of the planets (*gza' rta*) or sea monster (*makara*). bSe-byin, the daughter of the *btsan*, is dark red in colour and carries an iron chain and an excellent *kīla* (*mchog phur* or *bse phur*, that is a *kīla* made from human leg bone). She wears a trailing robe of red silk and rides upon a red horse of the *btsan* demons (*btsan rta*) or noose of lightning (*glog zhags*). Phag-byin, the daughter of the *klu*, is dark green in colour and carries a bell and turquoise *kīla*. She wears a long gown of blue silk and rides a blue-green horse of the *nāga* (*klu rta*) or sea horse (*chu rta*).

For an account of the manner in which these 12 goddesses were first elected to become protectors of the Kīla doctrines (*phur pa'i bsrung ma*), see Chapter Four, above. Cf. also below, Chapter Twelve, where their Rosewood, Iron and Conch brothers are discussed.

The next text in all collections and the one specified by name in the *them byang* as a partner to the above is the *Nag po dug gi 'khor lo* (A11, B19, C10, E11), also said to have been taught by Padmasambhava to his consort Ye-shes mtsho-rgyal in the lion's cave at sPa-gro stag-tshang. In this text the oath-bound servants, having satisfactorily been brought under control, are incited to perform their violent task of attacking and slaying

---

691 For their icons see L. Chandra, *Buddhist Iconography of Tibet* 154-158. These five are again depicted in the same collection within a single icon in both 899 and 905 where Rematī has *garuḍa* wings. As an independent deity, Rematī is depicted wielding a *kīla* in icon 900 where she is called Svayambhū-devī, and as the subduer of *nāga* in 903 she is shown with a *makara*-headed Kīla as her companion.

the enemy, here specifically said to be 'the ten kinds of beings who must be killed' (*bsgral ba'i zhing bcu*).[692]

As before, it is stated that this rite may only be performed by one who has successfully mastered the Vajrakīla *sādhana* and is capable of maintaining an imperturbable attitude of divine pride. Such a *yogin* should take up his dwelling in a charnel ground with all the appropriate characteristics and there, during the period of the waning moon, this rite of 'the transference of consciousness'[693] should be performed.

692 These are; (1) Those who cause harm to the Buddhist religion, (2) bring dishonour to the *triratna,* (3) embezzle the property of the *saṅgha,* (4) slander the Mahāyāna, (5) endanger the life (body) of the guru, (6) sow discord among the *vajra* brothers and sisters, (7) prevent others from attaining *siddhi,* (8) are without love and compassion, (9) abandon the sacred *samaya* and *saṁvara* vows, and, (10) have perverted views concerning *karma* and its retribution.

693 *mDa' 'phen* ('shooting the arrow') refers to the slaying of an enemy whose consciousness is then transferred to the realm of bliss.

The *yogin* should construct the violent *maṇḍala* an arrow's length in width and anoint it with poison and blood of various kinds.[694] In its centre he should build a triangular pit (*'brub khung*), one cubit deep and one cubit long. The first of the three tiers of this 'iron house' should be daubed with black paint, the second with red paint and the third with white. A *kīla* of thorny wood (*rtsang phur*, but C has *gtsang phur,* 'a pure *kīla*') should be enclosed within a circle ("bound with a garland") of skulls, the area within which is then smeared with blood and charcoal from the funeral pyre. The *maṇḍala* should be constructed with a red half-moon in its centre, a white border around the outside and a yellow courtyard in between. Upon it should be placed an effigy of the enemy made in the form of a rag doll with cloth from the one to be attacked (*dri ma'i gos,* "cloth having the scent" of its owner) stuffed with *kuśa* grass from the charnel ground.

A piece of shroud taken from a corpse in the cemetery should be prepared as an artist's canvas by smearing it with a paste of chalk (*sa dkar*) and it should be anointed with human flesh, poison and blood. Using as ink a preparation of blood, poison and charcoal from a cremated body that has been stirred with a sharp pointed weapon, an image of the enemy should be drawn upon that canvas using a knife or an arrow as a pen. The head, tongue and heart of that image should be marked with *cakra* having the form of four concentric circles. In their centres should be written the three *bīja* of 'the life support of blackness': HAṀ as the support of the lifespan (*āyus*), ŚA as the support of the breath (*prāṇa*) and NṚ as the support of the life force (*jīvita*). On half-moon seats[695] should be drawn the Mother God (*ma lha*), the Life God (*srog lha*) and the Enemy God

694 This line is unaccountably varied in the published texts. A adds ashes to the list of substances with which it should be anointed, B says that it should be anointed skilfully, C says that it should be anointed all the way out to its edges, and E says to anoint it "by means of a hearth (*thab pas*)".

695 These half-moons could equally well be intended as seats for the three *bīja* just listed. The text is ambiguous.

(*dgra lha*).[696] Finally that image of the enemy is to be enclosed within a series of six concentric triangles, expressed in the text as six bewildering (*'khrul mig*) iron houses.[697]

With his own body clearly visualised in the form of the deity Vajrakīla, the *yogin* should meditate upon the six secret *mantra* in due order, as they are given in the *bKa' nyan lcags kyi ber ka* text above. The *mantra* on his forehead and throat are to be arranged upon nine-spoked wheels and those

---

696 Tucci (*The Religions of Tibet* 193) writes of the group of five personal gods known as the *'go ba'i lha* who are born together with the person they protect. Throughout that person's life they reside on his or her body from where they function as guardians of the vital forces of life and well-being. The *mo lha* resides in the pit of the left arm, the *srog lha* in the heart and the *dgra lha* upon the person's right shoulder. These, then, are presumably the places upon which the *yogin* should draw those gods on the image of his enemy.

All Tibetans are probably familiar with the oft told tale concerning the death of the last of the line of early 'sky descended kings' as recounted in the *rGyal rabs gsal ba'i me long*. The assassination of this king was enabled by a subterfuge that caused him to wear the highly impure article of a fox's corpse upon his right shoulder. Offended by the corpse, the *dgra lha* (whose special function it is to protect one from enemies) abandoned his position and thus the king was rendered vulnerable to attack. This, of course, is the intended purpose of its inclusion within the present ritual and I presume it to be a uniquely Tibetan contribution to the rite.

Tucci (TPS 741) says "the mythology of the *dgra lha* is very complex" and he lists the names of a group of nine *dgra lha,* both male and female, some of whom "represent atmospheric phenomena" while others "have the aspects of birds". He concludes that they are clearly a legacy of the Bon tradition with no discernible Indian ancestry. In *The Religions of Tibet* (194), Tucci explains that the *dgra lha*, having materially protected a person from his or her foes throughout that person's lifetime, then goes on to "act as counsel for the defence" before Yama at the time of death.

Nebesky-Wojkowitz (*Oracles and Demons of Tibet* 332) describes the *dgra lha* as red in colour and wielding a hatchet.

Quoting from *dNgos grub rgya mtsho'i cha lag bsang brngan 'dod dgu'i rgya mtsho,* Tucci says (TPS 720) that the *ma lha* is to be depicted wearing an ornament set with gems, and Nebesky-Wojkowitz (*op.cit.* 327) adds to this that she is youthful, beautiful and dressed in white silk with a blue silk cloak. She holds a divination arrow in her right hand and a mirror in her left. Her function is to increase and guard the family (*ibidem* 332).

The *srog lha* is described by Nebesky-Wojkowitz (*ibidem* 327) as "a man with a powerful body of a white colour and riding a black horse with white heels. He wears a helmet and a cuirass of gold." It is also said that he carries a vase containing the nectar of long life and that his function is the preservation of the life force (*ibidem* 332).

697 The term *'khrul mig* may also refer to a lattice-like structure prepared of sharpened poison sticks, but such does not appear to be the meaning here. A11 104-105

in his heart upon a wheel with 18 spokes. Around the outside of the wheels run powerful *mantras* of sorcery (*thun sngags*) with 40 syllables, 32 syllables and 31 syllables respectively.[698] Rays of light radiate out from those *mantra* and accumulate within the sharp weapons that the *yogin* has on the table before him for use in the rite. Thus those weapons are empowered.[699]

As the *yogin* recites NṚ, he transforms the rag doll into the actual presence of the enemy and meditates that the enemy's consciousness is absorbed within it. That effigy is then imprisoned within the triangular pit by sealing its opening with an eight-spoked *cakra.*[700]

A second red half-moon should be drawn, divided into six parts: On the first part is placed frankincense that separates good from evil (*dbye ba'i gu gul*), and this should be offered in the morning (*zhogs*). On the second part is placed the white mustard seed of absorption (*stim pa'i yungs dkar*). On the third part is placed a bundle of green and red strings for the deeds to be done (*bya byed sngo dmar phung*). On the fourth part are placed the poisonous substances of sorcery that lead to madness (*smyo ba'i dug rdzas thun*). On the fifth part are placed weapons consisting of the three nails that strike (*gdab pa'i phur gsum mtshon*). On the sixth part is placed the glorious *bali* which is to be hurled (*btab pa'i dpal gtor*).

Upon the platform around the outside of the imprisoned effigy, the *yogin* should arrange all the articles required for the invocation and wor-

---

698 I presume that these three sets of *mantra* are to be derived from those given later in the text but can find no satisfactory correspondence between the *mantra* given there and the numbers of syllables required here.

699 A short text found in several of the collections (A16, B57, C32, E33) explains the meditation to be performed at this time. Having become one with the deity by sealing his body with *mudrā,* the *yogin* should radiate from his heart a syllable MA which transforms into a sun marked with a blue-black HŪṀ. From this causal syllable arise the letters of the *mantra* OṀ VAJRAKĪLI KĪLAYA SARVAVIGHNĀN BAṀ HŪṀ PHAṬ and this should be recited. At the outset of the recitation, from the chief *niṣevanakīla* emerges an emanation of the deity who summons the threefold Kīla *maṇḍala* and all *sugata.* As soon as the oath-bound protectors arrive, they offer their life essence and are ordered to fulfil their task of 'liberation'. The wrathful emanation then returns to the *kīla* on the altar, causing it to glow with exceeding brightness. A16 141

700 A fierce weapon in the form of a heavy metal discus with (eight) sharp blades that the ancients used to hurl at one another during times of warfare. Clear illustrations of their use in such rites as those currently under consideration are to be found in S. Karmay, *Secret Visions,* especially plates 20(1), 22D, 36, 40, 47 & 55.

ship of the deity, as well as those required for the fulfilment of his vows.[701] Magical necessities include the *hṛdaya* of the three groups, sprinkled with *amṛta* and wrapped up inside a skull, butter, oil, fat, honey, milk, blood, black pebbles, a child of incestuous union, a child of a young girl, the skull, heart and blood of a chicken, and the flesh and blood of a dog, wolf, fox and wild dog. To the sides and in front should be placed three castles[702] adorned with arrows to which silk ribbons have been attached and victory banners made from the hides of humans, dogs, crocodiles and birds. Small morsels of food should also be placed within those castles.[703]

The gods of the *maṇḍala* should be clearly visualised and summoned until they are actually present. The *yogin* then offers them gifts of food and so on and, remaining firm in his resolve, he should focus his attention upon the sharp weapons that he will use in the destruction of his enemy. The first task to be completed is the separation of the enemy from his protector gods (the *dgra lha* and the rest). The consciousness of the enemy is dragged forth by the *yogin*'s ferocious assistants and cast down into form by causing it to be absorbed within the effigy. It is held there by binding it with the weapons of green and red thread and, as the *yogin* hurls poisonous substances of evil magic (*dug thun*) at it, the protector gods flee and the enemy is driven insane. Those four deeds are to be accomplished by means of the substances arranged on the first four parts of the red half-moon, as above.

As for the actual rite of defeating the one to be subjugated (which euphemism is glossed by an interlinear note in A as 'killing the enemy'); this the *yogin* does by adding the *mantra* of summoning and slaying to the secret *mantra* of the deity. Thus: OṀ VAJRAKĪLI KĪLAYA, *So-and-so must be dragged forth* JAḤ HŪṀ VAṀ HOḤ. MĀRAYA VAŚAṀ KURU HAPARAYA HATANAYA HŪṀ PHAṬ. AVEŚAYA AVEŚAYA HŪṀ PHAṬ. ŚĪGHRAM ĀNAYA ŚĪGHRAM ĀNAYA HŪṀ PHAṬ. JALAPAYA JALAPAYA HŪṀ PHAṬ. OṀ VAJRAKĪLI KĪLAYA ACITTA APARACITTA MAMA VAŚAṀ TRAG MATAṀ MYAG KARA IMĀN JAYE VIJAYE KURU KARA IMĀN KAṬAṄKAṬE YA YETA KARA IMĀN DHADDHI MAMA KARMA

701 The personal accoutrements of a *yogin* such as the skull drum, thigh bone trumpet, bone ornaments, *khaṭvāṅga, vajra* and bell, and so on.

702 I understand that brass pots are normally used here. (Verbal communication from Prof. C.R. Lama.)

703 A11 105-106

ŚĪGHRAM KAṄKA KĀRAYE MĀRASENAPRAMARDANĪYE[704] *the enemy called So-and-so must be dragged forth* JAḤ HŪṀ VAṀ HOḤ. MĀRAYA CITTA NAN NṚ JAḤ JAḤ TADYATHĀ TADYATHĀ HŪṀ PHAṬ.[705]

These *mantra* are explained as follows: OṀ is the reality of the five *jñāna* and VAJRA is the *mūlamantra* of oneself as the deity. KĪLI is the assembly of *krodharāja* in the ten directions and KĪLA stands for their ten wisdom consorts. YA is the supreme nail son. These eight *bīja* of the secret *mantra* of blackness (*nag mo'i gsang sngags*) draw forth the heart and suck in the heart's blood.

By MAMA VAŚAṀ the four arteries are chopped to pieces. By TRAG the great Lord of Life (*srog bdag*) is summoned, and with MATAṀ he enjoys the *samaya* offering of life force.[706] Reciting MYAG, the *yogin* presses the offering of flesh and blood to his lips. Taking up the sword with KARA, the *yogin* slays the enemy with IMĀN. By means of this 18-fold secret *mantra* of the Mahātmādevī (on the spokes of the blue wheel in the heart), cuts are made that slice up the four arteries in the heart of the enemy.[707]

By JAYE the messengers are instigated to action, and VIJAYE indicates victory over the foe. By KURU KARA he is quickly 'liberated'. By means of these nine *bīja* of fierce spell belonging to the Śvanmukhā sisters in the nine-spoked red wheel, the centre of the enemy's throat is cut to pieces.

By KAṬAṄKAṬE the bSe-mo goddesses are incited, and by YA their brothers are called to devour the life force. Reciting YETA KARA, the blood of the brain is churned to a frenzy. By means of these nine syllables

---

704 As a collective term covering all unwholesome moral states, the term *māra-sena* is enumerated in the Pāli *Suttanipāta* 436-438 as passion, aversion, hunger, thirst, craving, sloth, torpor, fear, doubt, self-will, cant and various forms of self-exaltation. T.O. Ling, *Buddhism and the Mythology of Evil* 59. The epithet *mārasenāpamaddino,* 'the crusher of Māra's host', as applied to the Buddha is frequently met with in the Pāli canon. See, for example, *Dīghanikāya* III.196

705 A11 106-107

706 The *samaya* pledge of the *yogin* is to draw out this evil life force and dedicate it to the great Dharma protector known as Lord of the Life Force. Thus all 'demonic energy' is consumed and transformed into that which is of service to the Dharma and all living beings.

707 This section as given, however, contains only 12 syllables. In the previous chapter we noted the 18 syllables upon this *cakra* to be ACITTA APARACITTA MAMA VAŚAM HŪṀ MATAṀ MYAK KARA.

of secret *mantra* on the nine spokes of the white wheel in the centre of the brain, the body of the enemy is hacked to bits.[708]

In brief: by means of the six syllables DHADDHI MAMA KARMA, the assistants are summoned to act and, with ŚĪGHRAM, they are entrusted with their duties. These *mantra* apply equally to all the deities. Then there are the five syllables for the males (*pho'i 'bru*) KAṄKA KĀRAYE, nine for the 'butchers' MĀRASENAPRAMARDANĪYE, four syllables of summoning JAḤ HŪṀ VAṀ HOḤ, the three of slaying MĀRAYA, the six syllables that drag forth the enemy's consciousness CITTA NAN NṚ JAḤ JAḤ, and the eight that grind him to dust TADYATHĀ TADYATHĀ HŪṀ PHAṬ. If all these secret *mantra* are recited with strength then the result will be attained, as surely as fat is drawn forth from a side of mutton.

Becoming proficient in this practice of the life force of the oath-bound protectors, the *yogin* may speedily press them to his service. These evil wheels of *mantra,* which have the nature of sharp weapons, throw into total confusion the *cakra* in the three places of the enemy upon whom he meditates, severing the *nāḍī* and causing the life-sustaining *prāṇa* to cease. The first group are those in the *brahmācakra* which split open the head and confound the brain. The second group belong to the *cakra* in the throat and they drive their victim insane and cause him to vomit blood. The third group are associated with the *cakra* in the centre of the heart and they sever the four arteries and separate purity from pollution. This, in brief, is their function. If one merely wishes to scatter one's enemies, this can be achieved within three days by means of the eight syllables of fierce subjugation (OṀ VAJRAKĪLI KĪLAYA).

Thus, it is said, the *yogin* gathers the protectors of the *maṇḍala* together and immediately entrusts them to their various tasks. He who turns these wheels of secret *mantra* a thousand times each, both day and night, will achieve thereby the activities of sorcery (*thun gyi las*). Urgently performing the invocations at both dusk and dawn, the *yogin* should hurl the enchanted substances[709] against the effigy and thus strike down his enemy. Calling upon the irresistible force of the oath-bound ones, the *yogin* can gather together all the haughty gods and demons and slay them. He can then appropriate their personal splendour for himself and make a feast of their flesh and blood.[710]

---

708 A11 107

709 Listed in the text as blood and poison and so on.

710 A11 108-109

Thus the ritual concludes, but the text itself continues in the same vein with a shorter alternative rite designed to achieve the same purpose.

According to this second rite, a *yogin* who wishes to perform these violent acts of sorcery should place the male ingredient of poison and the female ingredient of blood together in a skull taken either from a border tribesman (*kirāta*) or from a person who is the last member of his family line. He should then take three of Māra's arrows with poison tips and a mixture of ingredients that cause insanity, and a curse should be placed upon those articles by means of evil spells. The victim should be summoned during the hours of daylight and slain in the dark of night. At the twilight times of dawn and dusk, the *yogin* should summon the male and female active messengers who will quickly fulfil the tasks allocated to them by whoever recites this long *mantra* completely free of distraction; OṀ ... etc.

The long *mantra* which follows in the text contains a number of indecipherably corrupt passages, apparently written in a mixture of languages. The separate manuscripts present us in several instances with entirely disparate readings, with even the interspersed Tibetan phrases being so garbled that it remains impossible to determine whether or not they were ever intelligible. Some, perhaps, are Tibetanisations of earlier Sanskrit or Prakrit forms now irretrievably lost, for there is about the entire passage a definite aura of antiquity.

One notable feature of this *mantra* is the application of the epithet Gaṇeśa (lord of the *gaṇa*) to the deity Mahākāla. In Hindu mythology, Gaṇeśa is the master of obstacles (*vighna*) and may be responsible either for their cause or removal. The *gaṇa* over which he rules are especially those inferior deities or demigods considered as Śiva's attendants.[711] Śiva, furthermore, is said to be Gaṇeśa's father. In terms of Buddhist mythology, however, Mahākāla himself is considered the manifest consciousness of the arch demon Śiva (Rudra), bound under oath to act as defender of the Buddhist faith and entrusted with the specific role of lord of the troops (*gaṇa*). His function is to rule over those inferior and often mischievous deities or demigods now included among the attendants of Heruka, many

---

711 The *gaṇa* are *pramatha, bhūta, yakṣa, rākṣasa,* etc., all that are deformed or ugly and "conceived of as *vighna*". V.S. Agrawala, "The Meaning of Gaṇapati", *Journal of the Oriental Institute* XIII.1 (1963) 1-4, Baroda.

According to STTS XI (*trilokacakra mahāmaṇḍala*), outside the circle of *krodha* kings are to be found *gaṇapati* (leaders of the troops), *dūta* (messengers) and *ceṭa* (slaves).

of whom were formerly in the retinue of Śiva. Both the current text as a whole and the previous *bKa' nyan lcags kyi ber ka* are concerned with the *yogin*'s status, whilst meditating upon himself in the form of Vajrakīla, as supreme commander of those unruly troops. It is interesting to find here yet further confirmation of an Indic origin for these myths and doctrines in their most primitive form.

Towards the end of the text we meet with the pun so often encountered in this literature in which it is said that "this rite of power which entwines[712] the three classes of oath-bound messengers" should be used to arouse them to action during periods of inertia. As they are imagined to descend upon the enemy, the *yogin* should see the belly of that *rākṣasa* demon deluged beneath a welter of poison, blood and sharp weapons, his life force burned to ashes by tongues of fire. The three Kīla (the three supreme sons) that bring about this total annihilation are the body, speech and mind of wrath to whom the final verses of the text are addressed;

བྱིན་རླབས་གོ་ཁྲབ་གོ་ས་རྗེ་༔
ཐོ་བ་ཅན་གྱིས་སྤྱི་ནས་བརྡེག་༔
སྣོ་དབལ་མདའ་ནི་མཐོ་ནས་འཕངས་༔

Oh Lords! You who wear the armour of blessings,
Strike from on high with the hand that holds the hammer and
Shoot your sharp pointed arrows from above!

གཤིན་རྗེ་གཤེད་ཀྱིས་སྤྱི་བོར་གདབ་༔
ལུས་ཀྱི་གནས་སྦྱངས་ཚངས་རྩ་གཏུབས་༔

Yamāntaka, hurl yourself against the enemy's crown!
Purify the place of the body and hack at the vein of Brahmā!

རྟ་མགྲིན་དབང་ནི་མགྲིན་པར་བཏབ་༔
ངག་གི་གནས་སྦྱངས་ཁྲག་རྩ་གཏུབས་༔

712 The word used here is *'dril ba*, 'to entwine, envelop, roll up' and this rite which 'entwines' the three classes of unruly messengers is brought about by 'rolling' (*'dril ba*) the three *kīla* between the palms of the hands.

Hayagrīva, attack the throat!
Purify the place of speech and sever the arteries of blood!

བདུད་རྩི་འཁྱིལ་པ་སྙིང་ཀར་བཏབ༔
སེམས་ཀྱི་གནས་སྦྱངས་སྲོག་རྩ་གཅོད༔

Amṛtakuṇḍalin, descend upon the heart!
Purify the place of the mind and slice through the vein of life!

ཚེ་སྲོག་བཀུག་མདངས་རང་ལ་བསྡུ༔
དྭངས་མ་ཆོས་ཉིད་བདེ་བར་བསྒྲོད༔
སྙིགས་མ་ཤ་ཁྲག་དྲེགས་པ་རོལ༔

Gathering the life span, energy and glory to oneself,
The vital essence should be transferred to bliss
in the *dharmatā* and
The impure dregs of flesh and blood may be enjoyed
by the haughty ones as a feast![713]

Thus *yogin* appropriates for himself the remaining lifespan, vital force, charisma and power of the conquered enemy[714] but his 'essence'[715] should be released into the bliss of the *dharmadhātu*. The impure sediments of flesh and blood are to be enjoyed by the unruly troops of assistants who hacked it to bits with their terrifying swords and then the text says that a glorious *bali* should be presented to the assembly of *krodha* kings.

This wheel of ferocious sharp weapons, belonging to the three groups of red and black oath-bound protectors, terrifies even the king of the gods. So what needs to be said about its effect on others? (A note in ms A obligingly informs us that by "others" is meant the enemies and

---

713 A11 109-111

714 Although the lower *yāna* teach the karmic result of killing to be a short and miserable lifespan, the Vajrayāna presents this as a skilful means through which the *yogin*'s life force may be enhanced. Cannibals and head-hunters in primitive societies all over the world also hope to appropriate just such intangible qualities of heroic prowess from their victims.

715 *Dvangs ma, rasa,* 'juice', in this context refers to consciousness (*rnam shes, vijñāna*).

obstructors.)[716] Only B tells us that this text was taken from the golden southern section of the Byang-gter treasure cache at Zang-zang lha-brag.

Although those two are the sole texts specifically named in the *them byang,* intended as a guide exclusively to the literature of the *mahottara-kīla* cycle, several other documents present similar instructions for the incitement of the fierce protectors. It seems pertinent, then, to deal briefly with those texts of the black deity cycle from the iron cache in the north which are also to be found in common within several of the collections.

The short *Drag po'i bzlas pa* (A16, B57, C32, E33) deals with only two topics: the contemplation appropriate to the radiating and gathering of light, and the appropriate contemplation for the moment of slaying. The first of these topics has been dealt with above in note 699. With regard to the act of slaying, the text states that while the fierce *mantra* is being recited the *yogin* should visualise an imaginary *kīla* flying out from the material *kīla* in his hand and attacking the enemy in his own place. Thus, while the material *kīla* is being stabbed into the head of the effigy, the imaginary *kīla* enters the victim's crown and travels down through his body until it reaches the soles of his feet. When it is finally withdrawn from the top of his head, the enemy's body is dead. It then lands on the tongue and enters the throat. Having buried itself in the windpipe, when it re-emerges from the tongue the speech is dead. Finally it sinks into the heart until it revolves within the 'cavity of life' (*srog khong*). As it re-emerges from the heart, all the subtle traces (*vāsanā*) are known to be destroyed. Thus, as the material *kīla* is stabbed into the head of the effigy and along the entire length of its body, the victim is surely killed. "This meditation should roll forth like an unimpeded wave rolling on a vast ocean."[717]

In the *Las thams cad kyi don bsdus pa* (A20, B60, C23, E36), the *yogin* finds further guidance for the preparation of a ritual effigy. The existence of an effigy is apparently taken for granted in redactions A, B & E, for only C23 begins with the instruction to "create or draw an effigy of the enemies and obstructors and place it upon a *cakra.*" Details said to be derived from the *Vidyottama-tantra* are then given concerning the *mantra* of wrath to be inscribed upon the effigy. Thus; OṀ VAJRAKĪLI KĪLAYA

716 A11 111

717 A16 141-142

snying khrag shad JAḤ ACITTA APARACITTA are the 19 syllables of the *mātaraḥ* and butchers which should be inscribed upon the head of the effigy and recited. MA RAKMO YAKMO KĀLARŪPA *snying rtsa la* YAṀ YAṀ THIB THIB are the 16 syllables which should be inscribed upon the right hand of the effigy and recited. CITTA *srog la* THUNG THUNG *srog la* YAṀ YAṀ JAYE VIJAYE *myags myags sod sod* CAKRASENA *btubs* are the 24 syllables of the male and female haughty ones which should be inscribed upon the left hand of the effigy and recited. *sNying phril phril srog la* CHUṀ CHUṀ KAṬAṄKAṬE *snying rtsa la* YAṀ YAṀ *snying kha rak dun* TRI are the 21 ferocious syllables of the Śvanmukhā sisters which should be inscribed upon the right leg of the effigy and recited. MAMA VAŚAṀ KURU DHADDHI MAMA KARMA IMĀN ŚĪGHRAM TAṀ NYA KĀRAYE MĀRASENAPRAMARDANĪYE HŪṀ PHAṬ are the 33 syllables of the male and female confusion-mongers which should be inscribed upon the left leg of the effigy and recited. If the *yogin* then strikes with the iron *kīla,* the *mantra* and the magic articles (*thun rdzas*), it is said that the enemies and obstructors will die at that moment.[718]

Within the short *Man ngag rtsa thung* (A37, B56, E42), Padmasambhava explains that when the three groups of goddesses came to him during his period of meditation and offered these *mantra* of their life essence, they promised that their fierce spells would act for the benefit of *yogins,* "like butchers of the life force or a burning fire against all trouble-makers." Consequently, it is said, any *yogin* who wishes to practise the rites of Vajrakīla without knowledge of these *mantra* is like a dog chasing a bird in the sky (with no chance of catching it). OṀ is to be understood as Vajrakīla and VAJRA, his consort Tṛptacakra. KĪLI is the *daśakrodharāja* and KĪLA their ten fierce wives. YA indicates the supreme son. SARVA means 'all together' and VIGHNĀN are the oppressive enemies and obstructors. BAṀ means that they should be bound with iron fetters. HŪṀ is the heart essence of the deity and by PHAṬ the emanations are sent forth. JAḤ calls in the *siddhi* and HŪṀ means that they are gathered to oneself. ĀḤ establishes those *siddhi* firmly in the mind-stream of the *yogin.* MA RAKMO refers to the Mahātmādevī, YAKMO to the Bhūmipati sisters and KĀLARŪPA indicates the Śvanmukhā. *sNying rtsa la* YAṀ YAṀ stands for the four brothers of Rosewood, and *srog la* YAṀ YAṀ to the long-armed butchers. *sNying la khril khril* stands for the male and

718 A20 163

female killers. *Srog la* CHUṀ CHUṀ indicates the life force of the enemy, while CITTA *srog la* THUNG THUNG is the Lord of Life (Srog-bdag) himself. *sNying khrag shad* indicates the Master of Activity (Las-mkhan) and *thum ri li li* stands for the form of the enemy. *sNying rtsegs rtsegs ur ur* is sound and light, while by *shig shig gul gul* are indicated the 'devourers'. *Myags myags sod sod* DHADDHI MAMA is the black host (of Mahātmādevī) and KARMA ŚĪGHRAM KĀRAYE stands for the bSe-mo goddesses. MĀRASENA are the *rgyal po* and *btsan mo* demons, and by PRAMARDANĪYE PHAṬ is meant Śvanmukhā and her sisters.[719] With this in mind, the *yogin* should bless the iron *kīla,* transform his body into the *maṇḍala* of gods, place the effigy of the enemies and obstructors within the *cakra* and slay it.[720]

The final text of this category to be found within several collections is again reputed to be based upon the experience of its author Padmasambhava as he "bound the eight classes of gods and demons under oath" to act as protectors of the Buddhist doctrines. Called the *sDe brgyad bsrung bzlog* (A30, B58, C29, E40), this text explains the manner in which the fierce *mantra* are employed in the production of a paper amulet that, as well as being (a) the means of commanding the unruly hosts of oath-bound protectors, may also be used (b) in rites of consecration (*pratiṣṭhā*).

(a) The first function is discussed under the three familiar rubrics: (i) outer, (ii) inner and (iii) secret (*phyi nang gsang gsum*). 'Outer' refers to an amulet to be worn upon the body, 'inner' refers to offerings to be presented to the protectors and the 'secret' aspect is the inner meditation associated with recitation of the *mantra*.

(i) For the purpose of outer protection, the *yogin* should draw the magic *cakra* on a piece of Chinese paper (*rgya shog*) or human skin, using as ink either burnt horn, filth scraped from the skin or fingernails (*rta bon*) or sulphur. A drawing (*dpe chung*) of the enemy should be prepared with poison and blood and within the belly of Vajrakumāra should be written the *mantra* of ferocious averting. All of these articles should then be

---

719 Final two attributions reversed in text.

720 A37 280-282

smeared with frankincense, solidified cattle-bile, elephant musk,[721] sandalwood, *Acorus calamus* [722] and realgar.[723]

(ii) The section dealing with the 'inner protection' consists simply of an obscure list of requisite magical substances, including *Costus speciosus* (*ru rta*), *ya dha* (?), magnolia (? *ka li* for *ka li ka*), umbilical cord (? *lte bur*), areca nuts (? *kra ri*), clay (? *lder po*), water (*chu*), fat (*tshil*) and asafoetida (*rtsi bo*), etc. "All of these should be collected together on the *cakra* and fumigated with black *guggul* incense." It must be supposed that such substances are considered to delight the eight classes of spirits and that their presence within the rite therefore increases the magical potency of the amulet itself.

(iii) Secret protection is afforded by the *mantra* met with above, which the *yogin* should inscribe upon the *cakra* and then set it down in front of a standing nail honoured as the *niṣevanakīla*. He should then imagine a *vajra* arising from the syllable HŪṀ which is his own mind and this, in turn, transforms into the deity Vajrakumāra. Keeping the visualisation clear, the *yogin* should recite the deity's *mantra* and the long razor spell (*spu gri'i sngags ring,* the DHADDHI *mantra*), all the while imagining rays of light to radiate out from the *kīla*. Whirling around like a mass of sharp weapons, those light rays strike the *cakra* and, as they are absorbed into it, the *cakra* begins to emit ferocious sparks "like sharp weapons" which circle around in a clockwise direction and hack the enemies and obstructors to pieces. This done, those sparks become *vajra* which whirl around in an anticlockwise direction and create a great blazing wall of fire. The *yogin* then imagines himself standing in the centre of that mass of flames in the form of a golden nine-pronged *vajra,* grinding all trouble-makers to a pulp. When his meditation has reached the stage of heat, the *yogin* should assume the divine pride of the deity beyond imagination (*mi dmigs*).[724]

(b) When the *cakra* is to be used within a rite of consecration, upon its reverse side should be inscribed the three syllables (OṀ ĀḤ HŪṀ) and the

---

721 All manuscripts read *glang rtsi* at this point. But see below where all read *gla rtsi*.

722 An aromatic root described as being bitter in taste and "useful in the treatment of insanity, epilepsy and afflictions by *rākṣasa*."
Vaidya Bhagavan Dash, *Materia Medica of Indo-Tibetan Medicine* 38

723 Said to cure poisoning, affliction by evil spirits and skin diseases.
Vaidya Bhagavan Dash, *op.cit.* 407

724 A30 206-208

'formula of dependent origination'.[725] These should each be recited aloud 121 times and the *mantra* (on the obverse) of the *cakra* should each be read out 21 times. Flowers should be scattered and a prayer of benediction offered. The *yogin* then invites the *jñānasattva* by means of his *samādhi* and offers them praise and gifts. If the article to be consecrated is solid he should imagine that, with the twirl of a silk tassel, rays of light are transferred from the *cakra* to the material or object. Otherwise the *cakra* itself may be enclosed within an iron amulet or concealed within the chest cavity[726] of a statue, etc.

Finally the text states that, in order to maintain the continuity of protection, whatever path of action the *yogin* follows (such as the prescribed path of *mantra* recitation and *samādhi* four times per day) he should at all times continuously maintain the divine pride of himself as the deity. If he does this without a break, all the unruly *'dre* and *srin* will be subdued. "Even an army of gods will certainly be repelled. This *upadeśa* on the protective method of keeping the arrogant ones at bay is a piece of paper that acts as a castle for the life force of *yogins*. Vows. Triple seal."[727]

Appended to the end of the text is a brief commentary supposedly taught by Padmasambhava concerning the outer, inner and secret three *cakra*. From what has been written above, however, it seems that a hiatus in the text may have resulted in a conflation of the outer and the inner here, for items listed in the two groups, above, are combined within a single list and the text itself jumps directly from the outer to the secret.

Describing the material *cakra,* this commentary says that the letters of the 'secret name' (*gsang ba'i ming*) should be clearly inscribed in substances that are known to possess a special occult affinity with the eight classes of demons. For the *btsan* demons one should use burnt horn (*rva gshob*), and filth (*rta bon*) for the *rgyal po*. For the *'chi bdag* one uses sulphur (*mu zi*), and musk (*gla rtsi*) for the *gza'*. *Acorus calamus* (*shu dag*) is

---

725 YE DHARMĀ ... etc. This well-known verse summary of the Buddha's doctrines formulated by the sage Aśvajit is said to have been spoken to Śāriputra and Maudgalyāyana, resulting in their conversion to Buddhism. First recorded in the Pāli *Vinaya* i.40.28-29, it was repeated in the *Mahāvastu* and is even included in the closing passages of the *Kālacakra-tantra*.

726 *mChan khung* usually means 'armpit' but in this context I take it to mean the hollow chest of a statue or image being consecrated.

727 A30 208

suitable for the *klu,* and wolf dung (*sphyang brun*) for the *ma mo*. For the *gnod sbyin* one uses frog flesh (*sbal sha*), and for the *bdud,* wood (*shing*).

As for the secret *mantra* protection, this is achieved by means of the spell that is taught in the texts for the worship of the deity; OṀ VAJRAKĪLI KĪLAYA SARVAVIGHNĀN BAṀ HŪṀ PHAṬ JAḤ HŪṀ ĀḤ MA YAKMO RAKMO KĀLARŪPA *dregs pa'i snying rtsa la* YAṀ YAṀ *snying la* KHRIL KHRIL *srog la* CHUṀ CHUṀ CITTA *srog la btung btung snying khrag srog la shad shad* JA *thum ri li li sde brgyad kyi snying tsegs tsegs ur ur shig shig gul gul myags myags sod sod* DHADDHI MAMA KARMA ŚĪGHRAM KĀRAYE MĀRASENAPRAMARDANĪYE *gnod byed che ge mo* MĀRAYA HŪṀ PHAṬ VAJRAKĪLI KĪLAYA VAJRAYAMARĀJA MĀRA-VAJRA YA TRI KOT NĀGA RAKMO YAKṢAGRĪVĀYA MAHĀ RAṀ YAṀ KHAṀ KṢATAŚATRŪN MĀRAYA MĀRAYA *sod bzlog* BHYO. Reciting this secret *mantra* four times per day with the god held clearly in mind, the *yogin* should strike the effigy of whatever trouble-makers there are with the purified iron *kīla,* the invocation of the god and the *mantra*. In times of great trouble, this powerful method provides more effective protection than the rites of *sīmābandha,* hurling the magic weapon (*zor*) or imprisoning within the triangular iron box. By this recitation alone, all arrogant ones are kept under control.

"These are the words of the guru, taken out as treasure from the iron cache in the north."[728]

[728] A30 208-210

CHAPTER TEN
A display of wrathful power

Chapter Three of the root BRT makes it clear that the function of the Vajrakīla *maṇḍala* is "to pulverise all the enemies and obstructors in the ten directions" and, accordingly, the Byang-gter texts in our collections include a large number of violent rituals calculated to bring this about. The *them byang* explains that 'the heart of the fierce rites' consists of three primary aspects: scattering (*zor*),[729] burning (*sreg*) and trampling down (*mnan*) – activities mentioned in the eighth chapter of the root *tantra* and elaborated in virtually every ritual text thereafter. In particular, the essential features of these three activities are clarified in the tripartite text *mNan bsreg 'phang gsum* (A13, B20, C11, E12)[730] as follows:

Scattering

Prior to commencing the rite of scattering,[731] the *yogin* should fill either 'a skull with evil signs' (*thod pa mtshan ngan*)[732] or the horn of a yak that twists to the right (*gYag ru gYas pa'i skyogs*) with various kinds of poison and blood. The text also says that poison and blood should be mixed with the seeds of white mustard to be thrown (*yungs kar thun brabs*) and then a 'golden libation' (*gser skyems*) should be offered to the local gods and demons. Detailed instructions for this libation are to be found in the dance manual (*'Cham yig*) by the present sTag-lung-tse sprul-sku who explains that, as the liturgy of invitation and praise to the various deities and demi-

---

729 This activity is variously known in the texts as *zor* ('magic weapon'), *'phang* or *gtor* (both of which mean 'scatter' or 'cast'). The noun *gtor ma* indicates that which is scattered, which, in the context of these rites, refers to the *zor* which is hurled against the enemy. The result of such rites is called *bzlog pa* (sometimes *log pa)* 'turning away', 'reversing' or 'averting' evil influences.

730 This text was taken from the golden southern section of the treasure casket and thus belongs to the *mahottarakīla* cycle. Incorporated into that three-part text is A39 (A40).

731 The *maṇḍala* for this rite of scattering is described in the *Khro bo rol pa'i gtor bzlog* as a yellow *cakra* with ten spokes, drawn within a black border and surrounded by a *vajra* fence and fire wall, etc. A43 306

732 The skull of a murder victim is considered to have the greatest occult power. The skull of one whose life was cut short by disease or violent accident is said to possess medium power but that of a person who passed away peacefully in old age is ritually powerless. Oral communication from C.R. Lama.

gods is recited, dancers wearing the garb of 'black hat sorcerers' whirl around in a circle so that goblets held in their hands are caused to scatter their contents of alcohol and grain ('gold') over a wide area. These libations being enjoyed by the invisible inhabitants of every direction, the *yogin*s appeal to the deities for their help in the subsequent main section of the rite.

Proceeding with the magic weapon to an unobstructed site on elevated ground (which is an occasion of much splendour and pomp when the ritual is performed by an entire monastic assembly), the participants should clearly visualise the form of Vajrakīla, holding in his hand a freshly severed head "streaming with blood and beautiful with long hair". The role of the deity is assumed in the rite by an appointed expert (*zor mkhan* or *'phen mkhan*) who should be fully adorned in the attire of the deity. As the liturgy of invocation and the root *mantra* of the deity are recited "in a melodious voice of wrath", the weapon (the severed head)[733] is hurled in the direction of the enemy. Being flung like a stone from a sling (*'ur rdo brgyab bzhin*), it whizzes through the air against the array of inimical forces.

The oath-bound protectors are summoned with the chant, "BHYO Don't be idle, don't delay, you who are bound under oath!" (*ma gYel ma gYel dam can rnams*) and they are urged to arrest and bring before the court all malicious wrong doers. The Triple Gem are exhorted to be present as judge and jury, final arbiters in the trial that distinguishes gods from demons. Thus the good elements are carefully separated from the bad (*legs nyes srid pa'i lha 'dre brtsis*) and the three groups of red and black protectors are incited to rain down pestilence and disease upon the households of the enemy and avert their power.[734]

Much of the imagery employed in this text is similar to that of the *Nag po dug gi 'khor lo* above but, whereas the former document concerned itself primarily with the inner aspects of the rite, the present readily lends itself to dramatic interpretation. Indeed, within Buddhist communities this imagery is regularly put to spectacular effect for the edification of the lay faithful, the rite being annually performed as a masked dance in which the participants present a gorgeous pageant of lavishly attired divine beings. The *'Cham yig* cited above quotes the liturgy for every section of

---

733 The *Khro bo rol pa'i gtor bzlog* names the weapons as *gtor ma,* arrow *zor,* blood *zor* and mustard *zor*. A43 307

734 A13 117-118

the rite as it is given in the *Khro bo rol pa'i gtor bzlog* (A43), a text far more elaborate that the one being dealt with here. That liturgy is then broken down into its component parts and for every syllable there are instructions for both dancers and musicians. In accordance with these stage directions, the entire rite[735] may be performed by a large company of players (normally the assembly of monks in any given monastery) who thus dramatically bring these difficult symbolic teachings to life as they annually reenact the enduring religious motif of the triumph of good over evil.

Burning

Instructions for the *homa* rite are found in several of the texts in the three collections. Each of the original *gter ma* texts (A12, A39, B21, E29) outlines in brief the wrathful (*raudra*) rite and it is only in the long and detailed liturgy by Padma 'phrin-las (A46) that instructions are given for the three 'gentle' (*mañju*) attainments.

Padma 'phrin-las begins by considering the nature of the site: An area in which the sky has the aspect of an eight-spoked wheel and the earth the form of an eight-petalled lotus is said to be suitable for the rite of pacification. Where there is found a mountain like a heap of jewels is good for increase. A delightful garden in which there stands "a wish-fulfilling tree" is an auspicious place for the rite of overpowering. The wrathful rite should be performed in a charnel ground, by a solitary tree, at a crossroads, a place frequented by wild animals, where the sky is like a knife and the earth triangular, a place with thorny trees to one side, etc.[736] This text also provides verses for the invocation of the Earth goddess, presentation of payment for the use of the site, its ritual purification, and so on.[737]

In performing the fierce rite of burnt offerings, all sources state that a pile of wood with thorns should be arranged within a triangular hearth and kindled with fire taken from the house of a widow. The specifics of the hearth, however, are variously described in the several texts. Neither A12 nor A13 (A39) give any details but B21 and the long commentary by Padma 'phrin-las are quite explicit.

---

735 Dalai Lama V prepared an elaborate choreography for the entire Vajrakīla *sādhana*. See René de Nebesky-Wojkowitz, *Tibetan Religious Dances*

736 A46 418

737 A46 420-421

B21 deals with a *homa* ritual dedicated to 'the solitary hero' (*ekalavīra*) Vajrakīla (a term meaning 'without consort'),[738] said to have been taken from the black northern treasure of iron. This very clear text discusses the rite under three rubrics: 1) the fireplace and fuel, 2) the collection of articles for burning, 3) the generation of deities.

1) With regard to the fireplace and fuel: The hearth should be triangular in shape with each side measuring one cubit in length, standing one handspan in height. It should be painted black with charcoal from a funeral pyre and in its centre should be placed an effigy of whichever enemies and obstructors one wishes to kill. It is constructed with three borders, each four inches wide, which rise up like steps. On the first step one should draw *vajras*, on the middle step should be depicted a multitude of weapons and on the top step one should sketch a mountain of fire. Then a pile of thorny firewood should be built up in a triangle, the shape of which is maintained by binding it with the hair of a widow.

2) Next, as well as general offerings for the enjoyment of the assembly (*gaṇacakra*), the following articles for burning are required: Various kinds of flesh and blood, poisonous oil, an article belonging to the enemy that has been smeared with blood,[739] an effigy chopped up into pieces, a pair of sacrificial ladles and specially prepared lengths of firewood (*yam shing*). All of these must be gathered together.

3) With regard to the generation of deities, this has two sections: The generation of the *yogin* himself as a deity and the generation of the gods in front. Having generated himself as the solitary hero, the *yogin* brings the articles to be burned near to the hearth and blesses them all as the flesh and blood of the enemies and obstructors. Purifying the fireplace with nectar,[740] he blesses it as the triangular symbol of *tathatā*.[741]

---

738 All other sources describe the *yuganaddha* deity.

739 In the absence of any actual article belonging to the enemy, a slip of wood upon which his name has been inscribed (*ming byang*) may be burned.

740 Padma 'phrin-las points out that the nectar used here should swirl in an anti-clockwise direction, while clockwise-swirling nectar is appropriate to the three gentle rites. A46 431

741 At A12 113 the hearth is described as the *dharmodaya* arisen from the syllable E. This use of a triangular fire altar for the annihilation of rivals apparently stems back to a Vedic tradition which adds that, when the end is desired for both the present and the future, the shape of the altar should be that of a six-pointed star composed of two interlocking triangles. See N.K. Majumder, "Sacrificial Altars: Vedīs and Agnis", *Journal of the Indian Society of Oriental Art* VII (1939) 39-60

He then generates the deities in front and these are threefold: Agni,[742] Vajrakīla, and the retinue. For the generation of the fire god, the *yogin* imagines a brown billy goat arising as the transformation of the brown seed syllable TRI within the fireplace. He imagines the sun as a cushion placed upon that goat and a blue syllable RAṀ upon that cushion. Then, as he mutters AGNIDEVARṢI RAṀ HŪṀ, the fire god arises with a blue body having one face and two hands. He has three eyes. In his right hand he holds a *triśūla* and with his left he counts the beads of a rosary. He is seated upon his mount, the brown billy goat, and is adorned with the bone ornaments of Karmaheruka. His body, speech and mind should be consecrated with the three syllables (OṀ ĀḤ HŪṀ) and thus the *samayasattva* Agni is produced.[743]

The *jñānasattva* is then aroused with the prayer; "HŪṀ Oh mighty sage, god of fire. In former times you consumed the offerings burned for the gods. Now we invite you here and present you with gifts and, as a result of our faith and commitment, you must come here. Oh, great element, come! You must come through the power of our bond. AGNAYE SAMAYA JAḤ." And the text instructs the practitioners to snap their fingers while reciting this. Agni is then invited with the words; "HŪṀ Through faith and commitment, you must come here. Oh, great element, come! King of the fire gods, supreme among sages, we pray that you will come here to this place in order to accept the food offered with the sacrificial ladles and, having come to this very place, we pray that you will happily stay firm. AGNIDEVARṢI JAḤ A." And the text instructs the practitioners to beckon with the thumb while reciting this. Now the practitioners should imagine the inner offering of human flesh to be clearly visible before them and, muttering JAḤ HŪṀ VAṀ HOḤ, they should merge the *jñānasattva* and the *samayasattva* into non-duality.

Following that, respectful salutations are offered to the deity; "HŪṀ The long hair of your head is wound up in a bun, your teeth are showing like a great white rose and the light of fire is in your eyes. We pay homage to you, great sage. AGNIDEVARṢI ATIPŪHO."

Then the offerings are poured onto the fire. First the oil and then, one by one, the other articles are burned. "HŪṀ Oh, mighty sage, this ambrosial food arising through the power of *samādhi* is like nothing ever

---

742 According to A13 it is not necessary to generate the god of fire separately within the fireplace. A13 118

743 B21 46-47

offered before. Being purified, it is prepared as an offering of sanctity and therefore, moving your mind by wisdom and compassion, we beg you to accept it. AGNIDEVA HAVYA KAVYA STAVYA KHĀHI KHĀHI *So-and-so must be killed* HŪṀ PHAṬ!"

Next, singing his praises; "HŪṀ Son of Brahmā, lord of the world. King of the fire gods, supreme among sages, incarnate through the power of compassion for the sake of protecting all beings. Greatest of the *ṛṣi* who have mastered the spells and formulae. Burner of defilements,[744] wisdom light[745] that blazes like the mass of fire at the end of an aeon. Mounted on a goat that is the emanation of skilful means, you bear a vessel containing the essence of nectar and with the nectar of Dharma you soothe (all troubles) completely. Holding a rosary as you count the recitations of *mantra,* you are the compassionate one made lovely by tranquillity. You abide in the world and yet you have transcended misery. Salutations, offerings and praise be to you."

Then Agni is requested to fulfil his function in the rite; "Ho! Agni, great sage. Please remain here as one with the blazing fire and convey to the mouths of the wisdom gods all the foodstuffs offered in this burnt sacrifice."[746]

Following which, the assembly of deities should be generated either in his stomach or heart. Muttering BHRŪṀ CAKRAMAṆḌALA, the *yogin* imagines a dark blue triangular *maṇḍala* with four doors. In its centre is a sun, moon and eight-petalled lotus upon which is the syllable HŪṀ from which the lord Vajrakīla arises as his *mantra* is recited. The *yogin* then generates the remaining deities of the retinue, including the four supreme sons above the four doors and the twelve oath-bound protectors around the periphery. The liturgy for this is to be taken from the *sādhana* discussed above in Chapter Seven and the deities are to be consecrated with the power of body, speech and mind.

---

744 Since ancient times in pre-Buddhist India, Agni has been "generally regarded and worshipped as the mighty protector against demons, goblins, sorcerers, hostile magic and any other evil influences".
J. Gonda, *Rice and Barley Offerings in the Veda* 195-196

745 Citing the *Taittirīya-brāhmaṇa,* Gonda says that the light of fire counteracts evil; "Agni, the brightly flaming ... light, purifying drives away the demons".
J. Gonda, *op.cit.* 196

746 B21 47-49

The wisdom deities are then called forth with the well-known verse; "HŪṀ In order that empowerments, *siddhi* and the successful accomplishment of the *bhavakīla* may be attained, you deities of wisdom wrath must please come here ... etc." ending SAMAYA HO JAḤ HŪṀ VAṀ HOḤ, by means of which they are inseparably united.

Muttering OṀ VAJRAKĪLI KĪLAYA and the rest and adding ATIPŪHO they are saluted and then the outer and inner offerings are presented by means of *mantra*. Pieces of the effigy are offered and then the practitioner offers in succession all the remaining articles to be burned. Finally he presents the *ming byang* with *mantra* after stabbing it with the *kīla*. Casting it into the fire, the *yogin* recites;

> HŪṀ From within the depths of blazing fire like that at
> the end of an aeon,
> Upon piled-up cushions of haughty great gods,
> Overawing the enemies and obstructors with the heroic mode
> of his stance
> Is the lord Mahāśrīvajrakumāra, with three faces,
> Six arms and adorned with apparel from the charnel ground.
> From his heart blazes forth a mass of wisdom fire like that at
> the end of time.
>
> Into this swirling pit of fire, within the vastness of wisdom,
> Are offered the sacred articles of slaying the enemies
> and obstructors.
> Accept them!
> Burn the trouble-makers!
> The demons must blaze!
> Kill the vow-breakers!
>
> Enemies and obstructors MĀRAYA!
> OṀ VAJRAKĪLI KĪLAYA KHĀHI KHĀHI!
> *So-and-so* MĀRAYA HŪṀ PHAṬ!
>
> HŪṀ Within the four doors of the divine *maṇḍala* palace
> Are the four wrathful emanations from the heart,
> The four door-keepers that perform the violent activities.
>
> Into this swirling pit of fire ... etc.

Enemies and obstructors MĀRAYA!
VAJRAKĪLI KĪLAYA JAḤ HŪṀ VAṀ HOḤ KHĀHI KHĀHI!
So-and-so MĀRAYA HŪṀ PHAṬ!

The three classes of vow keepers
emanated from your body, speech and mind
And the many further emanations
Must kill the enemies and obstructors without remainder!

Into this swirling pit of fire ... etc.

Enemies and obstructors MĀRAYA!
OṀ VAJRAKĪLI KĪLAYA REMATĪ REMAJĀ REMAJŪ REMAJĪ
(and so on..)
ŚVANMUKHĀ SRIRA SṚGĀLA KUKKURA
(and so on..)
KUMADARI ŚULA CAMUDARI KAṄKADARI[747]
So-and-so MĀRAYA HŪṀ PHAṬ!"

With these words he burns the *ming byang.*[748]

When all the articles have been offered, five pieces of thorny wood should be cast into the fire with the curse "May *So-and-so* be reduced to dust!" Then offerings should be made to the lower classes of servants and they also should be given their orders. When the ritual is over, all participants should circumambulate the Kīla *maṇḍala* in the hearth[749] and perform the

747 By position in the text it is apparent that the names given here are intended to refer to the Bhūmipati sisters but such appellations are unattested elsewhere.

748 B21 49-51

749 This ritual circumambulation is to be performed in an anticlockwise direction in the case of the fierce rite. A46 434. Other minor points mentioned by Padma 'phrin-las as appropriate to the fierce rite are that it should be performed during the dark of night (419), in the winter (419), using a rosary of bone or *rudrākṣa* seeds (429), with the left leg extended (429), with the little finger outstretched (439), and so on. Other times, seasons, rosaries, body postures and the rest are indicated for the three gentle rites and it is explained that whatever omens are considered inauspicious for those three rites are deemed excellent in the case of the fierce rite. A46 440

dance of pacification whilst muttering the *mantra* of SUMBHA and NISUMBHA.[750]

This "*homa* ritual of the solitary hero" is said to have been composed on the basis of the *Vidyottama-tantra* by Padmasambhava in the Upper Yak's Horn Cave (gYag-ru-gong) for the protection of the teachings and assembly of Nālandā monastery.[751]

Pressing down

One who wishes to press down the enemies and obstructors in order to arrive at the end of the fierce activities should mix the ashes of the wrathful *homa* rite with black clay and fashion from it an effigy in the likeness of the enemy and a model of a camel.[752] He should then insert the heart (the name on paper, together with a curse) of the enemy into the effigy[753] and securely bind it with lengths of green and red string. Loading the effigy upon the camel's back, he should place it within a skull of evil portent and, separating the enemy from his protector gods, he should summon his consciousness to be bound within the effigy's form. Imagining the camel to be real, the *yogin* places it to the north bearing the burden of the enemy upon its back.[754]

He should then take a *bali* offering for the local *nāga* and *bhūmipati* and so on and go either to a great charnel ground or to a place where gods and demons reside (*lha 'dre gnas pa'i sa,* usually crossroads). At that

---

750 See above, Chapter Two, note 266.

751 B21 51-52. For further details of this and other Vajrakīla *homa* rituals, see *A Blaze of Fire in the Dark* (forthcoming in this ongoing series of *Vajrakīla Texts of the Northern Treasures Tradition*).

752 The consciousness after death is carried upon the back of a very subtle life-bearing wind which, in this ritual, is replaced by a camel. See Jeffrey Hopkins & Lati Rinbochay, *Death, Intermediate State and Rebirth* 49. In Chapter Two of the *Mahāvajrabhairava-tantra* we read; "Then, if the *mantrin* wants to drive someone away, he should make a camel out of earth from the seven places and should then imagine on its back a wind *maṇḍala* in the shape of a half-moon transformed from the syllable YAṀ. Above it he imagines the victim and on his back he imagines the form of Yama holding a staff in his hand. He thinks that the victim is beaten with that staff and is lead off facing south." B. Siklós, *The Vajrabhairava Tantra* 100

753 C reads *snying kha gtsugs* ("tear out the heart") here for *snying khar bcug*.

754 Although the north is the quarter generally associated with Vajrakīla's fierce rites of destruction, the way to Yama's abode lies to the south and this is the direction we should expect here.

place he should dig a triangular pit in the ground, one cubit deep, and bury that skull and its contents within it. Making the gesture of the sword (*khaḍgamudrā*) and muttering VAJRATĪKṢṆA-KHAḌGA HŪṂ, the *yogin* strikes the ground and imagines it rent asunder as a mass of black fire comes bursting forth. In the midst of that fire, arising from the *mantra* OṂ KṚṢṆAYAMĀRI HŪṂ JAḤ, the *yogin* is instructed to imagine the sudden real appearance of the black Yama of *karma* (Karmayama).[755] It should be noted here that Kṛṣṇayamāri is not normally Yama but rather his adversary, 'the enemy of Yama', a form of the Buddhist deity Vajrabhairava (a wrathful emanation of Mañjuśrī) who subdued the Vedic Yama and bound him under oath to protect the Buddhist Dharma.[756] Originally, however, the epithets Yamāri and its virtual synonym Yamāntaka were indeed applied to Yama himself who was known as 'Death, the enemy' or 'Death, the ender'.[757] These terms were later reinterpreted to mean 'the enemy of Death' and 'the ender of Death' when applied to the overthrower of Yama who succeeded in crushing his power.[758] The question then arises – Does our Byang-gter text have its roots in a time when Kṛṣṇayamāri was actually an epithet of Yama, or did the author of the text (said to be Padmasambhava) simply confuse their (current) discrete identities?

The invited god is then to be presented with a *bali* offering and requested to fulfil his task as follows; "HŪṂ You who dwell in a doorless iron house[759] in the dense wind beneath the dark depths of the great ocean below the mighty foundation of the king of mountains (Sumeru).[760] You, the black-bodied one with coarse stunted limbs, from whose mouth issues forth the foul vapour of death. Mounted upon your black buffalo steed,

---

755 The *Vimalaprabhā* says that the nature of Karmayama is threefold: as a ghost (*preta*) he inhabits a plot of earth, as the lord of death (*mṛtyu*) he dwells in the body of living beings and as defilement (*kleśa*) his abode is the mind. A. Wayman, "Studies in Yama and Māra" 126

756 B. Siklós, *The Vajrabhairava Tantra* 38

757 These and other epithets of Yama are listed in the lexicon *Amarakośa*. A. Wayman, "Studies in Yama and Māra" 44-45

758 W.D. O'Flaherty, *The Origins of Evil in Hindu Mythology* 232

759 Described as having 16 very sharp edges, reminiscent of the sharp-edged discus (*cakra*) employed in so many Vajrakīla rites to press down upon demons. A. Wayman, "Studies in Yama and Māra" 127-128

760 The *pretakaṇḍa* of the *Garuḍa-purāṇa* devotes Chapter XXXIII to a description of Yama's realm and XXXXVII to a description of the river Vaitaraṇi which lies at the threshold of Yama's city.

you hold in your hands a skull club and noose. Your land is known as 'the World of Black Blemish' ('Jig-rten rme-nag) and for those who are born there it is a place of no escape.[761] Oh lord of death, king of the Dharma (Dharmarāja), you who have the power of great insight (*abhijñā*) and the performance of miracles (*ṛddhi*). Discriminate now between virtue and vice. This enemy is entrusted to your hands, oh Yama. Oh lord of death who maintains the *samaya,* do not release the entrusted enemy!"[762]

Then, muttering once more the name *mantra* of the black Yamāri, the *yogin* imagines himself pressing food to his lips and inviting him to eat the flesh of the enemy, to drink his blood, devour his heart and consume the entrails and sense organs.[763]

After that the *yogin* should recite the DHADDHI *mantra* as he imagines that wind camel (*rlung gi rnga mo*) travelling to the land of Yama with the enemy upon its back. Muttering IMĀN VIGHNĀN STAMBHAYA NAN, the *yogin* meditates upon a *kīla* as the actual Amṛtakuṇḍalin and nails it into the effigy. Then a slab of stone upon which have been drawn Mount Meru and the four continents of Buddhist cosmology is placed over the burial chamber and this presses down upon the enemy with the whole weight of the universe. This stone slab should be covered over with earth so as to make it invisible and the celebrants perform dances of the four activities upon its surface.

---

761 According to the *Vajrabhairavākhyāna-kalpa,* Yama's city (named there as Galava) contains 16 gateless iron dwellings, 32 houses, etc.

B. Siklós, *The Vajrabhairava Tantra* 177

Chapter V of the *pretakāṇḍa* in the *Garuḍa-purāṇa* describes the torments suffered by the deceased as he is dragged away to the south in the direction of Yama's realm. There are said to be 16 cities to pass through *en route;* Yāmya, Sauripura, Nāgendrabhavana, Gandharva (Gandhamādana), Śailāgama, Krūrapura, Krauñca, Vicitrabhavana, Bahvāpada, Duḥkhada, Nānākrandapura, Sutaptabhavana, Raudra, Payovarṣaṇa, Śītāḍhya and Bahubhīti. *Garuḍa-purāṇa* II.V 81-154

V. Fausboll, *Indian Mythology* 136, gives the name of Yama's city as Saṁyamana.

762 The character of Yama is thought to exhibit two clearly distinct facets. As the god of death he is the much feared destroyer of life whose retinue consists of dreadful diseases and whose messengers drag the deceased through barren lands devoid of shade and water towards his realm in the south. Within his wondrous palace, however, Yama is the wise and just judge of the dead, the righteous king of Dharma whose laws and nature have their roots in the *karma* of the one who stands before him to be judged.

V. Fausboll, *Indian Mythology* 138

763 A13 119-121

Finally, as a benediction for the site, a golden Mount Meru should be visualised upon the road and there, in a ritual vase, one should meditate upon the lord Amoghasiddhi[764] in the company of his inconceivable retinue.[765]

764 The *tathāgata* who presides over the northern quarter of the *maṇḍala,* the peaceful equivalent of the wrathful Amṛtakuṇḍalin.

765 A13 121-122

CHAPTER ELEVEN
For the benefit of yogins

Those *yogins* who have accomplished the rite of the *bhavakīla* and wish "to postpone the termination of either their own or another's lifespan" are instructed in the process of this achievement by the *rDo rje phur pa'i tshe sgrub* (A18, B22, C12, E13), a longevity ritual apparently based upon the 21st chapter of the Vajrakīla *Garland of Flames Tantra* (*Me lce'i 'phreng ba*) (A31, C13, E15).[766]

Opening with a homage to Vajrakīla as 'the deity of *vajra* life' (*rdo rje tshe'i lha*), this ritual instructs the *sādhaka* to assemble the necessary articles such as the long-life vase (*tshe'i bum*)[767] and the various life-prolonging medicines[768] and perform the Kīla *sādhana* in a solitary place, inserting the rite of longevity in the section devoted to the assembled

---

766 Chapter XXI alone appears extant of this otherwise unknown *tantra,* taught by 'the *bhagavat heruka* king' (*bcom ldan 'das khrag 'thung gi rgyal po*) in response to a request made by the deity Vajrakīla. It is possibly also the primary source for the *rDo rje phur pa'i tshe dbang* found as A19, B23, E14.

767 The *Garland of Flames* says that this jewelled vase should contain five kinds of gem, five kinds of medicinal herb, five sorts of grain, five fragrances, five essences (not listed individually but see A. Wayman, *The Buddhist Tantras* 81), the three sweet substances (sugar, honey and molasses) and white mustard, 'the supreme seed' (*'bru mchog*). It should be filled to the top with water, covered over with a red half-moon and richly adorned with ornaments before being placed in the very centre of the *maṇḍala*. The text then gives the *mantra* required in order to invoke the presence of the Kīlas of the five *kula* which are imagined to take up residence within the belly of the vase. They are said to be generated and invited "in accordance with former rites" (see chapters 5–7, above). Once present, those deities are honoured with incense and flags and the *maṇḍala* itself should be surrounded by the necessities (*yo byad*) of the ritual. A31 213. The *tshe dbang* text fills the vase with beer instead of water, closes its mouth with 'a long-life teat' (*tshe'i 'brang rgyas*), seals it in four places around the outside with HRĪḤ and finally binds it with five-coloured thread. A19 154

768 Unspecified in the text. Generally, however, Tibetan lamas collect together an assortment of ingredients both sacred (relics of diverse sorts) and medicinal (herbs, minerals, etc.) which are ground to powder, bound together with roasted barley flour and moulded into pills. These pills are then consecrated in the process of the ritual to become 'long life medicine'.

offerings (*gaṇacakra*).[769] There the *yogin* should contemplate that from the syllable BHRŪṀ arises a jewelled *maṇḍala* palace, square with four doors and replete with all adornments. In its centre, arising from the transformation of the syllable HRĪḤ, Buddhāmitāyus rests upon cushions of lotus and moon. He is white in colour and holds a long-life vase on his lap. In front of him, to the east, is the blue Vairocanāmitāyus with the yellow Guṇāmitāyus to the south, the red Amitābhāmitāyus to the west and the green Karmāmitāyus to the north. All of them hold long-life vases upon their laps and are held in non-dual embrace by the leading ladies of the five *kula*.[770] Surrounding them are the eight offering goddesses: Lāsyā, Mālā, Gītā, Nṛtyā, Dhūpā, Puṣpā, Ālokā and Gandhā,[771] and the four gate-guardian goddesses holding the hook, noose, fetters and bell. The *yogin* is instructed to visualise all of these deities clearly so that no confusion

769 In this regard it is interesting to note the explanation given by the *Garland of Flames* in which it is said that, in a superior practice such as this, the activities of presenting offerings to the deity and so on are perfected by maintaining an awareness of utter purity. This text also glosses "the radiating and gathering of the recitation syllables" (normally imagined internally in the form of light) as "right speech (*samyagvāk*), within which neither confusion (for others) nor error (in oneself) arise" and says that this is the manner in which the ritual is to be performed. A31 214

770 Instead of generating the *pañcakula* Amitāyus in front, the *Garland of Flames* describes self-generation in four-armed form. According to this *tantra*, the *yogin* should imagine rays of light streaming out from the syllable A in the centre of a *viśvavajra* in his heart. As those light rays gather together and return to his heart, he himself becomes Amitāyus, shining white like a snow mountain with one smiling face and four arms. In his two right hands he holds a *viśvavajra* and a bag made of mongoose skin. In his two left hands he holds a bell and a vase of nectar. He is adorned with strings of jewels and seated in non-dual embrace with his consort. A31 214

771 The *Garland of Flames* and the *tshe dbang* text list only four of these eight goddesses. Lāsyā to the east is white and she carries a vase of crystal. In the south is the blue Mālā (all mss: Lāsyā) who has a garland of turquoise and a jewelled vase. In the west is the red Gītī, goddess of song who has a vase of coral, and in the north is the green Nṛtyā, goddess of dance whose vase is made of beryl. All are said to summon the lifespan and to contain within their vases the essence of the five nectars, with which they nourish life force and vitality, restoring the weak. A31 218-219

In the *tshe dbang* text, their vases are filled with the distilled essence of flowers, juices, fruits and forest herbs respectively. A19 157

arises in his mind concerning their colour, form or insignia. Each of them is said to be adorned with all the usual attributes.[772]

When the visualisation is stable, the wisdom counterparts (*jñānasattva*) of those deities should be invited, praised and presented with offerings and their *mantra* recited. For, it is said, it is precisely by means of standard meditative procedure that the attainment of long life is gained. OṀ ĀḤ HŪṀ NṚ BHRŪṀ VAJRĀYUṢE HŪṀ Ā.[773]

That this *siddhi* of longevity is considered a natural corollary of orthodox yogic praxis is then demonstrated in the text as it goes on to cite from the *Garland of Flames Tantra* the adage; "One should perform the acts of devotion (*sevā*), secondary devotion (*upasevā*), evocation (*sādhana*) and great evocation (*mahāsādhana*) for long life".[774] The *yogin* is then instructed to imagine that the entire animate and inanimate world dissolves into light and is absorbed into himself and into the 'long life substances' upon the altar before him.

Now, as for summoning the lifespan; calling HRĪḤ the *yogin* contemplates Buddhāmitāyus in the non-dual embrace of his consort Caṇḍālī[775] and invokes the *siddhi* of long life and glory (*śrī*) from the *maṇḍala* of their non-dual heart. Then he calls to Vairocanāmitāyus and his consort from the eastern direction, Ratnāmitāyus and his consort from the southern direction, Padmāmitāyus and his consort from the western direction and Karmāmitāyus and his consort from the north. He calls to the god-

---

772 Details of colour, form, attribute, position in the *maṇḍala, mudrā, mantra,* etc., of the minor deities mentioned here are to be found in SDPT (*passim*), where Vajraghaṇṭā is called Vajrāveśa.
For their icons see Lokesh Chandra, *Buddhist Iconography of Tibet* 177-184

773 A18 146

774 *Tshe bsnyen dang ni nye bsnyen dang, tshe sgrub dang ni sgrub chen bya.* The verse in the *tantra* ends; *las rnams yongs su rdzogs par bya.* "(Thus) one fully accomplishes all activities". A31 213. These four categories of praxis, within which are included the stages of both *utpattikrama* and *saṁpanna-krama,* are discussed at length in Alex Wayman, *Yoga of the GST* (*passim*) where the term *upasevā* is replaced by *upasādhana.*

775 The *Garland of Flames* presents the rite of the consort as a backup technique to ensure the attainment of *siddhi.* If the signs of success are not fully attained by means of the previous rite, it says, the *yogin* should invoke the white goddess Caṇḍālī from the heart of Amitāyus by muttering OṀ VAJRA-CAṆḌĀLĪ HA JA JA HŪṀ. Blazing in a mass of fire she appears with one face and four hands within which she holds a *vajra* made of gems, a precious vase of nectar, a jewel and a casket. She has jewels in her hair and from her body radiate countless emanations which fill the ten directions of the six destinies and grind to dust all those who hold false views. A31 216

desses Lāsyā, Mālā and the rest, to Vajrāṅkuśā, Vajrapāśā, Vajrasphoṭā and Vajraghaṇṭā. He imagines that all of these deities hold 'life silks' (*tshe dar,* arrows festooned with silks of five colours) in their right hands which they wave in all directions and 'life vases' in their left which are filled with the nectar of immortality. By means of these articles they bestow the blessings of long life upon the fortunate ones (those of meritorious *karma*).

"HRĪḤ Oh lord Mahāśrīvajrakumāra and the great divine mother Tṛptacakra, bestow the attainment of long life upon we fortunate ones!"

The *yogin* then proceeds systematically to appropriate for himself the lifespans and attractive qualities ('glory') of the denizens of the universe. This he achieves through the agency of the *daśakrodha* kings and their consorts, the overlords of all those who dwell in the ten directions.

"HŪṀ The span of life that pertains above in the realm of Brahmā must be brought forth by the *krodharāja* Hūṁkāra. His consort Śabdavajrā must preserve the glory." With such words as these, the *krodha* couples of the ten directions are urged to bring forth the lifespans and merits of the *gandharva* from the east, of the retinue of Agni from the southeast, of Yama from the south, of the *rākṣasa* from the southwest, of the *nāga* from the west, of the wind gods from the northwest, of the *yakṣa* from the north, of Īśāna from the northeast and of the *bhūmipati* from below. OṀ ĀḤ HŪṀ NṚ BHRŪṀ VAJRĀYUṢE HŪṀ.[776]

The text continues in this manner with a further series of ten verses exhorting the animal-headed 'devourers' and 'killers' to gather in the lifespans and protect the glory that are to be found in the sky, in the southern forests, on rocky mountains, on open plains, in the borderland of snow and slate (the snow line), in areas of farmland, within the shadows on the

---

776 A18 147-148. According to the *tshe dbang,* the *mantra* given here is to be added in turn to that of each individual deity in the *maṇḍala*. A19 154

western face of forests, in the wild regions of snowy mountains, upon the northern plains and within the depths of the great oceans.[777]

"The goddesses with the hook, noose, fetters and bell – those four goddesses who guard the *maṇḍala* gates – must gather in the lifespans and all the oath-bound protectors must preserve the glory."[778]

The *Garland of Flames* explains that whatever demons there are in the ten directions of the world are subdued and annihilated by the recitation of the *mantra* and that their lifespan is to be drawn in with the syllable NṚ. It is also said that the *yogin* may use this technique in order to gather the 'essential nectar' (*rtsi bcud*) of the elements or the *bodhicitta* of all the buddhas in the ten directions, which he then either unites with himself or dissolves into the vase (or sacred food and drink) upon the altar so that it becomes "like the wish-fulfilling gem", supreme among jewels. Thus, the text says, "the excellence of the vase is that it contains the auspicious qualities of the lifespans of others and makes them immediately available for the benefit of the *yogin*."

In order to reap the maximum benefit of this appropriation, the *yogin* should absorb the lifespan and other qualities into himself in the form of enlightenment, visible either as the three syllables OṀ ĀḤ HŪṀ or as the five syllables OṀ on the crown of his head, AṀ on the top of the tongue, HŪṀ on the heart, TRAṀ on the navel and A on the soles of both feet. This absorption may be completed either simultaneously or in stages and then the *yogin* should protect the attainment and keep it hidden "within the blissful dance of natural awareness".[779]

The *yogin* having thus vastly enriched the store of longevity abiding within his life vein (*jīvitanāḍī*), the texts then deal with the method of hiding away that lifespan so as to conserve it. The *Garland of Flames* says that the essential vitality (*snying po bcud*) is to be sealed by means of

777 These 42 deities of the Vajrakīla *maṇḍala* are to be visualised holding iron hooks in their right hands (with which to capture the lifespan) and vases in their left (containing the stored nectar of immortality). From the three places of each deity radiate innumerable 'Lords of Boundless Life and Wisdom' (*aparimitāyurjñānanātha*) so that the entire world is filled with wrathful wisdom beings who, having taken the best of all things, restore whatever is impaired, distorted, dissipated or unstable for the *yogins* and their sponsors. Otherwise, the captured lifespan of all worldly gods and demons is dissolved into the vase in the form of the syllable A and the vase is seen to glow with light. A19 154-155

778 A18 148-149

779 A31 214-215

a *vajra* weapon within the closed container of a *viśvavajra* (presumably within his heart),[780] whereas the *tshe sgrub* instructs the *yogin* to visualise a green syllable NṚ (the syllable that attracts the life force of humans) and imagine that the entrance to his life vein is guarded on the outside by Hayagrīva and on the inside by Amṛtakuṇḍalin, both of whom arise from HRĪḤ and stand like soldiers with their feet together.[781]

Alternatively, that 'lifespan with excellent qualities' may be concealed within the *dharmadhātu,* where even a buddha will not perceive it. In either case, this 'precept of longevity' is said to be an excellent activity which possesses the unexcelled armour (*kavaca*) of *mahāśūnyatā,* armour with the seal (*mudrā*) of protection against perverted views. The *Garland of Flames* says that, of all armours, knowledge of *śūnyatā* is supreme for it destroys all objective weapons. The *yogin* should therefore conceal his acquired lifespan within the sphere beyond imagination, where obstructors and misleaders can do it no harm.[782] "By donning the indestructible *vajra* armour, one is protected from the demons of mistaken ideas." OṀ VAJRA-KAVACA HŪṀ.

"HOḤ The hosts of gods of deathless *vajra* life must take up and gather in the lifespans of we *yogins* here and straighten out whatever is crooked, replace that which has broken off, renew whatever has become worn out, and nourish that which has become weak. Please bestow upon us the blessings of a lifespan that has never been born, a lifespan which is the nectar of immortality, an undying lifespan, a lifespan which is a banner of victory that never droops, a lifespan of unchanging great happiness and all the good fortune of long life, power and merit."[783]

The *Garland of Flames* concludes with a few lines that indicate the normal significance of 'immortality' in this world – the begetting of children so that the name (and especially the religious tradition) of the *yogin* may live on after death.[784]

---

780 A31 219

781 These two deities are to be imagined holding clubs in their right hands and making the *tarjanīmudrā* with the left. The *tshe dbang* has them standing guard over the lifespan contained within a 'wisdom palace' arisen from the syllable HŪṀ on the forehead, not within the heart.
B23 66-67 (page missing in A)

782 A31 220

783 A18 150

784 A31 220

The text claims that, through the proper performance of this ritual, even a hermaphrodite or a barren woman or a decrepit old person will receive the empowerment of life and their family lineages will be increased, so what more need be said? Either the family line will be increased with unending virtue[785] or, if the results are not applied in that (mundane) way, the *yogin* who practises this rite will blaze like Bhairava in the *maṇḍala* of ferocious deities. From such a one will emanate various hand symbols and weapons that will spread out and cut down all demons in the ten directions of the world and the glorious attributes of Hayagrīva will drag them forth from whichever place they stay. The various weapons such as the *vajracakra* will 'liberate' the powerful gods, even those long-lived gods of the higher heavens, and thus the *yogin* will gather the lifespans of the five classes of beings under his power.[786] By means of the ploughshare and other such weapons that till the fields and overturn the world beneath the surface of the earth, the *yogin* subjugates Yama, the *nāga* and other (subterranean) troublesome beings and, 'liberating' them, he gathers them under his power. By means of the iron hook and the discus, etc., the unimaginable weapons of the dangerous ones filling the whole of the sky, the eight classes of *bhūta*[787] are liberated in an instant.[788]

It is also stated in the *Garland of Flames* that this method of enhancing longevity should be practised "in accordance with the stages of secret Vajrayāna" by the *yogin* joining in a *samādhi* of union with a youthful woman whose body possesses the appropriate signs and symbols. Then the precepts and *siddhi* of this rite should be transmitted to any children born of that union, to whom also should be given the empowerments of the *pañcatathāgata* – the crown consecration and the wisdom consecration and the rest.[789]

In the case of these *siddhi* of long life being bestowed by a guru upon his disciple at the time of the latter's *abhiṣeka,* the *tshe sgrub* instructs that the various preliminaries such as the expulsion of obstructing demons and so on be completed first. Then the disciple should take a purificatory bath, present the *maṇḍala* of offerings to his teacher, take refuge in the *triratna,* generate *bodhicitta,* pledge himself to protect the *samaya* and

---

785 Text A reads, "virtue will increase".

786 Text A reads, "will gather it up in the form of light".

787 Enumerated in the text as "*btsan, bdud, the'u rang* and the rest".

788 A31 217

789 A31 220

saṁvara vows, and respectfully request his guru for the great method of prolonging his lifespan. "These preliminaries should all be performed in accordance with the authoritative texts of Vajrakīla."

The disciple then makes a request for empowerment by reciting the well-known verse from the Vajrakīla *mūlatantra,* met with so often above; "HŪṀ Empowerments and blessings must be bestowed in this place ..." etc. He then recites the *mūlamantra* of Vajrakīla and his retinue, adding the words ABHIṢIÑCA MĀṀ (consecrate me) at the end. And for the vase consecration he recites BUDDHA- VAJRA- RATNA- PADMA- KARMA-KALAŚA-ABHIṢIÑCA BHRŪṀ.

"HRĪḤ Glorious lord, Vajrāmitāyus, the sovereign whose form extends to the limits of space, we pray that you will bestow the empowerment of the lifespan of the *vajra* heart and the enjoyment[790] of dominion with the all-pervading *vajra* body."[791] Thus, says the text, the empowerment of all the good qualities and enlightened activities of the various *kula* are received in unity. Also the empowerments of 'the seven precious things' (*saptadhanāni*)[792] and 'the eight auspicious symbols' (*aṣṭamaṅgala*)[793] are gained.

Then the guru and disciple imagine the *siddhi* of long life being gathered in from the sacred field (*kṣetra*) of Lotus Light (Padma-'od) in the west. As they contemplate Vajrāmitāyus arisen from the syllable HRĪḤ, they imagine that from the amulet of half-moon and *śrīvatsa* in his heart flows the *bodhicitta* of longevity in the form of red light. By means of

---

790 Text A reads *brnyes pa* (*prāpta*), 'got, received'. B & C read *mnyes pa* (*toṣita*), 'delighted'.

791 The longevity of the *trikāya* alluded to here is bestowed in three separate verses in the *tshe dbang*. A19 161

792 A wealth of faith (*śraddhā*), a wealth of moral conduct (*śīla*), a wealth of shame (*hrī*), a wealth of modesty (*apatrāpya*), a wealth of learning (*śruta*), a wealth of renunciation (*tyāga*) and a wealth of wisdom (*prajñā*). These spiritual attributes are symbolised in ritual consecrations by seven jewels or 'the seven attributes of a *cakravartin*' which are his magic wheel (*cakra*), elephant (*hasti*), horse (*aśva*), jewel (*maṇi*), queen (*strī*), home minister (*gṛhapati*) and military general (*pariṇāyaka*). Cf. SDPT 79 n.11

793 Regarding these, Buddhaguhya says, "*Yoga* displays itself as the eight emblems on the true nature of body; the endless knot (*śrīvatsa*) which is lotus-like, the wheel (*cakra*) which is frightening, the banner (*dhvaja*) which is victorious, the umbrella (*chattra*) which is dignified, the lotus (*padma*) which is luminous, the flask (*kalaśa*) of acute mind, the conch (*śaṇkha*) of purity and the golden fish (*matsya*) of auspicious mind."
A. Wayman, *The Buddhist Tantras* 108

this, "all those present here must receive the *siddhi* of long life and be blessed with this great secret of longevity." Thus the *siddhi* are gained.[794]

When the ritual is over, whether or not it had been the occasion of a disciple's *abhiṣeka,* the usual benedictions (*maṇgala, svastika*) and distribution of merit (*pariṇāmana*) should be performed.

So much for the magical enhancement of the lifespan. According to the *them byang,* however, for the benefit of *yogins*, the Vajrakīla cycle should also provide the means of enhancing wealth.

With regard to this provision, in the *Garland of Flames* it is said that the ten *krodha* kings, their queens and animal-headed assistants are to be visualised brandishing *vajras* in their upper right hands (with which all those who hold false views are overthrown) and iron hooks in the left (by means of which their lifespans are drawn forth). In the right hands below those, the gods hold bags full of gems from which wealth is bestowed upon all the poor and needy, while from precious caskets held in the left, glory and lordliness are dispensed to all whose merit is exhausted. "Especially the glory and splendour of the threefold world is to be bestowed upon virtuous *yogins*."[795]

Apart from this, however, no root *gter ma* text in any of the Vajrakīla collections at our disposal is seen to focus itself specifically on means to the enhancement of wealth (*nor sgrub*).

The collections do, however, provide for the enhancement of the *yogin*'s food and drink in a number of texts.[796] Of these, the only title to be found in common in three of the collections (A23, B24, C14) gives merely the briefest outline of the steps in the ritual procedure, leaving the liturgical details (if required) to be supplied from elsewhere. Opening with a salutation to Śrīvajrakumāra, this short text, said to have been written by Padmasambhava, styles itself 'the *samādhi* within which the *yogin* should dwell on all occasions when eating (or drinking)'. It begins with a general outline of the ritual procedure for the blessing of food and drink and then adds those details deemed to be specifically appropriate for practitioners

---

794 A18 150-151. The *tshe dbang* names the buddhafield as Padma-dbang. A19 161

795 A31 218

796 According to 'Jigs-med gling-pa, the technique of taking food and drink ('the objects of enjoyment') as the path to enlightenment is a special characteristic of the Vajrayāna. T. Thondup, *Enlightened Living* 132

of the Kīla cult. In general, it is said, the *yogin* should gather all his food and drink together within 'the great vessels' (*snod chen*)[797] without indulging in mental discriminations of 'pure' and 'defiled'. Imagining himself to be in the presence of the lord, he should generate the mind of enlightenment[798] and meditate upon himself in the form of the deity. Purifying and blessing the food by means of the three syllables, it should be offered. The *yogin* may then entrust the deities to perform the four *karma,* gather from them the *siddhi* and enjoy the food in the nature of truth. Finally the left-overs are presented, the deities are dismissed and prayers are dedicated to the welfare of all beings. So it is said.

Having thus outlined the topics to be discussed, the text goes on to elaborate only very slightly. We are now told that those *yogin*s who are accomplished in the practice of Vajrakīla should, on all occasions, gather their food and drink on a plate and recite RAṀ YAṀ KHAṀ[799] so as to render it pure. By OṀ ĀḤ HŪṀ the six goddesses of all desirable qualities infuse it with their blessings and then the guru[800] and the host of divinities are invited and the food and drink is presented to them as an offering with the words, OṀ VAJRAKĪLI KĪLAYA KRODHA KHRODHĪ HA HE PHAṬ DHADDHI MAMA KARMA KAṄKA KĀRAYE KHA KHA KHĀHI KHĀHI. Making prayers to those deities, the *yogin* should imagine that they bestow *siddhi* upon him so that he becomes full of satisfaction and joy.

After eating, he presents a feast of the remainders with the words SARVAPŪJĀ KHĀHI and then entrusts the remains-taking guests with the four activities by adding ŚĀNTIṀ PUṢṬIṀ VAŚAṀ MĀRAYA PHAṬ. They are then dismissed under oath to protect the doctrines.

Finally, the *yogin* should recite a benediction: "Ho! Salutation to the hosts of joyful gods. With a wealth of benefit and vast in blessings, enjoying permanent blessings, having purified the two obstructions and amassed the two accumulations of merit, may all things (beneficial) without exception be increased! A LA LA HO."[801]

In that way, initiates in the cult of Vajrakīla transform the everyday act of eating and drinking, uplifting it from the mundane so that it becomes,

---

797 By this is indicated the *yogin*'s imaginative transformation of his own ordinary plates and utensils into the divine vessels (skull cups) of the gods.

798 This line missing in B.

799 These are the seeds of fire, air and water respectively.
Cf. above, Chapter Seven, note 649.

800 Text B says "oneself".

801 A23 175-176

in miniature, a sacred rite along the lines of the *gaṇacakra* discussed above in Chapter Seven. Such a procedure is the logical corollary of the *yogin*'s self-transformation into the deity. Further demonstration of its importance is to be seen below in the final chapter of this work.

CHAPTER TWELVE

Rites designed to make good any deficiencies in yogic praxis

The first text in this category (A24, B24, C14, E19) is a brief outline of the meditations to accompany the preparation of *sāccha*.[802] The extraordinarily corrupt condition of the text in all redactions seems indicative of a general disinterest in this procedure on the part of Kīla initiates. Although the orthographic standard of the entire corpus of material presently being studied is generally low, this particular text seems to have been written out with a singular lack of attention. Said to be an original *gter ma,* the text bears neither attribution of authorship nor any reference to its sources.

Following the homage to Śrīvajrakumāra, this text stipulates that an area of sanctified ground should be sprinkled with fragrant perfumes and upon it should be arranged the various necessities (unspecified) for offering to the deities. The *yogin* should then generate himself in the form of the god and recite the *hṛdaya* of Vajrakīla as many times as possible. He should prepare a mixture of clay using mud, powdered gemstones, sandalwood and perfumed water[803] and he should bless this lump of clay by placing upon it the three syllables OṀ ĀḤ HŪṀ, which he radiates out from his heart. Then, muttering OṀ DHARMADHĀTU OṀ ĀḤ HŪṀ A, the *yogin* imagines rays of light to stream forth from those three syllables upon the heap of clay. Gathering in the rays of light and returning them to their source, the *yogin* imagines that the syllables dissolve into light and he contemplates the void nature of the clay.[804]

Imagining his own body to be marked with the syllable BHRŪṀ, the *yogin* visualises light rays emanating from that syllable and then, as he mutters BHRŪṀ VIŚVAVIŚUDDHE VAJRAJÑĀNACAKRA BHRŪṀ, he imagines the light returning to the syllable and his body transformed into a palace of the gods (*vimāna*). He then recites the deity's *hṛdaya* OṀ

802 *Sāccha* (Tib. *tsha tsha*) are small relief images prepared by impressing clay into a metal mould. Sanskrit and Tibetan sources relating to Avalokiteśvara are discussed at length in my *Illuminating Sunshine*, but see also: Li Jicheng, *The Realm of Tibetan Buddhism* (New Delhi 1986) 170-176 for clear photographs of *sāccha* being stamped out with a metal mould, a brief description of the process and close-ups of the finished articles.

803 A surprising omission from this list is ashes belonging to a deceased guru or other holy person, for these *sāccha* are regularly manufactured in Tibet as reliquaries of the dead. See *Illuminating Sunshine* for more details.

804 This section missing in B.

VAJRAKĪLI KĪLAYA OṀ ĀḤ HŪṀ and is thereby further sealed with the *mudrā.*[805]

At this point both the *yogin* and the clay have been fully prepared so that the manufacture of the *sāccha* can begin. The text, however, gives no instructions concerning either the form or the quantity of *sāccha* to be made in order to fulfil the purpose specified in the *them byang* of restoring broken vows and making good any defects in yogic praxis. It seems natural to assume that the clay will be stamped in the likeness of the deity Vajrakīla but the text is not specific on this point and its instructions undoubtedly hold good for *sāccha* modelled in other forms such as miniature *stūpa,* etc. Indeed, the texts are particularly corrupt at this point with text A having four lines more than B, C or E. The only instructions given for the actual manufacture of the *sāccha* concerns the non-dual unity of wisdom and means, which the *yogin* must recognise as inherent within both himself and the small lumps of clay that are to be moulded into shape, "all forms arising from the sphere of the *dharmadhātu*".[806]

Once the *sāccha* have been manufactured, however, they should be consecrated (*pratiṣṭhā*) as divine palaces, each inhabited by a host of gods. Thinking thus, the *yogin* should hold flowers in his hand and recite seven times the formula of dependent origination, YE DHARMĀ, etc. He should then cast the flowers onto the *sāccha* and imagine that all aspects of cause and result have been fully perfected. Following that he may worship the *sāccha* in whatever manner he deems suitable.

"Ho! Whatever (buddhas) there are who are desirous of passing into *nirvāṇa,* I implore you compassionate ones not to pass beyond this realm of sorrow so long as *saṁsāra* abides." Saying this, the *yogin* should scatter flowers and imagine that (the compassionate buddhas) remain until *saṁsāra* has been emptied.

This is the means of manufacturing *sāccha* with the purpose of obtaining the complete enlightenment of oneself and others. Vows. Triple seal.[807]

---

805 This line found only in A. I take it to mean that the presence of the deity is installed within the palace of the *yogin*'s body by the three seals of Body, Speech and Mind.

806 A24 177

807 A24 177-178

The final text to be found in four of the collections is a summary of votive rites for those initiated into the *maṇḍala* of Vajrakīla, simply referred to as 'the Appendix' (*zur 'debs*) (A28, B25, C16, E20).

Described in its colophon as a treasure from the golden southern cache, this document commences with the deity's *hṛdaya* and informs us that the body of the glorious *mahottara* Vajrakumāra is dark blue in colour with nine heads and 18 hands. His three faces on the right are pale yellow, red and blue. Those on the left are dark yellow, maroon and green while his central three faces are white, yellow and dark blue.[808] All are wrathful with gaping mouths, eyes that stare in opposite directions (*spyan bzlog*) and beards that bristle like fire. The long brown hair on his head is described as twisting upwards and the implements said to be held in his 18 hands have been given above in Chapter Three, Table 1. With his eight legs in the *pratyālīḍha* posture, he advances to the left and tramples upon Rudra, the enemies and obstructors. His form is fully adorned with the eight articles of the charnel ground and, with his *vajra* wings, he overawes the *tribhava*. The great mother Tṛptacakra is blue in colour, with a single face and two hands. She holds a *vajra* in her right hand[809] and, with her left hand, she presses a skull full of blood to the lips of her lord. The divine couple are vast with rough limbs and they emit terrifying roars.[810]

The *yogin*'s awareness (*vidyā*) should instantly arise in that form without stages in the process of generation. Then, with a spontaneous sound of joy, the *daśakrodha* kings and their entourage, the supreme sons, the guardian goddesses of the gates and the rest, all arise as the unity of appearance and emptiness (*prabhāsa-śūnyatā*), filling the ten directions and setting the wheel of Dharma into motion. Vast numbers of oath-bound messengers should be dispatched in pursuance of their tasks and the entire vision is seen to blaze with light like the raging inferno at the end of time.

Following this description of the *maṇḍala* of Mahottarakīla, the text continues with verses from the BRT and *Thugs kyi 'phrin las* (A45),[811] two texts pertaining to the black deity cycle. Thus, the intention of the rite is declared with "HŪṀ All those who hold the awareness of Vajrakumāra ... etc." and "HŪṀ Empowerments and blessings must be bestowed in this place ... etc." The section ends in the usual fashion with *mantra* for the

808 Cf. above, Chapter Three.

809 Not the *khaṭvāṅga* of Chapter Three.

810 A28 184

811 A45 407/6-409/1

empowerment of the *maṇḍala;* OṀ ĀḤ HŪṀ OṀ HŪṀ SVA AṀ HĀ KĀYA-VĀK-CITTA-GUṆA-KARMA-SIDDHI-ABHIŚIÑCA HŪṀ.

The wisdom deities are then invited to enter this consecrated *samaya-maṇḍala* with the usual "HŪṀ In order that the empowerments, *siddhi* and successful accomplishment of the *bhavakīla* may be attained ... etc." and verses follow in which the deities are asked to accept offerings, bestow *siddhi* and remain firm until the two purposes are fulfilled.[812] With verse and *mantra,* the deities are praised.[813]

In that way the *yogin* should clearly bring to mind the *maṇḍala* palace and its retinue of gods. With an understanding of non-duality he should then respectfully salute the deities with his body, speech and mind – ŚRĪVAJRĀYA NAMAḤ – and present them with offerings.

First there is the offering of *bodhicitta* nectar, which is to be understood as the distilled essence of all consciousness, an effective counteragent (medicine) for all wrong views, represented on the physical plane by *semen virile:* "HŪṀ Self-arising from desire and very pure, with eight major and one thousand minor ingredients,[814] this offering of nectar medicine (*bdud rtsi sman*) is offered to Mahāśrī (Vajrakīla) and his retinue. Please bestow the *siddhi* of body, speech and mind.[815] MAHĀSARVA-PAÑCĀMṚTA KHĀHI."

---

812 The supreme *siddhi* of enlightenment for the benefit of the *yogin* and the various mundane *siddhi* of pacification, enrichment, etc. for the benefit of others.

813 A28 185

814 The eight major ingredients are the eight *vijñāna,* while the term "1,000 minor ingredients" refers to the countless thoughts and sensations derived from these. By this offering to the deities, all consciousness is purified.

The *Che mchog gi 'phrin las* further characterises this *bodhicitta* nectar as "the reality of the five *samaya* substances of the five *kula,* the article of the total fulfilment of the five wisdoms". It is said to be the nectar which clears away the five poisons and to be derived from the slaying of all sentient beings in the six *gati.* B11 548

815 The *Che mchog gi 'phrin las* explains the absorption of the deity's *siddhi* thus: Having satisfied the gods with nectar, the *yogin* sees three syllables radiate out from the three places of all those satisfied deities and descend in the form of light in the centre of the nectar. He then takes up the nectar and, muttering OṀ ĀḤ HŪṀ KĀYASIDDHI OṀ VĀKSIDDHI ĀḤ CITTASIDDHI HŪṀ, the *yogin* places a few drops upon his tongue and contemplates its absorption into his own three places. B11 549

Next, the offering of *bali* in which all manifest phenomena are included, produced by the union of semen and menstrual blood;[816] "HŪṀ This amazing great *bali* cake prepared with pure ingredients, emanating from the depths of the unborn *dharmatā,* fully adorned with the five qualities of desire,[817] must satisfy the sacred hearts[818] of Mahāśrīvajrakīla and his retinue. OṀ VAJRAKĪLI KĪLAYA MAHĀBALIM TE KHĀHI."[819]

The offering of blood (*rakta*) is the female counterpart to the male seeds of *bodhicitta*. It is the wisdom of *śūnyatā* that underpins the effective medicine of *upāya*: "HŪṀ The great red blood of *saṁsāra* obtained by slaughtering the afflictions is swirling in the skull cup.[820] We press this to the lips of Mahāśrīvajrakīla and his retinue in order that the *traidhātuka* may be emptied. OṀ VAJRAKĪLI KĪLAYA MAHĀRAKTA KHĀHI."

Next is the offering of killing, in which the primary *kleśa* are destroyed;[821] "HŪṀ Having slain all the enemies and obstructors, to the mouths of Mahāśrīvajrakīla and his retinue we offer ignorance as a quivering mound of great flesh,[822] desire as a shimmering ocean of blood, and hatred

---

816 Even in Vedic times, the sacrificial cake was considered to have regenerative properties, the mixing of water and flour in its preparation being viewed as the uniting of male and female.
J. Gonda, *Rice and Barley Offerings in the Veda* 5

817 As the *yogin* presents the *bali* offering he imagines all manner of sensual pleasure being offered to the *maṇḍala* deities by beautiful goddesses who delight the six senses. B11 549

818 *Thugs dam bskang,* a term that refers to the fulfilment of vows. By this offering the deity is satisfied and the *yogin*'s broken vows are restored.

819 A28 186

820 *Kapāla* have been the designated vessels for sacrificial offerings in India since the prehistoric period. In the Veda, however, the term referred to "pieces of pottery (not necessarily potsherds)".
J. Gonda, *Rice and Barley Offerings in the Veda* 4

821 This great offering of the slaughter of the entire three realms arises as a result of the annihilation of all attachment and desire. Outwardly it is composed of the slaughter of the ten classes of enemy to be killed. Inwardly it is the symbolic form of the *kleśa,* the greenish corpse of the overthrown Rudra. B11 549

822 *Mahāmāṁsa* usually indicates human flesh but since the 'enemies and obstructors' are deemed to be of both human and non-human types, I have chosen here to render the word more literally as 'great flesh'.

as a glistening pile of broken bones. MAHĀMĀṀSA-RAKTA-KEMNIRITI[823] KHĀHI."[824]

The offering of union is presented with the closing lines of BRT Ch.V; "HŪṀ Within the shining *yoni*s of the wrathful queens are the blazing *vajra*s of the *krodha* kings. The pounding of those *vajra* hammers is sufficient to kill even those who are gods! KATHAṀ KATHAṀ KATHAṀ HŪṀ HŪṀ HŪṀ PHAṬ PHAṬ PHAṬ VAJRAYAKṢA KRODHAVIJAYA KHĀHI KHĀHI KHĀHI HA HA HA HŪṀ HŪṀ HŪṀ PHAṬ PHAṬ PHAṬ."

The prayer of the proclamation of truth (*satyavacana*); "Ho! Please listen to me. By the truth of *dharmatā,* the blessing of *guhyamantra* and the power of the buddhas, the time for the wrathful act has come.[825] The severe deed must be performed! By this method, through the power of the wonderful rites of secret *mantra,* I pray that I and all sentient beings will be blessed within the circle of the lord Śrīvajrakumāra to enjoy throughout the aeon (i.e. for all time) the inexhaustible body, speech, mind, good qualities and perfect activities of the deity himself."[826]

Then praise; "HŪṀ Arise, all you who have attained knowledge of Vajrakīla! Arise from the *dharmadhātu* and, by the truth of *dharmatā,* perfect the form that encompasses the wisdom of all the buddhas! Manifest the clear light of *dharmatā* in the form of nine wisdom faces, the epitome of wisdom wrath! The upper three faces subjugate all those who are to be converted by means of love and compassion. The middle three faces bless all beings with the consecrations and attainments, while the lower three faces purify body, speech and mind." The text then goes on to collocate Vajrakīla's 18 arms and the symbols that they hold with various powers and lines from the root text. Thus the first pair of hands are associated with the lines "Anger must be destroyed by means of *vajra* wrath" (right) and "The *bindu* arises in the centre of the sky" (left). For the second pair are "Arousing the mind of supreme *bodhicitta*" (right) and "Their hearts must be burned on the pinnacle of *vajra* fire" (left). The third pair hold "The blazing great blue weapon" in the right and the *khaṭvāṅga* of body, speech and mind in the left. Fourthly are "Must seize! Must pulverise!"

---

823 This word is attested in all manuscripts. Unknown in the lexicons, it perhaps derives from a lost Prakrit for *kaṅkāla* (skeleton).

824 As the effigy of Rudra is dismembered, so the *yogin* should liberate appearances and let go of the view of subject and object. In that manner he makes the highest offering of *dharmatā*. B11 550

825 Line missing in C.

826 A28 187-188

which is represented by the hammer in the right hand, while the great hawk (here called *garuḍa*) held in the left is the ABHICĀRA *mantra*. The *viśvavajra* in the fifth right hand is indicative of buddha activity, while the fifth left hand wields the *bhavakīla*. The sixth right hand is Hūṁkāra who has the power of life, while Amṛtakuṇḍalin is represented by the vase in the left. The seventh pair of hands hold the iron hook of love and compassion (right) and the *kartṛkā* which slays the misleaders (left). In the eighth pair are the pounding *vajra* hammer (right) and the blazing *yoni* of the wrathful mother (left). The ninth pair wield the battle axe that chops to pieces (right) and the jewel that fulfils all desires (left). The eight legs spread wide are associated with the phrase "The time has come!"[827]

The arising of this powerful figure, the very embodiment of the Kīla *tantra,* immediately renders powerless all those who obstruct the progress of *yogin*s, whether those trouble-makers be gods or demons. Trampling them down, "the performance of skilful means for the benefit of all sentient beings is accomplished" and empowerments and blessings are bestowed upon the meditator. With the life force arising as the *jñānasattva,* Hayagrīva and his consort are established in the heart and, by means of light rays radiating from the heart *mantra,* the ten directions of space are filled with the ten *krodharāja*. The *yogin* should meditate upon his consciousness in the form of 'the Wisdom *Vajra*', adorned with the ornaments of universal accomplishment and blazing with unbearable wrath. "Such is the form of the lord who is the embodiment of all the buddhas, the chief of wrathful *heruka,* master of all *mātaraḥ* and *ḍākinī,* the body, speech and mind of the assembly of *sugata,*[828] the supreme emanated son who subdues all those to be converted, who dispatches the three classes of red and black emanations as his messengers. Great being, to you be praise!" Saying thus, he is praised.[829]

Then summoning or 'drawing in' (*bskul*), beginning with the holders of the Vajrakīla lineage (*vidyādhara*); "HŪṀ The time has come for all you *vidyādhara* who are heirs to the buddhas of the three times to arouse the supreme mind of *bodhicitta* and descend!" The text then invokes the early Vajrakīla masters Padmasambhava, Vimalamitra, Śīlamañju and Padma-

827 A28 188-189. Cf. above, Chapter Three, Table 1.

828 These epithets are omitted from B. Text C ends at this point, although that collection does include a *skul ba* (C36) through which Padmasambhava is invoked in his eight names.

829 A28 189-190

sambhava's Tibetan disciples, each one being urged to come forth from a site where once he or she demonstrated some miracle power gained through Vajrakīla praxis.

Then the summoning of the deities; "HŪṀ *bhagavat* Mahāśrīvajrakumāra, wrathful king who subdues through anger, arise from the *dharmadhātu* in the embrace of Tṛptacakra! The time has come for you to perform your great deeds. Drawing forth the trouble-making demons and obstructors, immediately destroy them! HŪṀ From your blissful union of wisdom and means arise the ten *krodha* kings and their consorts upon cushions of the piled-up bodies of enemies and obstructors, the lords of the ten directions and the sun and moon."

Together with these major deities are their 20 *piśācī* emanations and all of them are urged to act in accordance with their sacred oaths. The *krodharāja,* their consorts and emanated assistants are invoked by name, each one being summoned individually from the appropriate direction and told "The time has come for you to do your terrible[830] deed!" They are followed by the supreme sons and the four guardian goddesses of the gates.[831]

The summoning of the oath-bound protectors; "BHYO You oath-bound goddesses of the evening!" (There follows a description of the four Śvanmukhā sisters.) "BHYO You oath-bound goddesses of midnight!" (There follows a description of two of the four Mahātmādevī. "BHYO You oath-bound goddesses of the morning!" There follows a description of two of the four Bhūmipati sisters.)[832]

The text then calls forth their twelve brothers.[833] The four *skyes bu* (*puruṣa*) are the brothers of Rosewood and they stand to the right of the four Śvanmukhā sisters. From the east comes Rākṣasa skyes-bu, the great champion of the *rākṣasa,* white in colour wielding a *kīla* of conch shell. From the south comes Yama skyes-bu, also known as Kālayama. He is black in colour and wields a *kīla* made of iron. From the west comes Yabdud skyes-bu of Mongolian descent (*sog po mi rigs*). He is red in colour

830 The specific nature of this terrible deed is changed with each repetition of the line.

831 A28 190-192

832 For descriptions of these twelve, see above, Chapter Nine. There is a lacuna in all manuscripts of the present text so that two goddesses of the morning follow immediately after the first two midnight goddesses. A28 193-194

833 These correspondences are clarified at A53 679-680, citing the authority of mNga'-ris paṇ-chen.

and wields a *kīla* of copper. From the north comes Yakṣa skyes-bu the Mon-pa,[834] blue in colour wielding a *kīla* of turquoise.

The four *bdud po* are the brothers of Iron and they accompany the Mahātmādevī. In the east is the white *māra* who bites his lower lip and wields a *kīla* of conch. In the south is the blue *māra* with long hair wielding a *kīla* of turquoise. In the west is the black *māra* who wields a *kīla* and a noose. In the north is the green *māra* wielding *kīla* and sword.

The four *kiṁkara* (*ging*) are the brothers of Conch who stand to the right of the Bhūmipati sisters. The military commander of the east is Karmarāja, the *kiṁkara* of the *rākṣasa*. He is white in colour and carries a *kīla* of conch. The military commander of the south is Yamarāja, the *kiṁkara* of the *yama*. He is blue in colour and carries a *kīla* and knife. The military commander of the west is Daśagrīva, the *kiṁkara* of the *māra*. He is red in colour and carries a *kīla* and knife. The military commander of the north is Yakṣagrīva, the *kiṁkara* of the *yakṣa*. He is yellow in colour and carries a *kīla*.

The *yogin* invites all those oath-bound protectors who guard the precepts of Vajrakīla to accept an offering of *bali*. He then commands them to drag forth the enemies and obstructors and slay them immediately. The text ends with the exhortation; "You must accomplish your tasks as you promised!"[835]

834 The term Mon is applied in Tibetan texts to "all kinds of groups throughout the Himalayas with whom the Tibetans came into contact", a non-specific designation for any "southern or western mountain-dwelling non-Indian, non-Tibetan barbarian". M. Aris, *Bhutan* xvi

835 A28 194-195

CONCLUSION

Within the earlier chapters of this book it was conclusively demonstrated that all the basic doctrines and rituals of Vajrakīla had their origin in India.[836] Sufficient Sanskrit material remains extant in that country to have facilitated charting the development of the deity from an aniconic wooden spike to the multi-faced and multi-armed god of great wrath exalted today. It is known that wooden spikes were employed from a very early period to secure the boundaries of chosen plots of land, and that such spikes were considered in Vedic ritual to possess the power to ward off evil.

At some stage, the general rite of *sīmābandha,* by means of which a sacred area is rendered ritually secure, was supplemented by (and, to a certain extent, replaced by) the specifically tantric procedure of *kīlana,* in which the boundaries of the chosen area are pegged out so as magically to render them impregnable to such hostile forces as malignant spirits or demons. By the eighth century CE, knowledge of this technique seems to have been as widespread among the Hindu *tāntrika*[837] as among the Buddhists. Buddhism, however, having been eradicated from its homeland during the 13th century, presents us now with a legacy of burned books from which much vital information is missing. Sufficient literature remains, nevertheless, to enable us to collect together in piecemeal fashion 100,000 snippets of knowledge such as may once have been honoured with the epithet '*Vidyottama-tantra* in one hundred thousand sections'. Such a title I suppose to refer in a non-specific way to the entirety of accumulated magico-religious beliefs concerning the *kīla*, both documented and undocumented .

According to the chronicles of the Vajrakīla cult as propounded by Tibetan historians, it was in Nepal during the eighth century CE that this entire corpus of early and medieval Indian *kīla* lore, including affiliated ritual technique, was codified and harmonised into a single unitary system of religious philosophy and procedure. This project having been undertaken by the three Buddhist scholars, Padmasambhava, Vimalamitra and Śīlamañju, their approach to the task at that time was simply to gather

---

836 A few further Sanskrit references of interest in this respect are to be found below, in Appendix II.

837 Robert Svoboda, *Aghora* 48 *& passim*

together all of the *kīla* lore that they could find, and amalgamate it into the general schemata of Vajrayāna Buddhism. We have seen that, already by the eighth century, Buddhist texts contained an enormous wealth of *kīla* lore, but I suppose that the three *ācārya* also incorporated into their definitive résumé all details of cult and practice found acceptable to them – whatever their school of origin. All such lore was then tailored by them to fit neatly into the system of a Vajrakīla *maṇḍala*. The probable effect of this ratification was actually to create a cult of Vajrakīla where none existed before, and thus to divide all *kīla* lore into two camps: Vajrakīla cult and non-Vajrakīla cult. Subsequent to this, the cult of Vajrakīla having been propagated in Tibet by its originators, it flourished there and continued to evolve. Perhaps it also flourished in Nepal and India for some time, for Tibetan historians contend that it did so, but thus far we have seen little evidence to support this. Later Indian exegetes, such as the peerless Abhayākaragupta, and later canonical texts such as the *Kālacakra-tantra*, describe the rite of *kīlana* without reference to the deity Vajrakīla.

Among Tibetan texts, the *Phur 'grel 'bum nag* in 115 folios presents itself as the complete explication (*bshad 'bum,* 'the hundred thousand words of elucidation') of Kīla lore, and claims to represent the thoughts or intention (*dgongs pa*) of the three *ācārya*. It is said to have been transmitted by Padmasambhava to Ye-shes mtsho-rgyal who was entrusted with the dissemination of its knowledge. It is a *bka' ma* text, respected as authoritative by all Tibetan schools – both *bka' lugs* and *gter lugs*. This text, then, is held to stand at the turning point in the formation of a Vajrakīla cult from the 'one hundred thousand ideas' concerning the ritual *kīla*.[838]

When discussing the Vajrakīla *maṇḍala*, the *Phur 'grel 'bum nag* speaks of five supreme sons: Buddhakīla, Vajrakīla, Ratnakīla, Padmakīla, and Karmakīla. The fundamental deities of the *maṇḍala* are thus 51 in number: Vajrakīla and Tṛptacakra in the centre, the five supreme sons, the *daśakrodharāja* and their consorts, their 20 animal-headed messengers, and the four goddesses who guard the gates. As we have seen above, however, the Byang-gter tradition presents the *maṇḍala* with an irregular number of supreme sons: often three, sometimes four or five, occasionally twenty-one. Our Byang-gter tradition thus appears to contain archaic elements, perhaps directly derived from Indic lore, representing earlier

838 This text has been translated in full in my *A Bolt of Lightning from the Blue*.

stages in the evolution of the Vajrakīla *maṇḍala*, for it is only in the later commentarial literature of this school that we meet with references to Kīla of the five *kula*.

SDPT 313 shows that within the *yogatantra,* eight *krodharāja* are accompanied by eight animal-headed messengers: lion-, tiger-, owl-, crow-, bull-, snake-, stag- and pig-headed assistants. Thus we suppose that later Indian texts describing ten *krodharāja* may well have presented these kings together with an expanded series of animal-headed assistants. Eventually their number reached twenty. Early sources seem ambiguous with respect to the gender of these emanations. The Tibetan *bka' ma* tradition presents them in pairs; males to the right and females to the left. The Byang-gter tradition studied here presents them all as female. Such details, therefore, may well have remained still undetermined at the time of their original transmission to Tibet. Only through the continued study of Indic documents may we hope to develop a clearer picture of the evolutionary path trodden by these 20 gods.

As for the fundamental texts upon which the Northern Treasures tradition is said to be founded (especially the two root *tantra* analysed above in Chapter Five), we have seen that these contain a great deal of material in common with the VKMK, the sole root *tantra* to be included within the *bKa' 'gyur.* These texts, however, are unlikely to be known in schools other than the Byang-gter, for each of the many different Buddhist traditions of Vajrakīla in Tibet presents itself as stemming from separate root texts. Of particular interest in this regard are those Byang-gter documents dealing with the episode of the scorpion guru and the aetiology of the *mahottarakīla* cycle. It seems that this is one area of Kīla myth that is dealt with only marginally in the literature of other traditions. According to the *Phur 'grel 'bum nag*, the *mūlatantra* of Vajrakīla doctrines is the *rTsa thung rdo rje khros pa* (NGB 317, 17 folios).[839] Elsewhere, also, a great number of other *mūlatantra* are cited, and all of them are supposed to have come from India.

Although there can be no certainty at this stage that the various *mūlatantra* of Vajrakīla were actually written in India, there can surely be no doubt that their contents are of Indic origin. This mass of Indian material, however, may have been only partially systematised at the time of its

---

839 This is possibly, also, the text referred to above on page 189. Note, however, the caveat in footnote 447 concerning the firm identification of these texts.

transference to Tibet. In many respects, the eighth century texts of the *bka' ma* traditions appear better organised than the later *gter ma* discoveries of Rig-'dzin rgod-ldem. Since the overwhelming majority of documents in the Byang-gter school are said to have been delivered as oral instruction by the teacher Padmasambhava, it seems that we witness in these documents vital phases in the evolution of the cult of Vajrakīla.

Many of the rites of Vajrakīla, said to have been derived from these *mūlatantra,* are self-evidently modelled on paradigmatic norms of tantric Buddhist praxis. The rites of assembled offerings (*gaṇacakra*) and longevity (*āyurvidhi*)[840] and so on, looked at above, differ in no fundamental fashion from their counterparts in the religious cycles of other Vajrayāna deities. I suppose, therefore, that the three *ācārya* of India and Nepal took the basic fivefold pattern of the *yoganiruttara maṇḍala* as their starting point and carefully wove into that pattern all their combined knowledge of the *kīla.* Working this knowledge into a Buddhist framework must have involved some moral re-evaluation of the material to hand, much of which was possibly derived from village witchcraft of unsavoury character. Thus, the Buddhist *yogin* entering the *maṇḍala* of Vajrakīla takes a vow of 'wrathful compassion' and strives to master the rites of the *kīla* by means of which his vow will be fulfilled when the world is liberated from evil. Outwardly, the rites are explained for the slaying of wrath. Inwardly, they are explained for the destruction of desire, and, secretly, for the destruction of ignorance. These, however, are merely rites on the level of mental construct (*prapañca*). Ultimately, the yogin strives for the nail of the *trikāya* which is free of any such fabrication and, piercing the *dharmadhātu,* he slays all characteristics in their own place and realises unbounded buddhahood for the benefit of all beings.

840 Compare the longevity rites detailed above in Chapter Eleven with those explained by Tibetan physicians on the basis of Indian medical *tantra.* Yuri Parfionovitch *et al, Tibetan Medical Paintings*, plates 52-53

APPENDIX I

Contents of the *Phur pa dril sgrub* (collection A)
(Except for a few minor changes, noted below, this collection has been reproduced as Vol.14 of the *Phur pa phyogs bsgrigs* compilation)

A1) Phur pa che mchog gi them byang rin chen gter mdzod (1) (2 folios)
(Included within the longer text C15, E2)

A2) rDo rje phur pa spu gri nag po rab tu gsang ba'i rgyud (5) (7 folios)
(*Śrīvajrakīlapotrihala-tantra* Found also as B31, C19 & E21)
(Missing from *Phur pa phyogs bsgrigs*)

A3) rDo rje phur pa thugs gsang ba sku'i rgyud (19) (10 folios)
(*Vajrakīlacittaguhyakāya-tantra* Found also as B10, C1 & E3)
(Replaced with a new ms in *Phur pa phyogs bsgrigs*)

A4) rDo rje phur pa'i bka' sgo (39) (3 folios)
(Replaced with a new ms in *Phur pa phyogs bsgrigs*)

A5) rDo rje phur pa'i 'dzab rig 'dzin chen po'i gter ma (45) (Single folio)
(Found also as B43, E6 & D47)

A6) rDo rje phur pa'i bstod pa (47) (6 folios)
(Found also as E24. Cf. B35 etc.)

A7) Phur bsrung gi bskul (59) (4 folios. Unique to this collection)

A8) Phur pa che mchog gi dbang chu (67) (12 folios)
(Found also as B12, C5 & E8)

A9) dKar po lam gyi sgron ma (91) (4 folios)
(Found also as B15, C6 & E9)

A10) bKa' nyan lcags kyi ber ka (99) (2 folios.) (This and the next text;)

A11) Nag po dug gi spu gri (103) (5 folios) (are both found also as B19 & C7, in which the two texts are placed together under a single title.)
(Found also as C10 & E10)

A12) bCom ldan 'das 'phrin las phur pa'i sbyin sreg gi cho ga bskal pa'i me dpungs (113) (Single folio. Copied out by different hands twice in this volume. Found also as E29)

A13) rDo rje phur pa'i mnan bsreg 'phang gsum (117) (3 folios)
(Found also as B20, C11 & E12)

A14) rDo rje phur pa'i spu gri nag po'i dbang chog (123) (8 folios)
(Found also as B63, C20 & E30)

A15) rDo rje phur pa'i rgyun gtor gyi rim pa (139) (Single folio)
(Found also as E32 & as the first part of C32 which is a longer, more comprehensive text)

A16) rDo rje phur pa'i drag po'i bzlas pa (141) (Single folio)
(Found also as B57 & E33 & included in C32)

A17) rDo rje phur pa'i chos nyid kyi bzlas pa (143) (Single folio)
(Found also as B61 & E34)

A18) rDo rje phur pa'i tshe sgrub (145) (4 folios)
(Found also as B22, C12 & E13)

A19) rDo rje phur pa'i tshe dbang (153) (5 folios)
(Found also as B23 & E14. Missing from *Phur pa phyogs bsgrigs*)

A20) rDo rje phur pa'i las thams cad kyi don bsdus pa drag sngags kyi rtsa ba (163) (Single folio. Found also as B60 & E36)
(Included within the "compendium of *mantra*" C23)

A21) rDo rje phur pa'i za tshogs rgyas pa (165) (2 folios)
(Found also as A22 & E17)

A22) rDo rje phur pa'i bza' tshogs rgyas pa (171)
(taught by Padmasambhava) =A21 =E17

A23) rDo rje phur pa zas tshogs (175) (Single folio)
(Found also as B24 & C14)

A24) rDo rje phur pa'i tsha tsha (177) (Single folio)
(Found also as B24, C14 & E19)

A25) gSang ba'i rin po che'i dngos grub blang ba (179) (Single folio)
(Found also as C15 & E26 & included as a preface to C1)

A26) Drag sngags kyi rdo rje phur pa'i 'di khyad par 'phags pa'i lo rgyus (181) (Single page. Found also as B51)

A27) rDo rje phur pa gong khug ma (182) (Single page only)
(Quoted in B4 and included as an appendix to C21)

A28) Phur pa'i zur 'debs (183) (7 folios. Found also as B25, C16 & E20)

A29) Phur pa drag sngags kyi sgrub thabs rgyun khyer lha brag gter gyi yang bcud (197) (4 folios. Found also as E38)

A30) rDo rje phur pa'i lugs kyi sde brgyad bsrung bzlog (205) (3 folios)
(Found also as B58 & E40, included in C29)

A31) Phur pa me lce'i 'phreng ba'i le'u nyi shu pa khol du byung ba (211)
(5 folios. A solitary chapter from a lost *tantra*.
Found also as C13 & E15)

A32) dPal rdo rje phur pa'i rtsa ba dril sgrub kyi sgrub thabs (221)
(5 folios. A *sādhana* taught to Padmasambhava by the early *atiyoga* master Śrīsiṁha. Found also as B41, B53 & C33)

A33) Phur pa'i rgyu tshad dbyibs sbas tshul mnga' gsol dus tshod dang bcas bstan pa (231) (7 folios. Unique to this collection but extensively quoted in B4. Cf. B30 & B55)

A34) rDo rje phur pa'i spyod lam rgyun gyi rnal 'byor (245) (Single folio)
(Found also as C26)

A35) rDo rje phur pa drag sngags spu gri'i sgrub thabs (247) (3 folios)
(A *sādhana* taught to Padmasambhava by the early *atiyoga* master Śrīsiṁha. Found as the first of several texts in B32, etc.)

A36) bCom ldan 'das dpal rdo rje gzhon nu'i 'phrin las thun mong ma yin pa (253) (13 folios. Found also as A48 & E44)

A37) rDo rje phur pa'i man ngag rtsa thung (279) (3 folios)
(Found also as B56 & E42)

A38) rDo rje phur pa spu gri'i bskul (285) (2 folios)
(Unique to this collection)

A39) rDo rje phur pa'i sbyin sreg (289) (Single folio)
(Found also as A40, included in the 3-fold rite at A13, etc.)
(Missing from *Phur pa phyogs bsgrigs*)

A40) rDo rje phur pa'i sbyin sreg (291) =A39

A41) rDo rje phur pa'i rgyun 'khyer gtor bsngos (295) (3 folios)
(Found also as E28)

A42) rDo rje phur pa'i mnan pa'i las (301) (2 folios)
(Unique to this collection)

A43) Phur pa yang gsang gi khro bo rol pa'i gtor bzlog (305) (11 folios)
(Found also as A49 & E39)

A44) Byang gter phur pa 'bring po spu gri'i bsnyen sgrub kha 'phral ba'i lhan thabs yang yig 'dod dgu'i gter mdzod (327) (38 folios)
(A liturgical arrangement by Padma 'phrin-las, copied out by the scribe Padma bun-bde. Also found as E55)

A45) Byang gter rdo rje phur pa'i thugs kyi 'phrin las (403) (6 folios)
(A xylograph found also as mss at B42 & C35)

A46) Byang gter phur pa spu gri las bzhi'i sbyin sreg 'phrin las kun 'grub (415) (26 folios)
(Written by Padma 'phrin-las in 1695. Found also as B9)

A47) Byang gter phur pa'i brgyud 'debs (467) (3 folios)
(Written by Padma 'phrin-las. Found also as B29 & B46)

A48) Khro bo bcu'i phur pa dril sgrub kyi las byang sbrul gyi chun po gnam lcags spu gri (471)
=A36 =E44 (with added prayers by Blo-bzang mthu-stobs)

A49) Byang gter phur pa khro bo rol pa'i gtor bzlog bdud sde phyer 'thag (by Dalai Lama V) (513)
=A43 =E39 (which include extra liturgy by Padma 'phrin-las)

A50) Rang bsrung zab mo (by Padma las-'brel-rtsal) (561) (2 folios)
(Unique to this collection)

A51) Byang gter phur pa'i sri gnon gyi ngag 'don chog khrigs rdo rje'i lhun po (by Padma 'phrin-las) (565) (26 folios. Found also as E58)

A52) Phur pa'i sri chung bcu gsum mnon pa'i lhan thabs rab gsal me long (Written by Padma 'phrin-las in 1701) (617) (8 folios) (Found also as B64 & E59)

A53) bCom ldan 'das rdo rje gzhon nu 'bring po spu gri'i sgrub chen gyi chog khrigs lag len snying po rab gsal (633) (48 folios) (Written by Padma 'phrin-las in 1686. Found also as B3 & E60)

Contents of *Phur-pa Texts of the Byang-gter Tradition*
(collection B) Volume 1
(Except for a few minor changes, noted below, this set of texts has been reproduced as Vol.13 of the *Phur pa phyogs bsgrigs* compilation, 46-58)

B1) Phur pa dril sgrub thugs kyi 'phrin las ngag 'don bklags chog tu bkod pa (by ’Phrin-las bdud-’joms) (1) (481) (14 folios) (Unique to this collection)

B2) Phur pa drag sngags kyi smad las dgra bgegs sgrol byed drag po zor gyi man ngag rno myur las kyi mtshon cha (29) (509) (19 folios) (Written by 'Phrin-las bdud-'joms. Unique to this collection)

B3) bCom ldan 'das rdo rje gzhon nu 'bring po spu gri'i sgrub chen gyi chog khrigs lag len snying po rab gsal (Written by Padma ’phrin-las) (69) (549) =A53 =E60

B4) Byang gter phur pa'i dbang gi lo rgyus legs par bshad pa nor bu'i do shal (173) (653) (16 folios) (Written by 'Phrin-las bdud-'joms. Unique to this collection)

B5) Byang gter phur pa spu gri'i dkyil 'khor du dbang bskur ba'i cho ga rin chen bum bzang (207) (687) (70 folios) (Written by Padma 'phrin-las. Also found as E57. Cf. C40)

B6) Byang gter phur pa lugs gsum gyi bsnyen sgrub las sbyor bya tshul bdud sde'i gYul las rnam par rgyal ba (347) (827) (10 folios) (Written by Dalai Lama V in 1660. Unique to this collection)

B7) Lha brag phur pa'i bsnyen yig gsal ba'i sgron me (367) (846) (Written by Dalai Lama V at the request of sTobs-ldan dpa'-bo 6 folios. Unique to this collection)

B8) 'Dod 'jo'i bum bzang gi nang dkyil sogs kyi dris lan (379) (A text unrelated to the Vajrakīla cycle. Written by sMin-gling lo-chen Dharmaśrī. 34 folios. Missing from the *Phur pa phyogs bsgrigs*. Unique to this collection)

B9) Byang gter phur pa spu gri las bzhi'i sbyin sreg 'phrin las kun 'grub (by Padma ’phrin-las) (447) (857) =A46

B10) rDo rje phur pa thugs gsang ba sku'i rgyud (499) (Missing from the *Phur pa phyogs bsgrigs*) =A3 =C1 =E3

B11) rDo rje phur pa che mchog gi 'phrin las (523) (909) (20 folios) (Found also as C4 & D5)
B12) Phur pa che mchog gi dbang chu gter ma (563) (949) =A8 =C5 =E8
B13) dPal rdo rje phur pa che mchog gi lo rgyus (591) (977) (3 folios) (Unique to this collection)
B14) bCom ldan 'das rdo rje phur pa smad nag po dug gi 'khor lo rab tu gsang ba (597) (993) (5 folios. Unique to this collection)
B15) rNam gsum srog gi 'khor lo (607) =A9 =C6 =E9
B16) rDo rje phur pa che mchog gi dam can gnad stabs kyi man ngag 'khor lo bri lugs dang bcas pa (615) (1001) (3 folios) (Unique to this collection)

Contents of *Phur-pa Texts of the Byang-gter Tradition*
(collection B) Volume 2
(Except for a few minor changes, noted below, this set of texts has been reproduced as Vol.13 of the *Phur pa phyogs bsgrigs* compilation, 1-45)

B17) bCom ldan 'das rdo rje phur pa'i smad las nag po dug gi spu gri rab tu gsang ba (1) (9 folios. Unique to this collection)
B18) Phur pa'i sri mnan (19) (4 folios) Also found as E48, commented upon by A50 and expanded with commentary in the ritual texts A51 & A52, etc.)
B19) rDo rje phur pa'i sgrub chen bka' nyan lcags kyi ber ka (27) =A10 + 11 (=C10 =E10), =C7
B20) rDo rje phur pa'i mnan sregs 'phang gsum (39) =A13 =C11 =E12
B21) rDo rje phur pa'i sbyin sreg gi cho ga (45) (4 folios) (Unique to this collection)
B22) rDo rje phur pa'i tshe sgrub (53) =A18 =C12 =E13
B23) Phur pa'i tshe dbang (61) =A19
B24) rDo rje phur pa'i zas tshogs dang tshva tshva (71) =A23 + 24, =C14
B25) rDo rje phur pa'i zur 'debs (81) =A28 =C16 =E20
B26) Phur pa rig 'dzin gyi bskul (95) (3 folios. Found also as C36 & E46)
B27) Phur pa rig 'dzin skul (101) (11 folios. Unique to this collection)
B28) Bse lcags dung gsum srog gi tsitta (123) (5 folios) (Unique to this collection)
B29) Phur pa byang gter gyi brgyud 'debs dpe grangs dang bcas pa (133) (2 folios. Related to texts A47 & B46 but not identical)
B30) rDo rje phur pa'i drag sngags zab pa'i lo rgyus (137) (4 folios) (Found also as B55, C18 & E31)
B31) dPal rdo rje phur pa spu gri nag po rab tu gsang ba'i rgyud (145) =A2 =C19 =E21

B32) Thugs kyi snying po gsang ba phur gcig ma'i sgrub thabs rdo rje phur pa'i drag sngags spu gri'i sgrub thabs (159) (7 folios) (Includes A35 as the first of 7 short but seemingly unrelated texts. Found also as C21, C22 & E52)

B33) Phur pa drag sngags kyi 'phrin las (173) (20 folios) (The longest of the *gter ma* texts. Found also as C24 & E23)

B34) rDo rje phur pa yang gsang spu gri phur gcig ma'i nyams len rgyun khyer (213) (4 folios. Unique to this collection)

B35) dPal rdo rje phur pa drag sngags spu gri nag po'i bstod bskul (221) (5 folios. Found also as B39 & C25)

B36) dPal rdo rje phur pa'i srung ma'i bskul te dam can sgos bskul (235) (3 folios. Unique to this collection)

B37) rDzas kyi phur pa shin tu zab pa (243) (3 folios) (Unique to this collection)

B38) Phur pa'i bstod pa chen mo (249) (3 folios) (Unique to this collection. Cf. B35, etc.)

B39) rDo rje phur pa'i bstod bskul (255) =B35 =C25

B40) Phur pa rtsa ba'i sgrub thabs kyi gleng gzhi (271) (4 folios) (Unique to this collection)

B41) dPal rdo rje phur pa'i rtsa ba dril sgrub kyi sgrub thabs (279) =A32 =B53 =C33

B42) bCom ldan 'das dpal rdo rje gzhon nu'i thugs kyi 'phrin las (299) =A45 =C35

B43) rDo rje phur pa'i 'dzab rig 'dzin chen po'i gter ma (308) (2 folios) (Found also as A5, B43 & E47)

B44) (Untitled offering ritual) (311) (Single page) (Unique to this collection)

B45) rDo rje phur pa skyed la bcang ba'i man ngag (313) (4 folios) (Unique to this collection)

B46) Lha brag phur bu'i brgyud 'debs byin rlabs gter mdzod (321) (3 folios. Written by Padma 'phrin-las. Unique to this collection as an independent text, but Cf. A47 & B29)

B47) Lha brag gter byon gyi phur pa lcags khang drag sngags spu gri'i las byang 'jigs med rdo rje pha lam (327) (25 folios.) (Written by Dalai Lama V in 1643. Unique to this collection)

B48) Phur pa spu gri las tshogs rdzas kyi mthu chen bco brgyad (377) (4 folios. Found also as E41)

B49) rDo rje phur pa'i spyod lam rgyun gyi rnal 'byor gyi man ngag brgyad pa (385) (2 folios. Found also as E35)

B50) Ser ba dong bzlog (389) (2 folios. Found also as E27)

B51) rDo rje phur pa spu gri drag sngags lugs kyi khyad par 'phags pa'i lo rgyus (392) =A26

B52) rDo rje phur pa spu gri lha nag srog gi spu gri'i gsal byed (393) (2 folios. Found also as B54, E37 & E51)

B53) dPal rdo rje phur pa'i rtsa ba dril sgrub kyi sgrub thabs (397) =A32 =B41 =C33

B54) rDo rje phur pa srog gi spu gri (413) =B52 =E37 =E51

B55) rDo rje phur pa drag sngags zab mo'i lo rgyus dang rdo rje phur pa'i rgyu dang tshad bstan pa (417) =B30 =C18 =E31

B56) rDo rje phur pa'i man ngag rtsa thung (423) =A37 =E42

B57) rDo rje phur pa'i drag po'i bzlas pa (427) =A16 =E33, included in C32

B58) rDo rje phur pa'i lugs kyi sde brgyad bsrung bzlog (431) =A30 =E40, included in C29

B59) dPal rdo rje gzhon nu'i nyams len rgyun 'khyer (437) (2 folios) (Found also as E45)

B60) rDo rje phur pa'i las thams cad kyi don bsdus pa'i rtsa ba (441) =A20 =E36, included within C23

B61) rDo rje phur pa'i chos nyid kyi bzlas pa (445) =A17 =E34

B62) Drag sngags kyi ti ka bse sgrom ma (449) (2 folios) (Unique to this collection)

B63) rDo rje phur pa spu gri nag po'i dbang chog (453) =A14 =C20 =E30

B64) Phur pa'i las mtha' sri chung bcu gsum mnan pa'i lhan thabs rab gsal me long (589) (465-479) =A52 =E59

B65) Byang gter phur pa drag sngags kyi gtor ma'i dpe'u ris blo thog nas bris pa (605) (Missing from the *Phur pa phyogs bsgrigs*) (4 pages that must be placed side by side in order to complete the drawings thereon. Unique to this collection.)

Contents of the *Byang gter phur pa'i skor* (collection C)

C1) rDo rje phur pa thugs gsang ba sku'i rgyud (1) =A3 =B10 =E3

C2) Dam can lto log gi ngan sngags (21) (3 folios) (Unique to this collection)

C3) lCags sgrog 'khril ba'i man ngag (27) (3 folios) (Unique to this collection)

C4) Phur pa che mchog gi 'phrin las (33) =B11 =E5

C5) Phur pa che mchog gi dbang chu (63) =A8 =B12 =E8

C6) dKar po lam gi sgron ma (rNam gsum srog gi 'khor lo) (81) =A9 =B15 =E9

C7) bKa' nyan lcags kyi ber ka (87) =A10 + 11, =B19

C8) rDo rje phur pa'i dam can gnad rem (97) (2 folios) (Unique to this collection)

C9) rTsa gsum zang gyi sgo 'byed (101) (3 folios)
(Unique to this collection)
C10) Nag po dug gi 'khor lo'i spu gri (107)
=A11 =E11 (included in B19 & C7)
C11) Phur pa'i mnan sreg zor gsum (117) =A13 =B20 =E12
C12) rDo rje phur pa'i tshe sgrub (123) =A18 =B22 =E13
C13) rDo rje phur pa'i tshe chog (129) =A31 =E15 =E16
C14) rDo rje phur pa'i zas tshogs dang tsha tsha (139) =A23 + 24, =B24
C15) rDo rje phur pa'i che mchog gi dbang gi brgyud rim them byang zab mo (143) (2 folios) = E2, incorporating A1
C16) Phur pa'i zur 'debs (147) =A28 =B25 =E20
C17) rDo rje phur pa gsum kyi rnal 'byor (155) (3 folios)
(Unique to this collection)
C18) rDo rje phur pa'i drag sngags zab pa'i lo rgyus (161)
=B30 =B55 =E31
C19) dPal rdo rje phur pa spu gri nag po rab tu gsang ba'i rgyud (167)
=A2 =B31 =E21
C20) rDo rje phur pa spu gri nag po'i dbang chog (177) =A14 =B63 =E30
C21) Shi ri sing has gsang ba phur gcig ma thugs kyi snying po (189)
=B32 =C22 =E52 Includes A27 as an appendix.
C22) Yang snying thugs kyi phur gcig ma (201) =B32 =C21 =E52
C23) Phur pa thams cad kyi rtsa ba bsdus pa drag po sngags kyi rtsa ba dang phur pa drag sngags kyi rtsa ba dang phur pa bsam sgral ma dang phur pa srog gi spu gri dang phur pa lus la bcangs thabs rnams (215) (6 folios) (A compendium of *mantra* including A20, B60, E36)
(Unique to this collection)
C24) rDo rje phur pa drag sngags kyi 'phrin las (227) =B33 =E23
C25) Phur pa lcags rkang nag po'i bstod pa (267) =B35 =B39. Cf. A6
C26) rDo rje phur pa'i spyod lam rgyun gyi rnal 'byor (279) =A34
C27) Drag po'i 'dzab dgongs (283) (Single page only)
(Unique to this collection)
C28) Phur pa drag sngags 'dus pa (285) (10 folios)
(Unique to this collection)
C29) rDo rje phur pa gcig lugs kyi sde brgyad bsrungs bzlog (305)
(6 folios. Bears the same title as A30, B58 & E40 but lengthened by the addition of many supplementary *mantra,* etc.)
C30) Phur pa yang gsang spu gri'i las mtha' 'sdung po sri nan pa (317)
(4 folios. Unique to this collection)
C31) bDud kyi bar chad 'dul ba'i thabs (325) (5 folios)
(Unique to this collection)
C32) rDo rje phur pa'i rgyun gyi spyod lam (335) (4 folios)
(Unique to this collection but includes A16, B57, E33)

C33) rDo rje phur pa'i rtsa ba dril sgrub (343) =A32 =B41 =B53
C34) rDo rje phur pa'i dril sgrub kyi 'phrin las chen mo (361) (7 folios) (Unique to this collection but related to A32, B41, B53 & C33)
C35) bCom ldan 'das rdo rje gzhon nu'i thugs kyi 'phrin las phur pa'i dril sgrub gyi 'phrin las (375) =A45 =B42
C36) rDo rje phur pa'i bskul (383) =B26 =E46
C37) Las tshogs rin chen khang bu las phya 'phrin nor bu'i mchog rgyal bla dgu (389) (19 folios. A Byang-gter *tantra* unique to this collection. Unrelated to the Vajrakīla cycle, this text describes a conversation between the gods Indra and Brahmā.)
C38) Phur mchod dang 'phrin brtsol sgrags pa (427) (5 folios) (Unique to this collection)
C39) Phur pa'i snying thig yang gsang spu gri 'bar ba'i bsgrub thabs (437) (8 folios. Followed by a commentary in 4 folios by Bla-ma mgon-po. Unique to this collection)
C40) sPu gri'i dkyil 'khor du dbang bskur ba'i cho ga klags chog ru brkod pa Vaidurya'i bum bzang zhes bya ba (461) (58 folios) (Written in 1766 by 'Phrin-las bdud-'joms) (Modelled on B5, a previous ritual by Padma 'phrin-las called *Rin chen bum bzang*. Unique to this collection)

Contents of the *Lha nag gi chos tshan*, by bsTan-'dzin nor-bu (collection D)

Thog mar dkar chag (List of contents plus preamble) (1) (4 folios)
D1) Byang gter sngon 'gro gzer lnga (9) (4 folios) (Unique to this collection)
D2) dPal chen rdo rje gzhon nu'i phrin las kyi khrigs kha sgrol byed drag po'i rno mtshon gdug pa tshar gcod (17) (29 folios) =E53
D3) Chad tho (75) (Single folio. Unique to this collection)
D4) rJes chog smon lam (77) (Single folio. Unique to this collection)
D5) O rgyan smon lam gyi don bsdus (79) (Single folio) (Composed by Ye-shes mtsho-rgyal. Unique to this collection)
D6) bKra shis kyi rim pa (81) (4 folios. Unique to this collection)
D7) rDo rje gling pa'i gter byon rtsa gsum spyi'i bskang bsdus (89) (4 folios. From the treasure revelations of rDo-rje gling-pa, this text is widely used in Byang-gter rituals)
D8) Drag po rang byung rang shar gyi rgyud las byung ba'i dong sprugs (97) (7 folios. Unique to this collection)
D9) Phur pa'i dkyil 'khor yongs rdzogs kyi bshags pa (111) (Single folio) (Unique to this collection)

D10) Byang gter guru drag rtsal mthing kha'i sgrub thabs rnal 'byor par nyer mkho gtor bsngos don gnyis lhun grub ma (113) (3 folios) (Unique to this collection)
D11) dPal ye shes mgon po phyag bzhi pa'i phrin las (119) (14 folios) (Unique to this collection)
D12) mGon po bstan bsrung yongs rdzogs kyi phrin las (147) (4 folios) (Unique to this collection)
D13) Ekajaṭi'i gsang ba yang snying 'dus pa'i phrin las (155) (4 folios) (Unique to this collection)
D14) bKa' bsrung gter bdag mchod pa'i las rim (163) (19 folios) (Unique to this collection)
D15) gZa' bdud dug gi spu gri'i skor las gza' bdud kyi gsol kha (201) (4 folios. Unique to this collection)
D16) rGyal po sku lnga 'khor bcas kyi gsol kha phrin las don bcu ma (209) (20 folios. A Treasure revelation of mNga-bdag nyang-ral. Unique to this collection)
D17) rGyal chen sku lnga'i gsol kha nor bu'i phreng ba (248) (Single folio) (Unique to this collection)
D18) gNod sbyin tsi'u dmar po'i gsol kha rgyas pa mnga' ris paṇ chen rin po che'i gter byon rtsa ba'i don rgya cher bkral ba dbang drag dus kyi pho nya (250) (19 folios. Unique to this collection)
D19) gNod sbyin chen po'i gsol kha'i sgrub thabs (288) (6 folios) (Unique to this collection)
D20) Chos skyong gnod sbyin tsi'u dmar po'i bskang bshags (294) (Single folio. Unique to this collection)
D21) gNod sbyin bstod bskul bsdus pa (296) (Single folio) (Unique to this collection)
D22) Ja mchod thun min zhig (297) (Single folio) (Unique to this collection)
D23) bKa' bsrung bsdus mchod (299) (Single folio) (Unique to this collection)
D24) bCom ldan 'das dpal rdo rje gzhon nu'i drag po gtor ma'i las rim 'phang gzor gyi khrigs kha gnam lcags rdo rje'i thog 'bebs (301) (29 folios. Unique to this collection)
D25) Brubs khung bskyed chog dang 'gugs bzhugs (359) (3 folios) (Unique to this collection)
D26) Lha dbye'i rim pa (364) (Single folio. Unique to this collection)
D27) Byang gter dpal chen rdo rje gzhon nu'i bzlog chung (365) (4 folios) (Unique to this collection)
D28) bKa' brgyad bzlog pa (373) (Single folio. Unique to this collection)
D29) dKon mchog spyi bskul (374) (3 folios. Unique to this collection)

D30) Thugs sgrub hūṁ gi bde gshegs spyi bskul (380) (4 folios)
(Unique to this collection)
D31) bCom ldan 'das phrin las phur pa'i sbyin bsreg gi cho ga go bde bklags chog bskal pa'i me dpung (388) (9 folios)
(Unique to this collection)
D32) 'Jig rten me lha thab bsal bya ba (406) (Single folio)
(Unique to this collection)
D33) Byang gter rdo rje phur pa'i sgrub chen gyi phyag len snying po sbyor ba bklags chog zur du bkol ba (408-448) (21 folios)
(Unique to this collection)

Contents of the *dPal chen rdo rje gzhon nu'i chos skor phyogs bsgrigs*
(Short title: *Phur pa phyogs bsgrigs*) Volume 12 (collection E)

E1) Byang gter phur pa'i sgrub bskor chos tshan kyi dpe tho (1)
(2 folios. Unique to this collection)
E2) dBang gi rim pa gsang ba rin po che'i dngos grub blang ba'i rim pa zhes bya ba rdo rje phur pa'i mi 'gyur rin chen mdzod kyi them byang (5) (3 folios) = C15, incorporating A1
E3) rDo rje phur pa'i thugs gsang ba sku'i rgyud zhes bya dbus phyogs bzhugs (11) (14 folios) =A3 =B31 =C19
E4) Phur pa'i bka' bsgo (39) (3 folios) =A4
E5) Che mchog rdo rje gzhon nu'i 'phrin las (45) (23 folios) =B11 =C4
E6) rDo rje phur pa'i 'dzab bskul (91) (3 folios) =A5 =B43 =D47
E7) rDo rje phur pa'i bstod pa dad bskul gyi rim pa rnams (97)
(11 folios) =A6 & 7
E8) Phur pa che mchog gi dbang chu rin po che dbang gi mdzod (119)
(14 folios) =A8 =B12 =C5
E9) dKar po lam gyi sgron ma zhes bya ba rnams gsum srog gi 'khor lo (147) (5 folios) =A9 =B15 =C6
E10) bKa' nyan lcags kyi ber ka (157) (3 folios) =A10 =C10
E11) Nag po dug gi spu gri (163) (6 folios) =A11 =C10
E12) rDo rje phur pa'i mnan bsreg 'phang gsum dbu phyogs (175)
(4 folios) = A13 =B20 =C11
E13) rDo rje phur pa'i tshe sgrub (183) (5 folios) =A18 =B22 =C12
E14) rDo rje phur pa'i tshe'i las byang (193) (6 folios) =A19 =B23
E15) Phur pa'i me lce 'phreng ba'i le'u nyi shu pa khol du phyung ba (205) (6 folios) =A31 =C13 =D16
E16) rDo rje phur pa'i tshe chog (217) (7 folios) =A31 =C13 =D15

E17) rDo rje phur pa'i bza' tshogs rgyas pa (231) (6 folios) =A21 =A22

E18) rDo rje phur pa'i bza' ba rgyun gyi ting 'dzin gyi rnal 'byor (237) (2 folios. Unique to this collection)

E19) rDo rje phur pa'i tsha tsha'i las rim (241) (2 folios) =A24 =B24 =C14

E20) dPal rdo rje phur pa'i zur 'debs dbu phyogs (245) (9 folios) =A28 =B25 =C16

E21) dPal rdo rje phur pa'i spu gri nag po rab tu gsang ba'i rgyud (263) (9 folios) =A2 =B31 =C19

E22) Tshogs kyi mchod pa lhag ma dang bcas pa (281) (6 folios) (Unique to this collection)

E23) rDo rje phur pa'i drag sngags kyi 'phrin las (293) (33 folios) =B33 =C24

E24) dPal rdo rje phur pa'i bstod pa (359) (9 folios) (Unique to this collection)

E25) Phur pa spu gri las pho nya 'gugs 'dren gyi las byang (377) (3 folios. Unique to this collection)

E26) dPal rdo rje phur pa'i brgyud rim gsang ba rin po che dngos grub blang ba (383) (2 folios) =A25 =C15

E27) dPal rdo rje gzhon nu'i ser ba gdong bzlog (387) (2 folios) =B50

E28) dPal rdo rje phur pa'i rgyun khyer gtor bsngo (391) (3 folios) =A41

E29) bCom ldan 'das 'phrin las phur pa'i sbyin sreg gi cho ga bskal pa'i me dpungs (397) (3 folios) =A12

E30) rDo rje phur pa'i spu gri nag po'i dbang chog (403) (8 folios) =A14 =B63 =C20

E31) rDo rje phur pa'i drag sngags zab mo'i lo rgyus dang rdo rje phur pa'i rgyu dang tshad bstan pa (419) (4 folios) =B30 =B55 =C18

E32) rDo rje phur pa'i rgyun gtor gyi rim pa (427) (3 folios) =A15, included in C32

E33) rDo rje phur pa'i drag po'i bzlas pa (433) (2 folios) =A16 =B57, included in C32

E34) rDo rje phur pa'i chos nyid kyi bzlas pa (437) (2 folios) =A17 =B61

E35) rDo rje phur pa'i spyod lam rgyun gyi rnal 'byor gyi man ngag brgyad pa (441) (2 folios) =B49

E36) rDo rje phur pa'i las thams cad kyi don bsdus pa'i rtsa ba (445) (2 folios) =A20 =B60, included in C23

E37) rDo rje phur pa srog gi spu gri (449) (4 folios) =B52 =B54 =D51

E38) Phur pa drag sngags kyi sgrub thabs rgyun khyer lha brag gter gyi yang bcud (457) (4 folios) =A29

E39) Phur pa yang gsang gi khro bo rol pa'i gtor bzlog (465) (10 folios) =A43 =A49

E40) rDo rje phur pa'i lugs kyi sde brgyad bsrung bzlog (485) (4 folios) =A30 =B58, included in C29

E41) Phur pa spu gri'i las tshogs rdzas kyi mthu chen bco brgyad (493) (6 folios) =B48

E42) rDo rje phur pa'i man ngag rtsa 'thung (505) (3 folios) =A37 =B56

E43) rDo rje phur pa'i dril sgrub kyi 'phrin las (511) (13 folios) =A36 =A48 =D44

E44) bCom ldan 'das dpal rdo rje gzhon nu'i 'phrin las thun mong ma yin pa phur pa'i dril sgrub gyi 'phrin las (537) (13 folios) =A36 =A48 =D43

E45) dPal rdo rje gzhon nu'i nyams len rgyun 'khyer (563) (2 folios) =B59

E46) rDo rje phur pa'i bskul (567) (3 folios) =B26 =C3

E47) rDo rje phur pa'i dzab bskul (573) (3 folios) =A5 =B43 =D6

E48) Phur pa las kyi sri chung bcu gsum mnan pa'i sngags (579) (5 folios) =B18

E49) rDo rje phur pa'i las mtha' nor sgrub pa zab mo dzam bha la rigs brgyad kyi sgrub thabs (589) (4 folios)
(Written by Padma 'phrin-las. Unique to this collection)

E50) rDo rje phur pa gong khug ma zab mo'i lo rgyus (597) (2 folios)
(Written by Padma 'phrin-las. Unique to this collection)

E51) rDo rje phur pa spu gri lha nag srog gi spu gri'i gsal byed (601)
(Written by Padma 'phrin-las. 3 folios) =B52 =B54 =D37

E52) Thugs kyi snying po gsang ba phur gcig ma'i sgrub thabs rdo rje phur pa'i drag sngags spu gri'i sgrub thabs (607) (4 folios)
(Written by Padma 'phrin-las) =B32 =C21 =C22

E53) dPal rdo rje gzhon nu'i 'phrin las kyi chog khrigs sgrol byed drag po'i rno mtshon (615) (19 folios)
(Written by Padma 'phrin-las) =D2

E54) sTobs ldan dpa' bo ral pa'i thor tshugs can gyi mdzad pa'i phur pa'i bsnyen thabs (653) (8 folios)
(Written by sTobs-ldan dbang-po. Unique to this collection)

E55) Byang gter phur pa 'bring po spu gri'i bsnyen sgrub kha 'phral ba'i lhan thabs yang yig 'dod dgu'i gter mdzod (669) (40 folios)
(Written by Padma 'phrin-las) =A44

E56) Byang gter phur pa'i bsnyen bsgrub zungs 'brel gyis yi ge 'phrin las rab rgyas (749) (4 folios)
(Written by Padma 'phrin-las. Unique to this collection)

E57) Byang gter phur pa yang gsang spu gri'i dkyil 'khor du dbang bskur ba'i cho ga rin chen bum bzang zhes bya ba (757) (69 folios)
(Written by Padma 'phrin-las) =B5

E58) Byang gter phur pa'i sri gnon gyi ngag 'don chog khrigs rdo rje'i lhun po zhes bya ba (895) (23 folios)
(Written by Padma 'phrin-las) =A51

E59) Phur pa'i sri chung bcu gsum gnon pa'i lhan thabs rab gsal me long (941) (9 folios) =A52 =B64

E60) bCom ldan 'das rdo rje gzhon nu 'bring po spu gri'i sgrub chen gyi chog khrigs lag len snying po rab gsal (959) (59 folios)
(Written by Padma 'phrin-las) =A53

E61) Byang gter gyi chos skor rnams kyi spyi chings rin chen phreng ba zhes bya ba (1077) (62 folios)
(Written by Padma dbang-chen. Unique to this collection)

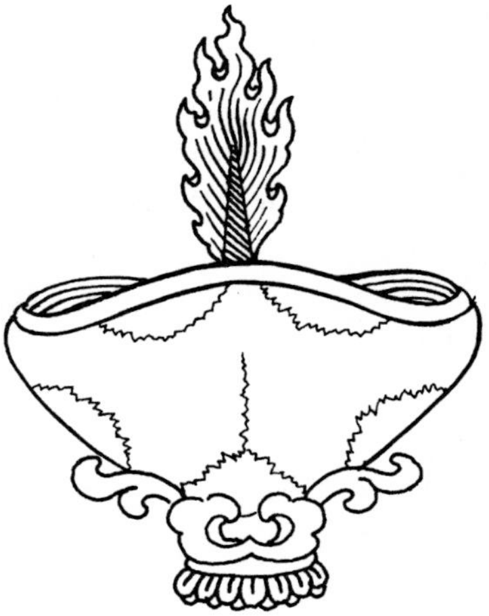

APPENDIX II
Kīla references in Sanskrit texts

Miscellaneous quotations of relevance for a study of *kīlanavidhi*, taken from a selection of Vajrayāna Buddhist texts:

Amoghapāśakalparājā [3b.3]

अगरुधूपेन सीमाबन्धो भस्मोदकेन सर्षपखदिरकीलकाद्यैः ॥

The boundaries are to be sealed using incense made of aloe wood, a mixture of ashes and water, with mustard seeds, or with *kīla* made of acacia wood, and so on.

[3b.5]

पञ्चरङ्गिकसूत्रमेकविंशतिवारान्परिजप्य चतुर्षु खदिरकीलकेषु बध्वा चतुर्दिशं निखन्तव्या महासीमाबन्धा भवन्ति ॥

The great sealing of the boundaries consists of reciting the *mantra* 21 times over a cord of five colours and tying it to four *kīla* made of acacia wood which are to be imbedded in the four directions.

Āryāmoghapāśanāmahṛdayam

सीमाबन्धं पञ्चरङ्गिकसूत्रमेकविंशतिवारान्परिजप्य चतुर्षु खदिर-कीलकेषु बध्वा चतुर्दिशं निखातव्यं सीमाबन्धो भविष्यति ॥

As for sealing the boundaries: With threads of five colours that have been empowered by 21 recitations of *mantra*, one ties together four acacia wood *kīla* that have been embedded in the four directions. Thus the boundaries become sealed.

Āryamañjuśrīmūlakalpa [p.37]

Speaking of the ground chosen for the construction of the *maṇḍala*:

तं पृथिवीप्रदेशं भूयो निःप्राणेनोदकेन पञ्चगव्यसन्मिश्रेण नदीकूल-मृत्तिकया मेध्यया वल्मीकमृत्तिकया वा यत्र प्राणका न सन्ति तया मृत्तिकया पूरयितव्यम् । पूरयित्वा च स्वाकोटितं समतलं समन्तात्

त्रिविधं मण्डलं यथेप्सितं कारयेत् । चतुर्दिक्षु चत्वारः खदिरकीलकां निखनेत् । क्रोधराजेनैव सप्ताभिमन्त्रितं कृत्वा । पञ्चरङ्गिकेण सूत्रेण सप्ताभिमन्त्रितेन क्रोधहृदयेन कृत्वा समन्ता तन्मण्डलं चतुरश्राकारेण वेष्टयेत् । एवं मध्यमे स्थाने एवमभ्यन्तरे चतुरश्राकारं कारयेत् ॥

That spot of earth which has been chosen as the ground is to be filled up and made good with mud, using filtered water,[841] with mud from the bank of a river mixed with the five products of a cow, or with the potent and ritually pure earth taken from an ant hill within which no living creatures were dwelling. Then, having made it good, properly level and smooth in all directions, one should construct the threefold *maṇḍala* in accordance with one's wishes. One should nail down four *kīla* made of acacia wood in the four directions, and they should be empowered by seven recitations of [the *mantra* of] the wrathful king. Then, with threads of five colours, empowered by seven recitations of the heart *mantra* of wrath,[842] that *maṇḍala* should be enclosed all around with the figure of a square. And, in the same way, one should mark out an intermediate square and an inner square.

Jñānodayatantra [p.1]

In discussing the correspondences between the human body and the layout of the *maṇḍala*, the text states: *romāṇi kīlakān*, "the hairs on the skin are *kīla*."

Āryamañjuśrīmūlakalpa [p.29]

Following a lengthy apotropaic *mantra*, the text states:

मुद्रा चात्र भवति महा शूलेति विख्याता सर्वविघ्नविनाशिका । अस्यैव क्रोधराजस्य हृदयम् । ॐ ह्रीं: ज्ञी: विकृतानन हूं सर्वशत्रूं नाशय स्तम्भय फट् फट् स्वाहा । अनेन मन्त्रेण सर्वशत्रूं महाशूलरोगेण चतुर्थकेन वा गृह्णापयति । शततजपेन वा यावद् रोचते । मैत्रतां वा न प्रतिपद्यते । अथ करुणाचित्तं लभते । जापान्ते मुक्तिर्न स्यात् । मृयत इति रत्नत्रयापकरिणां कर्तव्यं नाशेषं सौम्यचित्तानां मुद्रा महाशूलैव

841 "Without life," i.e. filtered so as become free of insects and fish, etc.

842 "The heart *mantra* of great wrath" is defined as OṀ ĀḤ HŪṀ at MMK p.25

प्रयोजनीया । उपहृदयं चात्र भवति । ॐ ह्रीं: कालरूप हूं खं स्वाहा । मुद्रा महाशूलयैव प्रयोजनीया । सर्वदुष्टां यमिच्छति तं कारयति । परमहृदयं । सर्वबुद्धाधिष्ठितं एकाक्षरं नाम हूं । एष सर्वकर्मकर: । मुद्रा महाशूलयैव प्रयोजनीया । सर्वानर्थनिवारणम् । सर्वभूतवशंकर: संक्षेपत: । एष क्रोधराज सर्वकर्मेषु प्रयोक्तव्य: मण्डलमध्ये जाप: सिद्धिकाले च विशिष्यते ॥

And with regard to this matter there is also a *mudrā* known as 'the great spike' which destroys all obstacles. This, furthermore, is the heart *mantra* of the wrathful king: OṀ HṚĪḤṀ JÑĪḤ VIKṚTĀNANA HŪṀ SARVAŚATRŪN NĀŚAYA STAMBHAYA PHAṬ PHAṬ SVĀHĀ. As a result of this spell, one causes all enemies to be gripped by severe colic ('great spike disease') or recurrent illness ('every four days'). Or, by reciting it constantly, for as long as the spell shines forth, [the enemy] will find no friendship. Now, [the sorcerer] should be possessed of a sympathetic mind and not allow death ('liberation') to come about at the end of the recitation. Those who think "Let him die!" offend the triple gem and they should not be given the complete teachings which are bestowed upon those of compassionate disposition. The *mudrā* to be employed is that same 'gesture of the great spike.' And, for that purpose also, this is the secondary heart *mantra* (*upahṛdaya*): OṀ HRĪḤṀ KĀLARŪPA HŪṀ KHAṀ SVĀHĀ. The *mudrā* to be employed is that same 'great spiking.' Whatever [the *yogin*] wishes, he may command all evil ones to perform. The supreme heart *mantra* (*paramahṛdaya*), renowned as the single syllable encompassing the power of all the buddhas, is HŪṀ. It is this that can perform all activities. The *mudrā* to be employed is that same 'great spiking.' It overcomes all hindrances. In sum, it is the subjugator of all demons. It is, oh wrathful king, the one to be applied in all rites. It is to be recited in the centre of the *maṇḍala* and especially at the time of accomplishing *siddhi*.

Āryasarvatathāgatoṣṇīṣasitātapatrānāmā vidyārājñī
[*Dhīḥ* 33 (2002) 150-151]

In a long spell for the eradication of a large number of evil influences (beginning: *sarvavighnān*, 'all obstructors'), the chant: *chindayāmy asinā, kīlayāmi vajreṇa*, "I cut them off with a sword, I nail them down with a *vajra*," is repeated 37 times.

Caṇḍamahāroṣanasādhana by Prabhākarakīrti

मदनेन पुत्तलिकां कृत्वा चतुरङ्गुलप्रमाणतः तस्या हृदये साध्यनाम-सहितं भूर्ज्जमन्त्रमभिलिख्य प्रक्षिपेत् । कण्टकेन तु तस्या मुखं कीलयेत् । प्रतिवादिमुखं कीलितं भवति । पादौ कीलयेत् । गतिं स्तम्भयेत् । हृदयं कीलयेत् । रोषं स्तम्भयति । मानुषजङ्घास्थिकीलकेन लोहकीलकेन वा नाम गृहीत्वायान्यङ्गानि कीलयेत् तानि तस्य नश्यन्ति । अरिद्वारे निखनेदुच्छादयेत् । अभिमन्त्रितश्मशानभस्मना द्वारपटे निक्षिप्तेनो-च्चाटयति । खड्गमभिमन्त्र्य संग्रामे प्रविशन् जयमासादयति । यस्मिन् कार्ये समुत्पन्ने बलिमुपसंहरेत् तत् तस्य सिध्यति । यद् यदिच्छति मन्त्री तत् सर्वं शुभमशुभं वा कर्म करोति जपमात्रेण ॥

Having made an effigy out of beeswax, four inches in length, one should inscribe the *mantra* on birchbark, incorporating the name of the victim, and insert it into the effigy's heart. Then, by fastening (*kīlaya*) the mouth of the effigy with thorns, the contentious mouth [of the opponent] will be closed (*kīlita*). By nailing down the two feet, one paralyses his movements. By piercing the heart of the effigy, the enemy's anger will be stopped. Using a *kīla* made of the lower leg bone of a human, or a *kīla* of iron, if one were to take hold of that effigy and pierce it in any place, the corresponding organ of the victim would be destroyed. By pegging it down in the enemy's doorway, he will be driven away. He may also be driven away by reciting the *mantra* over ashes from the charnel ground and casting them onto his door. If one recites the *mantra* over a sword before entering into battle, one will be victorious. Whatever the deed that is being performed, one should offer a *bali* cake and that will ensure the success of the act. Whatever it is that is wished for by the knower of *mantra*, whether it be good or bad, he will be able to perform all rites by the recitation of *mantra*.

Buddhakapālatantra VIII

ॐ मारय मारय कीलय कीलय सर्वशत्रून् नाशय हूं फट् । आत्मानं हेरुकं भूत्वा श्यामवर्णं क्रूरचेतसा नाशयन् तु सर्वशत्रून् तत्क्षणादेव न संशयः ॥

Having oneself become Heruka, dark in colour and with a mind of wrath, [by the recitation of] OṀ MĀRAYA MĀRAYA KĪLAYA KĪLAYA SARVAŚATRŪN NĀŚAYA HŪṀ PHAṬ (OṀ *all enemies must be killed, must be killed, they must be nailed down, nailed down, they must be destroyed* HŪṀ PHAṬ), all one's enemies will certainly be destroyed at that very instant. Of that there is no doubt.

Also, in chapter XII of the *Buddhakapāla-tantra*, within a discussion concerning the appropriate rosaries to be employed for the accomplishment of various rites, the rite of nailing down the heart of an enemy is said to be achieved using a rosary prepared from the bones of a cow (*go asthikena kartavyaṁ śatruhṛdayakīlanam //*)

Nityakarmapūjāvidhiḥ [*Dhīḥ* 33 (2002) 160]

इन्द्रादयो महावीरा लोकपाला महर्द्धिकाः ।
कीलयन्तु दशक्रोधा विघ्नहर्ता नमोऽस्तु ते ॥

May Indra and those others of great power,
Chief guardians of the world,
Be nailed down! (*kīlayantu*)
Oh, you ten wrathful kings who annihilate obstructors,
Homage to you!

Śrīguhyasamājamaṇḍalopāyikāviṁśatividhiḥ V.1 by Nāgabodhi

कीलयित्वा ततो विघ्नान् प्राकारं पञ्जरादिकम् ।
ध्यात्वा वज्रमयीं भूमिं सूत्रितामधिवासयेत् ॥

Having nailed down the obstructing demons in this manner,
One should meditate upon the palace walls
And the protective enclosure, and so on.
Then one should prepare the *vajra* ground
By marking out the lines.

Cakrasaṁvarasamādhiḥ [*Dhīḥ* 36 (2003) 149-150]

Having explained that, at the sound of HŪṀ, the fourfold SUMBHA *mantra* issues forth from the four faces of the deity (Cakrasamvara) in the form of rays of light, it is said that (on the first recitation) these give rise to Kākāsyā and the rest in the four cardinal directions and (on the second recitation) they give rise to Yamadāḍhī and so on in the intermediate directions, starting with the southeast. These goddesses in the corners are to be worshipped as having two colours each. The text then continues with the recitation:

ॐ सुम्भनिसुम्भ हूं हूं फट् । ॐ गृह्ण गृह्ण हूं हूं फट् । ॐ गृह्णापय गृह्णापय हूं हूं फट् । ॐ आनय होः भगवन् विद्याराज हूं हूं फट् ॥

OṀ *Sumbha and Nisumbha* HŪṀ HŪṀ PHAṬ. OṀ *Seize, seize!* HŪṀ HŪṀ PHAṬ. OṀ *Cause them to be caught, cause them to be caught!* HŪṀ HŪṀ PHAṬ. OṀ *Bring them forth* HOḤ *Glorious king of awareness* HŪṀ HŪṀ PHAṬ.

काकास्या कृष्णा । उलूकास्या श्यामा । श्वानास्या रक्ता । शूकरास्या पीता । यमदाढी कृष्णपीता । यमदूती पीतरक्ता । यमदंष्ट्री रक्तश्यामा । यममथनी श्यामकृष्णा । एता देव्यो वामहस्ते कपालपरिणामेन सुम्भ-राजकीलकं नाभेरधः शूलाकारम् उर्ध्वं नाभे रूपकं धृत्वा दक्षिणहस्ते कर्तिपरिणामेन वज्रमुद्गरहस्ताः ॥

The crow-faced goddess is black. The owl-faced is dark. Dog-face is red and the pig-faced goddess is yellow. Yamadāḍhī is yellow-black, Yamadūtī is yellow-red, Yamadaṁṣṭrī is dark red, and Yamamathanī is dark green. Each of those goddesses holds a *kīla* in her left hand, transformed from her skull cup. The upper half of each *kīla* has the wrathful body of Sumbharāja, but below the waist it has the form of a sharp spike. In their right hands, those goddesses hold *vajra*-hammers which have arisen as the transformations of their curved flaying-knives (*kartṛkā*).

तदनु आकाशे रं परिणतसूर्यमण्डलमध्ये हूंकारेण विश्ववज्रं हूंकाराधिष्ठितं तद्रश्मिना यवफलप्रमाणं वज्रकर्णिकारूपेणागतेर्वज्रमयभूमिं विभाव्य । ॐ मेदिनीवज्रीभव वज्रबन्ध हूं हूं फट् । ॐ वज्रप्राकार हूं वं हूं । ॐ वज्रपञ्जर हूं पं हूं । ॐ वज्रवितान हूं खं हूं । ॐ वज्रशरजाल त्रां सं त्रां । ॐ वज्रज्वालानलार्क हूं हूं । इति दिग्बन्धनम् ॥

Then, in the sky, appears the syllable RAṀ which is transformed into a sun disc. In the centre of that sun appears the syllable HŪṀ which transforms into a *viśvavajra* marked by a syllable HŪṀ the size of a grain of barley. Rays of light spread out from that and, by their blessing, one should contemplate that the ground rises up in the form of an unshakeable prominence and becomes composed of *vajra*. Then the directions are held firm by the recitation of *mantra* for the *vajra* earth, the *vajra* walls, the *vajra* cage, the *vajra* canopy, the *vajra* network of arrows, and the *vajra* blazing fire. Thus, the four quarters are made safe.

प्राकारवर्त्तिहूंकारनिष्पन्नेषु अष्टकूपेषु निवेशितानामिन्द्रादिविघ्नानां हृदये कीलकं धृत्वा वज्रमुद्गरेणाकोटयेत् । ॐ घ घ घातय घातय सर्वदुष्टान् हूं हूं फट् । ॐ कीलय कीलय सर्वपापान् हूं हूं फट् । ॐ हूं हूं हूं वज्रकील वज्रधर आज्ञापयति सर्वविघ्नविनायकानां कायवाक्चित्तवज्रान् कीलय कीलय हूं हूं फट् । इति कीलनम् ॥ ॐ वज्रमुद्गर वज्रकीलमाकोटय आकोटय हूं हूं फट् । आकोटनम् ॥

इति रक्षाचक्रविधिः ॥

In a circle around the walls, eight pits are generated from HŪṀ syllables and into those pits are thrown Indra and the rest of the obstructors. Holding a *kīla* to each of their hearts, one should hammer them down by striking them with a *vajra* hammer, saying: OṀ *Slay, slay! Kill, kill all malignant ones* HŪṀ HŪṀ PHAṬ! *Nail down! Nail down all evil doers* HŪṀ HŪṀ PHAṬ! OṀ HŪṀ HŪṀ HŪṀ *Oh Vajrakīla, Vajradhara orders that you nail down the vajra body, speech and mind of all obstructors* HŪṀ HŪṀ PHAṬ! This is the *mantra* for nailing down. OṀ *Vajra hammer, you must beat down upon the vajra nail! Beat down!* HŪṀ HŪṀ PHAṬ! This is the *mantra* for hammering.

That is the ritual for the circle of protection.

Maṇḍalasādhanavidhiḥ [*Dhīḥ* 34 (2002) 141-142]

In the *sūtraṇavidhi* section (laying down the lines of the *maṇḍala*), having established the centre of the *maṇḍala* by means of the lines of Brahmā:

ततो मण्डलनाभौ चतुरङ्गुलप्रमाणमयोमयमध एकसूचिकमुपरि पञ्चसूचिकवज्राकारं हूंकारजकीलकं विचिन्त्य कीलनमन्त्रेणाष्टोत्तरशतं परिजप्याकोटयेत् । मन्त्रः । ॐ वज्रान्त महाक्रोध सर्वदुष्टविघनानां कायवाक्चित्तं कीलय कीलय हूं फट् । ॐ वज्रमुद्गर वज्रकीलकं आकोटय हूं फट् । ततः ऐशानीं दिशमारभ्य प्रदक्षिणतो वर्तुलसूत्राणि पातयेत् । ततः सूत्रणावसाने बलिपूजापूर्वकम् ॥

Then, into the centre of the *maṇḍala*, one should hammer down a *kīla*, four inches in length and made of iron, and it should be visualised as arisen from the syllable HŪṀ, with a single spike at its lower end and its upper end in the form of a five-pronged *vajra*. Whilst hammering it down, this *mantra* of nailing should be recited 108 times: OṀ VAJRĀNTA MAHĀKRODHA SARVADUṢṬAVIGHNĀNĀṀ KĀYAVĀKCITTAṀ KĪLAYA KĪLAYA HŪṀ PHAṬ. OṀ VAJRAMUDGARA VAJRAKĪLAKAM ĀKOṬAYA HŪṀ PHAṬ. (*Oh great wrathful one with a vajra at the end, you must nail down the body, speech and mind of all evil obstructors* HŪṀ PHAṬ. *Oh vajra hammer, you must beat down upon the vajrakīla* HŪṀ PHAṬ.) Then, beginning in the northeastern corner, one should inscribe the circular lines in a clockwise direction. When the drawing of the lines is completed, one should offer a *bali* cake, as before.

(When all the lines have been drawn, the text states:)

ततो मण्डलनाभिस्थितकीलकं चतुःहूंकारेणोत्पाद्य हस्तस्थितवज्रे धियान्तर्भाव्य । मन्त्रः । ॐ वज्रकील उत्कीलय सर्वकीलान् वज्रधर आज्ञया हूं हूं हूं हूं फट् स्वाहा । कीलगर्तं पञ्चरङ्गैः पूरयेत् । पं लां घं स्तुत । अथ घण्टाध्वनिभिर्वज्रगीतिकाभिर्दुर्निमित्तमपनीयम् ।

धर्मधातुरयं शुद्धः सत्त्वधातुप्रमोचकः ।
स्वयं वैरोचनो राजा सर्वतथागतालयः ॥

सर्वदोषविनिर्मुक्तश्चक्राभ्यन्तरे संस्थितः ॥

Then, that spike which was situated in the centre of the *maṇḍala* is pulled out with the recitation of four HŪṀs, and one contemplates it being absorbed into the *vajra* which is held in one's hand. This is the *mantra*: OṀ VAJRAKĪLA UTKĪLAYA SARVAKĪLĀN VAJRADHARĀJÑAYĀ HŪṀ HŪṀ HŪṀ HŪṀ PHAṬ SVĀHĀ. (OṀ *Oh Vajrakīla, by command of Vajradhara, all kīla are to be pulled out.* HŪṀ HŪṀ HŪṀ HŪṀ PHAṬ SVĀHĀ) And the hole that was made by that spike should be filled up with the five colours. Praise. With *vajra* songs and the ringing of bells, all evil omens are banished.

This is the pure Dharma realm,
The realm of liberation for all beings.

The king of this place is Vairocana
But it is the abode of all buddhas.

Thus, the centre of the circle is established as freed from all impurity.

Āryavajravidāraṇā nāma dhāraṇī [*Dhīḥ* 40 (2005) 162]

ॐ छिन्द छिन्द भिन्द भिन्द महाकिलिकीलाय स्वाहा । ॐ बन्ध बन्ध क्रोध क्रोध वज्रकिलिकीलाय स्वाहा । ॐ चुरु चुरु चण्डकिलिकीलाय स्वाहा । ॐ त्रासय त्रासय वज्रकिलिकीलाय स्वाहा । ॐ हर हर वज्रधराय स्वाहा । ॐ प्रहर प्रहर वज्रप्रभञ्जनाय स्वाहा । ॐ मतिस्थिरवज्र श्रुतिस्थिरवज्र प्रतिस्थिरवज्र महावज्र अप्रतिहतवज्र अमोघवज्र ऐहिवज्र शीघ्रं वज्राय स्वाहा । ॐ धर धर धिरि धिरि धुरु धुरु सर्ववज्रकुलमावर्ताय स्वाहा । अमुखं मारय फट् । मम सर्वशत्रून् मारय स्वाहा ॥

OṀ Destroy, destroy! Split apart! Praise to the great Kilikīla! OṀ Suppress, suppress! Rage furiously! Praise to Vajrakilikīla! OṀ Make them disappear! Praise to the ferocious Kilikīla! OṀ Terrify them! Make them tremble! Praise to Vajrakilikīla! OṀ Remove them! Carry them off! Praise to Vajradhara! OṀ Strike! Attack! Praise to the Vajra Destroyer! OṀ Vajra of unwavering resolution, Vajra of unwavering listening, Vajra of unwavering opposition, great Vajra, irresistible Vajra, unfailing Vajra, Vajra of the here and now, speedy one. Praise to the Vajra! OṀ Support, sustain, nourish, maintain! Praise to the one who holds the centre for all those who revolve in the Vajra family! *So-and-so* must be killed! PHAṬ All my enemies must be killed! SVĀHĀ

Kālacakratantra III.12

कीलकं चाष्टभेदैर्न्यग्रोधाश्वत्थकास्थीन्ययसखदिरजं चूतबिल्वार्कजं च ॥

And *kīlaka* are to be divided into eight types: those made of wood from the banyan tree, the bodhi tree, bone, iron, acacia wood, mango, wood-apple, or copper.

Commenting on this verse, the **Vimalaprabhā** says:

इह शान्तिके न्यग्रोधकीलकाः । दशदिक्कीलनार्थं पुष्टौ अश्वत्थाः । मारणेऽस्थिमयाः । उच्चाटने आयसाः । वश्ये खदिरजाः । आकृष्टौ चूतजाः । मोहनेऽर्कजाः । स्तम्भने बिल्वजा इति कीलक नियमः । सार्वकर्मिके उदुम्बरजाः ॥

Here, in rites of pacification, the *kīla* should be made of **wood from the banyan tree**. For pegging down the ten directions, and in rites of increase, the *kīla* should be made of **wood from the bodhi tree**. In rites of slaying, they should be made of **bone**. *Kīla* of **iron** are used in rites of driving away, and the *kīla* should be made of **acacia wood** in rites of overpowering control. The *kīla* should be made of **mango** wood in rites of attraction, made of **copper** in rites intended to drive the victim insane, and they should be made of **wood-apple** in rites of paralysis. These are the rules for the *kīla*. *Kīla* made of wood from the cluster fig tree may be used in all rites.

Vimalaprabhā *ad* Kālacakratantra III.22

येनैव स्तम्भनं तेनैव कीलनं कर्तव्यम् । किन्तु कीलने शत्रूद्वर्तनेन पञ्चामृतसहितेन प्रतिकृतिं कृत्वा मदनकण्टकैः षट्चक्रेषु कीलयेद् हस्तपादसन्धिषु । शेषः स्तम्भादिवत् ॥

The rite of nailing down (*kīlanam*) is to be performed in just the same way as the rite of paralysis (*stambhanam*), except that here, in the rite of nailing down, an effigy [of the enemy] should be fashioned out of something derived from the enemy, mixed together with the five nectars. Then one should pierce (*kīlayet*) the six *cakra* of that effigy, as well as the hands and feet, with infuriating thorns.[843] All the rest is just as it is in the rite of paralysis.

---

843 *madanakaṇṭaka* may be thorns that infuriate or drive mad, or they may be spikes of the acacia tree or thorn apple bush.

Catuṣpīṭhatantra III, section 3, a ritual of attraction (*ākṛṣṭiprayoga*) incorporating the commentary of Bhavabhaṭṭa
[With thanks to Péter-Dániel Szántó]

खदिरकीलकमष्टस्य रक्तमण्डल कारतः ।
परिपूर्णबलिसंयुक्तं मध्ये नामं तु आलिखेत् ॥३८॥

Having outlined a red *maṇḍala* with eight *kīla* made of acacia wood,
One should also present a full *bali* offering and inscribe the name
[of the one to be summoned] in the centre. (38)

खदिरेत्यादि । तस्य गोचर्मप्रमाणस्य रक्तगन्धमण्डलस्याष्टसु दिक्षु खादिरा अष्टाङ्गुलप्रमाणा एकशूकवज्राकारा अष्टौ कीलका निखातव्याः । कारत इति । मण्डलं कृत्वेत्यर्थः । परिपूर्णबलिसंयुक्तमिति । सर्वमिदं बलिदानपूर्वकं कर्तव्यमिति भावः ॥

As for the verse beginning, **made of acacia wood**: In the eight directions around that *maṇḍala* drawn with red fragrant powder, the size of a cow hide, one should embed eight spikes (*kīlaka*) of acacia wood. [These spikes] have the form of single-pronged *vajra*s, measuring eight inches in length. **Having outlined** means, after having made the *maṇḍala*. **One should also present a full *bali* offering.** The intended meaning is that all this should be done preceded by an offering of *bali*.

रक्तसूत्रं तु जापेन प्राकार सप्त वेष्टयेत् ।
वज्राङ्कुशेन आकृष्य अस्य मन्त्रं तु जापितम् ॥३९॥

Reciting *mantra*, [the *maṇḍala*] should be wound around seven times
with red string.
Then one should repeat the name (*mantra*) of the one to be summoned,
drawing him/her forth with an iron hook. (39)

रक्तसूत्रं त्विति । तेषां कीलकानामग्रे रक्तसूत्रेणाष्टशताभिमन्त्रितेन सप्त वेष्टनानि कुर्यात् । एतदेवाह । प्राकार सप्तेति । प्राकारशब्देन वेष्टनं वेष्टयेदिति कुर्यात् । वज्राङ्कुशेनमाकृष्येति । वज्राङ्कुशपाशहस्तं वज्रडाकिनीरूपमात्मानं चिन्तयित्वा पाशेन गलके बद्ध्वाङ्कुशेन हृदये बिद्ध्वा समाकृष्यमाणं साध्यं पश्यन्मन्त्रं जपेत् । एतदेवाह । मन्त्रं तु जापितमिति ॥

The verse beginning, **red string**: On the tip of those spikes, one should make seven loops with red string which has been empowered by 108 repetitions of *mantra*. This is what is meant by the statement, **wound around seven times**. The word "around" refers to an enclosure, which one should make by winding those threads [around the *maṇḍala*]. As for, **drawing him/her forth with an iron hook**: Visualising oneself in the form of Vajraḍākinī holding an iron hook and a noose, one should repeat the *mantra* whilst imagining the person upon whom one meditates to be caught around the neck with the noose and pierced through the heart with the iron hook, so that the target is pulled inwards, caught around the neck. This is stated here with the words, **reciting *mantra***.

शतयोजनभिर्बाह्ये निवर्त्ते तस्य कर्मणः ।
मण्डलबन्धेति कर्मस्य सिध्यन्ते नात्र संशयः ॥४०॥

By this ritual, any person may be dragged forth
from a hundred leagues distance.
Thinking that the one upon whom one meditates is
constrained within the *mandala*,
They will succeed, of this there is no doubt. (40)

प्रयोगमाहात्म्यमाह । शतेत्यादि । शतयोजनानन्तरितोऽप्याकृष्यते योगेनानेनेति भावः । मण्डलेत्यादिना प्रयोगोपसंहार उक्तः ॥

Now, with the words, **a hundred** and so on, [the Lord] teaches the greatness of this applied ritual. The intended meaning is that, by this *yoga*, even one who is at a distance of a hundred leagues will be drawn forth. The last line, with the words **maṇḍala** and so on, brings the discussion of this rite to a close.

Śrīguhyasamājamaṇḍalavidhi by Dīpaṅkarabhadra
[*Dhīḥ* 42 (2006) 109–154 vv.162-164]

First of all, a *vajra* dance is performed, and then:

भूमेः परिग्रहं कृत्वा निर्विघ्नाय प्रकीलयेत् ।

Having taken possession of the site (by means of that dance), it should be imbedded with *kīla* for the removal of impediments:

ॐ घ घ घातय घातय सर्वदुष्टान् फट् कीलय कीलय सर्वपापान् फट् हूं हूं हूं वज्रकील वज्रधरो आज्ञापयति सर्वदुष्टकायवाक्चित्तवज्रं कीलय हूं फट् ॥

OṀ GHA GHA GHĀTAYA GHĀTAYA SARVADUṢṬĀN PHAṬ KĪLAYA KĪLAYA SARVAPĀPĀN PHAṬ HŪṀ HŪṀ HŪṀ VAJRAKĪLA VAJRADHARO ĀJÑĀPAYATI SARVADUṢṬAKĀYAVĀKCITTAVAJRAṀ KĪLAYA HŪṀ PHAṬ

अधः शूलोर्ध्वविघ्नारिं धिया मध्ये प्रकीलयेत् ।
विघ्नौघान् घातयेत् सर्वान् दशदिक्संव्यवस्थितान् ॥

Meditating upon [that *kīla*] with its lower half in the form of a spike, above which is the enemy of all obstructors, one should nail it into the centre [of the ground] and thus one destroys the entire assembly of obstructing demons, everywhere in the ten directions.

संवीक्ष्य क्ष्मां सुनिर्विघ्नां तीक्ष्णज्वालाकुलप्रभाम् ।
सीमाप्राकारदिग्बन्धान् धिया कृत्वाधिवासयेत् ॥

One should visualise the ground as completely free of impediments, blazing with a mass of sharp-pointed flames. Contemplating the boundary walls as having been made secure in every direction, one may begin to install [the *maṇḍala*, etc.].

(And in verse 246):

द्वेषो वक्रया मृत्युश्छिन्नया गुरुशिष्ययोः ।
अप्रदक्षिणपाते तु रजसां कीलनं भवेत् ॥

A cruel person, who, with malicious intent, causes death or the separation of teacher and disciple, in such an inauspicious case, certainly, the evil one should be nailed down with a *kīla*.

Parikramapadopāyikā by Śrīkīrti
[Manuscript transcription & note courtesy of Péter-Dániel Szántó]

ततः प्राग्वत् सलीलनृत्यं कृत्वाभिमुखं वज्रमुष्टिद्वयं वामकटिप्रदेशे संस्थाप्य । आक्षेपानुपसंहृत्य मध्ये ईशानादिकोणेषु च यथाक्रमं स्थापयेत् ॥ अनन्तविजयमेघनादमहोदरजयाख्यान् पञ्च कीलकान्

पञ्चाधिपतिस्वभावान् क्रोधरूपाविर्भूतान् नाभेरध एकसूचिककीलकान् ओं घ घ घातयेत्यादिमन्त्रेण निखत्य तैश्च रसातलं यावदाकीलितं विभावयेत् ॥

Then, having performed a graceful dance, as described earlier, one makes the two hands into *vajra* fists and positions them, face to face, on the left side of the hip. When the dance is over, one takes up (five *kīla*) and imbeds them in the centre and the four corners beginning with the north-east, in due order. The five *kīla* are known as Endless (Ananta), Great Conqueror (Vijaya), Roaring Cloud (Meghanāda), Big Belly (Mahodara) and Victorious (Jaya) and they have the nature of five deities, in the forms of wrathful protectors with spikes going down to a single point from below the waist. Imbedding them with the *mantra* OṀ GHA GHA GHĀTAYA GHĀTAYA and so on, one imagines that they penetrate right down to the foundation of the earth.[844]

Śrīguhyasamājamaṇḍalopāyikāviṁśatividhi by Nāgabodhi

In the *vighnopaśamanavidhi* section of this text, at first the *yogin* performs an elaborate *vajra* dance to subjugate the earth and cleanse it of all hindrances, and then:

एवमाक्षेपकैर्मन्त्री सन्तर्ज्येन्द्रादि सद्गणान् ।
दिक्पालान् कीलयेत्सम्यक् स्वभावज्ञो यथायथम् ॥

Threatening the lords of the directions with these challenging gestures, the follower of *mantra* who knows his own nature, just as it is, should now decisively nail down Indra and the rest, together with their faithful followers.

अष्टाङ्गुलप्रमाणं तु कीलं संगृह्य खादिरम् ।
एकशूचिकमधोगं सौगताङ्गुलमानतः ॥

844 Note that the ultimate source for this work and the names of the five pegs is the *Māyājālatantra*. The four corner pegs are also mentioned by name in Ch.III of Kuladatta's *Kriyāsaṁgrahapañjikā*. With the *ācārya* positioning himself in the centre, Meghanāda is embedded in the SE, Mahodara in the SW, Jaya in the NW, and Vijaya in the NE.
See above, p.86, & *A Bolt of Lightning from the Blue* 6-7

Taking hold of a *kīla* made of acacia wood, eight inches in length, the lower half of which ends in a single spike, one thinks of it as the finger of the Buddha.

पञ्चशूचिकमूर्द्धर्वन्तु रक्तचन्दनलेपितम् ।
पञ्चरंगिकसूत्रेण वेष्टयेत् तद् यथाक्रमम् ॥

Crowned on the top with a five-pronged *vajra* and smeared with a paste of red sandalwood, those *kīla*, in due order, should be wound around with threads of five colours.

अभ्यर्च्च्य गन्धपुष्पाद्यैः स्थापयेन्नवभाजने ।
हस्तेन संस्पृशन्कीलं त्र्यक्षरेणाभिमन्त्रयेत् ॥

Honouring them with perfume and flowers and so on, they should be placed in new containers and, touching each *kīla* with one's hand, they should be empowered with the *mantra* of three syllables.

एवं सुसंस्कृतं कीलं संवृत्तेर्भावदर्शनात् ।
पुनर्ध्यानमयं कुर्यात् क्रमेणानेन बुद्धिमान् ॥

Thus the *kīla* should be properly prepared in this way, by focussing upon their relative nature. Then, further, the wise one should perform this meditation in accordance with proper procedure:

ॐ सुम्भनिसुम्भ हूं गृह्ण गृह्ण हूं गृह्णापय गृह्णापय हूं आनय होः भगवन् विद्याराज हूं फट् ॥

OṀ SUMBHA NISUMBHA HŪṀ GṚHṆA GṚHṆA HŪṀ GṚHṆĀPAYA GṚHṆĀPAYA HŪṀ ĀNAYA HO BHAGAVAN VIDYĀRĀJA HŪṀ PHAṬ

अनेन क्रोधरूपेण प्राकृष्यैवं विनायकान् ।
कीलयेद्विधिवत्सर्वान् प्रयोगेण तु बुद्धिमान् ॥

By means of this *mantra*, wrathful forms will drag forth all heretical misleaders. The wise one who knows the method should nail them down with a *kīla*, in accordance with the rite.

वज्रामृतमहाराजं वज्रकीलं विभावयेत् ।
नीलोत्पलदलश्यामं ज्वालामालाकुलप्रभम् ॥

The great king Vajrāmṛta is to be generated as Vajrakīla, dark like the petals of the blue lotus, blazing with an aura of a mass of flames.

नाभिदेशादधोभागं शूलाकारं विभावयेत् ।
ऊर्ध्वं क्रोधाकृतिं चैव त्रिमुखाकारषड्भुजम् ॥

Contemplating him in the shape of a sharp spike from the waist down, his upper portion has the form of the king of wrath, with three faces and six arms.

वज्रमुद्गरमेकेन कीलं वामेन धारयन् ।
निसुम्भरूपधृक्वज्री मन्त्रेणानेन कीलयेत् ॥

Holding the *kīla* in his left hand, the *yogin* assumes the form of Nisumbharāja and nails it down with a *vajra* hammer whilst reciting this *mantra*:

ॐ घ घ घातय घातय सर्वदुष्टान् फट् फट् कीलय कीलय सर्वपापान् फट् फट् हूं हूं वज्रकील वज्रधरो आज्ञापयति सर्वविघ्नानां कायवाक्चित्त-वज्रं कीलय हूं हूं फट् फट् ॥

OṀ GHA GHA GHĀTAYA GHĀTAYA SARVADUṢṬĀN PHAṬ PHAṬ KĪLAYA KĪLAYA SARVAPĀPĀN PHAṬ PHAṬ HŪṀ HŪṀ VAJRAKĪLA VAJRADHARO ĀJÑĀPAYATI SARVAVIGHNĀNĀṀ KĀYAVĀKCITTA-VAJRAṀ KĪLAYA HŪṀ HŪṀ PHAṬ PHAṬ (OṀ *Begone, begone all evil ones* PHAṬ PHAṬ *Nail down, nail down all sins* PHAṬ PHAṬ HŪṀ HŪṀ *Oh Vajrakīla, Vajradhara orders that you nail down the body vajra, speech vajra and mind vajra of all obstacles* HŪṀ HŪṀ PHAṬ PHAṬ)

एवं कल्पितयोगेन विघ्नान्प्रोत्सार्य मन्त्रवित् ॥

Thus, the knower of *mantra* expels all obstructors by means of this meditative visualisation.

Later, in the *pṛthivīdevatākalaśādhivāsanāvidhi* section, this text says:

कीलयित्वा ततो विघ्नान् प्राकारं पञ्जरादिकं ध्यात्वा वज्रमयीं भूमिम् ॥

Then, having nailed down the obstructors, one should contemplate the *maṇḍala* walls and the protective enclosure and so on, and visualise the earth as made of *vajra*.

Note: At the end of the rainy season retreat, a ceremony is performed for the lifting of restrictions (Tib. *dgag dbye*, Skt. *pravāraṇā*). At this time, these are the instructions for the withdrawal of the *kīla* (*phur bu dbyung ba'i cho ga*):

रात्रौ कृतोपसंहारः प्रभातसमये पुनः ।
रजान्सि सर्वाण्याहृत्वा क्षिपेन्नद्यान् सपूजनम् ॥

The rites having been completed in the evening, on the following morning one should gather up all the coloured powders (used in the construction of the *maṇḍala*) and cast them into the river with all due ceremony.

अष्टदिग्मध्यगं कीलमुद्धरेदथ मुद्रया ।
संदंशया पठन्मन्त्रं प्रत्यालीढपदे स्थितः ॥

Then, with the gesture of pincers (*saṁdaṁśamudrā*), one should extract those *kīla* that had been embedded in the ground in the eight directions and the centre. Then, standing with the left leg extended in the *pratyālīḍha* posture, one should recite the *mantra*:

ॐ वज्रकील उत्कीलय सर्वविघ्नान् वज्रधर आज्ञापय हूं हूं फट् फट् होः ॥

OṀ VAJRAKĪLA UTKĪLAYA SARVAVIGHNĀN VAJRADHARA ĀJÑĀPAYA (*Oh Vajrakīla, the kīla are to be lifted up! Oh Vajradhara, you must command all obstructors!*) HŪṀ HŪṀ PHAṬ PHAṬ HOḤ

उद्धृत्य भाजने तस्य तथा सूत्राणि प्रोक्षयेत् ।
ततश्चन्दनवारिभ्यां मन्त्रेणानेन धावयेत् ॥

Extracting them from the ground, [those *kīla*] and the threads should be placed in a container and purified with a sprinkling of sandalwood water. This is the *mantra* to be used when washing:

ॐ आः हूं सत्त्वार्थं कुरु स्वस्ति स्वाहा ॥

OṀ ĀḤ HŪṀ SATTVARTHAṀ KURU SVASTI SVĀHĀ (OṀ ĀḤ HŪṀ *You must accomplish the welfare of living beings! May it be good! Praise!*)

क्रोधराजान्ततो मन्त्री बाह्याध्यात्मिकपूजनैः ।
संपूज्यगीतनृत्याद्यैर्बलिं दत्त्वा विसर्जयेत् ॥

Finally the *yogin* should perform the outer and inner rites of worship for the wrathful kings and, having completed the worship, he should present the *bali* offering with songs and dances and he should scatter it outside.

अथ मण्डलभूमिं तां गोमयेनोपलिप्य च ।
सत्त्वशिष्यकृपार्थं च होमं कुर्याच्च शान्तिकम् ॥

Then the ground upon which the *maṇḍala* had stood should be smeared with cow dung and, in order to ensure the welfare of his disciples and all living beings, [the master] should perform a fire sacrifice of pacification.

कीलोद्धरणविधिः

This is the ritual method of removing the *kīla*.

Catuṣpīṭhatantra III.4, concerning the symbolism of the *maṇḍala* walls and so on (*prākārādiviśuddhi*) incorporating the commentary of Bhavahaṭṭa [With thanks to Péter-Dániel Szántó]

Having explained the enclosing wall (*prākāra*) to be generosity (*dāna*, the first of the six perfections) free of subject and object, and the protecting cage (*pañjara*) to be moral conduct (*śīla*), the text now equates the ring of *kīla* with patient forbearance (*kṣānti*), thus:

क्षान्ति कीलेन निम्नस्य परपीडानुरोधिका ।
पञ्जरं कील प्राकारं दुष्टमारादिच्छारणम् ॥१०॥

Patient forbearance with respect to the torments of others,
Consists in pressing them down with a *kīla*.
The protective cage, the *kīla* spikes and the enclosing wall
Serve to keep wicked demons at bay. (10)

कीलकविशुद्धिमाह । क्षान्ति कीलेन निम्नस्येत्यादि । परापकार-मर्षदुःखाधिवासनाधर्मनिध्यानलक्षणा क्षान्तिः । तद्विशुद्ध्या कीलका निम्नस्य निखातव्या इत्यर्थः । परपीडानुरोधकेति क्षान्तिविशेषणम् । परपीडा परापकारः । आदिशब्दोऽत्र द्रष्टव्यः । ततो दुःखाधिवासना लब्धा । परपीडादुःखाधिवासनयोरनुरोधनं निराकरणं यस्यां सा परपीडानुरोधिका क्षान्तिः । पश्चादिकारक्षयः । अनुरोधकं च धर्मनिध्यानम् ॥

The *tantra* now explains the symbolism of the *kīla* spikes with the words, **Patient forbearance ... consists in pressing them down with a *kīla*** and so on. Patient forbearance is characterised by forgiving the offences of others, being able to willingly accept discomfort, and having a philosophical insight into the truth of Dharma. As a symbol of this, those *kīla* should be imbedded very deeply. This is the meaning. As for the words, **with respect to the torments of others**, this is an adjective qualifying patient endurance. The torments of others are those harms which one must endure as a result of wicked deeds committed by other people and it is understood that the words "and so on" are to be implied here. Thus, when speaking of "patient forbearance with respect to the torments of others", we include the two aspects of accepting ordinary suffering without being moved, as well as accepting those discomforts brought about by the wicked deeds of other people, because both of these are turned aside by patient endurance. And now we remove the letter 'i' [from the root text in Sanskrit] so that this statement also refers to having a philosophical insight into the Dharma.[845]

पञ्जरादिकं किमर्थमित्याह । पञ्जरमित्यादि । दूषयन्ति विकृतं कायादिकं कुर्वन्तीति दुष्टाः क्लेशस्कन्धमृत्युदेवपुत्राः त एव मारास्-तेषामादिच्छारणं निराकरणं तदर्थं पञ्जरादिकम् ॥

What is the purpose of the protective cage and so on? The *tantra* answers this question with the next line of the verse, beginning, **the protective cage**. Demons (*māra*) are called 'wicked' (*duṣṭa*) because they spoil (*dūṣayanti*) the body, speech and mind, making them corrupt. By "wicked demons" we are referring to the Māra of defilements, the Māra of the aggregates, the Māra of death, and the Māra who is a son of the gods, the ruler of the realm of desire. It is those very demons that must be opposed and thus the text speaks of **keeping the evil ones at bay**. That is the purpose of the protective cage and so on.

न मारो न च मारेण आत्मचेतं तु बन्धवत् ।
स्वचित्तदमनं यस्य कुतो मारेण पीड्यते ॥ ११ ॥

---

845 These are the three aspects of patient endurance (*kṣānti*) according to the authoritative texts of *abhidharma*. The root text is here manipulated by the commentator Bhavabhaṭṭa to conform to the Buddhist norm.

There is no Māra,
    nor does Māra cause one's mind to become restricted.
When one takes control of his own mind,
    how will he be tormented by Māra? (11)

Guṇabharaṇīnāmaṣaḍaṅgayogaṭippaṇī by Raviśrījñāna

मारवृन्दं विकल्पचित्तजालम् । उक्तं च मारः स्वचित्तं न परोऽस्ति मार इति ॥

The hosts of Māra are the network of discursive thoughts in the mind. Thus it is said: "There is no Māra other than the Māra of one's own thoughts."

BIBLIOGRAPHY

SANSKRIT TEXTS

Sanskrit Texts from the Imperial Palace at Peking
An 18th century Chinese encyclopaedia of Sanskrit *mantra* and *dhāraṇī* compiled by the Manchu emperor Ch'ien-lung and his Buddhist preceptor lCang-skya rol-pa'i rdo-rje
Published by Lokesh Chandra (22 vols.) New Delhi, 1966-1976

Acalapūjāvidhi (Unedited facsimile edition)
In *Sanskrit Manuscripts from Japan* Vol. 2
Published by Lokesh Chandra, New Delhi, 1972

Advayavajrasaṁgraha (19 short works by Advayavajra)
Edited by Haraprasad Shastri, GOS XL, Baroda, 1927

Āryamañjuśrīmūlakalpa (MMK)
Edited by Ganapati Sastri (3 vols.) Trivandrum, 1925
(Reprint) Sri Satguru Publications, Delhi, 1989

Śrīkālacakratantrarāja
Edited by Biswanath Bannerjee, The Asiatic Society, Calcutta, 1985

Kriyāsamuccaya by Jagaddarpana (Unedited facsimile edition)
Śatapiṭaka Series Vol. 237. New Delhi, 1977

Kriyāsaṁgraha by Kuladatta (Unedited facsimile edition)
Śatapiṭaka Series Vol. 236. New Delhi, 1977

Guhyasamājatantrapradīpodyotanaṭīkāṣaṭkoṭivyākhyā by Candrakīrti
Edited by Chintaharan Chakravarti, Patna, 1984

Śrīguhyasamājamaṇḍalopāyikāviṁśatividhi
Edited by Kimiaki Tanaka, Shunjusha Publishing Company, Japan, 2010

Guhyādi-aṣṭasiddhi-saṁgraha
Rare Buddhist Text Series 1. CIHTS, 1987

Jñānasiddhi by Indrabhūti & *Prajñopāyaviniścayasiddhi* by Anaṅgavajra
In *Two Vajrayāna Works,* edited by Benoytosh Bhattacharyya
GOS XLIV, Baroda, 1929

Jñānodayatantra
Rare Buddhist Text Series 2. CIHTS, 1988

Niṣpannayogāvalī by Mahāpaṇḍita Abhayākaragupta
Edited by Benoytosh Bhattacharyya, GOS CIX, Baroda, 1949

Vajrāvalī by Abhayākaragupta (Unedited facsimile edition)
Śatapiṭaka Series Vol. 239. New Delhi, 1977

Pañcakrama by Nāgārjuna
Edited by Louis de La Vallée Poussin, University of Gand, 1896

Vimalaprabhā by Kalki Śrīpuṇḍarīka
Vol.1 edited by Jagannatha Upadhyaya
Bibliotheca Indo-Tibetica XI. CIHTS, 1986
Vols.2 & 3 edited by Vrajavallabh Dwivedi & S.S. Bahulkar
Rare Buddhist Text Series XII & XIII. CIHTS, 1994

Sādhanamālā
Edited by Benoytosh Bhattacharyya (2 vols.)
GOS XXVI & XLI, Baroda, 1925, 1928

Sarvatathāgatatattvasaṁgraha (STTS)
Edited by Lokesh Chandra, with introduction & illustrations of maṇḍalas
New Delhi, 1987

Sekoddeśaṭīkā by Nāropa
Edited by M.E. Carelli. GOS XC, Baroda, 1941

TIBETAN LANGUAGE PUBLICATIONS

Collection A: *Byang gter phur pa lugs gsum gcig tu dril ba'i chos skor*
Smanrtsis Shesrig Spendzod Series Vol. 75, Leh, 1973

Collection B: *Phur-pa Texts of the Byang-gter Tradition* (2 vols.)
Published by Damchoe Sangpo, Dalhousie, 1977

Collection C: *Byang gter phur pa'i skor*
Published by Lama Dawa & Chopal Lama, Darjeeling, 1984

Collection D: *Byang gter phur pa lha nag gi chos tshan* (*sNga 'gyur byang gter phur pa lha nag thun min yol mo lugs su grags pa*)
by bsTan-'dzin nor-bu
Published by Tingkey Gonjang Rinpoche, Gangtok, 1994

Collection E: *dPal chen rdo rje gzhon nu'i chos skor phyogs bsgrigs* (*Phur pa phyogs bsgrigs*) Vol. 12
Published in 45 volumes by Bod-kyi shes-rig zhib-'jub-khang, Chengdu, 2002
(Note: Texts from the Northern Treasures cycle of Vajrakīla are mainly gathered together in Vols. 12, 13 & 14 of this large compilation.)

sNga 'gyur byang gter chos skor las 'don cha'i skor
Prayers and ritual texts of the Byang-gter tradition (4 vols.)
Published by Thub-bstan rdo-rje brag evam lcog-sgar monastery
Simla, 2000

bLa ma mchod pa'i cho ga nor bu'i phreng ba
Ritual texts of the Byang-gter tradition
Published by Brag-thog monastery in Ladakh (no date)

Lho brag mkhar chu bdud 'joms gling gi 'don cha'i skor
Liturgical texts from the mKhar-chu bdud-'joms-gling monastery in Southern Tibet (4 vols.) Published by 'Brug bum-than lho-brag-mkhar-chu grwa tshan, Jakar dzong, Bhutan, 1999

Byang gter 'don cha'i skor
Rituals of the Byang-gter tradition followed in the Nubri Valley of Nepal (2 vols.) Edited by Nub-ri-ba Chos-kyi nyi-ma rin-po-che

Vol.1: *Byang gter 'don cha'i skor stod cha sgrub skor rnam gsum yan lag dang bcas pa dngos grub mchog sbyin*
Vol.2: *Byang gter 'don cha'i skor smad cha bka' dgongs phur gsum yan lag dang bcas pa phrin las kun 'grub*
Published by Khenpo Shedup Tenzin & Lama Thinley Namgyal, Kathmandu, 2005

Byang gter sgrub skor
Containing: *Byang gter phur pa spu gri bsnyen sgrub zung sbrel gyi bsnyen yig go gsal* (instructions on the *sevāsādhana* of Byang-gter Vajrakīla practice by Brag-dkar-rta-so sprul-sku mi-pham chos-kyi dbang-phyug) & *Thugs rje chen po'i dkyil 'khor gyi cho ga'i rnam nges rin chen 'phreng ba* (teachings on the *maṇḍala* rituals of Avalokiteśvara by Rig-'dzin padma-'phrin-las). Reproduced from rare manuscripts in the library of bla-ma rGyal-mtshan of Yol-mo
Published by Lama Dawa & Chopal Lama, Darjeeling, 1974

Byang gter lugs kyi rnam thar dang ma 'ongs lung bstan
Collected biographies and prophesies of the Byang-gter tradition
Reproduced from manuscripts in the library of bla-ma Seng-ge of Yol-mo
Published by Sherab Gyaltsen & Lama Dawa, Gangtok, 1983

sBas yul spyi dang bye brag yol mo gangs ra'i gnas yig
Accounts of the various hidden lands, particularly Yol-mo gangs-ra (Helambu): Treasures of Rig-'dzin rGod-ldem & other Byang-gter masters
Published by Khenpo Nyima Dhondup, Kathmandu, 2003

Byang gter chos skor rnams kyi spyi chings rin chen 'phreng ba
by Se'i grub-chen Padma dbang-chen
Survey of Byang-gter literature and the rediscoveries of Rig-'dzin rgod-kyi ldem-'phru-can
Unpublished modern ms from Ladakh, available from TBRC (W23375)

Thub bstan rdo rje brag dgon gyi ngo sprod rags bsdus
Brief introduction to the monastery of rDo-rje-brag
Published at rDo-rje-brag-dgon in Tibet as a tourist booklet in Tibetan, Chinese & English languages (no date)

Thub bstan rdo rje brag dgon gyi byung ba mdo tsam brjod pa ngo mtshar baiḍūrya'i phreng ba
History of rDo-rje-brag monastery by Kun-bzang 'gro-'dul rdo-rje
Published in Tibet (?), 2004

WESTERN LANGUAGE PUBLICATIONS

Prasanna Kumar Acharya
An Encyclopaedia of Hindu Architecture (Reprint) Bhopal, 1978

Zahiruddin Ahmad
Sino-Tibetan Relations in the Seventeenth Century Rome, 1970

Bunkyo Aoki
Study on Early Tibetan Chronicles Regarding Discrepancies of Dates and their Adjustments Tokyo, 1955

Michael Aris
Bhutan; The Early History of a Himalayan Kingdom
Aris & Phillips, Warminster, 1979

Hidden Treasures and Secret Lives: a study of Pemalingpa (1450-1521) and the sixth Dalai Lama (1683-1706) RKP, London, 1989

... **with Aung San Suu Kyi** (eds.)
Tibetan Studies in Honour of Hugh Richardson
(Proceedings of the International Seminar on Tibetan Studies, Oxford, 1979) Aris & Phillips, Warminster, 1980

Arthur Avalon (Sir John George Woodroffe)
The Serpent Power Madras, 1950

Śakti and Śakta, Essays and Addresses on the Śakta Tantra-śāstras
Madras, 1959

Harold W. Bailey
"Vajrayāna in Gostana-deśa" JIABS I:1 (1978) 53-56

Hans Bakker
"Human Sacrifice (Puruṣamedha): Construction, sacrifice and the origin of the idea of the 'man of the homestead' (vāstupuruṣa)" in *The Strange World of Human Sacrifice*, ed. Jan Bremmer, Leuven, 2007

Daniel Barlocher
Testimonies of Tibetan Tulkus; a research among Buddhist masters in exile
Opuscula Tibetana XV (2 vols.) Rikon (Zurich), 1982

H. Bechert & R. Gombrich (eds.)
The World of Buddhism, London, 1984

Stephan Beyer
The Cult of Tārā: Magic and ritual in Tibet
University of California, Berkeley, 1978

Tarapada Bhattacharyya
A Study on Vāstuvidyā: Canons of Indian Architecture Patna, 1948

F.A. Bischoff
Ārya-Mahābalanāma Mahāyāna-sūtra. Tibétain (mss de Touen-Houang) et chinois Paris, 1956

... with Charles Hartman
"Padmasambhava's Invention of the Phur-bu. Ms. Pelliot tibétaine 44"
In *Études tibétaines dédiées à la mémoire de Marcelle Lalou* Paris, 1971

Anne-Marie Blondeau
"Analysis of the Biographies of Padmasambhava According to Tibetan Tradition" In Aris & Aung San (eds.), *Tibetan Studies* 45-52

"Le Lha-'dre bKa'-thang"
In *Études tibétaines dédiées à la mémoire de Marcelle Lalou* Paris, 1971

Alice Boner
Śilpaprakāsa; Medieval Orissan text on Temple Architecture by Ramacandra Kaulacara Leiden, 1966

Martin Boord
The Cult of the Deity Vajrakīla Tring, 1993

(Trans.) *Overview of Buddhist Tantra, by Panchen Sonam Dragpa*
LTWA, 1996

A Bolt of Lightning from the Blue Berlin, 2002

"A Pilgrim's Guide to the Hidden Land of Sikkim proclaimed as a treasure by Rig 'dzin rgod kyi ldem 'phru can" *Bulletin of Tibetology* Vol.39 no.1 Namgyal Institute, Gangtok, 2003

A Roll of Thunder from the Void Berlin, 2010

Illuminating Sunshine: Buddhist Funeral Rituals Berlin, 2012

Martin Brauen
Das Maṇḍala; Der Heilige Kreis im tantrischen Buddhismus Köln, 1992

Michael M.Broido
"Killing, Lying, Stealing and Adultery; A Problem of Interpretation in the Tantras" in Donald Lopez (ed.) *Buddhist Hermeneutics*, Honolulu, 1988

John Brough
"Nepalese Buddhist Rituals" *Bulletin of SOAS* XII (1948) 668-676

Cathy Cantwell & Robert Mayer
The Kīlaya Nirvāṇa Tantra and the Vajra Wrath Tantra: Two texts from the Ancient Tantra Collection
Österreichische Akademie der Wissenschaften, Vienna, 2007

Early Tibetan Documents on Phur pa from Dūnhuáng
Österreichische Akademie der Wissenschaften, Vienna, 2008

Barry Bryant
The Wheel of Time Sand Mandala Harper San Francisco, 1992

S.W. Bushell
"The Early History of Tibet from Chinese Sources"
JRAS XII (1880) 435-541

Lokesh Chandra
Buddhist Iconography of Tibet
(A New Tibeto-Mongol Pantheon Vols.I-XX)
Revised edition in 2 vols. with index Rinsen Book Co., Kyoto, 1986

The Thousand-Armed Avalokiteśvara Delhi, 1988

Alaka Chattopadhyaya with Lama Chimpa
Tāranātha's History of Buddhism in India Simla, 1970

Binayendra Nath Chaudhury
Buddhist Centres in Ancient India (Reprint) Calcutta, 1982

Chou Yi-Liang
"Tantrism in China"
Harvard Journal of Asiatic Studies VIII (1945) 241-332

Graham Clarke
"Lama and Tamang in Yolmo"
In Aris & Aung San (eds.), *Tibetan Studies* 79-86

"A Helambu History" *Journal of the Nepal Research Centre* 4 (1980) 1-38

Terry Clifford (ed.)
The Lamp of Liberation Yeshe Melong, New York, 1988

Edward Conze
The Large Sūtra on Perfect Wisdom
Berkeley, Los Angeles, and London, 1975

Daniel Cozort
Highest Yoga Tantra New York, 1986

Bruno Dagens
Māyāmātā; Traité Sanskrit d'Architecture (2 vols.)
(Sanskrit text with French translation) Pondichery, 1976

Anna Libera Dallapiccola (ed.)
The Stūpa; its Religious, Historical and Architectural Significance
Franz Steiner Verlag, Wiesbaden, 1980

Jacob P. Dalton
The Taming of the Demons: Violence and Liberation in Tibetan Buddhism
Yale University Press, New Haven & London, 2011

Eva M. Dargyay
The Rise of Esoteric Buddhism in Tibet MLB, 1977

Shashibhusan Dasgupta
Obscure Religious Cults Calcutta (3rd edition), 1969

Vaidya Bhagwan Dash
Materia Medica of Indo-Tibetan Medicine Delhi, 1987

Ronald M. Davidson
"Reflections of the Maheśvara Subjugation Myth"
in JIABS 14.2 (1991) 197-235

Indian Esoteric Buddhism: A social history of the tantric movement
Columbia University Press, New York, 2002

Tibetan Renaissance: Tantric Buddhism in the rebirth of Tibetan culture
Columbia University Press, New York, 2005

Kazi Dawa-Samdup
Śrī Cakrasaṁvara-tantra Calcutta, 1919

Ippolito Desideri
An Account of Tibet London, 1937

Dharmachakra Translation Committee
Deity, Mantra and Wisdom: Development stage meditation in Tibetan Buddhist tantra
Snow Lion Publications, Ithaca, 2006

DHĪḤ, Journal of Rare Buddhist Texts Research Department
Bi-annual publication of CIHTS, Sarnath

Andreas Doctor
Tibetan Treasure Literature: Revelation, tradition and accomplishment in visionary Buddhism Snow Lion Publications, Ithaca, 2005

Dodrub Chen Rinpoche
The Biography of Mahāpaṇḍita Vimalamitra Gangtok, 1967

Gyurme Dorje
A critical edition of the Guhyagarbha-tantra, together with the Phyogs-bcu mun-sel (a 14th century commentary by Klong-chen rab-'byams-pa)
Ph.D. thesis (3 vols.), SOAS, 1988

"The rNying-ma Interpretation of Commitment and Vow"
In T. Skorupski (ed.), *The Buddhist Forum* II (1991) 71-95

The complete Tibetan Book of the Dead
Penguin Books, London, 2005

... with Matthew Kapstein
The Nyingma School of Tibetan Buddhism; its Fundamentals and History, by Dudjom Rinpoche ('Jigs-bral ye-shes rdo-rje) (NSTB)
Wisdom Publications, Boston, 1991

Kenneth Douglas & Gwendolyn Bays
The Life and Liberation of Padmasambhava
The bKa' thang shel brag ma as recorded by Yeshe Tsogyal
(After the French translation of G.C. Toussaint) 2 vols. Emeryville, 1978

Nik Douglas
Tibetan Tantric Charms and Amulets Dover Publications, New York, 1978

Keith Dowman
"The Nyingma Icons" *Kailash Journal* III:4 (1975) 319-416

"A Buddhist Guide to the Power Places of the Kathmandu Valley"
Kailash Journal VIII:3-4 (1981) 183-291

Sky Dancer, the Secret Life and Songs of the Lady Yeshe Tsogyal
RKP, London, 1984

Masters of Mahāmudrā SUNY, New York, 1985

Power Places of Central Tibet RKP, London, 1987

Georges Dreyfus
"The Shuk-den Affair: History and nature of a quarrel"
JIABS 21.2 (1998) 227-270

Mark Dyczkowski
The Canon of the Śaivāgama and the Kubjikā Tantras of the Western Kaula Tradition MLB, 1989

Franz-Karl Ehrhard
"A 'Hidden Land' in the Tibetan-Nepalese borderlands"
in *Maṇḍala and Landscape*, ed. A.W. Macdonald, New Delhi, 1997

"The role of 'Treasure Discoverers' and their search for Himalayan Sacred Lands"
In *Sacred Spaces and Powerful Places*, ed. Toni Huber, LTWA, 1999

"A Forgotten Incarnation Lineage: The *Yol-mo-ba sPrul-sku*s (16th to 18th centuries)" in Ramon Prats (ed.) *The Paṇḍita and the Siddha: Tibetan Studies in Honour of E. Gene Smith* AMI Books, Dharamsala, 2007

Alice Egyed
"Notes on the Origin of Tibetan Religious Music"
In L. Ligeti (ed.) *Tibetan and Buddhist Studies* 1:191-198

Mircea Eliade
Rites and Symbols of Initiation New York, 1965

R.E. Emmerick
Tibetan Texts Concerning Khotan OUP, London, 1967

Elizabeth English
Vajrayoginī; her Visualizations, Rituals and Forms
Wisdom Publications, Boston, 2002

W.Y. Evans-Wentz
Tibetan Yoga and Secret Doctrines OUP, London, 1935

V. Fausboll
Indian Mythology London, 1902

Alfonsa Ferrari & L.Petech
mKhyen-brtse's Guide to the Holy Places of Central Tibet Rome, 1958

Eberhard Fischer & Haku Shah
"Treatment against ghosts and spirits; the bhagtai-ceremony of the Chodhri tribe in Gujarat"
German Scholars on India II (1976) 51-60 Delhi

Francesca Fremantle
A Critical Study of the Guhyasamāja-tantra (GST)
(Ph.D. thesis) SOAS, London, 1971

David N. Gellner
"Monastic Initiation in Newar Buddhism"
In R. Gombrich (ed.), *Indian Ritual and its Exegesis* OUP, Delhi, 1988

James Gentry
"Representation of Efficacy: The ritual expulsion of Mongol armies in the consolidation and expansion of the gTsang Dynasty"
In José Cabezón (ed.), *Tibetan Ritual*, Oxford University Press, 2010

Todd Gibson
"dGra-lha: A Re-examination"
Journal of the Tibet Society V (1985) 67-72

Captain H.H. Godwin-Austen
"Description of a Mystic Play as Performed in Ladak, Zaskar, etc."
JASB XXXIV (1865) 71-79

Richard F. Gombrich (ed.)
Indian Ritual and its Exegesis
(Oxford University papers on India, vol.2, part 1) Delhi, 1988

Jan Gonda
Rice and Barley Offerings in the Vedas Leiden, 1987

Prayer and Blessing; Ancient Indian Ritual Terminology Leiden, 1989

Sanjukta Gupta, Dirk Jan Hoens, Teun Goudriaan
Hindu Tantrism Leiden, 1979

Teun Goudriaan
"Tumburu and His Sisters" WZKSA XVII (1973) 49-95

The Vīṇāśikha-tantra; a Śaiva Tantra of the Left Current MLB, 1985

... with Sanjukta Gupta
Hindu Tantric and Śākta Literature

A History of Indian Literature Vol. II,2
Otto Harrassowitz, Wiesbaden, 1981

David B. Gray
"Eating the Heart of the Brahmin: Representations of alterity and the formation of identity in tantric Buddhist discourse"
History of Religions 45.1 (2005) 45-69

The Cakrasamvara Tantra: Discourse of Śrī Heruka (Śrīherukābhidāna)
Columbia University, New York, 2007

Janet Gyatso
"Signs, Memory and History: A Tantric Buddhist Theory of Scriptural Transmission" JIABS IX:2 (1986) 7-35

Tenzin Gyatso (Dalai Lama XIV)
The Kalachakra Tantra (edited by Jeffrey Hopkins) London, 1985

Erik Haarh
The Yar-Lung Dynasty Copenhagen, 1969

Kanai Lal Hazra
Buddhism in India as Described by the Chinese Pilgrims, AD 399-699
Delhi, 1984

J.C. Heesterman
The Ancient Indian Royal Consecration 's-Gravenhage, 1957

L.A. Hercus (ed.)
Indological and Budhist Studies: Volume in Honour of Prof J.W. de Jong on his Sixtieth Birthday Delhi, 1984

J. Hitchcock & R. Jones (eds.)
Spirit Possession in the Nepal Himalayas Delhi, 1976

Stephen Hodge (trans.)
The Mahāvairocana-tantra, with commentary by Buddhaguhya, translated from the Tibetan RoutledgeCurzon, London, 2003

Jeffrey Hopkins (trans.)
Tantra in Tibet: The Great Exposition of Secret Mantra by Tsong-kha-pa, part 1 London, 1975

The Yoga of Tibet: The Great Exposition of Secret Mantra by Tsong-kha-pa, parts 2 & 3 London, 1975

Death, Intermediate State and Rebirth, by Lati Rinbochay London, 1979

Siegbert Hummel
"Der Lamaistiche Ritualdolch (Phur Bu) und die Alt-vorderorientalischen Nagelmenschen" *Asiatische Studien* VI (1952) 1-4

John C. Huntingdon
The Phur-pa; Tibetan Ritual Daggers Ascona, 1975

Nobumi Iyanaga
"Recits de la Soumission de Maheśvara par Trailokyavijaya d'apres les sources Chinoise et Japonaise"
In M. Strickmann (ed.), *Tantric and Taoist Studies* 3 (1985) 633-745

David & Janice Jackson
Tibetan Thangka Painting: Methods and Materials
Serindia, London, 1989

Roger R. Jackson
Tantric Treasures: Three collections of mystical verse from Buddhist India
Oxford University Press, 2004

Ani Jinba Palmo
The Great Image: The life story of Vairochana the translator
Shambhala Publications, Boston, 2004

J.W. de Jong
"A New History of Tantric Literature in India."
(English precis of the Japanese work; *Mikkyo kyoten seiritsushi-ron,* by Yukei Matsunaga, Kyoto, 1980) *Acta Indologica* VI (1984) 91-113

Lal Mani Joshi
Studies in the Buddhistic Culture of India During the 7th and 8th Centuries AD Delhi, 1977

Eiichi Kaneko
Ko-Tantora Zenshū Kaidai Mokuroku (NGB catalogue) Tokyo, 1982

Matthew Kapstein
The Tibetan Assimilation of Buddhism Oxford University Press, 2000

Samten G. Karmay
"King Tsa/Dza and Vajrayāna"
In M. Strickmann (ed.), *Tantric and Taoist Studies* 1 (1981) 192-211

Secret Visions of the Fifth Dalai Lama London, 1988

The Great Perfection (rDzogs-chen); A Philosophical and Meditative Teaching in Tibetan Buddhism Leiden, 1988

The Arrow and the Spindle: Studies in history, myth, rituals and beliefs in Tibet Kathmandu, Vol.I 1998, Vol.II 2005

Leslie S. Kawamura & Keith Scott (eds.)
Buddhist Thought and Asian Civilisation; Essays in honour of Herbert V. Guenther on his sixtieth birthday Emeryville, 1977

Heidi I. Köppl
Establishing Appearances as Divine Snow Lion Publications, Ithaca, 2008

Stella Kramrisch
The Hindu Temple (2 vols.) Calcutta, 1946

The Presence of Śiva Princeton, 1981

Per Kvaerne
An Anthology of Buddhist Tantric Songs; a study of the Caryāgīti (Revised edition) Bangkok, 1986

"On the Concept of Sahaja in Indian Buddhist Tantric Literature"
Temenos XI (1975) 88-135

Marcelle Lalou
"Contribution à la bibliographie du Kanjur et du Tanjur
Les textes Bouddhiques au temps du roi Khri Srong-lde'u-btsan"
(The lDan-dkar catalogue) JA (1953) 313-353

Chhimed Rigdzin Lama
Byang-gter Teaching and Practice According to the Tradition of Khordong Monastery Series translated with James Low, *et al.* Vols. 1-20
Kalimpong, 1975-85

"The Twelve Months in the Life of a Monastery" In *Aspects of Buddhism* Commemorative Volume of the Sikkim Research Institute of Tibetology
Vision Books, New Delhi, 1981 147-159

C.R. Lama & James Low
The Origin of Heruka and the Twenty-four Places (n.d.)

Gega Lama
Principles of Tibetan Art (2 vols.) Darjeeling, 1983

Étienne Lamotte
History of Indian Buddhism (Translated from the French by Sara Boin)
Louvain, 1988

Ferdinand D. Lessing & Alex Wayman
Mkhas-grub-rje's Introduction to the Buddhist Tantric Systems
The Hague, 1968

Louis Ligeti (ed.)
Tibetan and Buddhist Studies Commemorating the 200th Anniversary of the Birth of Alexander Csoma de Körös (2 vols.)
Bibliotheca Orientalis Hungarica XXIX Budapest, 1984

L.H. Lindsay
"The *Makara* in Early Chinese Buddhist Sculpture" JRAS (1951) 134-138

Trevor O. Ling
Buddhism and the Mythology of Evil London, 1962

Rob Linrothe
Ruthless Compassion: Wrathful deities in early Indo-Tibetan esoteric Buddhist art Boston, 1999

Kennard Lipman
Secret Teachings of Padmasambhava
Shambhala Publications, Boston, 2010

John K. Locke
"Newar Initiation Rites"
Contributions to Nepalese Studies II:2 (1975) 1-23

Steven Lonsdale
Animals and the Origins of Dance New York, 1982

David N. Lorenzen
The Kāpālikas and Kālamukhas; Two Lost Śaivite Sects Delhi, 1972

A.A. Macdonell
Vedic Mythology Strassburg, 1897

N.K. Majumder
"Sacrificial Altars: Vedis and Agnis"
Journal of the Indian Society of Oriental Art VII (1939) 39-60

N.V. Mallaya
Studies in Sanskrit Texts on Temple Architecture (with special reference to Tantrasamuccaya)
Annamalai University Publications, Annamalainagar, 1949

E.W. Marasinghe
The Vāstuvidyāśāstra Attributed to Mañjuśrī
Bibliotheca Indo-Buddhica Series No. 67 Delhi, 1989

The Citrakarmaśāstra Attributed to Mañjuśrī
Bibliotheca Indo-Buddhica Series No. 81 Delhi, 1991

Thomas Marcotty
Dagger Blessing; the Tibetan Phurba Cult Delhi, 1987

Yukei Matsunaga
"A Doubt to Authority of the Guhyasamāja-ākhyāna-Tantras"
Journal of Indian and Buddhist Studies XII:2 (1964) 16-25

"A History of Tantric Buddhism in India with Reference to Chinese Translations" In Kawamura & Scott (eds.), *Buddhist Thought and Asian Civilisation* 167-81

"On the Date of the Mañjuśrīmūlakalpa"
In M. Strickmann (ed.), *Tantric and Taoist Studies* 3 (1985) 882-894

Robert Mayer
"Observations on the Tibetan Phur-ba and the Indian Kīla"
In T. Skorupski (ed.), *The Buddhist Forum* II (1991) 163-192

A Scripture of the Ancient Tantra Collection: the Phur-pa bcu-gnyis
Kiscadale Publications, Oxford, 1996

Georgette Meredith
"The Phurbu: The Use and Symbolism of the Tibetan Magic Dagger"
History of Religions VI.3 (1967) 236-253

C.A. Muses (editor)
Esoteric Teachings of the Tibetan Tantra Translated by Chen Chi Chang
Lausanne, 1961

Khenpo Namdrol Rinpoche
Vajrakilaya Dharmakosha, London, 1997

Bunyiu Nanjio
A Catalogue of the Chinese Translation of the Buddhist Tripiṭaka
Oxford, 1883

René de Nebesky-Wojkowitz
Oracles and Demons of Tibet Graz (2nd. edition), 1975

Tibetan Religious Dances: Text and translation of the Fifth Dalai Lama's 'Chams-yig The Hague, 1976

"The Use of Thread-Crosses in Lepcha Lamaist Ceremonies"
Eastern Anthropologist IV.1 (1950) 65-87

Eva Neumaier
"Einige Aspekte der gTer-ma Literatur der rNying-ma-pa Schüle"
ZDMG Suppl. 1 (1969)

"bKa'-brgyad rang-byung rang-shar, ein rDzogs-chen tantra"
ZDMG Band 120 (1971) 131-163

Ngari Panchen, Pema Wangyi Gyalpo
Perfect Conduct: Ascertaining the three vows
Translated by Khenpo Gyurme Samdrub & Sangye Khandro
Wisdom Publications, Boston, 1996

Jamyang Norbu (ed.)
Zlos-gar LTWA Dharamsala, 1986

E. Obermiller
History of Buddhism (Chos-'byung) by Bu-ston
(2 vols.) Leipzig, 1931-1932

Wendy Doniger O'Flaherty
"The Symbolism of Ashes in the Mythology of Śiva"
Purāṇa Journal XIII (1971) 26-35

Asceticism and Eroticism in the Mythology of Śiva London, 1973

The Origins of Evil in Hindu Mythology Berkeley, 1976

Tales of Sex and Violence Chicago, 1985

Blanche C. Olschak with Geshe Thubten Wangyal
Mystic Art of Ancient Tibet New York, 1973

Yuri Parfionovitch, Gyurme Dorje, Fernand Meyer
Tibetan Medical Paintings: Illustrations to the Blue Beryl treatise of Sangye Gyamtso (1653-1705)
(2 vols.) Serindia Publications, London, 1992

Pratapaditya Pal
Art of Tibet Los Angeles, 1983

Tibetan Paintings Basel, 1984

Khenchen Palden Sherab Rinpoche
& Khenpo Tsewang Dongyal Rinpoche
The Dark Red Amulet: Oral instructions on the practice of Vajrakilaya
Snow Lion Publications, Ithaca, 2008

Luciano Petech
China and Tibet in the Early Early 18th Century: History of the Establishment of a Chinese Protectorate in Tibet
(2nd edition, revised) Leiden, 1972

Ramon Prats
"Some Preliminary Considerations Arising from a Biographical Study of the Early gTer-ston" In Aris & Aung San (eds.), *Tibetan Studies* 256-260

"Tshe-dbang nor-bu's Chronological Notes on the Early Transmission of the Vimala sNying-thig"
In L. Ligeti (ed.), *Tibetan and Buddhist Studies* 2:197-210

Jean Przyluski
"Les Vidyārāja, contribution à l'histoire de la magie dans les sectes Mahāyānistes" BEFEO XXIII (1923) 301-368

"Heruka-Sambara" *Polish Bulletin of Oriental Studies* 1 (1937)

Marylin M. Rhie & Robert A.F. Thurman
Wisdom and Compassion, the Sacred Art of Tibet New York, 1991

Matthieu Ricard
Monk Dancers of Tibet Shambhala Publications, Boston, 2003

Hugh Richardson
Ceremonies of the Lhasa Year Serindia, London, 1993

High Peaks, Pure Earth: Collected writings on Tibetan history and culture
Serindia, London, 1998

Franco Ricca & Erberto Lo Bue
The Great Stupa of Gyantse Serindia, London, 1993

Tsepak Rigzin & Jeremy Russell
"Taglung Tsetrul Rinpoche, Dorje Drak and the Northern Treasure Tradition" *Chos-Yang Journal* (1987) 16-21

Staglung Tsetrul Rinpoche
A Brief History of Dorje Tag Monastery in Tibet and its Lineage Holders
Translated from the Tibetan by Tashi Rabgias, Leh, 1985

George Roerich
The Blue Annals, compiled by 'Gos Lotsawa Calcutta, 1949

Alexis Sanderson
"Vajrayāna: Origin and Function" in *Buddhism into the Year 2000. International Conference Proceedings* Bangkok, 1995

"The Śaiva Age"
In Shingo Einoo (ed.), *Genesis and Development of Tantrism*
University of Tokyo, 2009

Erik Hein Schmidt
The Great Gate; gTer-ma revelations of Chokgyur Lingpa
(3rd edition) Hong Kong, 1989

Miranda Shaw
Buddhist Goddesses of India Princeton University Press, 2006

Bulcsu Sikløs
The Vajrabhairava Tantras
Buddhica Britannica Series Continua VII, Tring, 1996

Lily de Silva
"The Symbolism of the Indrakīla in the Paritta Maṇḍapa"
In J.E. van Lohuizen de Leeuw (ed.), *Studies in South Asian Culture* 7 (1978) 234-250

N. Singh
"The Collective Vajrakilaya Retreat (Phur Drub)"
Tibet Journal XIV:2 (1989) 49-55

Tadeusz Skorupski
"The Cremation Ceremony According to the Byang-gter Tradition"
Kailash Journal 9 (1982) 361-376

"Tibetan Homa Rites" In Frits Staal, *Agni* (vol.2) 403-417

The Sarvadurgatipariśodhana-tantra: Elimination of all Evil Destinies (SDPT) MLB, 1983

Kriyāsaṃgraha: Compendium of Buddhist Rituals, an abridged version
Buddhica Britannica Series Continua X, Tring, 2002

Mary S. Slusser
Nepal Maṇḍala: A cultural study of the Kathmandu Valley
(2 vols.) Princeton University Press, 1982

David L. Snellgrove
The Hevajra Tantra (HT) (2 vols.) London, 1959

Indo-Tibetan Buddhism London, 1987

... with H. Richardson
History of Tibet London, 1968

... with T. Skorupski
The Cultural Heritage of Ladakh (2 vols.) Warminster, 1979-1980

Adrian Snodgrass
The Matrix and Diamond World Maṇḍalas in Shingon Buddhism
(2 vols.) Delhi, 1989

Per K. Sørenson & Guntram Hazod (eds.)
Thundering Falcon: An inquiry into the history and cult of Khra-'brug, Tibet's first Buddhist temple Vienna, 2005

Frits Staal (editor)
Agni, the Vedic Ritual of the Fire Altar (2 vols.) Berkeley, 1983

Sir Aurel Stein
Serindia; Detailed report of explorations in Central Asia and Westernmost China (5 vols.) Oxford, 1921

R.A. Stein
"Le liṅga des danses masquées lamaïques et la théorie des âmes"
In *Sino-Indian Studies (Liebenthal Festschrift)* 5:3 & 4 (1957) 200-234

Tibetan Civilisation Faber & Faber Ltd., London, 1972

"La gueule du *makara:* un trait inexpliqué de certains objets rituels"
In A. Macdonald & Y. Imaeda (eds.), *Essais sur l'Art du Tibet* 52-62
Paris, 1977

"À propos des documents anciens relatifs au phur-bu (kīla)"
Memorial Symposium, Bibliotheca Orientalis Hungarica XXIII
Budapest, 1978

Cyrus Stearns
King of the Empty Plain New York, 2007

John Stevens
Sacred Calligraphy of the East (Revised edition) Boston, 1988

Michel Strickmann (ed.)
Tantric and Taoist Studies in Honour of Professor R.A. Stein
Vol.1, 1981. Vol.2, 1983. Vol.3, 1985.
Mélanges Chinois et Bouddhiques XX-XXII
Institut Belge des Hautes Études Chinoises, Bruxelles

Gail Hinich Sutherland
The Disguises of the Demon: The development of the yakṣa in Hinduism and Buddhism SUNY, 1991

Robert E. Svoboda
Aghora: At the Left Hand of God Albuquerque, New Mexico, 1986

Musashi Tachikawa
A Catalogue of the United States Library of Congress Collection of Tibetan Literature in Microfiche (2 vols.) IIBS Tokyo, 1983-1988

Tarthang Tulku
Crystal Mirror V (A History of the Buddhist Dharma) Emeryville, 1977

Ryugen Tanemura
Kuladatta's Kriyāsaṁgrahapañjikā Groningen, 2004

Hans-Georg Türstig
"The Indian Sorcery Called Abhicāra" WZKSA XXIX (1985) 69-117

David Templeman
The Origin of the Tārā Tantra by Jo-nang Tāranātha LTWA, 1981

The Seven Instruction Lineages of Jo-nang Tāranātha LTWA, 1983

Tāranātha's Life of Kṛṣṇācārya/Kāṇha LTWA, 1989

Pema Namdol Thaye
Concise Tibetan Art Book Kalimpong, 1987

Michel Thevoz
The Painted Body; Illusions of Reality Skira/Rizzoli, New York, 1984

Tulku Thondup
The Tantric Tradition of the Nyingmapa; the origin of Buddhism in Tibet Marion, 1984

Hidden Teachings of Tibet; an explanation of the gTer-ma tradition of the rNying-ma-pa school of Buddhism Wisdom Books, London, 1986

Buddhist Civilisation in Tibet RKP, 1987

Buddha Mind; an anthology of Longchen Rabjam's writings on Dzogpa Chenpo Snow Lion Publications, Ithaca, 1989

Enlightened Living; Teachings of Tibetan Buddhist Masters Shambhala, Boston & London, 1990

Shiníchi Tsuda
"Classification of Tantras in dPal-brtsegs's lTa-ba'i rim-pa bzhad-pa and its Problems" *Journal of Indian and Buddhist Studies* XIII:1 (1965) 42-47

The Saṁvarodaya-tantra (selected chapters) Tokyo, 1974

Giuseppe Tucci
"Animadversiones Indicae" JASB (New Series) XXVI (1930) 125-60

Tibetan Painted Scrolls (TPS) (2 vols. & portfolio) Rome, 1949

The Religions of Tibet London, 1980

Indo-Tibetica (English translation) 4 vols. (7 parts) Delhi, 1988-1991

Hakuju Toh Ui (et al)
A Complete Catalogue of the Tibetan Buddhist Canons (bKa'-'gyur & bsTan-'gyur) Sendai, 1934

R.H. van Gulik
Hayagrīva; The Mantrayānic Aspect of Horse Cult in China and Japan Leiden, 1935

Sam van Schaik & Jacob Dalton
Tibetan Tantric Manuscripts from Dūnhuáng: A descriptive catalogue of the Stein Collection at the British Library Leiden, 2006

Kapila Vatsyayan (ed.)
Kalātattvakośa: A lexicon of fundamental concepts of the Indian arts Delhi, 1988

Roberto Vitali
Early Temples of Central Tibet Serindia, London, 1993

Glenn Wallis
Mediating the Power of Buddhas: ritual in the Mañjuśrīmūlakalpa SUNY, 2002

Alex Wayman
"Studies in Yama and Māra"
Indo-Iranian Journal III.2 (1959) 44-73, 112-131

The Buddhist Tantras; Light on Indo-Tibetan Esotericism New York, 1973

Yoga of the Guhyasamāja-tantra; the Arcane Lore of Forty Verses MLB, 1977

"Notes on the Phur-Bu" *Journal of the Tibet Society* 1 (1981) 79-85

Buddhist Insight
Essays, edited with an introduction by George Elder MLB, 1984

"The Sarvarahasya-tantra" *Acta Indologica* VI (1984) 521-569

"Imperatives in the Buddhist Tantra Mantras"
Berliner Indologische Studien, Band 1. Reinbek, 1985

Christian K. Wedemeyer
Āryadeva's Lamp that Integrates the Practices (Caryāmelāpakapradīpa)
Columbia University, New York, 2007

David Gordon White
The Alchemical Body: Siddha traditions in medieval India
University of Chicago Press, 1996

Kiss of the Yoginī: Tantric sex in its South Asian contexts
University of Chicago Press, 2003

Sinister Yogis University of Chicago Press, 2009

(ed.)
Tantra in Practice, Princeton University Press, 2000

Roderick Whitfield & Anne Farrer
Caves of the Thousand Buddhas: Chinese art from the Silk Route
British Museum Publications, London, 1990

Martin Willson
In Praise of Tārā London, 1986

... with Martin Brauen
Deities of Tibetan Buddhism Wisdom Publications, Boston, 2000

Turrell V. Wylie
The Geography of Tibet According to the 'Dzam-gling rgyas-bshad
Rome, 1962

"Ro-langs; The Tibetan Zombie" *History of Religions* 4:1 (1964) 69-80

A Tibetan Religious Geography of Nepal Rome, 1970

Zuiho Yamaguchi
"Methods of Chronological Calculation in Tibetan Historical Sources"
In L. Ligeti (ed.), *Tibetan and Buddhist Studies* 2:405-424

Chikyo Yamamoto
History of Mantrayāna in Japan Delhi, 1987

Mahāvairocana-sūtra (translated from the Chinese)
Śatapiṭaka Series 359 Delhi, 1990

Taiko Yamasaki
Shingon; Japanese Esoteric Buddhism
Shambhala, Boston & London, 1988

The Yeshe De Project
Ancient Tibet (Research Materials) Dharma Publishing, Berkeley, 1986

S. Yoshimura
The Denkar-ma, an Oldest Catalogue of the Tibetan Buddhist Canon
Kyoto, 1950

INDEX

Khordong Commentary Series

I MARTIN J. BOORD. *A Bolt Of Lightning From The Blue, The vast commentary on Vajrakīla that clearly defines the essential points.* edition khordong. Berlin, 2002. reprint: Wandel Verlag. Berlin, 2010

II JAMES LOW. *Being Right Here, Commentary on The Mirror of Clear Meaning by Nuden Dorje.* Snow Lion. New York & Colorado, 2004

II.dt JAMES LOW. *Hier und Jetzt Sein. Ein Kommentar zu „Don Sal Melong" – „Der Spiegel der klaren Bedeutung", ein Dzogchen-Schatztext von Nuden Dorje.* Edition Mandarava. Gutenstein, 2005

II.pl JAMES LOW. *Byc tu i teraz.* wydawnictwo A. Kraków, 2005

II.it JAMES LOW. *Esserci, Un commento a "Lo specchio del chiaro significato."* Ubaldini Editore. Roma, 2005

II.fr JAMES LOW. *Le Miroir au Sens Limpide: Trésor du dzogchen.* Éditions Almora, 2009

II.es JAMES LOW. *Aquí y ahora.* Ediciones Dharma, España, 2011

III JAMES LOW. *Being Guru Rinpoche, Commentary on Nuden Dorje's Terma: The Vidyadhara Guru Sadhana.* Trafford. Canada, 2006

III.pl JAMES LOW. *Byc Guru Rinpocze. Komentarz do Sadhany Guru Widjadhary z termy Nudena Dordże.* Wydawnictwo NORBU. 2006

III.dt JAMES LOW. *Eins mit Guru Rinpoche.* edition khordong. Berlin, 2007. reprint: edition khordong, Wandel Verlag. Berlin, 2012

III.fr NUDEN DORJE / JAMES LOW. *Dans le Mandala de Padmasambhava. La sadhana du Détenteur de Rigpa Padmasambhava et un commentaire de James Low.* Editions Khordong.France. Lyon, 2008

IV TULKU TSULTRIM ZANGPO (TULKU TSURLO). *The Five Nails – A Commentary on the Northern Treasures Accumulation Praxis.* edition khordong, Wandel Verlag. Berlin, 2011

IV.dt TULKU TSULTRIM ZANGPO (TULKU TSURLO). *Die Fünf Nägel – Ein Kommentar zu den Vorbereitenden Übungen der Nördlichen Schätze.* edition khordong, Wandel Verlag. Berlin, 2011

V RIG-'DZIN RDO-RJE (MARTIN J. BOORD). *A Roll of Thunder from the Void, Establishing the maṇḍala through guhyamantra, Vajrakīla Texts of the Northern Treasures Tradition, Volume Two.* edition khordong, Wandel Verlag. Berlin, 2010

VI CHIMED RIGDZIN RINPOCHE, JAMES LOW. *Radiant Aspiration, The Butterlamp Prayer: Lamp of Aspiration.* Simply Being. London, 2011

VI.dt CHHIMED RIGDZIN RINPOCHE, JAMES LOW. *Lichter der Weisheit, Das Butterlampen-Wunschgebet von Chhimed Rigdzin Rinpoche. Mit einem Kommentar von James Low.* edition khordong, Wandel Verlag. 2014

VII.tib TULKU TSULTRIM ZANGPO (TULKU TSURLO). *Boundless Vision. A Byangter Manual on Dzogchen Training. An Outline Commentary on the Boundless Vision of Universal Goodness (Kun bZang dGongs Pa Zang Thal).* Tibetan Text. edition khordong, Wandel Verlag. Berlin, 2012

VIII RIG-'DZIN RDO-RJE (MARTIN J. BOORD). *Illuminating Sunshine, Buddhist funeral rituals of Avalokiteśvara.* edition khordong. Berlin, 2012

IX.dt JAMES LOW. *Zuhause im Spiel der Wirklichkeit. Ein Kommentar zum Dzogchen Schatztext »Unmittelbares Aufzeigen der Buddhaschaft jenseits aller Klassifizierung« von Nuden Dorje.* edition khordong, Wandel Verlag. Berlin, 2012

X RIG-'DZIN RDO-RJE (MARTIN J. BOORD). *Gathering the Elements. An overview of the Vajrakīla tradition in all its facets. Vajrakīla Texts of the Northern Treasures Tradition, Volume One.* edition khordong, Wandel Verlag. Berlin, 2013

XI RIGDZIN PEMA TINLEY / KHENPO CHOWANG. *The Path of Secret Mantra: Teachings of the Northern Treasures Five Nails. Pema Tinley's guide to vajrayāna practice.* edition khordong, Wandel Verlag. Berlin 2014

XII MARTIN J. BOORD. *A Blaze of Fire in the Dark, Homa rituals for the fulfilment of vows and the performance of deeds of great benefit, Vajrakīla Texts of the Nor-thern Treasures Tradition, Volume Three.* edition khordong, Wandel Verlag. Berlin 2015

Other Titles

Die Geheimen Dakini-Lehren. Padmasambhavas mündliche Unterweisungen der Prinzessin Tsogyal. Ein Juwel der Tibetischen Weisheitsliteratur. Überarbeitete Neuausgabe. edition khordong, Wandel Verlag. Berlin, 2011

TULKU THONDUP. *Die verborgenen Schätze Tibets, Eine Erklärung der Termatradition der Nyingmaschule des Buddhismus.* Überarbeitete Neuausgabe. edition khordong, Wandel Verlag. Berlin, 2013

The Seven Chapters of Prayer, as taught by Padma Sambhava of Urgyen, known in Tibetan as Le'u bDun Ma, arranged according to the system of Khordong Gompa by Chhimed Rigdzin Rinpoche, incl. prayers of Byang-gTer and sMin-Grol-Gling tradition. Translated by CHHIMED RIGDZIN RINPOCHE & JAMES LOW. With an introduction by JAMES LOW. Practice text. edition khordong. Berlin, 2008. Reprint: Wandel Verlag. Berlin, 2010

Das Gebet in sieben Kapiteln gelehrt von Padmasambhava (Le'u bDun Ma), editiert von Chhimed Rigdzin Rinpoche, mit Gebeten für Byang-gTer and sMin-Grol-Gling-System. Übersetzt aus dem tibetischen von CHHIMED RIGDZIN RINPOCHE & JAMES LOW. Übertragung ins Deutsche von Jomo Gudrun & Camel Chhimed Wangpo. Praxistext. edition khordong. Berlin, 2008. Nachdruck: Wandel Verlag. Berlin, 2010

Die Fünf Nägel, Die vorbereitenden Übungen der Nördlichen Schätze. Überarbeiteter und ergänzter Praxistext. edition khordong, Wandel Verlag. Berlin, 2013

JAMES LOW. *Aus dem Handgepäck eines Tibetischen Yogi - Grundlegende Texte der Dzogchen-Tradition.* Überarbeitete Neuausgabe. edition khordong, Wandel Verlag. Berlin, 2013

KEITH DOWMAN. *Der Flug des Garuda, Fünf Dzogchen-Texte aus dem tibetischen Buddhismus.* Überarbeitete und erweiterte Neuausgabe.
edition khordong, Wandel Verlag. Berlin, 2015

In Preparation

DUDJOM RINPOCHE. *Die Klausur auf dem Berge. Dzogchen-Lehren und Kommentare.* Überarbeitete Neuausgabe.

TULKU THONDUP. *Boundless Vision. Manual of Jangter Dzogchen Yoga of Tulku Tsultrim Zangpo (Kun bZang dGongs Pa Zang Thal).* Restricted public.

JAMES LOW. *Gesammelte Schriften von Chhimed Rigdzin Rinpoche, ausgewählt, editiert und übersetzt von James Low.*

DUDJOM LINGPA. *Buddhaschaft ohne Meditation, Eine visionäre Beschreibung, bekannt als »Verfeinerung der eigenen Wahrnehmung (Nang-jang)«.*

The Five Nails, the accumulation praxis of the Northern Treasures. Practice text.

Die Sadhana von Chenresig, der alle Wesen befreit, Drowa Kundrol, die äußere Praxis des Drubkor Namsum, Terma von Rigdzin Godem ('Gro Ba Kun Grol). Praxistext.

The Sadhana of Chenresig, who liberates all beings, Drowa Kundrol – the outer ritual of the Drubkor Namsum cycle, ter of Rigdzin Godem ('Gro Ba Kun Grol). Practice text.

Vajrakīla Texts of the Northern Treasures Tradition

Volume 4: *A Tidal Wave of Blessings*
The Vase initiation and other rites of empowerment. *forthcoming*

Volume 5: *An Overwhelming Hurricane*
Averting disaster and turning back obstacles for the benefit of a wider world. *forthcoming*

Volume 6: *A Fortress of Solid Rock*
Completing the accumulation of the essential life force and consolidating all the elements of the tradition in order to remain firm in one's *samādhi*. *forthcoming*

Sarva Maṅgalam